MW01069132

BATTLESHIP COMMANDER

BATTLESHIP

THE LIFE OF VICE ADMIRAL WILLIS A. LEE JR.

COMMANDER

Paul Stillwell

Naval Institute Press
Annapolis, Maryland

This book has been brought to publication with the generous assistance of Edward S. and Joyce I. Miller.

Naval Institute Press
291 Wood Road
Annapolis, MD 21402

Library of Congress Cataloging-in-Publication Data

Names: Stillwell, Paul, date, author.

Title: Battleship commander : the life of Vice Admiral Willis A. Lee Jr. / Paul Stillwell.

Other titles: Life of Vice Admiral Willis A. Lee Jr. Description: Annapolis, Maryland : Naval Institute Press, [2021] | Includes bibliographical references and index.

Identifiers: LCCN 2021017418 (print) | LCCN 2021017419 (ebook) | ISBN 9781682475935 (hardcover) | ISBN 9781682475942 (epub) | ISBN 9781682475942 (pdf)

Subjects: LCSH: Lee, Willis A., Jr. (Willis Augustus), 1888–1945. | Admirals—United States—Biography. | United States. Navy—History—20th century. | World War, 1939–1945—Campaigns—Pacific Ocean. | World War, 1939–1945—Naval operations, American. | World War, 1939–1945—Biography. | United States. Navy--Biography. | Naval art and science—History—20th century.

Classification: LCC E746.L4 S75 2021 (print) | LCC E746.L4 (ebook) | DDC 359.0092 [B]—dc23

LC record available at https://lccn.loc.gov/2021017418

LC ebook record available at https://lccn.loc.gov/2021017419

Maps created by James M. Caiella.

Don Siders and Margaret Allen
Evan and Kate Smith
Guil and Mary Aertsen

Their generosity and kindness contributed substantially to this portrayal of Willis A. Lee Jr. as a naval officer and human being.

CONTENTS

CONTENTS

vii

MAPS

MAPS

ACKNOWLEDGMENTS

In gathering material for this volume, I am especially grateful to the three pairs of individuals to whom the book is dedicated. Their unstinting contributions provided far more material on Admiral Lee than I could otherwise have obtained. The account is much richer, especially regarding Lee's personal relationships, as the result of the help from those six.

In 1976, after going through a number of sources, I kept coming across the name Evan E. Smith, formerly of Cincinnati. Through a piece of serendipity and a Cincinnati telephone book, I reached Smith's daughter Margaret Ball. She in turn put me in touch with Mrs. Kate Smith. Her husband Evan had started researching a biography of Lee in the early 1960s but died before he could draft much of the manuscript. Evan Smith was a native of Owen County, Kentucky, as was Admiral Lee. During World War I, as an Army sergeant, Smith served overseas. He later became a newspaperman. In 1976 I wrote to Mrs. Smith, who was then living in Versailles, Kentucky. She invited me to come see her and turned over the many items that her husband had amassed. She told me she had wondered what to do with his research and got her answer when she received my letter. She provided her husband's collection of material, notably letters from people who had known Lee early in the twentieth century. By 1976 nearly all were deceased. They provided invaluable memories of their association with Lee.

That same year, I visited Lee's sisters-in-law and nephew in Rock Island, Illinois. Margaret Allen, whose sister was Lee's wife Mabelle, shared many recollections. She was essentially the family historian and supplied dozens of handwritten pages that contained information available nowhere else. Most welcome were copies of letters that Lee wrote to his fiancée/wife and letters she wrote to her sisters. Lee's nephew Don Siders was generous in providing material about his uncle's career. Don and I became friends. Over the years, he sent one package after another from material that the household had essentially inherited when Mrs. Lee died. He and his wife, Mary, provided kind hospitality on subsequent occasions. On 25 August 2005, the sixtieth anniversary of Lee's death, Don and I visited the admiral's grave at Arlington National Cemetery.

Two other people who were most helpful were Guilliaem Aertsen III and his wife Mary. Guil was Lee's aide and frequent companion from late 1942 until the day Lee died. Guil and I got together for multiple interviews, and he followed up with correspondence. Because he worked closely with Lee throughout most of the last three years of the war, his candid insights were particularly valuable on Lee's working style, his likes and dislikes, and his relationships to those with whom he came in contact. Mrs. Aertsen got to know Admiral and Mrs. Lee on a personal basis during the final two months of Lee's life and offered intimate vignettes that would have been available from no other source.

One of my most useful interviews for this project was with Admiral Arleigh Burke, who had key observations on Lee, both concerning the 1944 battles and in sending Lee to Maine in 1945. True to his personality, Burke was forceful, candid, and offered valuable insights into how Lee operated. And at times he was feisty. While the tape recorder was running, he said, among other things, "You're probably a historian, and I've got a couple of phobias about historians. First, by the very nature of the thing, they always look backward, and they ascribe . . . ideas that the commander couldn't possibly have had. . . . But the worst thing [is] that you like to match things up on little charts: ship against ship or aircraft against ships." Once the tape recorder was turned off, the admiral switched personas and became a congenial host: "Won't you have another dish of ice cream, Paul?" For the record, each of us had two dishes of ice cream. Vice Admiral Lloyd M. Mustin worked closely with Admiral Lee during World War II. His marvelously detailed U.S. Naval Institute oral history served as a valuable resource.

Rich Frank, a longtime friend and mentor, has provided a great deal of encouragement over the years and from time to time sent me useful source material. His review of the draft manuscript gave me a great deal of confidence in my approach to the subject. He also drew upon his vast knowledge of the topic, especially on Guadalcanal, to suggest useful word choices and to provide valuable corrections so I could fix errors before they got into print. The father-and-son combination of naval historians Tom and Trent Hone supplied useful advice and information.

Trent, like Rich Frank, is a fount of information on the subject areas covered in the book; he also supplied helpful corrections. Another in that category is Dr. Dave Rosenberg, whose knowledge of naval history is seemingly limitless. A valuable suggestion from Dave was that I add a section to the epilogue to describe Lee's posthumous legacy to the Navy he served so well. Another source of information and encouragement has been John Lundstrom, who shared useful nuggets about Lee's experiences in 1942. Bob Cressman of the Naval History and Heritage Command has urged me for years to get this project done. He and Mark Evans, also of the ship histories section at NHHC, provided valuable information. Dr. Malcolm Muir Jr., a professor of history for many years, supplied a copy of his doctoral dissertation on fast battleships. Thanks go to Samuel Loring Morison for sharing a portion of the wartime diary of his grandfather, Samuel Eliot Morison.

Ed Calouro, who has a considerable interest in the history of battleships, has been a source of encouragement and suggestions. He has also been a painstakingly thorough and effective proofreader of the manuscript. Phil Leerar, who wrote a manuscript of his own on Admiral Lee, generously turned his unpublished draft over to me and provided inputs to the first draft of this book. Jim Caiella created the superb maps that complement the text.

Three individuals of the Naval Institute staff were helpful in arranging for old interview tapes to be converted to digital format. Thanks go to Taira Payne, Mary Ripley, and Jon Hoppe. Janis Jorgensen of the USNI heritage division, a valued friend, has been supportive and helpful in a number of ways, in particular providing access to oral histories that constituted substantial parts of the Lee story. Glenn Griffith, acquisitions editor for the Naval Institute Press, has been both supportive and patient as the text came together; I am grateful for both qualities. Others on the Naval Institute Press staff who have contributed to the finished product are Adam Kane, Susan Corrado, and Rachel Crawford. Aden Nichols did the copyediting, Kathleen Dyson created the attractive cover, and Cleo Vastardis designed the interior appearance of the book.

Sadly, Dr. Jack Sweetman, who taught for many years at the Naval Academy, did not live to see the completion of this book. He frequently provided friendship and encouragement up to the time of his death in 2019. In addition, he suggested that I contact his father Arthur, who had served with Lee on board the battleship *New Hampshire* in 1914 during the U.S. incursion at Veracruz, Mexico. Another posthumous thank you goes to John Brown, who was executive director of the USS *Washington* reunion group. He invited me to attend gatherings of his former shipmates; I was able to meet and learn from men who had served in Lee's flagship. One of those reunions was in Wilmington, North Carolina. The director of the nearby Battleship *North Carolina* Memorial was retired Captain David Scheu, whom I had gotten to know when he was operations officer of the *New Jersey.* He and his staff were most hospitable.

Finally, I thank my dear wife Karen and our sons Joseph, Robert, and James. They have lived with me for many years as I lived with the Lee project. Now the sons have gone off to their own lives and have their own families, something that was far in the future when I started the Lee research. I cherish my relationships with all of them.

PREFACE

D r. Scott Mobley, a retired Navy captain who is now on the faculty of the University of Wisconsin, has studied naval history extensively. He put forth a convincing rationale for a biography of the largely unsung Admiral Lee: "I think Lee loomed larger in his own time than now, but he has much to offer naval officers of today." During his career, Willis Augustus Lee Jr. was highly respected within the naval profession. He had extensive knowledge of the sea, small arms, large-caliber gunnery, tactics, electronics, ship handling, and coordination of ship and aviation actions. Along with that package, he possessed a great deal of common sense and leadership ability; his subordinates enjoyed serving with him. He also had an innate quality of mental brilliance. George Street, who was later awarded the Medal of Honor as a submarine skipper, served under Lee's command as an ensign in the cruiser *Concord* in the late 1930s. Street often used an evocative term that aptly fits Lee: "bright as new money."

Why then is Lee so little known in the twenty-first century, even though he was skilled operationally and served as administrative type commander of all Pacific Fleet battleships during World War II? Several factors can help explain. His most important distinction was that he had tactical command during one of only two battleship-versus-battleship gunnery duels in the war. As the result of his leadership from the flagship *Washington* in November 1942, the Japanese lost the battleship *Kirishima* and were stymied in their efforts to deliver a pummeling bombardment of Guadalcanal. That victory was the turning point that essentially ended Japanese efforts to retake the island.

Then the role of fast battleships in a war that emphasized aviation-based offensive power was diminished as they were usually forced to serve in antiaircraft screens of aircraft carriers. That was instead of operating primarily as a battle line engaged in surface gunnery engagements—the mission intended for battleships up to the beginning of the war. After Guadalcanal, circumstances denied Lee the opportunity for an even greater victory. During the Marianas invasion in June 1944, he declined to engage in a tail chase of Japanese heavy ships because his ships had not operated together tactically, nor did the Japanese pose a threat to the Saipan beachhead. Lee's ships were unable to participate in the wide-ranging and controversial Battle of Leyte Gulf in October 1944. Because Admiral William Halsey refused to permit Lee's ships to guard San Bernardino Strait in the Philippines, another battleship-versus-battleship encounter was averted. Had Lee fought and won that potential engagement, his reputation would have been more widely known.

In addition, Lee's modest personality was one that avoided public recognition and acclaim. His goal was to fight and win, but he did not want to be lionized in the public media. He deliberately avoided the spotlight. Then, because he died only ten days after the end of hostilities in August 1945, he was not around to serve in the postwar Navy. Nor was he available to write a memoir, even though it is unlikely that he would have done so had he lived longer. The Navy did recognize his achievements by naming a destroyer leader, the USS *Willis A. Lee*, for him in the early 1950s. Though the service has often recycled ship names, no successor ship with his name has emerged after the scrapping of the first one. Because Lee was an Olympic medal winner as a marksman, for years members of the Naval Academy rifle team have visited his grave in the Arlington National Cemetery on the Sunday nearest the anniversary of his death.

This book is an effort to counteract Lee's relative obscurity in naval annals. My journey to this point started in 1969 when I received orders to serve in the crew of the battleship *New Jersey* as assistant combat information center officer. Coincidentally, Lee was an early proponent of the value of CICs. When the opportunity came to join that ship, I began a project to read naval history because the *New Jersey* had made so much history herself, including serving as Admiral Halsey's flagship at Leyte Gulf. Once I reported aboard, I found and perused a copy of the ship's cruise book from World War II. One page depicted the four officers who had flown their flags on board the ship during the war: Halsey, Admiral Raymond Spruance, Rear Admiral Oscar Badger, and Lee. That awakened a flicker of awareness. Once my tour in the *New Jersey* ended, I returned to civilian life and made a special trip to Sioux Falls, South Dakota, to see the memorial and museum that honored the state's namesake battleship in which Lee had served. Still later, I visited the museum ship *North Carolina*, another of his wartime flagships and a sister of the one in which he spent most of his time, the USS *Washington*. It was an honor to tour the *North Carolina*, especially the flag quarters in which Lee had lived and worked.

In 1974 I joined the staff of the U.S. Naval Institute in Annapolis as one of the editors of *Proceedings* magazine. Annapolis gave me proximity to the wealth of naval history source material in the Washington, DC, area and in the Naval Academy library. Research for this book began in the autumn of 1975 with searches of the records and by engaging in interviews and correspondence with individuals who had served with Lee. The goal here is to provide a narrative portrait of Lee as a human being and as a naval officer—his entire life, not just World War II. Descriptions of how he interacted with people are important in delineating his character and personality. By nearly every account, he was a pleasant man with a sense of humor—sometimes coming across as quiet and relatively unassertive. In all likelihood, the Leyte Gulf fiasco was the most disappointing and frustrating experience of his life. The essence of the man was that he cared deeply about the naval profession; he enjoyed what it offered and what he could offer it.

My research on Lee began more than forty years ago, and I am embarrassed that the completion of the project has only now come to fruition. Many other books, articles, and oral histories intervened on my agenda in the meantime. I am particularly rueful that all but a few of those who provided information for this book are no longer alive to read the result they helped to bring about. On the other hand, I am grateful that the admiral's story can now revive the reputation he acquired in his lifetime. In addition, as Captain Mobley suggested, the description of Lee's life can also serve as an inspiration to Navy professionals of this century.

MISCHIEVOUS MOSE IN KENTUCKY
1888–1904

For many years, long after he had left Owen County, Kentucky, Willis Augustus Lee Jr. was still known by local residents as "Mose." The nickname originated in the spring of 1888. Despite her advanced stage of pregnancy, his mother persisted in her pastime of fishing on Eagle Creek, which ran near the family home at Natlee. On 11 May she stayed at it so long, in fact, that she had to be rushed home from the creek for the birth of what proved to be her second son. She joked afterward that she might name him Moses, because she had taken him away from the water just as Pharaoh's daughter had rescued the biblical Moses from his hiding place among the bulrushes of the Nile River in ancient Egypt. The baby was named for his father instead, but the nickname stuck.[1]

The father was a thirty-five-year-old farmer and schoolteacher whose roots were in Kentucky. The baby's great-grandfather, Joseph R. Lee, had been born in the state in 1787, as had his grandfather, Nathaniel W. Lee, in 1825. Nathaniel was a farmer and licensed distiller of bourbon whiskey. He operated a mill on Eagle Creek for grinding grain into meal and flour. The rural hamlet in which the family lived was known originally as Lee's Mill and by 1888 had been renamed Natlee, a contraction of Nathaniel Lee's name.[2] Nathaniel died in 1891. Nathaniel Lee's brother, thus Mose's great-uncle, was Grandison R. Lee, born in 1827. During the

Civil War he served as a Confederate soldier under General John Hunt Morgan of the Second Kentucky Cavalry Regiment and was captured during the war. Grandison later became a physician; he died in 1905. Both brothers were buried in Owen County.[3]

Grandison's great-grandson, Allen Meacham, wrote of Mose's grandfather: "Nat was an ardent Confederate but necessarily inactive since it was his job to care for the farms, but at his distillery he maintained a tavern where his daughters liquored up the Union Soldiers to get intelligence as to Union Activities."[4]

Nathaniel Lee's son, Willis Augustus Sr., was born in Owen County in 1853. He later married Susan Ireland Arnold, daughter of Elijah Arnold, an undertaker and attorney in the nearby village of New Columbus. The census of 1880 listed the population of New Columbus at 84; Natlee was even smaller.[5] Owen County is an area of rolling farmland in north-central Kentucky, not far from the state capital at Frankfort. Its staple crop during the time young Lee lived there was burley tobacco, and farmers raised corn, alfalfa, and livestock as well.

In 1890 the family moved about fifteen miles north from the Natlee–New Columbus area to the county seat at Owenton when W. A. Lee Sr. became the county judge. In the census of 1890, Owen County had a population of 17,676; Owenton was a town of fewer than 1,000 inhabitants. The town was dependent on the surrounding farmlands for its economy. It had barns for the storage of tobacco and the usual facilities and services that made country towns natural meeting places: courthouse, general stores, blacksmith, hotel, harness shop, barber shop, law offices, churches, and schools.[6]

As a county judge, W. A. Lee was the chief fiscal and administrative officer, handling such diverse matters as road building, probate court, and small claims court. A circuit judge tried civil and criminal cases, so that county court day, held the fourth Monday of each month, was a well-attended social event. It attracted horse-drawn buggies from miles around as their owners gathered to trade horses, meet their friends, and be entertained by gypsies and traveling medicine men.

Judge Lee received a second four-year term in 1894 and then practiced law from 1898 until his death from a heart attack in 1931. He was also president of the People's Bank and Trust Company in Owenton and served for a time as city attorney. Like the rest of his family, the judge had dark brown hair and eyes. He was of medium height and became portly as he grew older. His personality was much the same as the one his son displayed as an adult: quiet, uncomplaining, shrewd, reliable, and purposeful. He was friendly and got along well with others, but he was not the hail-fellow-well-met type commonly known among career politicians. His wife Susan was a quiet person who, unlike her husband and children, spent much of her time at home. She suffered from heart trouble and died of a heart attack in 1913.[7]

The Lees settled into a two-story frame house at the corner of Roland Avenue and Seminary Street, about one-eighth of a mile from the county courthouse where Judge Lee worked. Out back of the home were a frame buggy house and an outhouse or two. Willis Lee Jr. had two older sisters, Lucy and Roberta, as well as a younger one, Alice. For a time the family also included Mose's older brother Clarence, who died of appendicitis when he was about eight or ten.[8] The household also included Mrs. Lee's brother, John Arnold, and a cook.

The Lees led a comfortable existence and were considered among the better families of Owenton, though they were not social climbers. Certainly they were among the most intelligent people around. All the children had excellent minds and did well in school. But they were not individuals to be bound by convention. They spoke their minds and did as they pleased, paying little heed to the gossip that followed. One subject of such talk was the family's failure to attend church. They were not attracted by the fire-and-brimstone preaching style of the Baptist Church, the most prominent denomination in Owen County.

Lucy, the oldest sister, married lawyer James Vallandingham; they had a happy marriage that produced three children. Vallandingham was later a circuit judge. By contrast, the two younger sisters lived undisciplined lives and set the gossips to chattering with tales of their behavior. Judge Lee's tolerant nature expressed itself in a live-and-let-live attitude toward gambling and bootlegging in Owenton. It was also manifested in the loose rein he kept on his children and helps explain why his younger son was allowed to become such a prankster. Mose was indeed mischievous, and generally his pranks involved some cleverness.[9]

Mostly young Lee played with other boys, but Florence Arnold qualified as an exception because she was a tomboy. On one occasion Lee and his friends asked her to join in a scheme involving her horse Bill because she was an accomplished rider. The boys killed some snakes and tied them to Bill's tail. Then Florence rode her horse through town with a group of boys running along behind. She stood in the stirrups and pretended to be frightened. The boys, young Lee among them, were calling such things as "Help! Help! This horse is running away with this girl. He'll kill her. Help! Help!" As it was calculated to do, the stunt brought the women of Owenton out to see what the fuss was about. More than seventy years afterward, the horse's rider recalled the incident and the reaction of the witnesses: "When they saw the dead snakes, they wanted to kill every one of us and instructed us in no uncertain terms, that we should know better than find our pleasure in such things as running people crazy for *nothing*, even though it seemed *fun* to us." Her conclusion, which was probably especially true in the case of Mose Lee: "I am doubtful any of us profited by the tongue lashing."[10]

On another occasion, Lee and his young male friends were walking along after obtaining a bag of caramel candy squares wrapped in paper. Some acquaintances saw them and asked for candy. They were put off for a time until Mose and his companions were able to get a bar of yellow soap, which they cut into caramel-size pieces and wrapped in the candy paper. After that, they shared the wrapped squares generously, to the consternation of the recipients.[11]

That was not the only time when Lee allowed something to be taken when it was other than what it seemed. He once was caught in school with a bag of Bull Durham tobacco in his pocket and the tag and drawstring dangling in view. The teacher confiscated the sack of tobacco and threw it into the school stove. Soon afterward, as if in demonstration that he had not learned his lesson, Lee again showed up at school with a tobacco sack in his pocket and the tag in view. The teacher took the second bag and pitched it into the stove, which then exploded. Lee had emptied the bag and refilled it with gunpowder. Afterward, he could claim, in a literal sense, that it was the teacher, not he, who had caused the explosion.[12]

A few black citizens lived in Owenton, and they generally got along well with the whites. The children of both races played together, even though their schools were segregated. None of Lee's close friends was black. Sometimes he and his chums teased and played tricks on Bill Lewis, a black youth who drove cattle to pasture. To the white boys it was doubtless playful fun, but they sometimes taunted Lewis to such an extent that he got angry enough to throw stones at his tormentors.[13]

W. T. Forsee, who would many years later become president of the First National Bank in Owenton, went to school with young Lee. He remembered him as an "uncouth youngster who was apparently oblivious to his personal appearance and what other people thought of him. Mose enjoyed the outdoors in that mostly rural area and took an interest in reptiles, bugs and freaks of mother nature." Lee's friends learned to be wary of him, because he might pull a snake, frog, or scorpion out of his pocket or some other hiding place and spring it on them. As Forsee put it: "In school most of the boys were rather leery of sitting with him in the double seats which we had to occupy in those days, for fear of introducing something of the undesirable species right during school hours."[14]

Because he was bright, Lee generally did well in school; it was a "family scandal," to use the words of his niece Elizabeth (Lucy Vallandingham's daughter), when Mose once flunked mathematics. He did so at Smith Classical School, a private institution he attended for a while before switching to the public one. Everyone else in the family excelled in math, so it was probably a case of letting his mind wander to things in which he was more interested. (As an adult, Lee demonstrated the facility for solving complex math problems and a tendency not to spend time on things that did not really interest him.) In any event, his sister worked with him to correct the deficiency.[15]

One tale of Mose's days in Smith Classical School became a classic in the annals of Owen County, for some version of it turned up in nearly every account of Lee's boyhood. His unkempt appearance (which, incidentally, was to be a lifelong trait, even when wearing naval uniforms) caught up with him one day when schoolteacher Smith reprimanded him for having dirty shoes. He admonished Lee to go home and shine his shoes before he came to class again. The boy did so, but he did not leave it at that. He carefully pulled a paper bag over each shoe and tied the top of it around his ankle. This, he explained to Smith, was his way of making sure that his shoes would stay shined. Alas, the teacher was not amused and proceeded to give the boy a thrashing for his impudence.[16]

Lee's interest in wildlife was not confined to bringing animals to school. Once he was in a store when the storekeeper remarked jokingly that he wished he had a blacksnake as a means of eliminating a population of rats. When Lee showed up three days later, he reached into his pocket and pulled out a blacksnake, which he deposited on the merchant's counter. The boy also kept a large squirrel cage in his backyard. From his ventures into the surrounding woods, he caught squirrels and kept them in the cage that was six feet high and ten feet across. Sometimes as many as ten squirrels were in it. Many times, though, Mose shot at forest creatures rather than bringing them back alive. One occasion did not turn out so well. Charles Yancey of Owenton recalled the time Lee encountered a skunk. The skunk did what skunks do, and Mose's clothes had to be burned afterward. (Charles' brother Evan later served with Lee in the cruiser *Concord* in the 1930s.)[17]

Judge Lee was an excellent shot and passed the knowledge of shooting along to his son. Many years afterward, Allen Cammack, who was a boyhood neighbor of the Lees, recalled that Mose seemed to have both an unlimited amount of ammunition and an unlimited enthusiasm for shooting it. Lee developed remarkable proficiency with small arms and his interest in guns remained with him, both personally and professionally, all his life. While in Owenton, he was sometimes called upon to rid the courthouse grounds of sparrows, and when there were no live targets to shoot at, he aimed at inanimate ones.

Cammack's sister Louise said of Lee that he was an "unusually bright boy [who] was born with a built-in sighting device and a shooting arm. Anything Mose aimed at he hit. Among his targets were the neighbors' window panes and the cupolas, lightning rods, and weather vanes of the well-to-do." Once he fired through an upstairs window in the Cammack house. Fortunately, Louise's sister Eleanor was not in the room, because the bullet shattered glass all over Eleanor's dolls, and her playhouse was near the broken windowpane.[18]

The boy's curiosity and familiarity with guns brought problems of another sort. One of his chums was a boy named Roy Holbrook. Lee's niece said of the two of them, "They were always in trouble together." Once the two of them decided to make a bomb. They took some gunpowder out of shotgun shells and put it under a tin can. Then they ran a trail of powder from the can as a fuse and lit the other end of it. Nothing happened for a while, so they went to investigate. When Mose got close, the "bomb" exploded in his face, and for a while there was some fear that he would lose his sight. The physician who cared for him was able to save his vision and treat his burned face so well that he had no permanent scars. From then on, however, Lee had damaged eyesight and wore thick glasses much of his life.[19]

Given his restlessness and adventurous nature, it was understandable that young Mose would seek something beyond the confines of Owenton. He could not see himself being cooped up with law books, even though his maternal grandfather, father, and brother-in-law were all attorneys. Instead, he sought to go to the Naval Academy. A friend who knew him at that time offered the opinion that he probably sought the opportunity to leave home because nothing in Owenton interested him.[20] Judge Lee's political connections in the overwhelmingly Democratic county were sufficient to gain Mose an appointment to Annapolis through Congressman South Trimble. He headed for the academy in the spring of 1904, when he had just turned sixteen and had not finished high school. Despite his intelligence, some in town questioned whether he would succeed at the rigidly disciplined academy, given his penchant for unconventional behavior. As former neighbor Louise Davis put it many years later, "The strict rules and regulations were tough on Mose but he stuck it out. This is the only thing he did which surprised the townspeople [who by then had probably lost nearly all capacity for surprise where he was concerned]. They had kind of expected him back somehow."[21]

■ 2 ■

NAVAL ACADEMY YEARS
1904–1908

Willis A. Lee's civilian existence ended on 9 July 1904. Up to then he and Oscar Smith, a Pennsylvania teenager, had been temporary boarders in Annapolis. They stayed at Miss Emma Atwell's house on Prince George Street, opposite Carvel Hall Hotel. (For many years the hotel provided housing for midshipmen's dates when they came to town for dances and other social events.) Smith and Lee took their oaths as midshipmen together that July day.[1]

When Lee arrived at the academy, most midshipmen lived in the New Quarters. "New" was a relative term in this case, since the structure had been completed in 1869. It was a four-story redbrick building with an illuminated cylindrical clock tower rising above it. In 1901 construction began on a much more modern gray-granite building, Bancroft Hall, in the then-popular Beaux-Arts style. The designer was noted architect Ernest Flagg, who produced a building that had dormers, a mansard roof, a center section with a rotunda, and two wings of rooms for midshipmen. The first occupants, including Lee's plebe class, moved into a wing of Bancroft in 1904. That original structure, completed in 1906, was designed for subsequent expansion, and now has eight wings. When Lee was there, the student body numbered fewer than one thousand. Now it is more than four thousand.[2]

One thing Oscar Smith prized about his relationship with the Kentuckian was that the Christmas boxes Lee received from home made his room a popular visiting spot. Years afterward, Smith wrote, "I still savor the delicious taste of the country hams that were always found among the gifts. . . . In those days there was no Christmas leave for Midshipmen and the Christmas boxes were treasured . . . by many a homesick boy in Bancroft Hall."[3]

Marc A. Mitscher from Oklahoma was a midshipman who entered the academy as a plebe in 1904. Another "mid" from that state, Peter Cassius Marcellus Cade Jr., had bilged out the year before for failing academically. The upperclassmen started ragging Mitscher as a surrogate for Cade. Mitscher had to repeat the name of the departed mid whenever asked. The strange upshot was that Mitscher thus acquired the lifetime nickname "Pete." Mitscher struggled academically, and he was also held culpable in a hazing scandal. In November 1905, Midshipman James R. Branch died in a fight among classmates. Investigation revealed that two hundred mids had been involved in hazing. Mitscher was compelled to resign, both for his part in the hazing and for the numerous demerits he accumulated. Even so, the young man was permitted to return to Annapolis and graduated in 1910, two years after Lee. Their paths would cross frequently forty years later in the Pacific.[4]

Lloyd C. Stark from Missouri was another plebe classmate. He graduated in 1908 and remained in the Navy until he resigned in 1911. He went home to join the family apple business and later was in combat as an Army major in World War I. He entered politics in 1928 and served as governor of his home state from 1937 to 1941. In 1940 he ran for the U.S. Senate and lost to Harry S. Truman. After his tenure as governor, he returned to work in the family nursery.[5]

Stark's time as a plebe is of interest because he left behind a diary of September and October 1904. Doubtless he took part in many of the same activities as did Lee. Among them were sailboat drill, steam-launch drill, and time on board the USS *Chesapeake*, a wooden-hulled, three-masted bark with auxiliary steam power; she was renamed *Severn* in 1905. According to Stark, the plebes rowed racing cutters and performed infantry drill and bayonet practice in the armory. Naturally, there was small-arms marksmanship practice as well. Further exercise included boxing, gymnastics, fencing, and swimming. All this was prelude to academic studies in the fall. At one point Stark recorded his weight as 137 pounds.[6] Photos of Lee from the period indicate that he, too, was skinny.

Nicknames were de rigueur at the academy for many years and the Kentucky native soon became "Wah Lee," on the basis of his initials, W. A. He also acquired another nickname that stuck for the rest of his life. John Earle, a fellow plebe, explained, "Lee was given the name 'Chink' by his classmates early in Plebe summer because, vaguely, he looked a bit like a Chinaman. About average in size, he had a round face, eyes that were slightly slanted and a skin yellowish in tone."[7] As the years passed, the nickname was modified to the less offensive "Ching," though many of his confreres stuck with the original version.

Lee spent part of the 1905 summer training cruise on board the *Nevada*, which he joined on 3 June. She was a shallow-draft, low-freeboard monitor with a main armament of two 12-inch guns. On 15 July he transferred to the *Hartford*. She was an old sailing vessel, a steam sloop of war. She had been Admiral David G. Farragut's flagship during the Civil War Battle of Mobile Bay in 1864. During one stop of the summer, Earle Buckingham and Lee were on liberty together in Rockland, Maine, and they passed a laundry with a sign that said, "Wah Lee." Buckingham and another midshipman persuaded Lee to ask the laundryman how to render the name in a Chinese character. Thereafter Lee used the character as an alternate signature.[8]

During three-and-a-half of his four years at the Naval Academy, Lee roomed with Edmund Randall Norton. The roommate marveled at Lee's ability to get by with little studying. Norton himself worked hard and stood second in the 201-man graduating class of 1908. Even though he had a great mind, Lee applied himself on only those things that really mattered to him. Norton observed that the two main categories that appealed to Lee were rifle shooting and freehand drawing.[9]

John Earle marveled at Lee's ability for intense concentration. He remembered that Lee could read a lesson assignment once and retain everything of importance. Earle wrote of Lee, "He never seemed to be in the least burdened by our studies, as were so many of us. On walking into Chink's room one seldom found him at his books. . . . He was particularly good at math, our hardest subject, and spent many hours trying to make dumb classmates see how simple math really was." Earle observed that Lee appeared to have a limited social life. He did not recall Lee being conspicuous at dances, adding, "I am sure he was much more interested in firearms than girls."[10]

Another classmate, Worrall Carter, was destined to have a substantial role in logistic support for the fleet in World War II. Years later, Carter recalled Lee's drawings. Even though Lee and his future wife would have no children of their own, Lee was fond of children and drew sketches to entertain them. As Carter remembered, "My own children had a great fancy for him."[11]

Just after the class of 1907 graduated, Lee began his final summer of training. During the cruise, Lee and classmate Walter Heiberg were assigned to the monitor *Nevada*. Other ships in the training squadron were definitely second line: the monitors *Arkansas* and *Florida* and the cruiser *Olympia*. The latter had been Commodore George Dewey's flagship during the Battle of Manila Bay nine years earlier. The squadron was at Hampton Roads, Virginia, for ten days in June to visit the Jamestown Exposition. The exposition lasted throughout much of the year. This world's fair commemorated the three-hundredth anniversary of the founding of Jamestown as the first permanent English settlement in what eventually became the United States.

During their ship's visit, Lee and Heiberg were often on the exposition's midway. The pair closed down several shooting galleries that hung silver dollars from strings. At a price of ten cents per shot, the marksmen won the dollars whenever their bullets snapped the strings. They were so successful that, according to classmate John E. Meredith, "This was long the subject of conversation in the Wardrooms of the fleets." As Meredith pointed out, the feat was mentioned in Heiberg's entry in the 1908 Naval Academy yearbook.[12]

John E. Iseman, a classmate, wrote, "When in company with [classmate Andrew Denney], we were looking over the shooting galleries on the Midway. Whenever we stopped, the proprietor begged 'Ching' to help himself to any of the prizes, but refrain from shooting up the place."[13] At the end of the 1906–1907 academic year, the school awarded prizes for "general excellence in target practice." The recipients were Willis Lee, gold medal; his friend Andrew Denney, silver medal; and his exposition partner, Walt Heiberg, bronze medal.[14]

From Virginia the *Nevada* proceeded to New England. While the ship was in New London, Connecticut, Lee received orders to report to the academy rifle team in Annapolis. When he was detached from the ship on 12 July, momentous events lay ahead. After undergoing practice at the Naval Academy, on 5 August he joined other marksmen for the National Rifle Association–sponsored national matches.[15] The site was Camp Perry, named in honor of Commodore Oliver Hazard Perry, who won a signal victory in the Battle of Lake Erie during the War of 1812. The camp was a National Guard training facility in northern Ohio—on the shore of Lake Erie. It was the first year the matches were held there, the result of efforts by the state's adjutant general, Brigadier General Ammon B. Critchfield, who sought to improve the marksmanship of Ohio soldiers. Shooters fired toward the open water of the lake; in between an earthen berm held the targets.

As he took part in the competition, Midshipman Lee had a ragamuffin appearance, far from the standard he was supposed to display at Annapolis. He was clad in a sailor-type wrinkled white uniform that bore his last name on the chest, a nondescript hat, and a cartridge belt. What he accomplished in one day was astounding: he won individual national championships in both rifle and pistol. Lee was the only American ever to win in both categories the same year. In the individual rifle category—as opposed to team competition—he was one of 684 contestants. He performed rapid fire at two hundred and three hundred yards, and slow fire was at six hundred, eight hundred, and one thousand yards. Even though he missed two targets at the maximum range, he eked out the victory over Lieutenant W. H. Clopton Jr., a cavalry officer, 318 to 316. With the pistol he shot slow fire, timed fire, and rapid fire at ranges that ran from fifteen yards to seventy-five yards. In that case he beat out his nearest competitor, 238 to 237.[16] His classmate Thomas C. Kinkaid talked with Lee after the triumphs at Camp Perry. Lee told him that he had finished the rifle competition early, so he entered the pistol matches "just to kill time." Clearly, he accomplished more than that.[17]

William Ward "Poco" Smith was also on the Naval Academy team. Smith wrote of Lee, "As an expert rifleman and pistolman, he might have been called a 'Nut' on this form of sport." On one occasion when they were shooting together, they were engaged in rapid-fire mode with bolt-action rifles—five shots in twenty seconds. Then Lee pulled what Smith termed a "stunt" during a match to determine who would make the team the following day. While Lee was shooting at a target two hundred yards away, a dog ran across the field, halfway between the firing line and the target. Smith reported, "Ching's rifle left the target as he sent his five shots at the dog. But nothing could keep him off the team." Because of his vision problems, Lee used different pairs of glasses while firing at different ranges.

Once, while firing at one thousand yards at Camp Perry, Lee confided, "Poco, at this range I cannot see the bull's eye. The entire target looks the size of a postage stamp." Smith observed that Lee aimed at the postage stamp and hit the bull's eye.[18]

Classmate Eugene Wilson was also a member of the rifle team. He emphasized that successful shooting by the Navy men was the result of effective teamwork. Members shot in pairs and coached each other. The rifleman firing the shot was responsible for the correct elevation of the piece, while his partner provided help on deflection—that is, coaching on horizontal aiming. He did so by observing the way wind moved the flags on the range, heat waves, clouds, and other factors that would affect the flight of the bullet during its trajectory to the target.[19]

Years later, John Earle, a fellow member of the rifle team, wrote to Lee's widow, "Lying prone in the boiling sun on the rifle range, through binoculars I would spot Chink's shots for him as he fired at long ranges. Then he, in turn, would do the same for me." He recalled that Lee often paused to wipe the sweat from his eyes and polished the lenses of the shooting glasses he wore. He also attested, as have many, that Lee was not flustered. As evidence of Lee's skill, Earle wrote, "I have seen him shoot chippy birds out of a bush with a Colt's .38—one, two, three, four—just as fast as he could pull the trigger."[20]

One of Lee's lifelong traits was his becoming sense of modesty. During his first-class year, he was in the same company with Midshipman William Kurfess, who was a plebe at the time. Kurfess explained that weekly personnel inspections were standard operating procedure. Midshipmen wore their full-dress uniforms, including medals. Lee did not comply, so the inspecting officer asked him where his medals were. Lee made an excuse—that they were being repaired or something else. The inspector finally lost patience and told Lee that if he did not show up with medals at the following week's event, he would be put on report. "The next Sunday," remembered Kurfess, "Lee did appear in formation with his chest so covered with medals that it was difficult to see his jacket."[21]

Poor eyesight dogged Lee throughout his naval career. He wore thick glasses and was always concerned about passing the vision portion of the annual physical. His classmate Thomas Kinkaid wrote that Lee memorized two lines of the eye chart that was no closer than twenty feet from a midshipman being tested. More than fifty years after they had been at the Naval Academy together, Kinkaid wrote that he still recalled the sequence of two vital lines: "FLOTDEXC" and

"CLVFOTZE." Once, when Lee and Kinkaid were walking together, Lee's vision was so poor that he was unable to recognize his roommate from across the street. As for personality, Kinkaid remembered Lee as unruffled and imperturbable and added, "I don't ever remember seeing him angry (nor anyone else angry at him)."[22]

Eugene Wilson of the rifle team knew Lee well. Like Kinkaid, he shared his midshipman recollections more than fifty years after the fact. Wilson recalled that Lee habitually failed the regular eye exam. The procedure called for a retest of those who flunked. By virtue of his name's place in the alphabet, Wilson took the regular exam near the end of the line. He was thus able to let Lee know which chart was in use that day. Lee could then recite the day's sequence of letters during the retest that followed right after the regular one. Remarkably, after all the intervening years, Wilson in 1962 recalled one line of letters that matched Kinkaid's memory: "FLOTDEXC." (Reaching ahead to discuss Lee's 1942 achievement at Guadalcanal, Wilson added, "When I heard the news of Chink Lee off Savo Island, I found justification for the little deceit we had perpetrated on the physical exams at Annapolis.")[23]

Among Lee's cartoons in the 1908 yearbook was a self-portrait that showed him with tousled hair, large-rim glasses, a big grin, and a chest full of medals. The latter were for his shooting prowess. Accompanying the sketch was a limerick:

This is a heathen Chinee,
Who is otherwise known as Wa Lee.
Take a look at the Chink,
And you surely will think
How jealous old Zimmy must be.[24]

The last line was a joking reference to Lieutenant Charles A. Zimmermann, bandmaster at the academy since 1887. In 1906 he composed the music for "Anchors Aweigh," the Navy's unofficial anthem.

In May 1908, not surprisingly, the Bureau of Medicine and Surgery reported that a physical examination of Midshipman Lee revealed that he had defective vision, a potentially disqualifying condition. His right eye tested at 11/20 and his left eye at 10/20. Nonetheless, the Navy's surgeon general recommended that he "be allowed to graduate with his class, subject to re-examination two years hence to determine his physical fitness for the service." The office of the Secretary of the Navy concurred in the decision.[25]

On 5 June 1908 Lee and his classmates graduated, after four years of study, drills, training cruises, and a generally confined life within the walls of the Naval Academy. Of the 201 graduates, Lee stood a middling 106 and was among the youngest. He had turned twenty less than a month earlier. His only younger classmates were Harry M. Hitchcock, born 7 June 1888 and Lee Pettit Warren, born on 20 June. Hitchcock was the youngest midshipman, admitted at the age of sixteen years, eight days. Lee, who did not finish high school, was also among the youngest admitted at just under sixteen years, two months. The level of attrition had been considerable in the years since he arrived: eighty-two of his original classmates did not make it to graduation.[26]

■ 3 ■

JUNIOR OFFICER
1908–1918

According to the practice of the era, graduates of the Naval Academy were required to serve two years in the probationary category of "passed midshipmen." The class of 1909 was the final one in that category. Starting in 1910, academy graduates became ensigns upon graduation, though still ranking in seniority behind the new ensigns who graduated in 1908 and 1909.

On the day after his class graduated, Lee had not far to go for his first assignment. After leaving the midshipman dormitory, he moved several hundred yards to the old sailing ship *Severn*, namesake of the river in which she was berthed. Lee and his classmates first encountered her as the *Chesapeake* during seamanship training in their plebe year. For Lee she provided a temporary home as he practiced with the Navy Rifle Team. He spent most of July and August with the team at Camp Perry, Ohio, the scene of his 1907 triumphs. That was not his first choice of duty. On 1 June, shortly before graduation, he had asked to compete for a spot on the U.S. team that would participate in an international rifle tournament in Bisley, England. The Bureau of Navigation, which directed personnel assignments, summarily turned him down.[1]

After he finished in Ohio, Lee spent thirty days of leave home in Kentucky. He was now ready to join the seagoing Navy, though his first ship turned out to be a lemon. He reported to the battleship *Idaho* on 2 October 1908.[2] She was brand new at that point, having been commissioned on 1 April. The ship was 382 feet long and displaced thirteen thousand tons. The British battleship *Dreadnought*, eponym of a new type, had entered service in 1906 and set a new standard for battleships with her main battery of all big guns.

The *Idaho* mounted the standard pre-dreadnought armament of four 12-inch guns, eight 8-inch, eight 7-inch, twelve 3-inch, and two torpedo tubes. It was truly a mixed bag. Not only that, she was built on the cheap. Previously Congress had provided basic characteristics so that each class would have the best armor, armament, and speed. But in 1905, in authorizing the *Idaho* and her sister, *Mississippi*, Congress restricted the tonnage, making them less capable than their predecessors. Battleship historian Malcolm Muir wrote that the two sister ships "proved a perfect example of false economy in defense spending. They were of such limited endurance and so slow that they hampered the performance of the whole fleet."[3]

The ship's wardroom comprised about three dozen officers, including passed midshipmen such as Lee. In November of that first year Lee was assigned to engineering duty. The ship could generate ten thousand shaft horsepower with two triple-expansion reciprocating engines. Fuel, as in all navies at that point, was coal. The *Idaho* could muster a top speed of only seventeen knots. Lee joined the watch-standing rotation, in port and under way. A few months later, on 22 February 1909, the ship was part of a large naval review at Hampton Roads, Virginia, to celebrate the return of the Great White Fleet to the United States. President Theodore Roosevelt had dispatched a squadron of battleships on a trip around the world. The title of the group came from hulls painted white, rather than the gray of the Spanish-American War. The superstructures and masts were tan in color, known as "buff" at the time. The circumnavigation was a test of operational capability and logistic support. International diplomacy was also involved as American sailors and officers mingled with citizens of other lands. Roosevelt was on hand to welcome the fleet home. It was his swan song as a naval-oriented president. He left office on 4 March.

Lee's tenure in his first ship ended in May 1909 when he returned to the rifle team and the *Severn* in Annapolis. His prowess earned him repeated spots in that capacity over the years. Indeed, he continued his small-arms shooting and coaching through the remainder of his life. An academy classmate, Bill Brereton, related an incident that demonstrated Lee's ability and coolness. During their time together in 1909, Navy shooters were trying out for the pistol team. Brereton wrote, "Lee had what was probably an overloaded cartridge in his revolver. At any rate his piece blew apart which [sic] he was firing. He turned to the guy behind him, after throwing down his gun, and said: 'Dan lend me your gun; I want to finish this string.' He finished the string with his *left* hand (his other was injured) making all bulls-eyes!"[4]

The competition for which the team was preparing was the annual meet of the New England Military Rifle Association, held at Wakefield, Massachusetts, in late July 1909. Lee's friend Andrew Denney won the Vaughn revolver reentry match at twenty-five yards, and Lee won the Sears timed-fire revolver match at fifty yards. Denney was the overall winner in the pistol competition. The *Boston Globe* crowed about beautiful weather and the quality of the competition.[5] From Massachusetts Lee proceeded to Camp Perry, Ohio, for further shooting.

Lee next spent a brief period on board the *Independence*, a former warship originally commissioned in 1814 as a square-rigger. She was the U.S. Navy's first ship of the line—that era's equivalent of a battleship. By 1909 she was a receiving ship at Mare Island Navy Yard in Vallejo, California, north of San Francisco. In that role she was a floating barracks that provided berths for those stationed at the shipyard and for transients such as Midshipmen Lee, Heiberg, and Denney.[6] Receiving ships were common in that era before the Navy had established considerable infrastructure ashore to house and feed men in transit. Often they were old warships that were long past useful roles in the fleet.

Lee then joined the protected cruiser *New Orleans*, which was being refitted at Mare Island for China service. A protected cruiser was one that had armor above her machinery spaces but not the side belt armor that characterized a similar type known as an armored cruiser. The 3,769-ton ship had a main battery of six 6-inch guns. She had been built in Britain for the Brazilian navy. In March 1898, with the Spanish-American War in the offing, the U.S. Navy bought the ship. She was renamed *New Orleans* and participated in the war off Cuba that soon followed. From 1899 to 1904, she was the flagship of Commander Cruiser Squadron, U.S. Asiatic Fleet. She was decommissioned in 1905.[7]

Lee's friend Eugene Wilson, another member of the class of 1908, was also at Mare Island. He was assigned to the destroyer *Hull*, which was undergoing overhaul. The young academy graduates—rifle team alumni—received overtures from an agent of a potential expedition. He sought to recruit them to overthrow the Manchu government of China. The inducements included "fantastic sums" to resign from the U.S. Navy and become sharpshooters for the adventure. Wilson remembered, "As a final offer, he guaranteed us the right to chop off as many Chinese heads as might suit our fancy, an offer that somehow did not appeal to Chink Lee at all."[8]

Instead, Lee and Denney were part of the cruiser's crew when she was recommissioned on 15 November. From California the new shipmates ventured across the Pacific and arrived at Yokohama, Japan, on 25 April 1910. She then patrolled in various Far Eastern waters. It was a reprise of the ship's earlier service in the Asiatic Fleet, and it was Lee's first in-person exposure to China. The *New Orleans* had served mainly as a seagoing taxicab to get the young men overseas.[9]

Though he was by no means a prolific writer, Midshipman Lee, along with his coauthor Andrew Denney, got an article published in the first 1910 issue of the U.S. Naval Institute *Proceedings*. The topic was revolver shooting, and certainly the two of them were well qualified to offer instructions. The six-page article was a primer on the subject and included hand-drawn diagrams to illustrate the shooter's desired stance and various views of the grip. Though the illustrations did not carry Lee's name, one was identified by his "signature" in a Chinese character. The approach was that anyone could learn to shoot well. One tip was, "Acquire accuracy before you try for speed." Then came this advice: "Remember first that the revolver is a very dangerous weapon, especially when *not loaded*." (Presumably they were referring to a pistol believed to be unloaded.) It was the only *Proceedings* article either of them ever published.[10]

On 6 June 1910, two years and one day after his graduation from the Naval Academy, Lee was commissioned as an ensign. (Surprisingly, when he took his promotion exams for what was then termed "final graduation," Lee flunked the navigation section with a mark of 2.16. He passed the re-exam held on 7 December of that year.) The *New Orleans* delivered Lee and Denney to Hankow, China, near current-day Wuhan, where they joined their next ship on 26 May.[11] The *Helena*, commissioned in 1907, served in both the Yangtze River Patrol and South China Patrol. She was distinguished in appearance by a tall foremast and tall smokestack; the latter helped disperse the heavy black coal smoke that came from her boilers. She was 251 feet long, 41 feet in the beam, and had a shallow draft of nine feet for navigating China's rivers. Her main armament consisted of four 4-inch guns.[12]

The purpose of the collection of ships in the area was to protect U.S. interests in the Far East. Typically, the locus was known as the "China Station," though the ships operated elsewhere as well, often in the Philippines. Some sailors "home-steaded" with the fleet, remaining there for tour after tour. Lore had it that such extended tours made a man "Asiatic," suggesting perhaps that he had slipped out of the mainstream and was inclined to behave oddly at times. For a young officer who sometimes signed his name with a Chinese character and went by the nickname "Chink," such an assignment seemed a natural.

It was also natural that he did a lot of shooting. In 1911 he crossed paths with one of his Annapolis classmates, Ensign Philip Seymour, who was then serving in the crew of the *Pompey*, a torpedo boat tender that arrived in Shanghai after a tour on the Yangtze River. Lee's ship was in the port at the same time, so he visited the *Pompey*. Seymour told him of an indoor rifle range ashore. Lee wanted to go there for practice if he could find some ammunition. An officer who frequented the range had a supply and agreed to "lend" Lee a few boxes of .22-caliber bullets. The next day Seymour learned that Lee had been stricken with cholera and hospitalized ashore. As his classmate recalled, "For a few days everyone was apprehensive and worried because [among] cholera patients very few recovered. However, I am glad to say he recovered in a short time and everyone felt relieved."[13]

Marine Second Lieutenant Adolph Miller, a shipmate who joined *Helena* in 1911, was a year behind Lee and Denney at the academy, though he didn't graduate. He described the pair as "inseparable friends—Gold Dust twins." Once Miller was part of the crew, the ship ventured in April of that year from Shanghai to Hankow because of rumors of a revolution between the Manchu government in Shanghai and the rest of the huge country. The revolt broke out in October in Hankow, where the ship was in port at the time. A landing force comprised of a company of Marines and two divisions of sailors went ashore from the *Helena* to protect American interests.[14]

The Imperial Army came south and clashed with the revolutionaries at Hankow. Those in power prevailed in the struggle. In his role as an intelligence officer, Miller was ashore for five months, and Lee commanded a division of sailors. During the five months of fighting, Miller kept a day-by-day record of the revolution. He and Lee joined in compiling a report that went to the Office of Naval Intelligence in Washington. Their further endeavors at looking after American interests involved what Miller called "an International Cocktail Tour." He and Lee made many liberties together in Shanghai and Hankow and at other ports on both sides of the Yangtze, all the way to Ichang, a thousand miles away. Their other activities included trips to China's interior to hunt for tigers, bustards, and pheasants.[15]

Around 1912 Lee and other members of an assembled team challenged people in various ports to rifle and pistol matches. Ensign Harold C. Train, who graduated from the academy in 1909, reported years later that he believed the Americans always won.[16]

On 29 January 1913, the Helena detached Lee with orders to return to the United States at the end of his tour. He took passage on board the collier Abarenda. He boarded her at Shanghai, China, and rode her to Nagasaki, Japan, and then to San Francisco. In April, he reported to the battleship New Hampshire but in June left for temporary additional duty with the Navy Rifle Team, for which his services were so frequently needed. The event was another series of matches in Wakefield, Massachusetts. Next was another stint at Camp Perry, Ohio. Afterward he reported to a receiving ship, the USS Franklin, in Norfolk to await the arrival of the New Hampshire. The Franklin had originally been commissioned as a screw frigate in 1867.[17]

On New Year's Eve of 1913, after spending more time on board the receiving ship, Lee returned to duty on board the New Hampshire, which was herself already obsolete. She had been commissioned in 1908 and had the dubious distinction of being the U.S. Navy's last pre-dreadnought battleship. She was 456 feet long, displaced sixteen thousand tons, and mounted a main battery of four 12-inch guns. She also had 8-inch and 7-inch guns.[18] In early 1910 the Navy had commissioned its first dreadnoughts, the South Carolina and Michigan, which were virtually identical to the New Hampshire in size and tonnage but mounted eight 12-inch guns apiece.

One of Lee's new shipmates was a young enlisted man, Quartermaster Third Class Arthur J. Sweetman. Years afterward he remembered the New Hampshire as a "happy ship" with a fine complement of officers. He recalled a distinct line between officers and enlisted men but not a sense of resentment. It was simply the way of life, said Sweetman, and it was one that did not sanction fraternization between the two groups. The routine required the enforcement of discipline, and it produced an "efficient" ship—the watchword of the time.[19]

One means the crew had for keeping in shape while on board was to pace the deck. A privilege granted to those with less than a year to go was being able to walk athwartships, that is, from side to side. All others had to pace fore and aft. Sweetman added, "Looking back this seems rather childish, but at the time it was an unwritten law that was strictly adhered to." For amusement while not on duty, crewmen played blackjack and shot craps. There was a written regulation against gambling, but "somehow the officers never seemed to come around at the right time to catch anyone."[20]

Frederick J. Egger, another enlisted man in the crew, was in the second division. The division officer was a lieutenant known as Dopey Shay. Egger did not recall the officer/enlisted divide as being so dramatic as Sweetman did. He wrote, "Lt. Shay evidently transferred to the ship after a tour of duty in China, and did not have that dignified attitude toward the enlisted men that officers did in those days. In fact, he hung out with the crew at every opportunity."[21]

In Egger's recollection, a friendly rivalry existed between Shay's division and that of Lee. Their crews manned whaleboats in a rowing contest won by Shay's men. Rumors among the crew were that the officers had a fifty-dollar bet on the outcome. Shay was so pleased with the result that he sent a boat ashore to buy bushels of mangos and treated his men to mango-flavored pies and ice cream at his expense. Lee, for his part, kept up his compulsive shooting. Egger recalled that the officer whom he referred to as "Bullseye Lee" would send crew members to the galley to bring up empty cans. Two crew members tossed cans into the air simultaneously, and they seldom fell into the sea intact.[22]

From June to December 1913, the *New Hampshire* joined other ships of the Atlantic Fleet in patrolling the Gulf of Mexico. The purpose was to protect U.S. interests, especially because relations were strained between the United States and Mexico. Sweetman said that there was no liberty for the ships' crews because of ill feeling toward Americans. When not steaming, the ship sometimes anchored off Veracruz and sometimes ventured to Tampico. On one return to the Veracruz area, he and his shipmates spotted the collier *Cyclops*, which caused dismay.

Loading the battleship's coal bunkers was hot, dirty, and onerous. It was unpleasant but necessary until oil became the standard fuel.[23]

In February 1914 the *New Hampshire* was operating in the vicinity of Cuba, as the Atlantic Fleet typically did during winter months. Lee was due to be examined both physically and on professional subjects for promotion to lieutenant (junior grade). He was concerned about his ability to pass the vision portion of the physical. Ensign Lee deliberately objected to having the eye exam ratified at the Norfolk Navy Yard unless he was there in person. He would not settle for the results of an exam held on board his ship in January. Events dictated that Lee's examination be postponed because the *New Hampshire* had pressing business elsewhere—Mexico.[24]

The atmosphere worsened in the spring of 1914, when an international incident blew up and led to hostilities. Nine American sailors went ashore in Tampico and entered an off-limits fueling station. The Mexican government arrested and later released the sailors. Rear Admiral Henry T. Mayo, commander of the Atlantic Fleet's Fourth Division, demanded an apology and a twenty-one-gun salute. He got the apology but not the salute. The situation was complicated when the Americans learned of the delivery of weapons to President Victoriano Huerta, who had taken control of Mexico the year before in a bloody coup. U.S. President Woodrow Wilson ordered a landing force to go ashore at Veracruz and seize the weapons from the local customs house.[25]

On the morning of 21 April, landing parties began going ashore from various ships. At that time there were no amphibious landing craft designed for the purpose. Instead, the ships' whaleboats, normally used to carry crewmen on liberty, were towed to the port, where the sailors and Marines clambered onto the land with orders to occupy the customs house, railroad terminal, and communications offices. Initially the landing was unopposed. That night, Rear Admiral Frank Friday Fletcher directed that the sailors and Marines expand their occupation beyond the port area to the entire city. That was too much for the locals, who began attacking the Americans.[26]

Captain Edwin Anderson, skipper of the *New Hampshire*, went ashore in command of the Second Seaman Regiment. Quartermaster Arthur Sweetman was with him to serve as signalman. The situation devolved into urban warfare as the outfit marched toward the Mexican Naval Academy in parade-ground formation and came under fire from locals. Anderson's men, out in the open, were convenient targets. The U.S. ships offshore then bombarded the academy. Into this hostile mix went Lee. He had shot at many things, both animate and inanimate, in his life up to then. Now Mexican snipers were on the menu. The snipers rarely showed themselves, sometimes poking out only a rifle barrel or a hand holding a pistol. Getting targets to respond required risk, but Lee baited them. During a lull, he sat on a curb in the open, with a borrowed rifle across his knees. As Arthur Sweetman's son Jack artfully put it years later in a book, Lee "went ahead, engaging in a competition in which there were no return matches."[27] Contingents of Marines later showed up and brought the city under American control. Lieutenant Colonel John A. Lejeune (who later served as commandant of the Marine Corps) was among those in command.

Captain Anderson wrote of the junior officer, "Ensign Lee was in the position of commanding the Second Company of seamen . . . on the occasion of the occupation of Vera Cruz. He displayed extraordinary heroism in rescuing a wounded man under very heavy fire from rifles and machine guns. He handled his company with conspicuous skill and courage throughout the entire engagement consequent to the occupation of the city and subsequently during the stay of the Naval Forces ashore."[28]

Afterward the *New Hampshire* steamed to New York, where Lee received a visit from his Naval Academy classmate John Earle. Earle wrote of the experience, "I remember having lunch with Chink aboard his ship in the Hudson River upon his return from the Mexican War and listening to his tales of picking Mexicans off the roof tops at Vera Cruz." As the modest Lee said to him, "Oh, I guess I got a few of them." The would-be snipers were silhouetted against a bright sky. "He said he drew a bead on a Mexican at perhaps eight hundred yards, pulled the trigger, and then watched as the man crumpled into the street below." As part of the visit, Lee went to his stateroom and pulled open a drawer crammed with shooting medals. As Earle put it, "They made my eyes pop."[29]

In July, when the ship had moved to the Norfolk Navy Yard, Lee again renewed his request to be examined by a statutory board for promotion, and he passed. The following month, while World War I was breaking out in Europe, Lee went on thirty days' leave. Perhaps he wanted a chance to wind down after dealing with all the bureaucracy involved with his promotion exams. Finally, on 29 September, he was commissioned a lieutenant (junior grade), with his date of rank set retro-actively as 6 June 1913—more than a year earlier. For seniority purposes, he had been an ensign for three years, and now he could finally wear the insignia of his new rank—and collect the difference in back pay.[30]

After he served in the battleship another year, while the United States was steadfastly neutral during the European war then in progress, Lieutenant (j.g.) Lee was detached from the *New Hampshire* on 3 December 1915—a few days after Thanksgiving. After a period of leave, he reported on 9 December to the Union Tool Company, a foundry in West Chicago, Illinois. There he served as naval inspector of ordnance. It was his first shore assignment, seven-and-a-half years since his graduation from the Naval Academy.[31]

The company's low-slung factory had the look of a warehouse—utilitarian rather than aesthetic. Lee's role was to act as a quality control observer. The location also served as a base from which he traveled to other sites that held Navy contracts. In January 1916, for example, the Bureau of Ordnance (BuOrd) authorized the young officer to make repeated trips to the Cutler-Hammer Manufacturing Company in Milwaukee, Wisconsin. There he inspected control appliances for turret motors that were long-lead-time equipment for battleships of the *Tennessee* class. Other travels took him to Minnesota, Michigan, Indiana, and Iowa. Obviously, factories in the Midwest were making their contribution to the construction and arming of ships that would operate on oceans far away.[32]

A letter of 16 March 1916 from the Bureau of Navigation (later the Bureau of Personnel) was the good news, bad news type: "You are advised that the Naval Examining Board before which you recently appeared found you mentally, mor-ally and professionally qualified for promotion and recommended you therefor. The Board of Medical Examiners found you not physically qualified for promotion because of 'myopia,' and recommended that you be further examined physically in six months in order to ascertain whether the present extent of your incapacity still exists at that time."[33]

The saga continued in January 1917, when Lee traveled from Chicago north to the naval training station at Great Lakes, Illinois, to be examined for promotion. The Bureau of Medicine and Surgery in Washington reported by radiograms to the Bureau of Navigation and to Great Lakes that the defective vision in Lee's right eye was 12/20 and in his left eye 10/20. Both could be corrected to 20/20 with glasses, and the medical examiners recommended that Lee be granted a waiver. The answer was slow in coming, so Captain Anderson, his skipper in the *New Hampshire*, sent a rousing letter on Lee's behalf. He noted that while Lee was in his ship, he was impressed by the young officer's ability to pick up objects such as sails and lights. In war games he was an excellent night spotter in spotting "enemy" torpedo craft. As a capper, Anderson wrote, "Lieutenant Lee was in command of a company of sailors at the capture of Vera Cruz and I personally observed him kill with a rifle two snipers who were firing upon my command after the other men of his company had failed to stop them."[34]

Another former *New Hampshire* officer, R. Z. Johnston, chimed in with a letter that echoed Anderson's. He said of Lee, "He wore glasses and appeared to be dependent upon them; but, with glasses on, he was very reliable." Still more support came from Captain Richard H. Jackson, who was Lee's commanding officer in the gunboat *Helena*.[35]

More and more paperwork flowed, red tape in overdrive, and Lee again underwent examination in September 1917. The waiver was granted. Finally, a letter from the Bureau of Navigation on 19 February 1918, after the nation had been at war since 6 April 1917, advised Lee that he had been appointed a lieutenant. His persistence and the recommendations of senior officers with whom he had served paid off. This time the retroactive date of rank was 29 August 1916. Remarkably, Lee did not even need to get his uniforms restriped as a lieutenant. Things were moving rapidly for a Navy involved in a war in Europe and the Atlantic Ocean in between. A letter of 19 April, this one from Secretary of the Navy Josephus Daniels, notified Lee that he was temporarily appointed a lieutenant commander with a date of rank of 1 January 1918—a time when he was still wearing the uniform of a jaygee.[36]

■ 4 ■

WORLD WAR I AND AFTERMATH
1917–1920

I n July 1917, while he was still going through the hassle of trying to get promoted to lieutenant, Lee was transferred to another shore billet. The United States had entered World War I three months earlier, and it still needed ordnance inspectors. One does not have to use much imagination to believe that a seagoing officer such as Willis Lee would have preferred to serve on board a warship that was going "over there" to support the Allied war effort in Europe.

The new job was in a town on the Mississippi River, all the way across the state from Chicago. His new base of operations was the Root and Van Dervoort Engine Company in East Moline, Illinois. It was a temporary geographical change that was to have a profound effect on the rest of his life. In 1918, at a party in Moline, he met an attractive young woman named Mabelle Allen.[1] She was vivacious and had a sense of humor, qualities that were bound to appeal to the young officer. Margaret Allen described her sister, Mabelle, as being slightly over five feet tall and having brown hair and a pink complexion.[2] Lee became increasingly smitten.

The company to which Lee was assigned had started business at the dawn of the twentieth century to provide engines for the fledgling auto industry. In 1910 the company introduced a new engine with an intriguing name, the "Moline Dreadnaught." Among the vehicles powered by the Dreadnaught was a luxury car, the Moline Knight. With the coming of World War I in 1914, Root and Van Dervoort got into the munitions business. It began producing projectiles and guns for the British and constructed additional room in its factory to keep up with demand. After the contract with the British expired, the company put its equipment in storage until the U.S. Navy contracted for the production of projectiles and naval guns.[3]

As the situation had been when he was based in Chicago, Lee's duties carried him to a variety of locations involved in producing war materials. Perhaps the farthest afield was a trip in the autumn of 1918 to Fort William, Ontario, Canada. His role there was to check on the bore-sighting of 4-inch guns furnished by the U.S. Bureau of Ordnance for French minesweepers. This also included teaching the French Navy men how to bore-sight the guns.[4]

On 7 October, soon after the Canada trip, Lieutenant Commander Lee submitted a request to be assigned to sea duty in European waters. He made the point that he had been serving on shore duty for nearly two years. Two days later, the ordnance inspector in Chicago wrote a favorable endorsement and said he had a potential relief for Lee standing by to be transferred to East Moline. Lee's request was granted; he was detached from the inspection job on 1 November. He took with him an identification certificate that reported he weighed 164 pounds, stood 5 feet, 10½ inches, and had brown hair and brown eyes.[5] Lee proceeded to New York and caught a ship to Queenstown, Ireland, which was then an active port for U.S. Navy ships. From there he went to Brest, France, where he reported on board the four-stack destroyer *O'Brien* on 20 November. But he had arrived too late for an opportunity to take part in World War I combat. Hostilities had ended nine days earlier.[6]

Lee was detached from the *O'Brien* on 18 December and ordered to temporary duty at U.S. naval headquarters at Brest. On 21 December he went on board another destroyer, the *Lea*. It was still another brief stay during the postwar chaos in which the Navy was shuffling ships and personnel. On 16 January 1919 Lee arrived at the London headquarters of Admiral William S. Sims, commander of U.S. Naval Forces Operating in European Waters. The next planned stop, in orders issued that January, was to be the U.S. naval base in Inverness, Scotland. But it was not to be, for he was directed instead to the U.S. Navy port office in Rotterdam, Netherlands.[7]

During the early months of 1919, Lee wrote some fairly long letters to his future bride. They were quite in contrast to the brevity of the ones he sent her later in life. During a stopover in London while awaiting transportation to Rotterdam, he wrote to Mabelle,

> Will probably not get back to the States inside of six months. That seems like a long time but remember that to date I have not received a letter and it already seems a year or so to me. I was going to tell you what an awful time I was having being true to you but the facts are that I find it the easiest thing in the world, since leaving you I have not found anyone who is the least bit attractive to me. It may be that distance lends enchantment to the view but you look good to me from here — what there is of you — 91 pounds 7 oz or thereabouts I guess. Dont be too nice to these returning heroes. . . . Havent written to my sister lately, so if you write her tell her I am well but lonesome for you. [Lee's punctuation was sometimes on the casual side, especially his aversion to apostrophes.][8]

In early February, after reporting to Rotterdam, he wrote to her, "If you cant read this it's because I am sitting with my feet on the stove and writing on my knee. This is a lovely place, in summer, so they say but the name seems to fit it." He told her that his duties involved providing routing instructions to ships that were carrying relief supplies of food to the Belgians, Dutch, and Poles, but he was having a hard time getting anything except boiled fish, for food was scarce.[9]

He reached Rotterdam from England on board a small steamer that carried German civilians who were interned in England during the war. The group included men, women, and children. He added, "Before leaving the boat they (except women) were searched by some British soldiers who had been prisoners in Germany — The soldiers seemed to enjoy it." He also teased her because he hadn't received any letters from her: "If you dont write to me I'll fall in love with a fat Dutch girl with a red nose and wooden shoes — (They wear more than that but I dont know exactly what). . . . If you have any spare time start studying French and someday I'll let you order me a dinner." As was typical in writing to her, he signed himself simply, "Lee." And that was how she addressed him and referred to him throughout their lives. His name for her in future years was "Chub" or "Chubby," though the weight he reported was unlikely to put her in that category.[10]

The following letter appears in its entirety because it demonstrates that he had time on his hands, that he missed Mabelle, and that a sense of humor was an integral part of his persona:

Rotterdam 4-6-19
Well small Child

Did you get my cable? Now you know how much I love you. I ran the last two words together to save 16ct. However that was only because I didnt have any more money with me. Had a hard time convincing the man at the cable office that my name was Lovely — He said I didnt look like it to him. I assured him however that I would to you — although I never heard you rave about it. Got a letter from A.T. dated sometime in Feb. — he evidently sent me some other letters but have never received them and am also apparently 6 or 8 letters short from you — Will probably get them when I get home.

Will probably be going away from here in a week or so — dont know where — worse place probably — If there is one. Dont see any chance to go home for some time and right now am not so very anxious as every body is down at Guantanamo so I wouldnt be much closer to you than here.

This blooming base over here will have to bust up sometime soon though of course they will have to have some of us until all the Army is back and everybody in the world is fed.

I can sympathize now with the waitress who is due to go off at 800 and sees a hungry individual come in at 755 and order a 5 course dinner.

Say what have you been doing with those letters you are writing me? — havent had one for about a month! You havent "forsook" me have you? Dont do it — cause I cant get even by finding a good looking Dutch girl — there aint no such animal.

Ive gotten so I dont do a darn thing but come home from the office and read English newspapers and try to study French — Havent been out of the house but once in a month — Went up to Amsterdam took in a Dutch show and a museum. Saw the portrait of every Dutchman's grandfather. All look alike — The only thing that did look good was the tulip beds on the way up — They have acres of tulips - just starting to bloom — raise them for the bulbs. The [sic] cut the flowers off and use them for fertilizer — sell bulbs to America — thousands of tons a year. The beds looked fine and would have enjoyed them more except for blinding snow storm which we ran into — we were in a car.

Everytime I go anywhere I think I might have a good time if I had you along to scold me or to get scolded — Saw a canal the other day that reminded me of the time we drove along on top for about 3 miles and you wanted me to back up! 'member it? How's the world treating you anyhow — cant you write a fellow now and then? Are you trying to get even? dont do it I'll be good and write more often — tisnt because I dont think of you but I never could write letters — have written more letters to you than I have sent home in 5 years. — I guess probably twice as many — nice prospect ahead of you — what? Well anyhow I like you and havent seen anybody else I even thouhgt [sic, line through the word] darn it – thought I liked half as much — I like you so much I cant tell you and you can see for yourself I cant write

Yours with love
Lovely[11]

He remained at the naval port office in Rotterdam until 9 June. A brief performance evaluation rated him as "calm painstaking loyal." He then took a circuitous route via London to Brest, France, from which he rode back to the United States on board the USS *Zeppelin*. She had been built in Germany as a passenger liner and retained her former name in her new life as a Navy transport. Once he left for the States, Lee concluded his first taste of Europe, though all the moving around probably did not make him an enchanted tourist. As it turned out, the immediate postwar period was the only time in his career in which he served on that continent.[12]

He arrived in New York on 27 June and took leave to go home for a visit to Owenton. He requested temporary duty with the Navy Rifle Team, then a tour in ordnance or in a destroyer. Either then or during a later visit, he did some shooting in his old hometown. Evan Yancey, a local teenager who years later graduated from the Naval Academy, wrote, "My first remembrance of Adm. Lee was around 14 or later when I saw him on the Court House lawn shooting sparrows. His marksmanship was 4.0."[13] That harked back to his younger days in

Owenton, before going to Annapolis, when he seemed to have all the ammunition he wanted and plenty of targets.

A dispatch to his home in Kentucky directed Lee to join the rifle team in Caldwell, New Jersey, on 15 July. But he had something else to attend to in the meantime. Lee and Miss Mabelle Elspeth Allen, daughter of John and Margaret Allen, were married on Monday, 14 July 1919. She was twenty-four years old at the time, having been born on 12 September 1894 in Gilchrist, Illinois.[14] Her new husband was thirty-one. The duty that beckoned in New Jersey did not permit a wedding in the bride's hometown, so Mabelle crossed the state to meet Lee in Chicago for the ceremony. The newlyweds had no time for a honeymoon. Afterward Mabelle went back to Rock Island, Illinois, to live with her family.[15]

A brief newspaper account on the day of the marriage did not waste space covering the bride's dress, the location of the ceremony in Chicago, whether it was civil or religious, or the composition of the wedding party. It did report that Mabelle had attended high school in Oskaloosa, Iowa, and Peoria, Illinois. At the time of her marriage, she worked as a clerk in the repair department of the Central Union Telephone Company in a town not disclosed in the article. Rather than indicating where the couple would set up housekeeping, the paper explained they would live wherever Lee's orders took him, though that often did not prove to be the case.[16] Years later, Admiral Jonas Ingram, a close friend of Lee, answered a question from his wife on what he thought of Mabelle. He said, "The only word I can use is 'effervescent.'" Mabelle played the piano, often without needing sheet music. Her sister Margaret described this talent as "improvising." Their younger brother Arthur put it slightly differently: "Chubby is imposing on the piano again."[17]

The day after the wedding, Lee reported as ordered to the newly constructed Navy rifle range in New Jersey to participate in the national rifle matches. Because the war had intruded, these were the first national matches since 1915. Caldwell advertised itself as being "45 minutes from Broadway."[18] The competition was supervised by the Navy and Marine Corps. For the first time small-bore .22-caliber matches were added to the program.

After the New Jersey interlude, Lee returned to shipboard duty, of which he had had little since before the war. Probably the most uncharacteristic stretch in the seagoing career of battleship-cruiser-destroyer man Willis Lee was his nine-month stint as executive officer of the submarine tender *Bushnell* from September 1919 to June 1920. (The ship was named for David Bushnell, a Revolutionary War–era inventor. He created a primitive submarine named *Turtle* that attacked a British warship in 1776.) It is likely that Lee was assigned to the ship for two reasons—to broaden his naval experience by including some contact with submarines and to "stash" him somewhere before going abroad to the 1920 Olympic Games with the U.S. Rifle Team.

He reported to the *Bushnell* on 5 September at New London, Connecticut.[19] The ship in which Lee served was yacht-like in appearance. She was 350 feet long, 46 feet in the beam, displaced 2,900 tons, and had a crew of around two hundred. The *Bushnell* had been commissioned in late 1915. She spent most of 1918 at Queenstown, Ireland, acting as a tender for submarines operating from there in World War I. After the armistice, she escorted surrendered German U-boats to England, Canada, and the United States.[20]

Willis Lee was an outsider, for the officers he was serving with were virtually all submariners. The *Bushnell*'s skipper, Commander Joseph V. Ogan, also doubled as Commander Submarine Division 15. The division comprised two of the latest U.S. submarines, the *S-3* and the *S-4*, and the surrendered German *U-111*. The commanding officers of the boats were lieutenant commanders, all of whom were junior to Lee. The division's mission was to evaluate the capabilities of the new S-boats and compare them with the similar *U-111*.

In contrast to today's practice of treating submarine operating characteristics as classified, the information was quite open in that period. *Scientific American*, for example, published the gist of the Navy Department's report of the *S-3*'s comparison with the *U-111*; it contained a bit of we-won-the-war chauvinism. It rated the American submarine superior in maximum speed, radius, and seaworthiness.[21] One of Lee's shipmates then was Ensign Roscoe Hillenkoetter, just a few months out of the Naval Academy. Despite the Navy reports, he remembered of the German submarine, "Without being unpatriotic, it was a damn good boat." To him the German diesel engines were better than their American counterparts.

For the first three months Lee was on board the *Bushnell*, the ship and her brood stayed pretty much in the New London area. With his typical curiosity, Lee tried to find out as much as he could about the undersea boats and how they worked. He went out in submarines from time to time, occasionally going down during dives. During these trips, Lee went along as a passenger, never in a position of command.

On 2 December, the *Bushnell* and her division left New London to go south for the winter. Their first stop was Hampton Roads, Virginia, where they spent most of the month.[22] Shortly after New Year's Day, the vessels left for the Dry Tortugas near Cuba. At mid-month in January, the division went to Havana. While ashore at the Hotel Inglaterra, the unpretentious executive officer did something that endeared him to Hillenkoetter. The ships' officers were drinking and in a good mood. Lee and the ensign were talking when the latter said, "Commander, what about this?" A civilian overheard the conversation, approached the pair, and said of Hillenkoetter's familiar manner, "Ensign, you can't talk to a commander like that."

Lee, whose back was to the civilian, did not even bother to turn around. He just said, "Hilly, tell that guy to go to hell."[23]

The traveling expedition spent the next few months around Florida and the Caribbean. After a couple of weeks in New York in early May, the tender and her brood finally made their homecoming to New England in the middle of the month. In June 1920, Lee was relieved as executive officer. His brief interlude with submarines was over.

■ ■ ■

The peripatetic lieutenant commander then traveled from Provincetown, Massachusetts, to the Marine barracks at Quantico, Virginia. World War I prevented Olympic Games from being held in 1916. Once the war ended in 1918, there was not much time available to plan for Olympics to be held a year and a half later. In April 1919 the International Olympic Committee awarded the Seventh Olympiad to Antwerp, Belgium, perhaps as a consolation for all the depredations that nation had experienced at the hands of the Germans during the war. To prepare for participation by the U.S. Rifle Team, the National Rifle Association sponsored tryouts at Quantico. Among those who vied for spots were some shooters who had done well in the games of 1908 and 1912. Based on his achievements in years past, Lee was a logical candidate and made the team. Of the seventeen men selected, only one was a civilian. The rest were officers and enlisted men of the Army, Navy, and Marine Corps.[24]

Getting the shooters to Belgium was a challenge in the wake of the war. Commercial liners were booked solid, so Lee made the crossing on board the Army transport *Antigone*. She was a former German liner that had served in the U.S. Navy during the war and then passed on to the Army. Lee boarded the ship at New York on 21 June 1920 and arrived in Antwerp on 6 July.[25] Other military members of the rifle team made it to Belgium on board the Navy's armored cruiser *Frederick*. Until 1916 she had been the USS *Maryland* but relinquished her name so it could be applied to a new battleship.

A challenge that faced the Olympic shooters was that the war had left the Belgian rifle ranges in rough condition; many had been destroyed. The terrain was rolling and barren and buffeted by winds that swirled the sandy surface of the ground. Marksmanship historian Jim Grossman wrote, "The crowning touch, though, was the series of pyramids. In order to get the shooters high enough to see over the hillock, rude pyramids of sand and sod were raised up above the surrounding ground 3 to 15 feet and the firing point was on top of the mound."[26]

The competitions involved a variety of shooting events. All told, Lee participated in fourteen events, including seven in one day. As a member in five-man team events, he captured the following medals: gold, men's 50-meter small-bore rifle; gold, men's 300-meter free rifle; gold, men's 300-meter military rifle, prone; gold, men's 300-meter military rifle, standing; gold, men's 600-meter military rifle, prone; gold, men's 300-meter plus 600-meter military rifle, prone; silver, men's 300-meter military rifle, standing; bronze, men's 100-meter team running deer, single shots.[27]

The captain of the U.S. Rifle Team, Commander Carl T. Osburn, had known Lee for some time; he had been two years ahead of Lee at the Naval Academy. All told, Osburn competed in the Olympics in 1912, 1920, and 1924. He won a total of eleven medals, including two for individual events. In writing about the results of the 1920 Olympics, Osburn emphasized the point that all of Lee's medals came as part of shooting team events. The U.S. team won three individual matches, but Lee was not a winner in those. Summing up years later, Osburn said, "Ching was a wonderful character, loyal, unselfish, and had a wonderful dry sense of humor."[28]

Not long after Lee and Mabelle were married, Lee took his shooting medals to the Allen family home in Rock Island. As his sister-in-law Margaret Allen recalled, he carried them tied up in a big silk scarf. She sought to make them more presentable by neatly pinning them to a black woolen cloth lined with green silk. Lee was pleased with the result. In time the silk wore out, and Lee got so many more medals—around seventy altogether—that she created a cloth the size of a card table upon which to display them.[29]

In the early 1920s, future midshipman Albert Mumma attended shooting matches with his father and older brother, both of whom were expert marksmen. The young man recalled Lee as patient and kind, and said he had a quality found in most top-notch riflemen—"good steady nerves." He recalled that Lee compensated for his poor vision with shooting glasses, which had only half a lens on the right side, to keep the rifle's bolt from hitting the glass and breaking it.[30]

On their return to the United States, Lieutenant Commander Lee and Commander Osburn reported to the building across the street from the White House that housed three governmental departments: State, War, and Navy (now known as the Eisenhower Executive Office Building). There they received congratulations from Secretary of the Navy Josephus Daniels. A photographer captured a picture of the three men with all of the recently earned medals laid out before them.

Soon, however, it was back to the real business of being a naval officer. The war period and its aftermath had permitted little sea duty. Lee had not served on board a combatant ship since he was detached from the battleship *New Hampshire* five years earlier. Now he was poised to assume his first command.

▪ 5 ▪

DESTROYER SKIPPER
1920–1928

O n 7 September 1920, after the Olympics were over, Lee received his regular
promotion to the rank of lieutenant commander, superseding the temporary
rank granted as of New Year's Day in 1918. On 28 September he took over
his first command, the four-stack destroyer *Fairfax*. She was a hurry-up job built
at the Mare Island Navy Yard in California for wartime duty. The shipyard laid
her keel on 10 July 1917, and she went into commission less than a year later, on
6 April 1918. The *Fairfax* was 314 feet long, had a beam of 32 feet, and displaced
1,247 tons. Her armament consisted of four 4-inch guns, two 3-inch, and twelve
21-inch torpedo tubes. She carried a crew of one hundred men and had a rated
speed of thirty-five knots.[1]

Lee's ship was based in Charleston, South Carolina, as a member of Destroyer
Division Eight, which comprised five ships. Divisions Eight, Twenty-four, and
Twenty-five together made up Destroyer Squadron (DesRon) Eight, which contained seventeen ships altogether. He and his wife lived in a large two-story house
on Tradd Street, not far from Battery Park. In mid-March 1921 Lee wrote to his
mother-in-law in Illinois, "I am probably the worst letter writer in captivity. I
have been hoping to answer your letter in person but dont see any chance of
it for some time. That being the case the only solution I can see is for you to

come and see us." He sent along a check for $150.00 to pay for the railroad fare for Mrs. Allen and Mabelle's sister Margaret. A day later, probably in response to a telegram, he learned that they would visit, so he wrote again. This time he said, "Maybelle was so tickled she couldn't sit still a minute." (At times he used an alternate spelling for his wife's name, in addition to calling her "Chub.") As with the letters he had sent his future wife from Europe, he signed "Love Lee" and added in a postscript that Mabelle's mother should bring along her recipe for lemon pie.[2]

Years later Margaret wrote, "Through the years I spent many vacations visiting Chubby and Ching." On this occasion the skipper entertained his relatives with a dinner party on board his destroyer. A bonus was seeing the moonlight on the water in the harbor, and a junior officer escorted Margaret to a dance. He described to her an incident when the *Fairfax* and accompanying ships first arrived in Charleston. Local citizens were holding a picnic on shore to welcome the crews. When Lee's ship got near land, one of the young engineers put on more speed than appropriate in confined waters. Margaret recounted the tale she had heard: "When Lee saw the situation, he remained calm as usual and guided the ship to safety, but maybe some of the greeters got a few sprinkles." Of her sister, she remembered, "Mabelle had a pretty pink and white complexion, sparkling azure blue eyes, and usually wore daintily colored organdy dresses and high heeled shoes." The two sisters enjoyed walking around the old southern city and viewing the flora, a number of which were different from the ones they knew back in Illinois. For instance, they saw lots of varieties of azaleas, as well as live oak trees draped with Spanish moss. To Margaret it "looked like a fairy land." And she discovered that in South Carolina the word "hear" has two syllables, pronounced as "he-ah."[3]

In Charleston, the Lees had a maid who shook her head while observing Mabelle's frantic pace and exclaimed, "Miss Lee, she's always in a hurry, she walk fast, she talk fast, she work fast." Also, remembered Margaret, Mrs. Lee had a tendency to lose patience if things didn't work smoothly or as quickly as she expected. That sense also applied to her appearance if she wasn't satisfied with the way her hair and clothes looked. Her sister added, "Meanwhile Lee who was always calm, would sit quietly watching with a gleam of amusement in his eyes, just thoroughly enjoying her show of annoyance. Then Chubby would glance at him and begin laughing. She could see the humor in the situation even when it concerned her."[4]

On board ship, Ensign John T. Bottom Jr. observed Lee's ingenuity in action. One of the unofficial denizens of the *Fairfax* was a rat that habitually traversed atop a steam pipe that led to the anchor windlass. The pipe was near the overhead of the officers' wardroom. Lee devised a method for executing the critter during one of its nightly trips. He set up a string stretched taut across the pipe, and the string, through a series of leads, went to the trigger of an air rifle that was propped up on pillows and held firmly in place on a wardroom transom by two heavy copies of Nathaniel Bowditch's book on navigation. The first attempt failed, because the rat managed to jump over the string. Lee made appropriate adjustments to the amount of lead given. The next time the air rifle made a direct hit that sent the rat tumbling to the deck, "where he was dispatched by gleeful and admiring J.O.'s wielding brooms."[5]

During Lee's time in command, the ship engaged in routine exercises off the East Coast. He also had additional duty as squadron gunnery officer, and from time to time he was given temporary command of other destroyers to convey them from Philadelphia to reserve fleet storage at Charleston. These other assignments suggest that the operations of the *Fairfax* were not all that taxing.

Lieutenant Commander Lee was detached from commanding the *Fairfax* on 1 June 1921 after slightly less than nine months. In a ceremony at Newport, Rhode Island, he became the commanding officer of the USS *William B. Preston*, a ship commissioned the year before and thus slightly newer than the *Fairfax*. In mid-1922, partway through Lee's time in command, the *William B. Preston* was ordered to the Far East. An amusing sidelight is that Commander Elijah H. Cope, a supply officer assigned to the New York Navy Yard, gave Lee a letter of introduction before departure. The letter was dated 17 June and addressed to Mr. Allan Colon in Annam, Hue, French Indochina. Cope asked Colon to introduce Lee to big-game hunting. He concluded, "I will always feel obligated to you if you find my good friend a TIGER."[6]

In 1924 (by which time the *William B. Preston* was in the Far East) Lee received a letter from Lieutenant Jerauld Wright, who was executive officer of the destroyer *John D. Ford*, then in Manila. Wright gave Lee the going rates for hiring guides, beaters, carts, and cooks for a hunting expedition in the Annam.[7] No available records indicate whether Lee was able to participate on this occasion, though his *Helena* shipmate Adolph Miller reported that the two of them did hunt tigers in China in the early 1910s.

The *William B. Preston* was a member of Destroyer Division Forty-Five and Destroyer Squadron Fourteen. The long transit took the ships across the Atlantic, through the Mediterranean, Suez Canal, then to the Indian Ocean, and on into the Pacific. The squadron commander was Captain Thomas T. "Tireless Tom" Craven. The skipper of the *Hulbert*, another ship in the same division, was Lieutenant Commander Frank Braisted. Many years afterward, he recounted a stop the ships made in Malta while going through the Med. He and Lee and other ships' captains stayed late in a bar. Braisted said that the people who ran the place tried to shut down the bar at midnight, "but we wouldn't let them close it." Tireless Tom called them together the following morning and didn't really ask any questions; it was more a case of letting the skippers know that he knew they had been involved in something.[8]

Braisted remembered that Lee was an excellent ship handler. He also saw Lee when all the commanding officers got together for conferences. He observed that Lee always had useful comments on the topics at hand. Braisted offered a terse evaluation of Commander Husband E. Kimmel, the division commander, who "was a little tough."[9] That was a characteristic of Kimmel throughout his career: energetic and demanding in preparing those under him for the challenges to be faced in wartime. Sadly, though, he was caught by surprise many years later, for he was commander in chief, Pacific Fleet when the Japanese attacked Pearl Harbor in December 1941. Twenty years after that, when asked to comment on the captain of the *William B. Preston*, Kimmel's memories went back to a happier time: "I knew Ching Lee well and liked him immensely both as an officer and as a man. . . . He was a fine naval officer who recognized the essentials and paid little attention to anything else. His crew worshiped him. . . . His ship was always near the top in gunnery and other activities which make an efficient fighting unit."[10]

Braisted recalled something else of interest. When he visited the *William B. Preston*, he went to Lee's cabin, where the skipper opened a couple of drawers under his bunk and revealed a cache of rifles and pistols. Doubtless the ship had an official armory in which weapons were locked up. The captain had his own private supply. When the ships shot target practice, they sometimes used a procedure known as "ping-pong," in which a .22-caliber rifle was attached to the top of a 4-inch gun, with the target some distance away. When the gun was moved up and down, the rifle went with it, and the bullets it fired were much less expensive than service ammunition.[11]

After her long journey, the *William B. Preston* joined the Asiatic Fleet. Her homeport was Manila in the Philippines, and in the summer she went to the cooler climes of Chefoo, China. Though far less robust than the U.S. fleets in the Pacific and the Atlantic, the Asiatic Fleet rated a four-star admiral as commander in chief. In August of 1922 the officer who took over that role was Admiral Edwin A. Anderson, Lee's skipper in the *New Hampshire* during the Veracruz operation in 1914. Anderson was among those who wrote testimonials that allowed Lee to remain in the Navy with a waiver for glasses.

A number of the wives of officers assigned to the division traveled to the Far East to be with their husbands; a small newspaper clipping from the era indicated that Mrs. Lee was among them. At some point during the early years of the Lees' marriage, Mabelle became sick while she was alone. She did not let on to her sisters about the problem until afterward. During a subsequent visit, she reported that she had rheumatic fever and had to be careful of overexertion. She was on digitalis the rest of her life and often remarked that she became nervous when in crowds.[12]

The *Truxtun* was another ship that made the long transit to Asia; she was a member of Destroyer Division Forty-Three. Lieutenant James L. Holloway Jr. was her executive officer. Holloway's wife and his son Jimmy accompanied him to his new assignment on board a transport. The youngster, James L. Holloway III (born in February 1922), made the trip in a baby carriage. A half century later he became a four-star admiral and served as Chief of Naval Operations (CNO) from 1974 to 1978.

The senior Holloway was the source of a story about Lee's approach to rats on board his new ship. In this version, the skipper improved upon his scientific applications in terms of extermination. The wardroom was small because the ship carried only a half dozen officers, including the commanding officer and executive officer. Atop the room were exposed I-beams, the lips of which were wide enough to accommodate rats that looked down at the officers eating their meals and saw the potential for food scraps. Moving beyond the strings and BB gun setup of the *Fairfax*, Lee concocted a miniature guillotine.[13]

On the beam, with the help of one of the ship's machinist's mates, he rigged up an electric solenoid connected to a razor-sharp six-inch knife. The solenoid was operated by a button on a wardroom table and connected to the knife by a wire so that the knife dropped after the button was pushed. As rats ran along, the men at the table had a good line of sight and took turns pushing the button when they hoped it would be the appropriate moment. There was a delay between the button push and the dropping of the knife, so it took some time and practice to develop the requisite skill on lead time before sending a victim to what Holloway called "rat Valhalla." Stunts such as this, said Holloway, displayed Lee's dry sense of humor and charmed the members of his crew.[14]

The *Preble* was another destroyer in the same division with the *William B. Preston*. Milton E. Miles was one of the ensigns on board in 1923; he graduated from the Naval Academy a year earlier. From his academy days and for the rest of his life he would be known by the nickname "Mary," because some wag in Annapolis thought his name was similar to that of a silent movie star of the era, Mary Miles Minter. He married an adventurous young woman named Wilma Sinton Jerman from Washington, DC. She was known as "Billie," so as a couple they were known as Mary and Billie.

Miles' widow Wilma presented still another version concerning rats as targets. She said that on several occasions her husband visited Lee on board the *William B. Preston* and that the skipper would get out a water pistol to shoot at the rats, at least one of which was given a name. It seems that Lee was invariably shooting at something. This was Lee's first meeting with Ensign Miles, and it was noteworthy because his career would be intertwined with Lee's years later.[15]

Hong Kong, then a British crown colony, was among the locales that the U.S. destroyers visited. One of the diversions was to hold shooting matches with the British on Stonecutters Island in Hong Kong's Victoria Harbor. The British won most of the contests, because they were able to practice ashore, while the U.S. destroyers had to go north to operate around the Chinese mainland. The U.S. ships put in appearances there in order to be available for possible evacuation of American citizens if trouble arose. Mrs. Miles suggested the possibility that the very presence of the U.S. ships prevented the sort of occurrences that would have made evacuations necessary.[16]

During one of the destroyer's excursions to the north in the summer, the British happened to see the Americans shooting. They noted that Lee was shooting poorly, but they didn't realize that the tricky American was doing so on purpose to set them up. When they later went back south for their actual matches in Hong Kong, one member of the U.S. team had to drop out, and the Americans asked if Lee could be a substitute. Because of Lee's thick glasses and the memory of his poor shooting earlier, the British accepted and made heavy bets on their team. The Americans won the matches and the bets. Evidently, the British were unaware of Lee's accomplishments in the Olympics a few years earlier.[17]

On Saturday, 1 September 1923, the Great Kanto Earthquake caused mass devastation on the main Japanese island of Honshu. Resulting fires and a tsunami led to thousands of deaths and a great deal of property damage and homelessness. Destroyers of the U.S. Asiatic Fleet were sent to the area to aid relief efforts. Despite the gravity of the situation, Lee still found an opportunity to have some fun when he took the *William B. Preston* to Yokohama. Knowing how security conscious and suspicious the Japanese were, he devised a ploy. He had his men bring up a table-sized meat-chopping block from the galley. The sailmaker—a Navy occupation rating at the time—made a canvas cover for the block and painted it. Then the crew mounted the contraption atop the ship's forward gun mount. As the ship entered the harbor, Lee sat on his bridge and took pleasure watching the Japanese take photos of the "new secret weapon."[18]

The Chinese milieu within which the *William B. Preston* operated during part of her tour in the Asiatic Fleet was the setting for Richard McKenna's marvelously evocative 1962 novel, *The Sand Pebbles*. As depicted in the 1966 film adaptation, Chinese men served as stewards and served the crew well, even though they were not themselves members of the U.S. Navy.

As always, Lee's focus was on accurate gunnery—and not just with small arms. The *William B. Preston*, along with the other ships in the division, periodically fired for practice at targets. Lieutenant (j.g.) William S. G. Davis was a member of the crew of the *Sicard*, one of the other ships in the division. He recalled a time when the ships were involved in long-range battle practice. Long before radar fire control was a factor, the ships used optical range finders. The devices proved inadequate because the "eyes" were too close together; that is, the base was too short to provide sufficient triangulation of the target. Lee's experimentation led to trying for a longer base by having crew members make simultaneous readings of the angles from the centerline of the ship when the number one and number four guns were on target. As Davis recalled, "Unfortunately, the brass arc on which the pointer registered 'degrees of train' gave readings too broad to permit the accuracy desired, but the innovation was typically 'Lee' and helped convince the Bureau of Ordnance of the need for better range-finders in the 'cans' of those days."[19]

On one occasion while the ships of the division were operating out of their northern base in Chefoo, China, Lee's ship was to be part of the raiding force during a night exercise. The object was to penetrate a harbor undetected under cover of darkness. The battle problem came to a sudden end when the other ships discovered that the *William B. Preston* had sneaked in among them, even though she had lights burning. The skipper, with his oft-practiced cleverness, rigged the ship with oil lights carried for use in case of power failure. They were located so as to give the impression that the vessel was a Chinese coastal craft entering port. To make it seem that the ship was wider than in reality, he had his men rig the lights on booms stretched out from the sides. Though Davis conceded he was not certain of his memory, he believed that Lee had taken the illusion even further by swapping the positions of the fore-and-aft lights and backing into the harbor. To give course instructions, he used the emergency conning station on the after deckhouse.[20]

In addition to the shooting matches in Hong Kong, Lee and his ship had other interactions with the British. In 1924, competing teams—one American and one British—sought to make the first aerial circumnavigation of the world. For the U.S. Army Air Service, Donald Douglas, head of the Douglas Aircraft Company, modified the DT-2 torpedo bomber the firm (then called the Davis-Douglas Company) had developed for the Navy. The new aircraft was dubbed the Douglas World Cruiser. It no longer had weapon-delivery capability; instead, it carried much more fuel than did the torpedo version. The logistics planning involved staging fuel, spare engines, and other spare parts at various places around the globe. The team of four American planes manned by Army pilots got under way on 6 April 1924 in Seattle and headed to Alaska.[21]

Meanwhile, British aviator Archibald Stuart Charles Stuart-MacLaren had taken off thirteen days earlier in an attempt to win the circumnavigation honor for his nation. His was a private venture rather than a government-sponsored initiative. He and his two-man crew took off in their Vickers Vulture from a base near Southampton, England, and flew eastward. They encountered many mishaps in that primitive era of aviation. Their route included France, Italy, the Mediterranean, Egypt, and India. While en route to Rangoon, Burma, radiator problems forced them down at Akyab Island in the Bay of Bengal, short of their destination. After repairs were completed, they attempted to take off and instead crashed. The plane was destroyed.[22]

First Lieutenant Lowell H. Smith, commander of the American flight, learned of the crash while staying at the Imperial Hotel in Tokyo. (The hotel, designed by American architect Frank Lloyd Wright, survived the earthquake while many other structures did not.) The British had a spare seaplane available at Hakodate on the northernmost Japanese island of Hokkaido. There was little prospect of the Royal Navy springing loose a ship to travel from Hong Kong to Hokkaido and thence to Burma—a potential voyage of eight thousand miles. In the spirit of sportsmanship, the U.S. Navy got permission to aid the fliers of the nation competing against the U.S. Army. On 28 May, Lieutenant Commander Carroll M. Hall, commanding the destroyer *Paul Jones*, got his ship under way from Yokohama, steamed five hundred miles north, and picked up the spare aircraft. The crew of the *Paul Jones* had to alter the ship a bit to shoehorn the British plane aboard. It was stored in three large boxes—one for the engine, another for the fuselage and wings, and a third for spare parts. The boxes wound up being stowed between the mainmast and engine room hatch. The Americans also took along a British mechanic to reassemble the plane in case MacLaren's people needed help.[23]

As he had in going to pick up the plane, Hall then cranked his ship up to twenty-five knots for the next leg of the journey, to Hong Kong. Who should be waiting there to take up the next leg of the relay race? Lieutenant Commander Willis Lee and the USS *William B. Preston*. Lee sent a radio message to MacLaren that the British aviator's new plane would reach Akyab Island no later than 13 June. The voyage was a challenging one as the destroyer was beset by a typhoon and rough seas. The ship crossed the China Sea, refueled at Singapore, steamed through the Strait of Malacca, and reached Akyab on 11 June.[24]

The next challenge was that of off-loading the boxes carrying the plane and spare parts, for the backwater port had only a two-ton crane, and the cargo boxes weighed four tons apiece. Thousands of Burmese and Indians gathered to watch the proceedings, as did hundreds of crows patrolling overhead. Carefully, the crane was chained down and the crew gradually swung a heavy crate toward shore. Once it was clear of the ship and almost in place ashore, the crane tipped over and dropped its contents the final three feet onto the dock. When MacLaren opened the crate, he found the contents undamaged. Journalist Lowell Thomas, who wrote of the incident, observed that whichever American naval officer conceived of the idea of using the *Paul Jones* for part of the trip used a wise bit of gamesmanship. He also concluded that John Paul Jones, hero of a notable victory over the British in the American Revolution, might have sat up in his grave.[25]

The end of the story is that the American team did win the race, despite the Britons' earlier start and the help provided by the U.S. Navy. The U.S. Army plane returned to Seattle on 28 September after having flown 27,553 miles in 175 days. The British effort came to an end on 4 August 1924 when the Lee-delivered plane had to make a forced landing in fog at the Commander Islands in the Bering Sea. The crew was rescued, but the aircraft was too badly damaged to continue.[26]

Lee's command of the *William B. Preston* ended on 29 July 1924 when he was detached at Chefoo, China. It was a tour of duty he must surely have enjoyed. He returned to the United States on board the USS *Argonne* and subsequently reported on 8 November to serve at the New York Navy Yard in Brooklyn. Few specifics are available on his duties there, though it is likely that his contributions were in the field of gunnery and ordnance inspection, as they had been during his World War I stint in Illinois. He did undertake other activities on the side, such as serving as president for the court-martial of a Navy physician. And he provided aid to a naval aviator who was soon to become world famous for his missions to the North Pole and Antarctica. He was Commander Richard E. Byrd, who had been put on the retired list as the result of sports injuries he had suffered as a Naval Academy midshipman. He sent gracious thanks to Lee for getting a dock assigned for his expedition's use and arranging for the storage of supplies.[27]

In 1925, when he was serving in New York, Lee received orders to report to the Naval Academy on 1 June for duty with—no surprise there—the Navy Rifle Team. That same month, Ensign Morton C. Mumma Jr. graduated from the academy. His father, Morton C. Mumma Sr., an Army colonel, was rated as an expert marksman. The son and six classmates were ordered to Camp Perry to try out for the rifle team and the national matches to be held there in August and September. Young Mumma and his fiancée had planned to marry that June, after his graduation. In that era it was customary to get permission from one's commanding officer to marry, and in this case his CO was Lee, the captain of the team. When Mumma asked, Lee's response was very quiet, courteous, and nonetheless direct: "Young man, I don't care if you get married, but if you want to shoot on the Navy Rifle Team, you will wait until the matches are over." Mumma had a quick conference with his future bride, and they agreed to wait until 7 October of that year to marry. In recalling the episode in 1962, Mumma said that the marriage was a "relationship we still enjoy."[28]

Mumma and two of his classmates made the Navy team and participated in the national matches that took place in the era when the national Prohibition against alcohol was in full swing. As each pair of contestants on the ten-man team completed its shooting in the final team match, Lee said to them, "Go back to my tent, and you will find something to relax and take the edge off." Mumma was in the fourth pair to compete; when he got to the tent, he saw the six previous shooters sitting on the tent floor. They were gathered around Lee's suitcase, which was filled with bottles of Canadian Club whiskey. When the fifth pair of teammates finished firing, and Lee had finished his "able coaching," they joined in to relax and receive Lee's compliments for their shooting. The team had achieved a second-place finish.[29]

In September 1926, Lee was promoted to the rank of commander, eighteen years after leaving Annapolis. He passed the promotion examinations with high marks, particularly in international law, strategy, and tactics. His retroactive date of rank was 2 April of that year. Lee's stint as executive officer in the target repair ship *Antares*, which was home-ported in Norfolk, Virginia, was another side trip from destroyers. He reported to the ship on 27 November 1926. It didn't have the excitement, or probably the pleasure, of destroyer service, but it was among the jobs that someone had to do, and for a while Lee did the job.

In the years before World War II, officers in battleships and cruisers made their professional reputations in gunnery exercises. The results were measured by practice firings against targets towed by tugboats or other ships. The targets themselves were wood-and-canvas contraptions built atop rafts. The procedure after a firing involved measuring the number of hits a ship achieved, and results were further broken down to specific turrets in each ship. Since the practice obviously called for making holes in the targets, target parties had to repair them between firings. That was where ships such as the *Antares* came in. At the time, the auxiliary-type ships that served the combatants were known collectively as the fleet train. Where the fleet went, the train followed. The *Antares* was the flagship of the commander of Train Squadron One, a place for the admiral to park himself. The ship also provided some logistical support for accompanying ships and had a photo lab on board to develop pictures that showed how well target practice went.

Ensign Thomas H. "Tommy" Dyer was one of the junior officers on board during Lee's tenure. Years later, Dyer was the Navy's top cryptanalyst in breaking Japanese codes. The results enabled U.S. forces to achieve a draw in the Battle of the Coral Sea in May 1942 and a decisive victory in the Battle of Midway the following month. In 1926 Dyer was still learning his craft as a seagoing naval officer, but his time in the *Antares* did not help. As he recounted many years later, the year was about as unproductive as any he spent in terms of furthering his professional qualifications. He was essentially just marking time. Very likely, it was much the same for Lee.

The ship spent part of the year at Guantánamo Bay, Cuba, a warm-weather training site for the fleet. One highlight of the *Antares*' time there was a challenge from a cruiser to the other ships present to participate in a series of competitions. As Dyer puckishly described it, the ships' crews faced each other in "tennis, swimming, whaleboat racing, bridge, acey-deucy, and right- and left-handed drinking. This last was unsuccessful because they could not keep the referees from imbibing also, but it did help to pass the time." Predictably, Lee added another activity for the benefit of the officers, teaching them the proper ways to handle the .45-caliber automatic pistol. After the training, he took them to a shooting range ashore, and they demonstrated their proficiency.[30]

When that tour ended, Lee took command of the four-piper *Lardner* on 7 October 1927 at Norfolk. He served in that capacity until relieved on 16 June 1928. During his time on board, the *Lardner* operated along the Atlantic Coast, made a winter cruise to the Caribbean, and often trained Naval Reservists.

While Lee was there, Lieutenant Dashiell L. Madeira was serving on board the destroyer *Lamson*. She and the *Lardner* were part of Destroyer Squadron Nine of the Scouting Fleet (the title assigned to the ships in the Atlantic). The Battle Fleet in the Pacific was the main force. At times Lee visited Madeira's house in Charleston, where Madeira was entertaining. He recalled that Lee "was a man whose crew loved him . . . because he always had a wisecrack, and one could never think of what he was going to do next."[31]

Lee's ship-handling prowess was especially vivid in Madeira's memory nearly a half century later. As an example, he said that one day somebody remarked that it would be impossible for one destroyer to come directly aft of another and "kiss" the stern with the bow (this was long before the era of sonar domes). The argument was that the wake of the leading ship would push away the bow of the pursuer. As Madeira recounted, "Ching stated it could be done and took his destroyer . . . out to the stern of another destroyer and kept pushing the engines ahead, jockeying the rudder to take care of the [propeller] wash, and finally kissed the stern of the destroyer ahead." He quoted Lee as saying, "You see, it can be done."[32]

With that proof of his ship-handling skills, Willis Lee's destroyer days were over.

During the 1928–29 academic year, Lee was a student in the senior course at the Naval War College. After leaving the *Lardner,* he arrived in Newport, Rhode Island, on 20 June. He and Mabelle moved into a rented house, because there was little government housing available for students. Lieutenant Commander Henry M. Kieffer was undergoing instruction at the same time as a member of the junior course. He observed that a sign on the front door of the Lees' residence contained the Chinese characters for happiness.[1] Lee's sister-in-law Margaret Allen provided a description from a visit she and her mother made to Newport. She wrote that Commander Lee and his wife were ensconced in a two-story house built on a terrace several feet above the sidewalk. The address was 5 Bliss Road—thus the Chinese for happiness.[2]

At this far remove, there is no indication of what the Lees paid for their accommodation. An author described the housing situation in Newport: "Student officers needed housing in a hurry, thereby placing themselves at the mercy of community realtors whose general reputation at the College was suspect."[3] One practice involved incoming students taking over lodging from those who had completed the previous year's course. Those who could not afford to rent separate houses often stayed in boarding houses.

As for the coursework at the war college, the curriculum was evolving. The school had not been fulfilling its traditional function during World War I because the would-be staff and students were involved in wartime pursuits. Gerald John Kennedy did a superb job of describing the renaissance the school underwent after the war and in tracing its evolution during the interwar years. Rear Admiral William S. Sims, an innovator who commanded U.S. Naval Forces Operating in European Waters during the war, resumed serving as the president of the institution in 1919. That meant a return to the job he held for two months in early 1917 before heading to Europe. Sims established principles that were followed with some modification in the years that followed.[4] (In keeping with the practice at the time, when an officer was no longer serving in a four-star billet, as Sims had been while in England, he reverted to his permanent two-star rank.)

Instruction at the college had to deal with the backdrop of the changing international political situation. The election of Warren G. Harding as president in 1920 came after he called for the nation to return to "normalcy" following the trauma it had undergone during the war. Included in the mix was an international naval conference that produced the Washington Naval Treaty of 1922. Among other things, it prevented the United States from fortifying locales west of Hawaii, notably Guam and the Philippines. In the case of the Philippines, it prevented further fortification. Primarily it called for a ten-year cessation on the construction of capital ships and mandated the scrapping of some older ships. It did allow for the conversion of partially built U.S. battle cruisers to the aircraft carriers *Lexington* and *Saratoga*, which were commissioned in 1927. By the time Lee and his fellow members of the senior class arrived, carrier aviation was demonstrating increasing potential as an offensive force rather than just a supporter of the battleships that were still considered "the backbone of the fleet."

Rear Admiral J. R. P. Pringle, who was the president of the war college when Lee studied there, had been on Sims' staff in London during the Great War and had also been a student and faculty member at the college. Strategy and tactics continued to be major topics, along with a mixture of world affairs, national policy, war games, international law, historical events, and logistics, though the study of logistics was downgraded by the time Lee arrived. The history studies included those from the Nelsonian era of the Royal Navy and World War I engagements, including Coronel, near Chile (November 1914), the Falklands (December 1914), Dogger Bank (January 1915), and Jutland (May–June 1916).[5]

The junior class studied and restudied Jutland from a tactical perspective. The purpose of reviewing these World War I confrontations was, according to historian Ronald Spector, not to study the tactics themselves but to show how actual battles would look as simulations on a game board. Others, such as Chester Nimitz, contended that the Jutland battle was studied so thoroughly as to be ingrained in his memory. The introduction of "quick-decision" games, in which the students had to plan and react to combat scenarios under pressure, was an innovation with Lee's class of 1929. Instructors set up scenarios on boards hidden by screens or curtains. Once the screens were pulled back, the players had to think on their feet in assessing the tactical situation and devising orders to their simulated forces. Once the students presented their orders to instructors, the games played out to fulfill those orders. Umpires assessed the results.[6]

War plans envisioned future conflicts against a few nations that were assigned colors. Great Britain was red, Japan orange, and the United States blue. By far the most likely scenario was blue versus orange. Plans anticipated a westward movement of the U.S. Fleet to establish advance bases from which to engage the Imperial Japanese Navy. Senior class members were required to write theses in the areas of policy and command and to participate in committee studies on various topics.[7] Sadly for the sake of reviewing Lee's career, his thesis is not preserved in the war college archives.

At the time of the arrival of the class of 1928–29, Admiral Pringle revised the organization of the school somewhat by emphasizing a change made by the previous president, Rear Admiral William V. Pratt. It recognized operations as a middle ground between strategy and tactics.[8] A newly established intelligence department replaced the former logistics department. Classroom lectures, divided between military and academic subjects, were the standard format of instruction. Those dealing with military and naval capabilities were often classified. The writing assignments and war games supplemented the lectures.

Some members of the senior class of 1929 wrote theses on the development of American foreign policy. They were Lee's contemporaries, having graduated from the Naval Academy around the same time. Commander Jesse B. Oldendorf, who would be involved in the Battle of Leyte Gulf fifteen years later, studied the

European situation rather than the Pacific. Commander John S. McCain, who was also a senior officer in the Pacific War, wrote of continuing to maintain the Open Door policy toward China. He said Japan had been aggressive in the past, and there was no doubt that "she [Japan] will try again when the time is ripe." McCain also cautioned against "entangling alliances." Commander Alan G. Kirk, who later commanded American naval forces during the 1944 D-Day invasion of Normandy, advocated a world in which the United States would exercise its leadership. Commander Thomas C. Kinkaid, one of Lee's Naval Academy classmates and another future participant in the Battle of Leyte Gulf, provided a historical narrative on the development of U.S. foreign policy.[9]

In sum, the war college experience broadened outlooks and provided a postgraduate educational opportunity in professional topics. Students learned the latest in institutional thinking and had a further bonding experience with contemporaries beyond connections they had made at the Naval Academy. The preponderance of Navy flag officers who made substantial contributions during World War II were Naval War College graduates.

In October 1960 Fleet Admiral Chester Nimitz, who served during World War II as commander in chief Pacific Fleet and Pacific Ocean Areas, made a presentation to the faculty and students of the war college. In it he said that "the war with Japan had been re-enacted in the game rooms [at the Naval War College] by so many people and in so many ways that nothing that happened during the war was a surprise—absolutely nothing except the kamikaze tactics towards the end of the war."[10] Some have debated the validity of the admiral's contention, but the kernel remains. The war college prepared naval officers for a naval war.

Once the academic year ended, Lee reported on 7 June 1929 to the inspector of ordnance in charge, Naval Ordnance Plant, Baldwin, Long Island, New York. The plant manufactured ammunition for the guns and magazines of the fleet. Replicas of battleship projectiles flanked its front entrance. Once again Lee, the gunnery expert, was cast into the same role he had performed during World War I. He ensured that the quality of the product was up to specifications and suitable for use. The job lasted less than a year; Lee was detached from the ordnance plant assignment on 24 May 1930.

He reported to the Naval Academy on 26 May as the non-shooting captain of the Navy Rifle and Pistol team. Ensign Alexander Hood, who graduated from the

Naval Academy in the class of 1930, was a team member. Now that he and Lee and other team members were back in Annapolis, they set up shop for practice. On Sundays, remembered Hood, Lee entertained a friend who played for the Baltimore Symphony Orchestra. The two played a Japanese board game called "Go." It involved strategy through the movement of black and white stones. (It was also a favorite of Japanese Admiral Isoroku Yamamoto.) As Lee and the musician played the game, they simultaneously posed calculus problems to each other to be solved in their heads. Hood recalled, "How any one man, let alone two together, could play the game of 'Go' and mentally solve calculus problems is beyond my comprehension—yet I saw it done."[11]

Following the previous pattern, after the stint in Annapolis the team went to Wakefield, Massachusetts, to prepare for its matches at Camp Perry, Ohio. Newly commissioned Ensign Walter T. Jenkins was a member of that year's team. Years later, his most prominent memories concerned the fatherly approach Lee took toward team members. He cited one example in which Lee gave a party so the "greenhorn" ensigns and their wives or dates could get acquainted with the more seasoned officers. Jenkins remembered the party as an icebreaker because up to then he had viewed lieutenants and above as officers to be feared and respected. But he said that Lee was "very friendly, considerate, a man of few words, but to the point and easy to converse with, and certainly an example of an officer possessing the quality of 'loyalty down' leadership. He made we young ensigns feel like officers and yet the officers and enlisted on the team were a family."[12]

During the matches, a shooter had the opportunity to challenge a ruling from the "butts," where the targets were, if he thought that a decision was in error. Jenkins' forte was long ranges, and he thought the ruling that he had missed the right target was incorrect. The procedure involved the shooter putting up a dollar to register a challenge. Jenkins was sure he had hit the right target, but it was a case of put up or shut up, and he had no money with him on the firing line. Because he did not pay to protest, he was not given credit for an accurate shot. The result was that he got a perfect score, minus five. He explained years later, "Instead of bawling out, Cdr. Lee was amused—I learned a valuable lesson in confidence from him: I should have borrowed from someone."[13]

Once the shooting competitions were completed, Lee reported on 22 September for duty at the Navy Department in Washington. It was the first of three tours he performed in the Fleet Training Division on the staff of the Chief of Naval Operations. This office was the repository for the results of gunnery exercises and engineering competiton from the fleet. It also kept track of the annual fleet problems, as war game engagements at sea were called. The work of the division was not the training of personnel in individual skills, but rather to assess the effectiveness of the performance of ships and groups of ships in their ability to perform wartime missions. A route to promotion in the Navy between the world wars was being a member of the "Gun Club," ordnance engineers who were involved in the design and production of weapons. Though Lee did not have a postgraduate degree in ordnance, he had great knowledge of such matters; indeed, some dubbed him a "scientist in uniform." His particular ability was in being able to apply the theoretical in real-world applications.

Lieutenant Harold Krick first learned of Lee while serving as main battery assistant and fire control officer of the battleship *West Virginia* in the early 1930s. He received a paper Lee had written that included a tabulation of the effect of the rotation of the earth on large-caliber projectiles fired at high elevation—the higher the elevation of the barrels, the longer the range. Krick wrote years later that he always used Lee's data when preparing ballistic corrections for long-range main battery firing practices and believed that the shooting was more accurate as a result. He recalled years later, when the *West Virginia,* "long since relegated to the junk heap and now possibly reincarnated in Japanese cars, stood first among the battleships of the Fleet—some 15 in those days—in 1932, 33 and 34."[14]

■ ■ ■

After a hiatus of more than fifteen years, Lee got back into battleship duty in the spring of 1931. Because of all his destroyer service in the 1920s, he had missed the billet of battleship gunnery officer that was a standard for up-and-coming surface officers of the era. By the time he reported to the *Pennsylvania,* he was a commander and too senior to be gunnery officer. Instead, he took over as navigator of the ship. Lieutenant George C. Dyer, then a rising junior officer (he retired as a vice admiral), observed that only top officers were assigned to the fleet flagship. Joining the ship, said Dyer, meant that Commander Lee "was riding right at the crest of the wave."[15]

The *Pennsylvania* was just finishing up a long modernization period at the League Island Navy Yard at Philadelphia. Gone were the cage masts of old. Now she had tripod masts and fire control tops that were much improved over those in her old incarnation. She also had a two-story conning tower and enhanced flag spaces because the renovation had prepared her for upcoming duty as flagship of the U.S. Fleet. Lee reported aboard on 5 May.

Once the remodeled warship got her post-overhaul tests and trials out of the way, she joined her sister ship *Arizona*, which was just completing her own substantial modernization. They linked up at Norfolk and departed on 1 August on the long trip that would take them to Cuba, Panama, and then to California.[16] There they would become members of the Battle Force. Navigation, of course, was second nature for a seasoned officer of Lee's seniority. He also fell heir to a duty that he probably would just as soon have avoided. Because of his rank, he frequently had to serve as senior member of summary courts-martial held on board the ship. Misdeeds that were considered too serious to be punished at captain's mast were referred to courts-martial for action.[17]

Soon after she reached her homeport of San Pedro, California, the *Pennsylvania* stepped into her new role. Admiral Frank H. Schofield, one of only four four-star admirals on active duty in the Navy, embarked with his staff. Schofield was commander in chief, U.S. Fleet (CinCUS). The ship really had two missions at that point. Because of her guns, she was a regular fleet battleship, and as such operated as part of a battleship division that had its own flagship. But she was also special in that the fleet staff was on board; she was more than just another battleship.

The *Pennsylvania*'s crew carried spit and polish to an even higher degree than the normally high standard of any battleship. The ship's quarterdeck sparkled; the cylindrical bitts that were used for mooring lines had brass sheets atop them that had to be polished laboriously and frequently by members of the ship's crew, especially since they were periodically given baths of salt water by the surrounding seas. Years later, one of the *Pennsylvania*'s officers succeeded in having the brass replaced with stainless steel to make maintenance easier.[18]

Soon the ship settled into a routine that included considerable time at anchor in San Pedro, because the Depression had forced the Navy to be frugal in its use of fuel. As in years past, gunnery was still of prime importance. When the various battleships went to sea, it was often in groups—either for tactical maneuvers, gunnery practice, or both. In the early 1930s aircraft carriers were becoming part of the fleet mix, and only gradually did the annual fleet problems reveal that their planes had potential as a striking force. In February 1932, while the flagship was moored at Ten-Ten Dock in Pearl Harbor, a U.S. carrier force commanded by Rear Admiral Harry Yarnell staged a highly successful mock air attack against defending forces in Hawaii.[19]

Later that month, the *Pennsylvania*'s skipper, Captain John M. Enochs, was so ill that he had to relinquish command of the flagship to her executive officer, Commander Jonas Ingram. Since he was several years too junior in rank for battleship command, Ingram probably had a good deal of "backseat-driver" help from the senior officers comprising the fleet staff. On 2 March, shortly before the commencement of Fleet Problem XIII, Captain Enochs was transferred to the hospital ship *Relief* for treatment. Still later he was put ashore at the naval hospital in San Diego, and there he died in early April. A new skipper, Captain William J. Giles, came aboard to take command, and in early May Commander Ingram departed. Lee relieved Ingram and for more than a month served as both executive officer and navigator. He relinquished the latter duty in mid-June.

As second in command, Lee was responsible for the internal operation of the ship: cleanliness, discipline, and the many things that came under the heading of administration. He went about the high-power job in a low-key way. In the area of discipline, for instance, he had to deal with Ensign Dick Steere, who had gotten so caught up in his celebration of the new year of 1933 that he forgot to report to the ship on time to stand a scheduled watch. Lee summoned him to his cabin, adjacent to the skipper's quarters at the stern of the ship. Steere was filled with apprehension over the possible punishment to be meted out, but Lee merely waved him away with his hand and said, "All right. Don't do it again." Steere concluded that he had probably punished himself as much with his worry about the situation as anything Lee could have delivered. Lee applied essentially no sanction and probably achieved the desired result just as easily as an exec who might have thrown the book at an offender.[20]

During their time in Southern California, Lee and his wife Mabelle rented a pink stucco bungalow at 121 Temple Avenue in Long Beach. Mabelle's sister Margaret and their mother visited the home during Lee's *Pennsylvania* tenure.

Years later Margaret remembered it as being "Bermuda Pink." It was an oblong structure topped with adobe roof tiles; the short portions were at front and back. A porch ran along one of the long sides. It was only a block from the main drag, Ocean Boulevard. A long flight of steps descended from that street to the beach. This area, wrote Margaret, was the desirable part of Long Beach. There were oil wells in the area, but they were far back in the hills and not an intrusion.[21]

During the latter part of Lee's *Pennsylvania* tour, he and Mabelle lived in a home at 430 39th Street, near Point Fermin on the San Pedro side of Los Angeles Harbor. As her sister explained, previously Mabelle had preferred to rent a furnished house, because that made it easier to move whenever there was a change of orders. But for this one she liked the view so much that she rented it and bought furnishings. She enjoyed watching ships far out on the water from the high vantage point and liked to watch their lights at night. For the most part, as Margaret Allen reported years later, Lee preferred living in a big house, but Mabelle often chose apartments. Apartments required less work and because of Mabelle's history of rheumatic fever, doctors did not want her to exert herself. During their time in the home, Lee often did professional reading in the evenings, and his wife spent her time reading, doing embroidery, or playing the piano.[22]

While Lee was pursuing his daytime duties on board ship, the mother and two sisters often walked to the waterfront. Even when they weren't swimming, they at least took off their shoes and went wading. With the harbor so close, the landing of the surf provided a soundtrack to the activities in the house. One time Lee and his wife invited their visiting relatives out to take a tour of the battleship, have dinner, and meet some of the officers. The ship was anchored in the harbor, so—just as Lee did every day to go to work—they rode a launch in order to reach the ship. The visit was a pleasant one. Years later, Margaret wistfully remembered, "Dancing under those big guns was a real thrill."[23]

The Navy was certainly not immune to economy measures imposed during the Great Depression. President Herbert Hoover directed that members of the armed services, along with the rest of federal employees, would be charged a month's leave without pay. This, in effect, amounted to a pay cut of one-twelfth of normal salary. Lieutenant Charles Wellborn Jr. said the cut did not adversely affect morale because the whole country was suffering, and those in the service at least had steady jobs. Another result of the budget cuts was a reduction of steaming hours for fleet ships in order to conserve fuel. That meant more time in port. Despite the cuts, retention of enlisted men was excellent: "We had a largely professional Navy in those days and, of course, it was all volunteer. And since jobs were hard to find when people left the service, a great many didn't leave. When their enlistments expired, they shipped over."[24]

Late on the afternoon of 10 March 1933 an unusual event occurred in the fleet's homeport: a devastating earthquake hit Long Beach. Ensign John Davidson was then serving in the *Pennsylvania*'s sister ship *Arizona*; he provided a vivid description of the result. He and his wife were entertaining friends in their Long Beach apartment when the whole building began to shake, sending their china—a wedding present—crashing to the floor. Years afterward he still had a mental image of looking at a building across the street that appeared to have been sliced open with a giant cleaver. The Davidsons and their guests could see into the now-exposed rooms of the nearby structure and observe the inhabitants' reactions.[25]

Earlier that afternoon, crew members from the various ships homeported in the area were ashore to hold contests in a park. As executive officer, Lee and his wife were at the park so he could present awards to the winners. Lieutenant (j.g.) George Wright, one of the ship's officers, and his wife Estelle invited the Lees to join them for dinner at their home in Long Beach. The exec countered that he had to return to the ship to sign some papers, so he invited the Wrights to join him and Mabelle for dinner on board. As they headed for the ship, those on board the boat felt a terrific jolt when the quake hit but thought perhaps the craft had struck a log. When they reached the *Pennsylvania*, the circumstances were obvious. After dinner, Estelle Wright recalled, Lee would not let the women go ashore, presumably because he was concerned for their safety. As a result, Mrs. Wright spent the night in the cabin of Admiral Richard H. Leigh, commander in chief, U.S. Fleet, and Mrs. Lee stayed in her husband's cabin.[26]

A few days before the earthquake, Admiral Luke McNamee, Commander, Battle Force, sent a letter to the Chief of Naval Operations with a recommendation for the next step in Lee's career. In stilted but effusive language, the four-star admiral wrote,

> During his current tour of sea duty as navigator and then executive officer of the U.S.S. PENNSYLVANIA, Commander W. A. Lee, Jr., U.S. Navy, has been of material assistance to battleship gunnery progress particularly

in such subjects as antiaircraft machine gun defense, ballistics, and the photographic analysis of antiaircraft bursts. His many tabulations and studies along these lines have been of considerable benefit and it is believed to be highly desirable that he should be assigned to some duty ashore where he will be in a position to further advise and assist in general gunnery progress and in the aforementioned still not entirely explored subjects in particular.[27]

Admiral Leigh heartily concurred in his endorsement. In other words, despite the official designations of the duties of his billets on board the flagship, Lee was still pursuing his perpetual interest—gunnery. Admiral McNamee's suggestion bore fruit. On 7 June 1933, Lee's time on board the *Pennsylvania* ended with his detachment, and he reported on 29 June for his second tour of duty in the Navy Department in Washington, DC. He was again assigned to the Fleet Training Division, where his principal duty was the revision of gunnery and tactical instructions.[28] (During his travel from California to Washington, his orders directed that he was to receive a per diem allowance of five dollars to cover expenses.)

Almost all Navy jobs involve some sort of collateral duties, and so it was with Commander Lee during that Washington assignment. A record exists of extra duty that he probably performed only reluctantly, because he eschewed publicity. In this case he delivered a speech on Navy Day, 27 October 1933, at the John Paul Jones Monument in Washington. The event was held under the auspices of the Military Order of the World War and the National Sojourners. The tone of the speech suggests that it was a product of the Navy's public information team and that Lee just read the words. The thrust of it was that other naval powers were building warships up to the quotas specified in treaties on limiting naval armaments, but the United States was not. The talk said that current building programs were not meant to be part of an arms race.[29] History records that the Vinson-Trammel Act of 27 March 1934 called for the construction of 102 new ships that would beef up the fleet considerably. Many other factors were at work than just the Lee speech.

In May 1934 came an example of the division's attention to interior communications. When Franklin D. Roosevelt became president in 1933, he inaugurated the New Deal to provide jobs for American workers. As part of the program, Public Works Administration funds paid for many of the shipyard workmen who constructed the aircraft carriers *Yorktown* and *Enterprise* at Newport News Shipbuilding in Virginia. Those two ships made valuable contributions when war came in the 1940s. In the meantime, Lee went to Rockland, Maine, to observe trials held by the Board of Inspection and Survey on the USS *Ranger*, the first American aircraft carrier built from the keel up for that purpose.

Lee's role during the trials was to observe interior control mechanisms and practices so that the lessons learned could be applied to the forthcoming *Yorktown* class. In September Lee went to the Bath Iron Works in Maine in connection with the pre-commissioning trials of the *Dewey*. She was the second member of the *Farragut* class. These newfangled ships were a considerable improvement over the old four-pipers and thus earned a nickname as "gold-plated destroyers." Their advantages were a raised forecastle for improved seakeeping, higher-pressure boilers, and the new 5-inch/38-caliber gun.[30]

Much of the work of the Fleet Training Division was routine, because the same ships and same airplanes kept going through gunnery and bombing practice year after year. The carrot that impelled performance was the competitive nature of the exercises, which would be reflected in officer fitness reports. Top-notch gunnery could earn prize money for the enlisted crews of guns and turrets—along with the honor of painting a white E, for excellence, on a turret or gun mount. In engineering, the sought-after goal was an E on a smokestack, signifying efficiency in the use of fuel. Some ships took the latter to an extreme, being miserly in the use of fresh water because fuel was needed to run the evaporators that distilled it from seawater. The result could be a reduction in the standard of living on board ship, so wise engineers sought to strike a reasonable balance.

Lieutenant Commander Malcolm F. Schoeffel monitored the performance of the aviation part of the fleet. He reported to Fleet Training in June of 1935 after commanding Scouting Squadron One on board the USS *Ranger*. Years later Schoeffel recalled that Lee had the battleship desk in keeping track of fleet performance. He described Lee as "a very pleasant shipmate in our shore job there." "Shipmate" is a special term within the Navy, describing a degree of bonding and shared experience. Interestingly, Schoeffel applied it even in an office on land. As with others, he thought Lee looked like a kindly farmer, usually wearing a shiny black alpaca coat, because civilian clothes were then the norm for officers on duty in Washington.[31]

As part of the staff of the Chief of Naval Operations, Fleet Training was housed in the Navy Department building on Constitution Avenue. It was a multi-wing structure constructed in 1918, during World War I, to provide temporary quarters for the service. Schoeffel described the interior arrangement in the Fleet Training wing as having desks arranged in a peculiar fashion. Inside the wall that had a public corridor on the other side was a parallel inner corridor that ran the entire length of the office. It was cordoned off into door-less stalls rather than individual offices. Each had a small cubbyhole off the inner corridor.

Lee and Schoeffel had adjacent stalls, and as the aviator put it, "Lee was a lot of fun." During a slack time in the schedule, Lee arranged a setup for his favorite activity—shooting. He brought in a rubber-band-powered pistol and set up a line of plastic birds on the backs of chairs to serve as targets. Then he put his feet up on his desk and began shooting at the birds. Schoeffel, meanwhile, was innocently sitting at his desk and working when he heard what he described as "plink-plist"—something that sounded like a wasp—fly past his ear. When he looked around, he saw no insects. Then came another round, accompanied by chuckling from his neighbor. Lee's ammunition of choice for firing at "these damned little birds" was BBs, which ricocheted off the wall and zinged at Schoeffel.[32]

Schoeffel's responsibility within the division included supplying cameras for the fleet camera party, which was housed in an auxiliary ship of the fleet train. Recording gunfire accuracy was a key part of monitoring and evaluating target practice. Finding the holes in a target certainly provided evidence of hits. Misses were evaluated from other ships with a device that resembled an upside-down garden rake. More information came when members of the camera party took both still and motion pictures in order to plot the fall of shots accurately.

Aside from being shot at by Commander Lee, Schoeffel found the routine in Fleet Training boring. After a year of what he likened to "just cutting out paper dolls," he let it be known that he was available for transfer. Lieutenant Commander Forrest "Fuzz" Sherman, then serving in the Bureau of Ordnance, also sought a change of scene. He wanted to get away and serve at sea and was told to find his own relief. He said to Schoeffel, "Red, I understand you're not all that desirous of spending another year in Fleet Training. Would you care to come over to Ordnance and relieve me?" Schoeffel was so happy that their desires meshed that he said he practically fell upon Sherman and kissed him on both cheeks. As a four-star admiral, Sherman served as Chief of Naval Operations from 1949 to 1951.[33]

One of the many ships on which Lee kept tabs during this period was the USS *Utah*. She had begun life as a battleship, commissioned in 1911. She was one of the battleships involved in the 1914 landings at Veracruz, Mexico. In 1931 she was redesignated as a miscellaneous auxiliary and mostly disarmed as the result of an international treaty. The Norfolk Navy Yard converted her into a radio-controlled target ship for gunnery practice. One or two other ships steamed in the vicinity and sent signals that operated her engineering plant and directed her course and speed. Once she passed her tests and moved to the Pacific, she proved her worth as a training vessel and also contributed to tactical development. Aviators got in their licks as well, dropping bombs and firing torpedoes. Dive-bombing was developing as a U.S. Navy skill in the mid-1930s, and the results of the exercises made their way to Fleet Training in Washington.[34]

Lieutenant Ernest Eller, the *Utah*'s gunnery officer from 1935 to 1938, would later serve with Lee in Fleet Training in the early 1940s. He remembered that the target practice drills were useful because the ship had the ability to maneuver at high speed and serve as an offset target or move with a target raft more realistically than one being pulled by a tugboat. In those cases, the crew members abandoned ship to be on the safe side. It was a little too dangerous to be on board when the 14-inch and 16-inch projectiles were approaching, even though they were dummies and did not carry explosive charges. When the *Utah* was hit, a repair party went back on board to patch up the damage.[35] (Ironically, the ship served as a real target during the shooting war that started a few years later. In 1941 the Japanese bombed her at Pearl Harbor, where she still sits as a memorial—partially capsized and mostly underwater.)

One assessment of Lee's performance during this period came from Rear Admiral Manley H. Simons, who was director of the Fleet Training Division. In 1936 he wrote, "I know of no officer in the Navy that I would prefer to have serve with me more than Commander Lee. He possesses zeal, ability, knowledge, and initiative that is far above the average. He has displayed exceptional knowledge of both theoretical and practical Ordnance in connection with his present duty.

He has lately been selected for promotion to Captain."[36] On 10 August Lee passed the physical exam for promotion. As before, his eyes were subpar, but glasses corrected his vision to 20/20. He had long since demonstrated that he could see well enough to do his job. He officially achieved the next rank on 26 August, with 1 July 1936 as the retroactive date of rank.

That promotion to four stripes would take him back to sea once again. In the meantime, during the last few days of August, Lee and his wife enjoyed a brief respite at the classy Shoreham Hotel in Washington, DC, before undertaking the long railroad trip across the country to California.[37]

▪ 7 ▪

CRUISER SERVICE
1936–1939

It is ironic that the man who commanded most of the U.S. Navy's battleships as an admiral during World War II did not command a single battleship as a captain. Following his second tour in Fleet Training Division, Willis Lee was due for his first major command. For surface officers of the day, the desired commands were battleships, heavy cruisers, and light cruisers—in that order. Having just received his fourth stripe, Lee was one of the Navy's most junior captains. In 1936, the Bureau of Navigation thus slated him for a light cruiser.[1]

He drew the 7,050-ton USS *Concord*, named for one of the Massachusetts towns where the Revolutionary War began. In some respects, the ship was an overgrown version of the several destroyers Lee had commanded. She had four smokestacks, a slim profile—555 feet long, 55 feet in the beam—and the same general lines. The ship, like her nine *Omaha*-class sisters, was armed with twelve slow-firing 6-inch guns, four of them in twin turrets and the other eight scattered in casemate positions at the corners of the superstructure.[2] Although she had been in commission only since 1923, Lee's ship was already obsolescent, particularly in armament. Her antiaircraft (AA) protection was virtually nonexistent. She was originally conceived as a scout cruiser that could accompany a team of destroyers steaming out ahead of the battle line to seek enemy warships. Shipboard naval aviation had come of age during the ship's lifetime, and airplanes had the advantage of being able to look ahead both farther and faster.

The *Concord*'s homeport was San Diego, but as Captain Lee traveled cross-country by train from Washington, he headed to San Francisco. The light cruiser had been at the nearby Mare Island Navy Yard in Vallejo since July and had only recently left dry dock. Commander Eugene T. Oates, the ship's executive officer, summoned Lieutenant (j.g.) Evan "Deacon" Yancey and told him to meet the new skipper at the railroad station. He would recognize Lee, said Oates, because the new captain would have a steamer trunk with him. No such introduction was necessary, because Yancey, like Lee, was from Owen County, Kentucky. He had known Lee since Yancey was in grade school.[3] The change of command took place on Tuesday, 6 October, on the ship's fantail, where Lee relieved Captain William T. Smith.

By all accounts, morale was high in the *Concord* under Lee's command. The enlisted members of the crew were topnotch because the labor situation during the Depression allowed the Navy to be choosy. The era of the pre–World War II Navy was approaching its end, but the fleet had not yet begun its buildup for that war. It still mostly comprised a small, elite professional group of men. Most of the officers were graduates of the Naval Academy, and a good many of the enlisted men were making careers in the service because the Navy life offered security during hard times. Few men in higher pay grades left, so there were few openings. Lieutenant (j.g.) Yancey observed that in one exam period for gunner's mate second class, forty gunner's mates third class took the test, but only one advanced. Yancey compared the professional knowledge and skills of a prewar petty officer third class to those of a wartime chief petty officer.[4]

Within a few days, the ship wound up her yard period, took on ammunition, and headed to her homeport. She spent the next several months conducting various training exercises off the coast of Southern California. On 23 October she became the flagship for Rear Admiral Walter N. Vernou, who was simultaneously commander of Cruisers Battle Force and Cruiser Division Three. Vernou was the type commander for the light cruisers and was in many ways a contrast to the captain of his flagship.

Vernou was a stickler for punctilious compliance with Navy regulations and customs. He insisted that flags be two-blocked at the top on their staffs, that proper terminology be employed, and that Navy men wear neat and correct uniforms. Vernou was a former naval aide to President Franklin D. Roosevelt and a fine physical specimen. When in command of a cruiser himself, Vernou had once called an in-port officer of the deck to task because he had not taken steps to eliminate a loose piece of line—an "Irish pennant" in navy lingo—during his four hours on watch.[5]

Lee was practically the antithesis of Vernou in his approach to the formalities of the Navy. In professional matters he did care and sought excellence. On the other hand, he was casual about appearances, because he didn't think such things were too important. His own uniform was a case in point: when wearing high-collared dress whites, Lee's collar might not be completely snapped, or the snaps might be mismatched. The fronts of his uniforms were often littered with ashes from his ever-present cigarettes. In blues, Lee's necktie knot frequently didn't go all the way to the inverted V of his collar.[6]

Lieutenant Commander Alvin Malstrom was skipper of Cruiser Division Three's aviation squadron, VCS-3, which comprised eight planes—two each for the *Concord*, *Cincinnati*, *Milwaukee*, and *Omaha*. Malstrom was part of Admiral Vernou's staff. He was in command of the planes when they were in the air, and those from the *Concord* came under Lee's command while on board ship. When the cruiser was in her homeport, the airplanes went ashore to the nearby North Island Naval Air Station.[7] The squadron flew Curtiss-built SOC biplanes with floats. Catapults launched the planes into the air, where they served as scouts and also provided aerial spotting during the ship's gunfire exercises.[8] Once they had finished their missions, they landed near the stern of the *Concord* and were hoisted aboard by a crane.

Lieutenant William D. "Andy" Anderson, a naval aviator, had a foot in each camp. As part of the ship's company, he was head of the aviation division in the gunnery department. He was also executive officer of the embarked cruiser scouting squadron. On one occasion Anderson, as the ship's senior watch officer, was officer of the deck and made a routine report to Captain Lee on the bridge. Lee acknowledged with an informal "Okay," instead of "Very well," which was the proper response. Lee quickly looked in the direction of Admiral Vernou, who was also on the navigation bridge because the ship had no separate flag bridge. Vernou apparently didn't overhear the captain's casual response, whereupon Lee turned to Anderson and said, "I got away with that."[9]

In another instance involving the admiral, Captain Lee was not nearly so casual. The ship was engaged in an exercise off the West Coast, and the admiral was the officer in tactical command. At one point Vernou gave an order to the *Concord*'s helmsman, whereupon Lee, who was conning the ship at the time, countermanded the order. He turned to Vernou and said, "I'm the commanding officer of this ship. I give orders to the helm. Please leave the bridge." Vernou did so and apparently apologized later for his action. This was a different Lee, for he was serious about things that were important to him. The line of demarcation between the two officers was clearly defined, and the usually correct admiral had overstepped it.[10]

Lee was also serious about ship handling. When he first assumed command of the *Concord*, he demonstrated to his officers that he knew the ins and outs of maneuvering the cruiser. Once he had done so, he turned the routine chores over to his junior officers so they could gain their own skills. Lee had them run man-overboard drills and take over the duties of the captain and navigator with the ship at sea detail for entering or leaving port.[11] Once, when the ship was approaching anchorage at Coronado Roads near San Diego, Lieutenant Anderson was acting as conning officer, and the ship's junior aviator was navigating. They had the ship headed toward the designated spot, but there was one hitch. The aircraft carrier *Ranger* was anchored in the path. Anderson held his course longer than the skipper thought he should, but Lee didn't raise his voice or reproach him harshly. Instead, he suggested—in his customary calm, quiet way—"Just remember, there is no rule of the road that gives you the right of way through another ship." Anderson took the hint, altered course, and headed toward the assigned anchorage.[12]

One Sunday when Lieutenant (j.g.) Marcus W. Williamson, another junior aviator during Lee's tenure, had the watch in port, Lee called him to the captain's cabin and asked him to bring along bombing data records. When Williamson arrived, the door was open. He walked in and saw that the skipper had a black-board set up. It was filled with bombing data and sketches of airplane bombing approaches at various altitudes. Mathematical formulas were scattered all over the chalkboard. Lee asked the aviator a number of questions, including whether the approaches he had drawn were feasible. Lee was in his shirtsleeves, and the Sunday newspaper lay unopened on a table.[13]

After the ship returned to her homeport from San Francisco, Captain and Mrs. Lee rented one floor in a modest house in Coronado. Lee didn't own a car, so he walked—at a brisk pace—from home to the fleet landing at the foot of Orange Street. There he caught the *Concord*'s gig and rode to work each morning, taking along other officers who lived in Coronado in order to save a trip by the ship's motor whaleboat.[14] When it was necessary to travel farther, Lee rode buses, trolleys, or taxis. With no car available, Mrs. Lee depended on her friends, such as Navy wives Estelle Wright and Margaret Simpson, to provide the transportation.[15]

Captain and Mrs. Lee received callers warmly, but they seldom participated in outside social activities. One junior officer recalled a cocktail party in which he observed the fireplace mantel covered with shooting trophies.[16] Lee preferred to stay home in the evening to work on naval problems, sometimes staying up until the wee hours of the morning by fortifying himself with cigarettes and coffee.[17] Those who knew Mabelle described her with a variety of terms: "tiny," "vivacious," "charming," "friendly," "down-to-earth," and "quite pretty." Like her husband, she was a heavy smoker and tried to kick the habit. Estelle Wright recalled that Mabelle would telephone her, and Mrs. Wright could hear coughs that seemed "so deep that they were coming up from her shoes." Mrs. Wright suggested she try candy when she had a craving for a cigarette, but it did not work.[18]

As for Lee's interests or "hobbies," they seemed directed at improving the ship's gunnery. One of the ship's officers who called on the Lees noticed some books on a table near the captain's chair. The volumes, which Lee described as his "light reading," dealt with the ballistics of small-arms ammunition.[19] The Lees once entertained Irma and Milt Fisher, visitors from Rock Island, Mabelle's hometown. The Fishers reached Coronado in the late afternoon and were eager to get out and see the ocean. While exploring the scenery by car, the two women sat up front, where they were well protected from the elements on a cool evening. Lee and Mr. Fisher were in the open rumble seat in the back, but had no warm clothing. Irma drove blithely along, unaware of the suffering by the two men riding behind. They tried to get Irma to turn around, but the wind prevented their pleas from being heard. At the end of the ordeal, remembered Mabelle's sister Margaret, the two men were shivering from the chill. She said that Lee remarked, "I can see how someone might by angry enough to shoot a person, but I do not understand how anyone could hate a person enough to make him ride in a rumble seat." Such were the travails of a sea captain when ashore.[20]

A good bit of the *Concord*'s operating schedule during those months was built around gunnery exercises in the San Diego area. Typically, during weekends the ship moored to a buoy in San Diego Harbor, then got under way early Monday morning for an operating area near San Clemente Island or off the strand of Coronado. She would anchor in the operating area late in the afternoon or sometime in the evening. The following morning the exercises started again. Sometimes she would stay in port all week to celebrate a holiday or conduct maintenance, but those weeks were relatively rare. Wednesday afternoons the crew got early liberty in a pleasant custom known as "rope yard Sunday." Saturday mornings were reserved for the captain's inspection of the crew and shipboard spaces. It was a routine the interwar Navy experienced for years.

Most of the Southern California exercises involved some form of gunnery practice, and Lee probably relished that part of his job more than any other. As Deacon Yancey observed years later, Captain Lee "was not a spit [and] polish man. But it was wise to have in your possession properly trained men and well [maintained] equipment." In surface gunnery exercises, the *Concord*'s pointers and trainers aimed at target rafts towed either by tugs or other cruisers. The speed of the target depended on the purpose of the exercise. It might be anywhere from five knots to nearly thirty. Yancey also stood deck watches on the bridge, and several times heard Captain Lee express the thought that the United States would have to fight Japan, adding, "He scanned every open foot of deck on the *Concord* to determine where we could install light AA guns." In practice, an airplane towed a target sleeve for the training of the ship's gunners.[21]

When a tugboat was towing the target raft during a firing exercise, Captain Lee often sent one of his officers along as an observer. Using a stopwatch, the officer recorded the elapsed time between when he heard the sound of a salvo and when he saw the splash from the fall of shot. Using the speed of sound in his calculations, Lee used the accumulated data to develop range tables for his guns and to check the accuracy of the range finders installed in the ship.[22]

December of 1936 passed relatively quietly with the observance of a holiday leave-and-liberty period at San Diego. The *Concord* continued her routine of training exercises in the San Diego area until 15 April 1937. That day, she and the *Cincinnati*, a sister ship in Cruiser Division Three, got under way for Bremerton, Washington. After a brief stay at the Puget Sound Navy Yard, the two light cruisers joined up with other units of the White Fleet's Alaskan Force. Fleet Problem XVIII was due to take place shortly, and the force the two cruisers were joining was scheduled to go first to the Aleutian Islands and then proceed to Hawaiian waters, the main arena for the forthcoming action. Rear Admiral Vernou, embarked in the *Concord*, was designated commander of the Alaskan Force.[23]

The passage to the Aleutians was fogbound and stormy. Even so, those in the *Concord* rode in relative comfort, for she was a good "sea boat." Her design allowed her to move with the action of the waves but not be tossed about as destroyers were. Thus, she pitched and rolled only moderately in a seaway. The heavy seas on that northern trip did give the crew more seasickness than usual. Lieutenant Ruthven Libby, executive officer of the two-year-old destroyer *Macdonough*, recalled years later that the ship rolled at times as much as 57 degrees in the rough seas. The rules that directed the war game prevented Admiral Vernou from changing to a more comfortable course.[24]

The ship got to Dutch Harbor, Unalaska, on 27 April. The day was windy as the *Concord* maneuvered to reach the *New Mexico* to refuel. Taking a cruiser alongside a battleship was an infrequent maneuver in those days, but Lee managed it with little difficulty.[25] The ship's engineer officer in 1937–38 was Lieutenant Commander John C. Lester. He received relatively infrequent visits from the skipper, whose attention was largely focused topside. Years later Lester recalled that Lee let him have free rein over his below-decks domain "as long as the ship got where she was needed to be and did well in the annual engineering competition."[26] She did exceedingly well. The *Concord* stood first among Cruisers Battle Force in the 1936–37 fiscal year. Her crew painted an E for excellence on a smokestack, and enlisted engineers could wear embroidered E's on their jumpers.[27] (A year later, Lee's ship stood first in communications efficiency among light cruisers.[28])

Lieutenant G. Angus Sinclair, the chief engineer's assistant, proved to be a real strength in the light cruiser's engineering department. A quiet, dour man, Sinclair knew his business.[29] Before a fuel economy run, for instance, he would get the ship's officers together to explain what would be involved and how best to achieve the objective. In those peacetime days, the careers of engineers rose and fell on their ability to scrimp on the use of fuel oil. If anything, Sinclair's counterpart on board the *New Mexico* was even more stringent. Lieutenant Hyman G. Rickover—future father of the nuclear Navy—had boosted his ship to the engineering E among the battleships of the Battle Force and kept her there. Among his methods were the practice of turning down the heat throughout the ship and turning off fresh water for drinking at times so the ship's evaporators would not consume as much fuel oil in the distillation process.

Coincidentally, Lieutenant William Smedberg, who was on Admiral Vernou's staff in 1937, was a newly commissioned ensign when he reported to the *New Mexico* in 1926. He later recalled an unethical task a more senior officer ordered him to carry out back then to help secure the engineering E. Prohibition of alcohol was then in force through the country. He was directed to bribe the master of a civilian tanker with a five-gallon can of alcohol in return for providing the battleship with off-the-books fuel oil.[30]

A confrontation between the likes of Sinclair and Rickover might be expected to be carefully watched as each sought to gain the advantage. In this case, that proved true to a comic extreme. The *New Mexico* provided two fueling hoses to the light cruiser, but Sinclair decided he needed only the forward one because his men had pumped the *Concord*'s oil aft. Thus the battleship's after hose was stopped off with a plug and allowed to hang goose-neck fashion over her quarterdeck. Someone in the *New Mexico*'s pump room apparently didn't get the word and opened the valves for both the forward and after hoses. The plug was blown out of the dangling hose, and heavy black oil cascaded onto the battleship's gleaming wooden quarterdeck. Her executive officer was standing nearby in his high-collared whites and got an unexpected shower of oil.[31]

Sinclair and his men on board the *Concord* recognized an opportunity, so they rushed across to the *New Mexico*, carrying dustpans, buckets, and squeegees. They put their buckets under the scuppers along the edge of the deck to catch oil going over the side and also scraped up as much as they could from the deck itself. Sinclair's men then raced back to the *Concord* and dumped the fuel into their own tanks so it wouldn't go through their meter and thus would still count against the *New Mexico*. It was "free oil" as far as the engineering competition was concerned. Pretty soon, however, Lieutenant Rickover learned what was happening and made Sinclair's men stop their scavenging. Soon after that, Rickover's people were up on deck with their own buckets and squeegees so they could salvage as much as possible.

Later that day, the pleasant but windy weather changed to something more typical of the Aleutians: rain, snow, and hail. The ships remained at Dutch Harbor until the final day of April, then got under way for the fleet problem near Hawaii. Once there, the ships split up, and the *Concord* joined the scouting line for the White Fleet. Over the next several days, Captain Lee's ship went in pursuit of the "enemy" Black Fleet and was involved in simulated combat. On 7 May, for example, the *Concord* sighted two enemy aircraft carriers, two light cruisers, and a number of destroyers steaming in company. She got into position and launched an attack against one of the carriers with torpedoes and her main battery. Once the attack was completed, she resumed her surveillance role of trailing the Black Fleet's ships.[32]

After several days of such maneuvering, Lee's light cruiser and her fellow members of the Battle Force steamed into Pearl Harbor for the crews to have some leave and liberty. The climate there was decidedly warmer than it had been in the Aleutians, and Willis Lee had a treat in that Mabelle came out from the mainland to spend some time with him. The Lees never had any children, even though they would have liked to. On the other hand, this meant they weren't tied down by a family, and Mrs. Lee could take off for a Hawaiian vacation when the opportunity presented itself. They could afford such treats partly because they didn't have the expense of rearing a family. And, unlike many families in the Depression-troubled 1930s, Lee was assured of a steady job, and his pay increased after being promoted to captain.

Following nearly two weeks at Pearl Harbor, the *Concord* got under way again. Mabelle said goodbye to her husband and boarded the passenger liner *Lurline* for the trip to San Francisco. Captain Lee was also taking a ship to San Francisco, but his wasn't quite a pleasure cruise. During part of the time the *Concord* steamed as a member of the anti-destroyer screen for the *California*, the flagship of the officer in tactical command, Admiral Claude C. Bloch, commander, Battle Force. The *Concord* was variously part of the Blue Fleet and the Black Fleet as colors changed with apparent convenience to suit the situation at hand. As Fleet Problem XVIII continued, the *Concord* was called upon to simulate gunfire a number of times against various enemy surface ships. She finally steamed under the Golden Gate Bridge and anchored in San Francisco Bay on 28 May, more than a month after she left Bremerton.[33]

On 12 June, the ship was back in San Diego after a brief dry-docking at Mare Island. The ship's crew gathered on the fantail that day for the customary Saturday morning personnel inspection, but this time it was special. Admiral Vernou presented Captain Lee with the Light Cruiser Unit Trophy for General Excellence in Athletics. It was a manifestation of the crew's interest in sports and the fact that the command fostered an atmosphere in which athletic participation was allowed to flourish. Sports served as a useful outlet for the U.S. Fleet of the 1930s.

The *Concord* enjoyed unusually good success—particularly for a light cruiser—in the annual Battenberg Cup races among pulling whaleboat crews. (The boats' motive power was supplied by men pulling oars.) The *Concord*'s results stemmed in part from the presence of a warrant officer, Machinist Paul C. Cottrell, who coached the whaleboat crews. In 1935 the *Concord*'s unheralded team staged an upset to win the Battle Force championship and then went on to win the U.S. Fleet competition as well. Whaleboats with long wooden oars were a throwback to an earlier era, but they did provide a means for the sailors and Marines to demonstrate their strength and stamina. One of the *Concord*'s officers observed later, "We had men standing in line and begging for a place to get out there and row their hands raw."[34]

Captain Lee gave his blessing as well. The attitude of the commanding officer could make a difference in such endeavors. It wasn't just a case of some people going off to row boats or box or play basketball or shoot small arms on their own time, although that was sometimes the case. It often meant that men had to stand watches for the athletes or get their work done for them. If the ship as a whole was in favor of the competition, then the substitution was done without complaint. And the esprit went even beyond that, for the matches—especially the Battenberg Cup—often involved heavy betting on the part of the cruiser's sailors.

Awarding the trophy was one of Admiral Vernou's last official acts as commander, Cruisers Battle Force. A little more than a week later, on 22 June, Rear Admiral Julius C. Townsend relieved him, and the flag shifted to the USS *Trenton*. Captain Lee took over as acting commander of Cruiser Division Three for the next few months. Lee's reporting senior was, of course, Admiral Townsend.

Lieutenant Harold Krick became Lee's flag lieutenant during the brief period that Lee was acting division commander. The aide's duties included inter-ship signals, inspection arrangements, and looking after Lee's few social engagements. He also supervised enlisted men—such as yeomen, radiomen, and stewards—who were part of the staff's flag allowance.[35]

With the ship back in San Diego following the fleet problem, it was time to return to the routine of being in port for a time and then out to the operating area for more exercises.[36] On 10 July Lieutenant Commander William F. Jennings reported to the cruiser division staff as flag secretary. Thus began a personal and professional association with Lee that continued for the next seven years. That same summer a quartet of ensigns reported aboard after having graduated from the Naval Academy in June. One was George L. Street III, who was awarded a Medal of Honor as skipper of the submarine *Tirante* in World War II. Syd Bottomley was another; years later he provided this word picture:

> One of our first duties following reporting was to report in person to the Captain, so I got into my best uniform, buckled on my sword, put on a clean white cap cover and gloves and knocked on the cabin door. Captain Lee was seated at his desk working with a slide rule on some mathematical problem when I entered. He was wearing spectacles, coat off, tie at half-mast and gave me a warm smile to put me at ease. All the senior officers aboard, especially the exec Cdr Tommy Oates and Capt Lee seemed as old as God to red-assed ensigns. Capt Lee's freckles and wrinkles seemed to enhance this image. He spoke in a slow Kentucky drawl, and never said more than was necessary.
>
> The Concord was a happy ship under Capt Lee. When he left, the new skipper Capt [Earle C. "Dutch"] Metz was as nervous as Lee was calm & serene. Metz was in all respects likeable and a fine officer, but he lacked the control that Lee exercised on the bridge and throughout the ship by his unruffled, taciturn demeanor. He [Lee] was an old shoe: one invariably could see his collar button above his tie, he had just enough stomach to make his clothes fit sloppily. But he got results.[37]

In mid-August the *Concord* arrived at Long Beach/San Pedro to begin a two-week maintenance period alongside the repair ship *Vestal*. Lee's brief period in command of the division ended on 7 September when white-haired, fifty-six-year-old Harold Raynsford Stark hoisted his two-star flag in the *Concord* as commander, Cruiser Division Three.[38]

Life on board the *Concord* was not all work and no play, despite the continuing routine of various exercises. In addition to the athletic competition, a number of officers and enlisted men formed a rifle team. One Sunday in late October, three officers—Lieutenant (j.g.) K. C. Walpole and two ensigns, Richard Bradley and Fitzhugh Palmer—took a contingent of sailors to practice at the Marine Corps rifle range at nearby Camp Pendleton. They were firing Springfield rifles at a distance of two hundred yards from the targets. Captain Lee showed up unannounced and asked how things were going. He was wearing his blue service uniform at the time, but that didn't matter. Shooting was more important than appearance. He took off his blue blouse, flopped down, and spread-eagled in a prone position on the canvas mats from which the cruisers' men were firing. He squeezed off a clip and scored five bull's eyes. Palmer had a healthy respect for the old Springfields. "They'd kick like a mule," he explained. "Until you learned how to use them, you'd wind up with a fat lip and a bloody nose."[39]

Bradley and Palmer were two contributions the *Concord* had received from the Naval Academy's class of 1936. Years later, both expressed gratitude at having been sent first to the cruiser. In those days, it was standard practice for newly commissioned academy ensigns to report to the fleet's battleships, carriers, or heavy cruisers. That enabled them to get their first experiences as commissioned officers in an atmosphere without a great deal of pressure or responsibility. With fewer officers in the light cruiser, the two of them got their initial upbringing at the hands of a capable bunch of wardroom officers, a group that was serious about professional performance and pleasant to be with. It was also a self-assured gathering, perhaps best typified by two lieutenant commanders: first lieutenant Francis X. McInerney and navigator T. Ross Cooley. Both of those men eventually rose to flag rank, and coincidentally the pair also later commanded the USS *Washington*, Lee's flagship during much of World War II.

After a trip to Oakland in November for Armistice Day festivities, the *Concord* and her sisters of Cruiser Division Three returned to their homeport. They moored in customary spots in San Diego Harbor, as did the three ships of Cruiser Division Two. The seamanship was quite precise in those prewar days, and flag officers watched their minions carefully to see which ones adhered to the prescribed methods and carried things off sharply. Navigator Cooley had the flying moor down cold, as he should have, because the ship used the same anchorage so often.[40]

Early in the new year of 1938, the *Concord* executed individual ship exercises in the San Diego area. Over the period of several months, there was a fair amount of turnover in the job of navigator. Ross Cooley was promoted to commander and reported to the Naval Academy as an instructor. First Lieutenant McInerney took over for a while, and he in turn was relieved by Lieutenant Commander Alf O. R. Bergesen, who stayed a few more months before leaving to become skipper of the submarine *Nautilus*. A few days before the end of 1937, Lieutenant Commander Charles Wellborn Jr. became navigator after having served in the Bureau of Ordnance and as commanding officer of the four-stack destroyer *Perry*. He remained in the ship's crew until Captain Lee relinquished command of the *Concord* the following July.[41]

Wellborn was a top-flight naval officer who later served as an aide to the Chief of Naval Operations, commanded the battleship *Iowa* in World War II, and eventually retired as a three-star admiral. After his forty-year career in the Navy, Wellborn described Willis Lee as "one of the most interesting people I've ever known. . . . He . . . had one of the keenest mathematical minds I've ever run across. He could carry in his mind the decimal figures for sines and cosines to any degree you wanted to give. He could multiply these decimals by some other number mentally and come out with the linear measures of sines and cosines." In essence, he described Lee as a human computer.[42]

Lee used this capability far from the classroom, for he spent little of his life in traditional academic pursuits. Rather, his concern was for the practical—the means by which his facility with numbers could be applied in naval operations. As navigator, Wellborn had a firsthand opportunity to observe. During division or fleet maneuvers, it was often the navigator's job to figure a new course and speed when the *Concord* was directed to take a new station in a steaming formation. The standard device for plotting these relative motion maneuvers was the mooring board, known today as the maneuvering board. It is familiar to anyone who has served as an officer of the deck.

Captain Lee, however, had an advantage over the navigator or officer of the deck trying to use the standard method. Lee used two superimposed compass roses that he carried in his pocket. The gadget was known as an "is-was" and was more commonly used by submariners to calculate attack courses. The device enabled Lee to come up with the two legs of the relative motion triangle: the range and bearing from the guide at the *Concord*'s present station and at the new station to which she would proceed. He figured the third leg in his head and then was able to supply the required course and speed. He did so because he had memorized the trigonometric functions of all the possible angles of a triangle and then was able to do the necessary calculations mentally. He was, of course, tolerant of people who didn't have his ability, but they had to go ahead and do the computations on paper to check his solutions. He was generally right within a degree or two.[43]

In his observations of Lee's persona, Wellborn recalled that his manner of speaking had the same "down-home" flavor as did his appearance. In one instance, those on the bridge of the *Concord* spotted a submarine ahead on the distant horizon. Lee remarked, "Oh, I ain't goin' that fur." He also observed that Lee seldom resorted to profanity—less than most Navy men of the era—but he did use it effectively for emphasis when the occasion called for it. He seldom used technical jargon in conversation, though he knew the technical terms well and used them when necessary. In other words, he was unpretentious. Wellborn noticed that Lee's fingers were often tobacco stained. When ashore, the captain always "enjoyed a couple of drinks and the swapping of sea stories." Summing up, the navigator said that the skipper truly enjoyed being a naval officer.[44] Lee also managed to get by with little sleep. Lieutenant Commander Horace Butterfield, the staff aviator, later reported, "I've seen him many times on the bridge—after being up all night—alert and pleasant."[45]

Lee didn't say a great deal while in his captain's chair on the bridge but did seem to enjoy the companionship provided by watchstanders.[46] He swapped stories with them on occasion. The relative rank of captain and junior officer or enlisted man seemed not to matter to Lee. The skipper was generally a patient man. He expected those with less experience to make mistakes, but he also expected them to learn from their mistakes. He calmly put up with things that were beyond an individual's control. He was less patient with individual stupidity and did not like to see the same mistake made twice. On one occasion, Lieutenant Commander Wellborn was at his chart table plotting compass bearings as the cruiser approached her assigned anchorage in San Francisco Bay. Hitting the right spot was important because the current was strong and might swing anchored ships into each other if they were too close together.

A chief quartermaster shooting bearings for Wellborn used the wrong object ashore, Wellborn plotted the bearing as given to him, and the cruiser anchored in the wrong position. The mistake was Wellborn's responsibility, because the quartermaster worked for him. Captain Lee quietly but firmly let him know that he expected an experienced navigator to get the ship anchored in the right place, and Wellborn never missed again. Lee could run the ship better than his officers of the deck, but he did not step in and do it for them. His calmness of manner undoubtedly put them under less strain than if they had been working for a screamer.[47]

The *Concord* arrived at Mare Island on 7 February 1938 to begin an overhaul that would last until early May. During that period, the cruiser missed participation in Fleet Problem XIX in the Caribbean, though Admiral Stark went as an observer. For the ship it was a time for remedying the inevitable effects of wear and tear during her operating periods. It was also a time for sports competition. The *Concord*'s sailors won eight straight basketball games to capture an all-service tournament sponsored by the Junior Chamber of Commerce in the San Francisco Bay area. Captain Lee and Ensign Henry Shonerd, the team's coach, accepted a plaque on behalf of the crew.[48]

After three months at Mare Island, the *Concord* returned to her homeport and usual operating area off Southern California. On 11 May, while she was at sea near San Clemente Island, the gracious Admiral Stark hosted a surprise fiftieth birthday dinner for Captain Lee. The admiral invited ten guests to join the celebration. The feature of the event was a two-layer cake decorated with fifty candles. The ship's newspaper, published by the crew, dutifully reported that the skipper blew out all fifty in one breath, and the guests wished him many more. Lee then cut the cake himself and passed out pieces.[49]

After sending people ashore to participate in a Memorial Day parade in San Diego, the cruiser weighed anchor a couple of weeks later and proceeded to San Pedro for the annual fleet matches to determine the winner of the Battenberg Cup. The *Concord* had again taken the honors among the cruisers of the Battle Force, but this time the fleet winner was the crew from the battleship *Tennessee*. In the cruiser competition against the *Trenton*, the *Concord*'s oarsmen had solid backing by their shipmates. The crew picked up several thousand dollars as a result of their team's victory. The loss to the *Tennessee* ended the cruiser's three-year reign as the fleet champion. The *Tennessee*'s crew was manned entirely by Marines, and their boat finished more than ten lengths in front of the fourth-place *Concord*. The men of the *Tennessee* completed the mile-and-a-half course in fifteen minutes flat.

In early July Rear Admiral Stark relieved Rear Admiral Townsend as commander, Cruisers Battle Force, and the *Concord* once again became the light cruiser type commander's flagship after more than a year of serving as division flagship only. In mid-July the *Concord* went to San Francisco once more to join in a fleet review by the commander in chief, President Roosevelt, who was on board the heavy cruiser *Houston*. The *Concord* spent the rest of the month in San Diego, and on 30 July Captain Willis Lee ended his nearly twenty-two-month tour in command of the ship. He remained on board in the newly created billet of operations officer on Admiral Stark's staff. Captain Earle C. Metz, Naval Academy class of 1910, became the new skipper of the *Concord*.[50]

As type commander, Stark's staff included Lee; Lieutenant Commander Well-born, gunnery officer; Lieutenant Commander Ellsworth E. Roth, engineer officer; Lieutenant Commander William F. Jennings, flag secretary; Lieutenant Commander Horace B. Butterfield, aviation officer; Lieutenant Commander Harold D. Krick, flag lieutenant; and Lieutenant William R. Smedberg III, communicator. A recent Walt Disney animated film, *Snow White and the Seven Dwarfs*, was popular then. Since Stark had white hair and seven staff members, they were soon nicknamed for the movie characters. Lieutenant (j.g.) Nick Doukas enjoyed a cartoon published on the front page of the ship's newspaper, *The Minute Man*. Drawn by Ensign Walt Keen, it depicted Stark with his shock of white hair; the seven staff members were shown taking part in various antics on the bridge. Captain Metz was shown in a corner with an unhappy expression on his face. The drawing amused Lee.[51]

So it was that Willis Lee stepped down from the only ship command he held in the grade of captain. It was unfortunate that someone with his innovative mind couldn't have had a chance with a ship of the new *Brooklyn* class instead of an outmoded member of the *Omaha* class. By the time Lee took the staff job, five ships of the new class were in commission, and Lee's classmates from 1908 had a virtual monopoly as skippers. Before 1938 was over, the two remaining ships of the class went into commission, also commanded by Lee's contemporaries, who were his friends as well. Moreover, as the senior staff officer for Admiral Stark, Lee was in a propitious spot to influence the employment and development of the entire class of these new vessels, not just one. That would have to wait a bit, for Admiral Stark remained in the *Concord*. She was on the West Coast with the bulk of the Battle Force and would be there until events in Europe dictated otherwise.

The new commanding officer of the *Concord* had a tough act to follow, and the resulting letdown in morale was probably inevitable. Lieutenant Commander Wellborn, still on board as a member of the staff, observed, "With Captain Lee, we had the feeling that we could do everything and do it better than anyone else. We didn't have quite that feeling with Captain Metz." The new man didn't have the same stature, and he had one other drawback in that the cadre of topflight officers who had served with Lee—Cooley, McInerney, Nicholas Van Bergen, and others—had gone on to other duties. Metz did arrive on the scene with a good exec already in place, Commander Herman Spanagel.

Human nature being what it is, the situation was potentially awkward. Lee remained on board the same ship he had just commanded, and he had to be there when the job wasn't being done as well as he had. Lee avoided the natural temptation to provide advice to his successor, even when he encountered Metz on the bridge. He still maintained a strong interest in the ship's gunnery, particularly antiaircraft, and made an effort to observe without interfering. That in itself must have been a challenge for a man who was accustomed to leading rather than observing.[52]

There was a dual nature to Willis Lee's personality. In things he cared about, he was extremely competitive. But in other areas he was less competitive and often unconcerned. If a letter or message came in that he was interested in, he would go right to it with vigor. But if it dealt with some area that didn't catch his fancy, he might well toss it into a desk drawer and forget about it. So it was fortunate that Stark's staff included an officer with a proclivity for standard paperwork and a willingness to get it done. Lieutenant Commander Bill Jennings was the man and he was quite well suited to the task. He'd had a previous tour of duty in a sister ship of the *Concord*, so he knew light cruisers, and he was literally a sea lawyer. Prior to reporting to Stark's staff, he had earned his law degree from George Washington

University and been admitted to the bar in the District of Columbia. He was the detail man that Lee needed; he was willing and able to ferret out the neglected papers from the desk drawer. As Stark's number two, Lee nominally filled the traditional billet of chief of staff, but he wasn't that in fact. He didn't run the staff in the way a captain normally does for an admiral. Lee attended to operations and gunnery while letting Jennings handle the administrative part of a normal chief of staff's job.

In late September 1938 a number of the ships, including the *Concord* and sister ship *Cincinnati*, were ordered to the Panama Canal and thence to the Atlantic because of a crisis in Czechoslovakia. The deployment was a contingency move in the event that American citizens needed to be evacuated from Europe. There was recent precedent. In the summer of 1936 the battleship *Oklahoma* interrupted a midshipman training cruise for that purpose. With the outbreak of the Spanish Civil War, the ship arrived at Bilbao, Spain, to transfer Americans and other refugees to safer havens.

Lieutenant (j.g.) Nick Doukas observed a mad scramble on 27 September as the ships made preparations for the unexpected deployment. Oil barges filled the *Concord*'s bunkers. Stores came aboard, as did curious reporters who were trying to find out what was going on. Admiral Stark permitted married men to go ashore for brief goodbyes with their wives. The *Concord* got under way that night, steaming in column with the *Cincinnati*. Doukas, who had been married in the spring, didn't see his bride again until Armistice Day, 11 November.[53]

In the meantime, while the ships were headed toward Panama, Prime Minister Neville Chamberlain of Britain met with Germany's chancellor, Adolf Hitler, in Munich. As a result of that encounter, Chamberlain agreed to cede the Sudetenland portion of Czechoslovakia to Germany in return for a German pledge of no more territorial acquisition. On his return to England on 30 September, Chamberlain waved a copy of the agreement saying it meant "peace for our time"—a term that would come back to haunt him because Hitler's ambitions were so rapacious. Edvard Beneš, president of Czechoslovakia, was forced to resign on 5 October 1938 after standing up to Hitler.

Once the *Concord* passed through the Panama Canal on 10 October, Stark, Lee, and Captain Metz went ashore to see the commandant of the Fifteenth Naval District. With the overseas situation seemingly defused, the *Concord* proceeded to Guantánamo Bay, Cuba, for training exercises.[54] Before leaving Panama, Lee encountered two *Concord* ensigns on shore leave. They were relaxing at a nightclub bar and the trio had a pleasant, informal visit. Lee challenged the pair to see which of the three had the steadiest hand by balancing a full jigger of liquor on the back of his hand. Lee won the contest; no doubt that same steady hand was a factor in his remarkable shooting ability.[55]

In early November a gathering of light cruisers arrived at Guantánamo. Included were some ships of the recently commissioned *Brooklyn* class, which had been designed and built as a consequence of the 1930 London Treaty on the Limitation of Naval Armaments. They certainly represented a step up from the *Concord* and her ilk. Each ship contained five triple turrets of 6-inch guns that had semi-fixed ammunition and could pump out projectiles at a high rate—ten to twelve rounds per minute per gun—from up to fifteen guns. The *Brooklyn* had steamed to Guantánamo in October 1938 to join up with a sister ship, the *Philadelphia*, which was the flagship of the recently created Cruiser Division Eight, commanded by Rear Admiral Forde Todd.

On 5 November Captain Lee and Lieutenant Commander Wellborn of Stark's staff transferred to the *Brooklyn* as an advance party to check out the characteristics and performance of the new class. It was a "welcome aboard" for Lee, because the skipper of the *Brooklyn* was his Naval Academy classmate Bill Brereton. Since there was no staff embarked in the ship, Lee took up residence in the vacant admiral's quarters. Brereton later recalled, "It goes without saying that there was close cooperation and understanding in the job we had, which was analyzing and evaluating the fighting value of the new class of ships."[56] Ensign John Wadleigh, one of the ship's junior officers, had reported aboard as one of the original crew members of the *Brooklyn* when she was commissioned on 30 September 1937. He recalled years later that his ship had been plagued by machinery and armament problems and had so far fired only structural tests of the main battery. It was Admiral Todd's job to train the ships into a cohesive unit, ready to join the fleet, which was scheduled to participate in a fleet problem.[57]

The ship took part in division gunnery practices with Lee observing the performance of the guns and their crews. In day and night practice, Wadleigh recalled, the *Brooklyn* was allotted ten rounds per 6-inch gun, a generous allocation in those days of economy. The *Brooklyn* fired off her full 150 rounds in slightly more than a minute. Accuracy was improved, because the new ships had much more capable fire control systems than did the *Omaha* class. Wadleigh added, "Comparing this with the 20 to 30 second loading intervals of the older six inch guns must have pleased Lee, an ordnance expert." He added that "by the time Lee observed us [shoot] he must have felt the fleet was getting an excellent weapons system."[58] With his puckish sense of humor, Lee once remarked to his wife's sister Margaret Allen that going to visit other ships within the command was like being a "mother-in-law"—able to visit when he pleased, stay as long as he wanted, and criticize his hosts.[59]

On 30 December 1938, at New York, Stark and his staff shifted to the *Honolulu*, one of the *Brooklyn*'s sisters. The commissioning skipper of the *Honolulu*, Captain Oscar Smith, had been sworn in with Lee at the Naval Academy in 1904. The *Honolulu* was a more suitable flagship than the *Concord* for a type commander when new doctrine was to be created. Though the main battery was a huge upgrade from that in the scout cruisers, the antiaircraft guns were still the old 5-inch/25 variety. The superior 5-inch/38 was entering the fleet about the same time. The dual-purpose 5-inch/38, effective against both air and surface targets, became the standard on board a large number of Navy surface combatants during World War II.

Lieutenant Commander Frederick I. Entwistle was the *Honolulu*'s gunnery officer when the staff embarked. He noted Lee's primary interest in the new 6-inch guns. A night-firing exercise off Guantánamo by ships of the division provided an especially vivid memory: "The [target] was completely demolished, about the only remainder was the raft (underwater) itself." The fire control in ships without radar was done with optical range finders. The doctrine for night engagements called for searching for the enemy by use of star shells and then illumination with more star shells once the foe was located. Though the cruisers were equipped with searchlights, the idea was to avoid using them if possible, because they would give away the position of one's own ship. As for Lee's personality, Entwistle recalled him as quiet and unassuming but not an introvert. He also described him as "democratic"—an interesting term for a senior naval officer—and completely devoid of pomposity. The contact between the staff and ship's company, he observed, was very close.[60]

As Charles Wellborn remembered of the *Honolulu*, it was a bonus to move to the much more modern ship with considerably more physical room available for carrying out staff functions. The newer ship had a separate flag mess. In the *Concord* the staff officers ate in the wardroom, and Lee dined alone in his cabin.

As staff gunnery officer, Wellborn had been scheduling the various ships for target practice and sending in administrative reports on the results. Now the international political situation dictated that the operation of the ships be geared more to potential wartime requirements.[61] Lieutenant Commander Harold Krick, Stark's flag lieutenant, saw that Lee personally observed both surface and antiaircraft target practice—and provided comments on the results—whenever other ships of the division were shooting. His vantage point was the flag bridge, a separate accommodation built into the new class.[62]

Krick shared another interesting recollection. On 29 December Mr. and Mrs. Talbot Jennings hosted a large dinner party at the ritzy Pierre Hotel in Manhattan. Talbot Jennings, a playwright and Hollywood screenwriter, was the older brother of Stark's flag secretary, Bill Jennings. (It is difficult to imagine the informal Lee at a black-tie gathering such as this.)[63] The host and hostess presented a ceramic namesake replica of a character in *Snow White and the Seven Dwarfs* to the admiral and each staff member. The dolls were beautiful figurines from the famous toy store FAO Schwarz. In recounting the experience, the retired captain wrote years later, "Bashful remains a member of the Krick household."[64] Subsequently, Lee's nephew Don Siders found among his uncle's possessions the doll that Captain Lee had received at the party. It depicted the dwarf Happy.[65] Wellborn reported that Lee was amused by the various dwarf designations.[66]

Stark and the staff returned to the *Concord* for a few weeks in January and headed for exercises in the Caribbean. On 4 February the admiral and staff returned to the *Honolulu* at Gonaives, Haiti, and at mid-month joined the White Fleet to participate in Fleet Problem XX. The scenario called for the White Fleet to simulate attacking targets in the Caribbean and off the East Coast of the United States. President Roosevelt personally observed some of the exercises from the heavy cruiser *Houston*. All told, the fleet problem involved 134 ships, 600 airplanes, 3,210 officers, and 49,445 enlisted men.[67]

As mentioned earlier, the cruiser staff had one naval aviator among its members, Lieutenant Commander Horace Butterfield. (Those with a memory of the Senate Watergate hearings of 1973 will recall that Alexander Butterfield created a sensation when he revealed the existence of a White House taping system.

The content of those tapes eventually led to the resignation of President Richard Nixon the following year. Alex was Horace's son.)

The senior Butterfield recounted an incident from the *Honolulu*'s winter sojourn at Guantánamo, Cuba. Sister ships of the class, including the *Savannah* and the *Brooklyn*, were also on hand. Their skippers were friends and contemporaries of Captain Lee. During a get-together at the officers' club, Lee bemoaned that the ship's store of the *Honolulu* had run out of Bull Durham tobacco. That was a concern, because Lee generally rolled his own cigarettes while at sea. Captain Robert C. "Ike" Giffen of the *Savannah* announced, "I'll take care of that." After the officers had returned to their respective ships, the captain's gig from the *Savannah* showed up at the *Honolulu* and delivered twelve packages of tobacco for Lee. Soon a visual signal went from the flagship to the *Savannah* for Captain Giffen: "Thanks for the services of your bull, signed Chink."[68]

After winding up her period of operating in the Caribbean, the type commander's flagship returned to her temporary homeport of New York City on 20 April. On 29 April the *Honolulu* moored in the North River west of Manhattan to celebrate the opening of the New York World's Fair in Queens. (The tomb of former President Ulysses S. Grant served was one of the shore points the navigation team used for taking bearings.) In late May she set out for Panama and the Pacific, where she would join the fleet. Admiral Stark was detached on 1 May to prepare for his new duties as the next Chief of Naval Operations. On 24 May the *Honolulu* departed New York City to begin a journey to Panama. That same day, Captain Lee left the cruiser to report to the Navy Department in Washington. He went there to prepare the U.S. Navy for the war that he and many others expected to come.[69]

▪ 8 ▪

THE WASHINGTON YEARS: PREPARING FOR BATTLE
1939–1942

War clouds were swirling throughout Europe when Admiral Harold R. Stark became the Chief of Naval Operations on 1 August 1939. Indeed, full-blown war broke out a month later when German forces invaded Poland at the behest of Chancellor Adolf Hitler. The United States was not yet an active combatant, but war seemed likely, probably inevitable. As Stark settled into his new role in Washington, DC, he brought with him several officers from his Cruisers Battle Force staff. Among them was Captain Lee, who returned to the Fleet Training Division (OP-22) on 30 June, a month before Stark took office. It was the shore duty for which the Navy considered his talents and experiences best suited.

When he reported to the Main Navy building on Constitution Avenue, the fifty-one-year-old Lee became the assistant director of the division. Rear Admiral Herbert Fairfax Leary, a gunnery man who had finished fifth—two spots ahead of Chester Nimitz—in the Naval Academy's class of 1905, served as director. Leary was brilliant, flamboyant, loud, and impatient. It was said of him that he didn't need a telephone to make a long-distance call—his voice alone would carry far enough.[1] Another officer described Leary as gruff, forceful, a high-order extrovert—a big man with a big voice, intelligent and bombastic. He had a superb memory and could repeat a conversation nearly verbatim some time afterward.[2]

The calm, quiet Lee served as a useful balance wheel and buffer between the admiral and the other fourteen officers who comprised Fleet Training. One of the junior officers in the division observed, "I always had the feeling that Captain Lee provided the majority of the detailed reasons in favor or against various projects. Admiral Leary then acted as a well informed and very effective moderator at . . . conferences."[3]

OP-22 prepared directives, reports, and analyses on all phases of fleet training and exercises. These included annual competitions in gunnery, communications, engineering, and overall battle efficiency. The division was subdivided into individual sections devoted to tactics, gunnery, engineering, damage control, and chemical warfare.[4] Lee concentrated on tactics and gunnery and left the details of running the individual specialties to the officers handling the appropriate desks. He was far less interested in which ships won E's for excellence than in determining the maximum capabilities of men, ships, and weapons, then finding the best ways to employ those capabilities. Above all, the division's mission was tactical training of the fleet for war.[5]

While in Fleet Training, as he had for years, Lee exhibited his intellectual capacity without being ostentatious. Commander Nealy Chapin, one of his subordinates, also observed Lee's sense of humor: "We learned that one of his methods of testing junior associates was to make some preposterous statement in order to observe the reaction."[6] (This was perhaps a reprise of the mischievous tricks he pulled in Kentucky as a youth.)

In addition to indulging his inquisitive nature while working in the Navy Department, Lee also undertook an extensive travel schedule outside of Washington. He often visited shipyards, both those of the Navy and of private companies. Much of the surface fleet that would win the Pacific War a few years later was in various stages of design and construction. Lee made the trips in order to bring an operator's perspective to the designs developed by the Navy's relevant material bureaus— Ordnance, Construction and Repair, Engineering—and after 1940, the Bureau of Ships. Often the graduates with the highest standing in their Naval Academy classes were routed into postgraduate education and assignments in the bureaus; Lee's experience was in the real world of going to sea and preparing for battle.

Within two weeks of arriving in OP-22, Lee received orders to proceed to the New York Navy Yard in Brooklyn to examine a full-size mockup of the conning tower designed for the *North Carolina* and *Washington*, the first new U.S. battle-ships in nearly twenty years. With twenty-seven-knot speed, they were also the first of the fast battleships. Wooden substitutes of parts of the ships enabled Lee to evaluate what later came to be known as "human factors" or "ergonomics"—how crewmen were likely to perform in such an environment and whether any changes were necessary. Later travels to Brooklyn included inspections of the replicas of plotting rooms, this time for both the *North Carolina* and *South Dakota* classes.[7]

Lee's odysseys in ensuing months took him to the Philadelphia Navy Yard, to Fort Monroe in Virginia to observe Army antiaircraft test firing, Bethlehem Steel's yard in Quincy, Massachusetts; an RCA plant for radio equipment; New York Shipbuilding in Camden, New Jersey; Norfolk Navy Yard; Atlantic Highlands, New Jersey, to see tests of fire control equipment; the Naval Proving Ground in Dahlgren, Virginia; Boston Navy Yard; Key West, Florida, for antisubmarine sound school; Long Island, New York, concerning fire control equipment. Other projects involved in these trips included *Baltimore*-class heavy cruisers, *Cleveland*-class light cruisers, and *Fletcher*-class destroyers.[8]

He was also involved in examining plans for the *Montana*-class battleships, which were designed to carry twelve 16-inch guns. Later, though, the Navy con-cluded that its shipbuilding resources could better be used for aircraft carriers, amphibious warfare ships, landing craft, and antisubmarine vessels. An alternate proposal arose that June; it suggested that a modified design of the *Iowa* class be substituted for the *Montana* class. Lee ruled against that option because it would add further delays to the shipbuilding program. In July 1943, before construction started, the *Montana* class was officially canceled because of the alternate priorities. Originally, the *Montana* was to be BB 65. That hull number and BB 66 were transferred to the *Iowa*-class ships *Illinois* and *Kentucky*. Both of those began construction but were never completed.[9]

The Navy also had plans to build six ships armed with 12-inch guns. They were known officially as large cruisers but were more commonly known as battle cruisers. The idea was that they could deal with similarly armed German and Japanese ships. Rear Admiral Richmond Kelly Turner of the Naval Operations (OpNav) War Plans Division recommended another four be added for a total of ten. The Navy's General Board endorsed Turner's idea. In August 1941, however, Captain Lee opposed the supplement to the original six, saying that the proposed cruisers would have questionable value, and the shipbuilding resources should go instead to aircraft carriers. Only two large cruisers, the *Alaska* and *Guam*, were built. They served in the Pacific during the war.[10] Historian Richard Frank observed that Lee's intervention "demonstrates [his] extremely impressive breadth of view. The CBs [large cruisers] were one of the few serious missteps in the combatant building program and Lee said so early and firmly."[11]

Within Fleet Training, Captain Lee practiced what is now known as "management by walking around." He was a peripatetic figure, strolling the corridors of Main Navy to find out the latest. One of his fellow officers thought a walkie-talkie would have been useful in order to keep up with him. In the large one-room office occupied by his division, Lee was frequently up and about. He went from desk to desk, not to interfere with the work of others, but to probe and learn. As an officer worked over a report or study or table of mathematical calculations, Lee would approach and ask, "Having any problems?" A quiet question here, a suggestion there, and the officer would work it out. The officer felt the better for it, because he had come to the answer himself. Lee had been only the catalyst, not one who forced his solutions on others.[12]

In this routine Lee often worked ten- or twelve-hour days at the Navy Department and then took work home with him in the evening. After a day of such wandering, it's no wonder he had to tackle his own full briefcase later. As with many other Navy offices, Fleet Training had to deal with a mountain of paperwork from the fleet and other sources. Lee put his penciled initials and notes on thousands of routing slips, reports, and carbon copies of outgoing letters.

After he and Mabelle had supper together, she often went to bed early because of her chronic health problems. Once she retired, her husband settled down in an easy chair. He did his homework far into the night. Sometimes, instead of going to bed, he picked up a detective novel and read some more before dozing off in the chair—perhaps as late as 0400. After a few hours of sleep, he put on his jacket and walked to work. Thus, if his clothes looked as if he had slept in them, he probably had.[13] Lieutenant Commander George Russell worked in the office of the Navy's top lawyer, the judge advocate general. He at times encountered Lee in the Navy Department building and later recalled, "Admiral Lee cleaned his glasses about once a month. We wondered how he saw through them."[14]

In 1938 and 1939, two of Lee's Naval Academy classmates took command of old battleships, as did a few more in 1940. Clearly, Admiral Stark believed Lee could do more good for the Navy as a whole in OpNav. Years later, speaking of that prewar period, Admiral Arleigh Burke said, "Battleships at that time were not good commands; nobody knew it, but they were not good commands . . . possibly due to the lack of innovation and aggressiveness of people in battleships."[15]

One of Lee's projects in 1940 involved photography. In June of that year Rear Admiral Ernest J. King, a member of the Navy's General Board, raised questions about readiness for war on the part of the Office of Naval Intelligence. His conclusion was that ONI was lacking in a number of areas. Later that month representatives of the various bureaus within the Navy Department gathered in the Fleet Training Division to discuss the state of photography in the Navy. Marion Cooper, a former Navy man who was an executive in Hollywood, suggested that the Navy ask for photographic help from the movie industry. Captain Lee was interested, and the Navy issued a directive concerning improvement of photographic training. Subsequently, naval officers went to Hollywood to get training in the art of photography.[16]

Things went a step further on the recommendation of Rear Admiral Robert L. Ghormley, then a special U.S. naval observer in London. He saw the results of what the British had been able to accomplish in the field of photo interpretation during the early months of the war. Lieutenant Commander Robert Quackenbush, a Naval Academy graduate and naval aviator, received permission to go to Britain to attend classes and observe the process. He set up the U.S. version of the school at the Anacostia Naval Air Station near Washington. The class trained hundreds of photo interpreters whose expertise proved invaluable during the war in the Pacific. In a campaign that involved capturing atolls and islands, aerial photography, using stereoscopic techniques, provided the intelligence that produced terrain maps of targets. These were useful in preparing for amphibious assaults and bombing raids.[17]

Fleet Training initiated another resource in learning from the Royal Navy. Lieutenant Commander Joseph H. "Gus" Wellings, one of the junior officers in OP-22, had an impressive pedigree from previous service. He had been flag lieutenant to Admiral William D. Leahy in that officer's billets as commander, Battleships Battle Force and later as commander, Battle Force. Leahy was Chief of Naval Operations just before Admiral Stark succeeded him in 1939. In the summer of 1940, Wellings was in Boston, slated to take command of the destroyer *Hopkins*. On 31 July he learned that the orders were cancelled.

Instead, he was to report back to Fleet Training, which he had left only a few days earlier. From there he was to go to England as an observer. In Washington, Admiral Leary told him about his upcoming trip: "Your official orders will assign you as assistant naval attaché in the American Embassy in London. However, after your experience as tactical officer for Admiral Leahy, and your two years' work here revising our regular tactical and convoy instructions, you will be of more value to our Navy by confining your duties to that of an observer in the British ships of the Home Fleet based at Scapa Flow [in the Orkney Islands, north of Scotland]."[18]

Finally, recalled Wellings, Lee, with whom he had worked closely up to then, told him to consider himself still part of Fleet Training. He explained, "Gus, you talked so much about the desirability of having U.S. naval observers in the British Fleet, we had your orders to *Hopkins* canceled. Send us all the information you think of value to the Navy in regard to tactics, gunnery, convoy operations, antisubmarine warfare, air defense, and the practical aspects of shipboard radar as far as reliability and performance are concerned."[19] The forceful Leary added the coda to the discussion: "Dammit, we are not going to fight the British. Tell them everything you know and get as much information out of them as you can. Let's make this one hundred percent exchange of information effective."[20]

In the ensuing weeks, the British approved Wellings' assignment to serve on board their combatant ships. He also received a series of briefings on the variety of topics he would be expected to observe and report. Before Wellings departed, Lee arranged for him to receive a life jacket, gas mask, and foul-weather gear. As the young officer explained in his memoir, these items would be useful in the "cold, rough and cruel North Atlantic." His wife was suspicious as to why these items would be necessary while serving in the attaché's office in London. Because his new assignment was secret, he could not tell her the real reason he was going and fibbed about needing protection on the way across the Atlantic and during German bombing of London.[21]

Then he was off to Halifax, Canada, and on to England. For the next eight months, he spent time both at sea and ashore while in the process of soaking up knowledge. Wellings remembered that it was Fleet Training that successfully pushed for complete interchange of information. Some within the Navy were opposed to the openness of the relationship. The Naval Research Laboratory, for instance, objected because it considered the U.S. Navy to be far ahead of the British in various categories. When Wellings got on board Royal Navy ships, he discovered that it was the British who were ahead, except in aircraft carrier operations.[22]

The young officer's British experience as a trailblazer for the observers that followed came to an end in June 1941. That was shortly after the battleship *Rodney* helped sink the German battleship *Bismarck*. Wellings wrote, "As I walked down the gangway of the *Rodney* I knew in my heart that one of the most instructive and happiest highlights of my navy career had come to a conclusion."[23] After his return to Washington, Wellings discovered that Lee (in conjunction with Captain Louis Denfeld of the Bureau of Navigation) played a key role in establishing antisubmarine warfare training schools at Key West and Miami, Florida. Readiness required trained personnel. Another effort was a push to develop an antisubmarine attack trainer, a simulator that enabled officers to develop proficiency.[24]

In the meantime, Lee was able to get a firsthand look at a modern British warship. In mid-January 1941, Prime Minister Winston Churchill dispatched Lord and Lady Halifax to Washington, where Halifax would take over as Britain's ambassador to the United States. Churchill went to the fleet anchorage at Scapa Flow to see off the Halifaxes and senior British officers. The latter would be involved in ABC-1 talks (American-British Conversations). The purpose was joint planning on how to deal with the German menace if and when the United States entered the war as a combatant. Their conveyance was HMS *King George V,* lead ship of a new class.

When it was time for the ship to return to England, Stark had obtained permission from the battleship's commanding officer to take American naval officers aboard as ship riders. Captain Lee was among them as the ship departed from Annapolis and steamed south in the Chesapeake Bay. The observers were able to talk with engineers and gunnery specialists in order to make comparisons with the newest classes of American battleships. Thus new information implanted itself into Lee's mental database.[25]

■ ■ ■

Lee didn't own a car. It was his practice to order two tickets for each Naval Academy home football game. One was for himself and the other for the taxi driver who took him to and from Annapolis and sat with him during the games.[26] During working hours, parking spaces were at a premium near the Navy Department building. Car pools—known as "driving squads" in that era—were frequent. The Lees lived in an apartment about two miles away at 1921 Kalorama Road. It was not far from Rock Creek Park and Connecticut Avenue in northwest Washington. Rear Admiral Nimitz was chief of the Bureau of Navigation at the time, and he wrote years later that he got to know Lee better during those years because of the long walks they took together:

> It was his custom . . . to join me in my office in the old Navy Dept Bldg on Constitution Ave—at the end of the working day and we would walk towards NW Washington—where both of us lived. This gave us much opportunity to exchange ideas and to discuss the state of the nation & the world. I was always impressed by his knowledge of world affairs—and by his sound wisdom. During the winter of 1940—on the coldest days—he would come prepared to walk—in a thin suit & without gloves—while I—clad in an overcoat & with warm gloves—still felt the cold. I marveled at his disregard for the weather and at his rugged physique.[27]

Nimitz's recollections also illustrate the point that the Navy was still relatively small as it girded for war. Many of the officers were well acquainted with each other and were known by what was called "service reputation." Lieutenant Commander John F. Crowe Jr., who served with Lee in Fleet Training, had his own take on Lee's reputation: "He seemed to be totally engrossed in the Navy and his work and, so far as I know, did not get involved in the social whirl here."[28]

Indeed, Lee's wife Mabelle spent very little personal time with her husband during that period. Estelle Wright was the wife of Lieutenant George Wright, who had served with Lee in the *Pennsylvania* in the early 1930s. She had also been a friend of Mabelle in Coronado when Lee commanded the *Concord*. When they were in Washington, Estelle received telephone calls from Mabelle nearly every morning. Lee's wife called to complain about her troubles. One complaint was that in going through the captain's pants pockets she had found money order stubs for a large amount of money that Lee had been sending to his nephew in Kentucky to put him through school. Mrs. Lee was irked that her husband had not consulted her about doing so. Mabelle also lamented that she had to skimp on food and drink on the rare occasions when the Lees hosted parties. Instead, she wanted to be able to reciprocate in kind for the hospitality they had received. Mrs. Wright had the impression that the Lees seldom went out, confirming Lieutenant Commander Crowe's observation. During a number of the telephone calls, Mrs. Wright concluded that Mrs. Lee had been drinking.[29]

Guilliaem Aertsen III, who served during World War II as Lee's flag lieutenant, offered some perspective on the relationship between husband and wife: "A lot of these men who saw fit to make the naval profession their livelihood recognized that one of the price tags was a rather tenuous domestic situation. The fact that Lee's domestic situation was tenuous did not surprise me at all—nor is it unusual." He added, "There were no kids. They loved each other dearly, but the competition [his demanding job] was a son-of-a-gun fact. And no doubt his lady hit the bottle for [that] reason. It wasn't because she didn't love him. It was because she did. . . . He was her whole life." M. C. Fisher, a friend of the Lees observed of the couple: "I sincerely believe that no heroine of fact or fiction ever was more devoted to lover or husband than was [Mabelle] for her spouse." But she got little of his attention, even when he was physically in the same apartment because of all the paperwork he brought from the office. His focus on improving the Navy's readiness for war was nearly all-consuming, and other considerations faded into the background.[30]

■ ■ ■

One of Captain Lee's many roles was as the senior member of the Antiaircraft Defense Board when it was established in August 1940. It included some individuals who would be quite influential in the future. Captain William H. P. "Spike" Blandy represented the Bureau of Ordnance, of which he would become chief in 1941 as a rear admiral. Commander Forrest P. Sherman represented the War Plans Division of OpNav. He later held that position for Pacific Fleet Commander in Chief Chester Nimitz. The board's agenda included a long laundry list of topics. Among those discussed in an August meeting were German dive-bombing tactics and exchange of information with the British. Other topics of interest included the establishment of AA gunnery schools, combined ship-and-shore practices, naval tactics, outfitting the former battleship *Wyoming* as an experimental AA training ship, and even the possibility of using smoke as a defense against planes operating at night and illuminating targets with flares.[31] Several months later, in a memo of 24 February 1941, Lee reported that the board was also considering the feasibility of using major-caliber main battery guns, ranging up to 16 inches, as AA weapons. Reports from Britain indicated that the Royal Navy had used the technique while fighting in the Mediterranean.[32]

During the operation of Fleet Training, officers considerably Lee's junior felt no awkwardness over the differences in ages, because he was approachable. Other officers often stayed late at the office, not because they were afraid of him but because the avuncular, storytelling Lee was interesting to be around. His philosophy was, "Don't give me a hard worker; I want an easy worker."[33] One such was Commander James L. "Jimmy" Holloway Jr. He had served with Lee in Fleet Training in the mid-1930s and returned in 1940, this time in the billet of gunnery officer. He took pride in a fitness report evaluation that Lee wrote about him: "This officer does not waste time searching for a perfect solution but takes a reasonable solution and goes ahead and gets something done."[34] As an aside, Holloway wrote of Lee, "I *never* heard him tell a dirty story, *nor* use vulgar talk. Unusually clean mind and heart."[35]

Holloway was one of "Uncle Ching's Boys," and there were others working nearby. Across the corridor from Fleet Training in Main Navy was the office of the Interior Control Board, of which Lee was chairman after June 1940. The members came from various bureaus and from divisions within OpNav. Commander Jeffrey C. Metzel and Lieutenant Commander Milton E. "Mary" Miles were the only officers whose primary duty assignment was board membership.

The board's purpose was to establish specifications and requirements for the construction of new ships and weapons. Miles kept a pot of coffee going in the board office, so it was often the site of mid-morning coffee breaks during which the men exchanged ideas. Lieutenant Commander Percival "Pete" McDowell of OP-22 joined the coffeepot group meetings in 1940. The ideas Metzel, Miles, and McDowell came up with were imaginative, sometimes even bizarre. Lee had the ability to direct these men into productive channels, encouraging them to follow up on topics that seemed useful. Some of the suggestions put forth at the morning meetings were far afield from the Interior Control Board's normal business. A prime example was a plan to send men to China.

At one board meeting in mid-1941, according to Miles' records, Lee said, "We know a lot about the German and British systems of making war, but so far as I can tell from the intelligence reports coming in, we do not know much about the precautions the Japanese are taking against the weapons that we have now. Do they know what we are planning? It seems to me that we should send someone out to China now, someone who may be able to obtain access to the Chinese Intelligence Services and who can find out about Japanese training methods. Also it may be possible to loan the Chinese some of our equipment to use so we can see how effective it is."[36]

During this same period, the Army was at work on a China plan, in part for reasons similar to the Navy's and in part to head off William J. "Wild Bill" Donovan. Donovan was a Medal of Honor recipient as a World War I Army officer, a lawyer, and a diplomat, and he aimed to create a super intelligence agency. He later accomplished that with the establishment of the Office of Strategic Services, the forerunner of the Central Intelligence Agency. The Army chose Brigadier General William Magruder, an intelligence officer, to head the mission to China. He had background knowledge as the result of having served as an assistant military attaché from 1920 to 1924. Captain Lee, who had China experience himself, suggested that Lieutenant Commander Miles be included in the military mission as an observer. The Army rejected that proposal and later set up its China mission in October 1941.[37]

Like Lee, Miles had spent years on the Navy's China Station. They had first met while serving in Asiatic Fleet destroyers in the 1920s. On his way to duty at the Navy Department, Miles and his hardy family had made a journey of hundreds of miles along the rugged, tortuous Burma Road. The Chinese had been enmeshed in a full-scale but undeclared war with Japan since 1937. As Lee had outlined, Miles envisioned putting a team of U.S. Navy men ashore in China to collect intelligence and to coordinate American efforts with those of the Chinese, comparable to what the Army was doing.[38] Lieutenant Commander Arthur H. McCollum, head of the Far East section of the OpNav Intelligence Division, joined the coffee break discussions as the plan was hashed out. So did Lieutenant

Commander Aubrey B. "Abie" Leggett, the officer who moved in under Miles in the Interior Control Board when Metzel left for other duty. Leggett's presence freed Miles to work on the China project.

Miles made contact with the Chinese embassy's assistant military attaché, Major Sin-ju Hsiao. The plan involved a rearguard action, including strengthening the Chinese Nationalists in their war against Japan and denying Japan access to natural resources in China. It was also a means of passing along weather reports, intelligence on the Japanese—including aerial and electronic surveillance—and monitoring the movements of the Japanese fleet. Still another potential purpose was to pave the way if Allied strategic planning decided upon an invasion of the Chinese mainland, though such an invasion did not actually come about during the war.

The Interior Control Board served as a cover for Miles' planning. Lee was invaluable in the process. In part it was because he supported the idea vigorously. Also, Lee's stature enabled him to cut across bureaucratic lines, observed Lieutenant (j.g.) Raymond A. Kotrla. Kotrla, who knew Miles, was assigned to the Office of Naval Intelligence and later served with Miles in China.[39] Lee's rank provided more horsepower than Miles had as a lieutenant commander. Because of the international implications, President Franklin D. Roosevelt and the State Department needed to approve the actions of the group. According to the plans, war with Japan was seemingly inevitable, and the operation would be activated when hostilities commenced.

■ ■ ■

At the end of 1940, Admiral Stark wrote a memorandum on Lee that made its way, via the chief of the Bureau of Navigation, Rear Admiral Nimitz, to President Roosevelt. The president, who served as Assistant Secretary of the Navy in World War I, maintained a keen interest in the seagoing service and its officers—certainly to a greater extent than he did in the Army.[40] Admiral Stark's biographer Tony Simpson opined that the purpose of the memo was to provide Roosevelt with more information on Lee regarding the plan for him to relieve Leary as head of Fleet Training. He added, "FDR made all the flag officer assignments. I am sure this nettled Stark and Nimitz, but they never breathed a word about it."[41]

Of his former shipmate, Stark wrote,

> Captain W. A. Lee, Jr., was my chief of staff on my last cruise at sea. I consider him to be one of the ablest officers in the service.
>
> Not only has he a brilliant mind but combined with it is a fund of common sense, feet one hundred percent on the ground, a coolness and calmness in an emergency which is little less than astounding, and the most uncanny ability to maneuver a ship into a proper position or to lead a division into a position in tactical maneuvers without the use of a mooring board or any other mechanical means, except his brain that I have ever known.
>
> Moreover, at the present time he is First Assistant to Leary whom it has been recommended he relieve and whose opinion of him is just as high as mine.
>
> In gunnery, Lee is likewise outstanding, particularly with regard to anti-aircraft.
>
> Finally, his subordinates are devoted to him.[42]

That final sentence might have been the highest accolade of all. Willis Lee was a walking exemplar of the maxim that "loyalty down begets loyalty up." Admiral Leary departed for other duty in January 1941, leaving Captain Lee as director of Fleet Training. By then, the routine business of running the exercises and competitions was still taking place, but its significance paled against the urgent need to prepare for war. Of the officers in Fleet Training then, one of Lee's closest associates was Pete McDowell. The two were kindred spirits, and it fell to McDowell to beef up the fleet's AA capabilities in conjunction with the Bureau of Ordnance. Lee and McDowell frequently tangled with Captain Garrett L. "Mike" Schuyler, director of BuOrd's Research Division, on the subject of anti-aircraft defense.

The two captains, Lee and Schuyler, were close personal friends and often had lunch together, but they were frequently at odds professionally. The BuOrd research head had a tendency to pontificate on his business, and Lee sometimes had to deflate him with a well-aimed remark. Lee had little tolerance for "pedigreed bunk," as he called it, and he could be quite stubborn on occasion—rearing back in his chair, putting both hands flat on his desk, and appearing "as immovable as a Missouri mule."[43] Schuyler championed 5-inch guns as the fleet's primary AA weapons. His rationale was that they had greater range than .50-caliber machine guns and 1.1-inch guns and thus could knock off attacking airplanes before they got close enough to hit.[44] Lee's people acknowledged the value of the 5-inch but contended that smaller guns were also useful to knock off planes that the 5-inch batteries missed. They were pushing for the acquisition of the 20-mm Swiss Oerlikon and 40-mm Swedish Bofors guns. Fortunately, the chief of the Bureau of Ordnance, Rear Admiral Blandy, was also working actively to get the foreign light AA guns into U.S. production.[45]

Lieutenant (j.g.) Blake D. Mills, who was assigned to BuOrd at the time, offered his opinion on the subject: "As much as I admired Mike Schuyler's technical abilities and perceptiveness, I'm not sure that his judgment of probable future battle effectiveness would be as reliable as that of a sea-going officer like Lee."[46] Lieutenant Commander Boynton L. Braun, a naval aviator, also observed Lee's interest in antiaircraft gunnery from within Fleet Training. He came to Washington from the staff of the commander of Aircraft Scouting Force; his specialties were gunnery and tactics. His job in Washington was to make up the rules for aviation gunnery exercises and summarize the results of the competition. He recalled years later that Lee never interfered with aviators and, curiously, demonstrated little interest in knowing the capabilities of aircraft as a means of shooting them down.[47] That contradicted the memory of Marcus Williamson, a junior officer under Lee in the *Concord*. Williamson recalled being summoned to Lee's cabin to discuss probable dive-bombing capabilities and approaches.

Pete McDowell, meanwhile, was frequently off traveling. He saw the need for antiaircraft training centers as the new light guns became available, so to an extent Fleet Training did have some involvement in initiating personnel training. With the advent of training facilities, ships that reached port would be able to send their men ashore. There they could blaze away at towed sleeves or drones so their shooting eyes would be sharper when enemy planes were approaching.

Lieutenant Commander Ernest "Judge" Eller spent six months in Fleet Training Division, from April to October 1941. Eller had just returned to the United States after nearly a year of observing antiaircraft guns and radar used in combat by the Royal Navy. Lee had met with Eller before he went to England, and now Lee debriefed him about what he had encountered in a fleet at war. The operational side of new weapons and tactics was included among the missions of the division. Sonar and amphibious warfare were included, though amphibious techniques did not get much attention in Fleet Training at the time.[48]

Captain Lee tasked Eller with finding a suitable location for the primary East Coast antiaircraft training center, for he saw an enormous potential demand as the nation moved closer to war. Eller scouted several locations, including Georgetown, South Carolina; a site near Wilmington, North Carolina; and Cape May, New Jersey. He finally settled on a spot at Dam Neck, Virginia, an area of cornfields and almost uninhabited coastline south of Virginia Beach. The latter was essentially a village at the time and not the thriving tourist attraction it later became. It took a while for the Navy to acquire the requisite land, and before Eller left Fleet Training, the site was up and running for smaller weapons: .50-caliber, 20-mm, and 1.1-inch. (The 40-mm Bofors was not yet in the inventory.) Eventually there were some ten antiaircraft training centers on each coast.

Developing effective aiming equipment for the light weapons was understandably something that Fleet Training strongly supported. Some background is in order. In the late 1930s the Navy sent four bright young lieutenants to the Massachusetts Institute of Technology for postgraduate work in ordnance fire control; they were Alfred G. "Corky" Ward, Horacio "Rivets" Rivero, Lloyd M. Mustin, and Edwin B. Hooper. The first two eventually became four-star admirals. Mustin and Hooper became vice admirals, and both served with Lee at sea during World War II. Mustin and Rivero teamed up on an extracurricular thesis project, that of developing a lead-computing sight. The principle is the same as a hunter uses in a duck blind. The shooter must figure out how far to aim ahead of the flying bird so that the shotgun pellets and the duck arrive at the same point at the same time. They worked with an MIT professor, Dr. Stark Draper, who years later was involved in the guidance that put men on the moon. Draper, meanwhile, was also working with the Sperry Gyroscope Company to develop such a gunsight.[49]

Draper had come up with a "black box" that turned out to be a sight designed for Army tanks, although it needed improvements in order to be used on board a ship that moved through several planes of motion. The device, which came to be known as the Mark 14 gunsight, was composed of two air-spun gyroscopes, one vertical and one horizontal. As a result, it could generate lead angles and the proper elevation for range. The gunner could keep his eye on the target rather than having to lead it, as was customary with the sights then in use. The Mark 14 sight was incorporated into the Mark 51 gun director. Still later, the basic Mark 51 concept was merged with a radar set and redesignated the Mark 57 director that could "see" the target even at night or in low visibility.

Historian Trent Hone explained, "A greater benefit was that the radar provided accurate ranges. One of the weaknesses of the Mark 14 was that its predicted lead angles relied on a manual range estimate by an operator. In fast-developing combat situations, operators would neglect to change the range setting as planes approached, throwing off their aim. Radar would not only 'see,' it could also update the range automatically, making the entire system much more accurate."[50]

In June 1941 two officers from the Bureau of Ordnance, Commander Ernest Herrmann and Lieutenant Commander Marion E. Murphy, went to MIT to examine the new sight. Two lieutenant commanders, Pete McDowell and John Opie from Fleet Training, made later visits. Initial tests at the Naval Proving Ground in Dahlgren, Virginia, were not impressive, but Sperry subsequently made improvements. Eller and McDowell observed later tests at Dahlgren, and the sight performed well with tracer ammunition. Officers assigned to OP-22 were helpful in developing confidence in the improved version. Miles, Holloway, and Lee also encouraged the adoption of the new gunsight, and Rear Admiral Blandy of the Bureau of Ordnance, approved production. Years later, Murphy wrote, "Capt. Lee undoubtedly talked to Admiral Blandy about it, though the latter probably needed no prodding."[51] Eventually the Navy purchased eighty-five thousand Mark 14 sights to control the multitude of light AA guns in the fleet.[52]

One of the best-kept secrets of those prewar months was the development of shipboard radar. Lee, who saw the device's potential, recognized the value of getting it installed aboard as many ships as possible to perform the functions of searching for targets and controlling gunfire against those targets. Lieutenant Commander Frederick R. Furth worked with Lee during that period. He originally served in the Communications Division of OpNav, the Fleet Maintenance Division, and later in the Electronics Division of the office of the Vice Chief of Naval Operations. He was involved in the specifics of numbers of radars allowed for ships and the ordering of equipment from manufacturers. He also reported to Lee on fleet communications competition and the state of training of communications personnel. As with his relationship with Admiral Blandy, Lee's interests required frequent updates with various other directorates involved in the quest for improved combat readiness.[53]

On 13 May 1941 Lee chaired a conference in his office to discuss installation of radar antennas and sets on board various ships of the fleet, beginning with battleships, heavy cruisers, and light cruisers. A record of the meeting detailed where the antennas would go in the superstructures of the ships and that some weight would have to be removed topside to compensate for the new gear. Topside weight has a deleterious effect on a ship's stability.[54] The following month Lee received a memo that reported on Lieutenant Commander Furth's evaluation of the capabilities and production of various types of radar. Hundreds of sets were on order but not yet completed.[55] Soon afterward, Lee recommended to the Bureau of Navigation that it should establish a class at the Naval Research Laboratory in Washington to train men to operate this marvelous new tool. The candidates for training were to include radiomen, fire controlmen, and electrician's mates.[56]

As the summer of 1941 turned toward autumn, good news arrived in the Lee household. At 0200 on a September morning, Commander Nealy A. Chapin, the Fleet Training duty officer, gave a pleased Mabelle Lee the news that her husband had been selected for rear admiral. She told him he was the first to inform them.[57] It wasn't that much of a surprise. Captain Lee had been serving in an admiral's billet in the months since Admiral Leary left, and the Chief of Naval Operations had utmost confidence in him. Once, Admiral Stark had jokingly graded Lee's military appearance "exceptional" on a fitness report. It wasn't all that great, but his typical sloppiness was an exception to the norm of high standards. When news of the selection came through, Lee's subordinates sent him a message: "Congratulations to the first man to make flag rank without two-blocking his tie." In other words, as indicated previously, the knot didn't go all the way to the top.[58]

A year earlier, Captain Jonas Ingram, Lee's longtime friend and *Pennsylvania* shipmate, had been selected for flag rank. About that time the *New Yorker* magazine published a cartoon that depicted a fat admiral who was clothed in an outrageously fancy uniform while attending a cocktail party. Two young ladies took a look at the Navy man, and one said, "He's only a rear admiral. That's the lowest type there is, you know." Lee had a copy of the drawing framed and sent it to Ingram, who tended to the rotund. Now, a year later, Lee was selected, and Ingram sent him copies of the same cartoon.[59]

On 7 December 1941 the Japanese struck Pearl Harbor and the nation was at war. The Lees were at home in Kalorama when a call from the Navy Department summoned Lee to the office. Unflappable as ever, he took the news in stride while some around him were devastated. He put Jimmy Holloway, head of Fleet Training's gunnery section, in charge of allocating .50-caliber ammunition, which was in short supply and dearer than gold. The half-million rounds on hand weren't enough for more than a few days of fighting. One reason for the scarcity was that the United States had been providing the bullets to the British through the Lend-Lease program, which was America's means of keeping the British afloat during the period before the United States got into the war itself. As Holloway put it later, "I had to dole it out in dribs and drabs because it was so damn scarce." The Bureau of Ordnance had the ammo; Holloway worked through the BuOrd liaison officer, Commander Freddie Withington, on where to send it.[60]

The workload increased dramatically for all hands in the wake of the Japanese attack. Up until then, Fleet Training didn't operate on Sundays. Now it was in a constant effort to expedite the development and production of new weapons. Civilian companies that had been involved in producing commercial products were converted to turn out the materials of war. In this process of procuring equipment, Lee was not a micro-manager. He relied on the expertise and resourcefulness of his subordinates.[61]

Admiral Ernest J. King, who had been serving as commander in chief, Atlantic Fleet, soon moved to Washington to become commander in chief, U.S. Fleet (CominCh). Admiral Stark remained as Chief of Naval Operations for a few more months, then went to duty in England when King became CNO as well. On 30 December 1941, Captain Lee reported to King's CominCh staff for temporary additional duty as assistant chief of staff for readiness. In a paper transaction, Fleet Training went out of business on 20 January 1942 and was reincarnated immediately as the Readiness Division (F-4) of the CominCh staff.[62] The duties and responsibilities remained much the same, although the new title was more descriptive of the division's function—to make the fleet ready for combat. Meanwhile, on 8 January, Admiral Stark administered the oath of office as Lee was promoted to the temporary rank of rear admiral. His date of rank was retroactively established as 4 November 1941. His permanent appointment to the new rank would come later.[63]

Lee wasn't fazed by the abrupt change from uncertain peace to certain hostilities. "As a matter of fact," recalled Holloway, "it was just the thing he needed, because now it meant we could get on with the business at hand—providing the fleet more to fight with than it had been getting up to then."[64] In this endeavor Lee and Blandy worked well together because they had been close friends for years. Neither was concerned about observing bureaucratic dividing lines.

Security was supposed to be important in a Washington at war. On one occasion, with Lee's permission, Lieutenant Commander Miles dressed up in the type of apron busboys wore in the Navy Department cafeteria. So attired, he got hold of a drawer of classified files from one office, loaded the material into a pushcart, and took it nearly a mile to the Federal Bureau of Investigation. He returned to his office without being detected, and the "theft" wasn't reported for two days. Lee himself also demonstrated the laxity of the building's security, coming and going at will with a picture of Adolf Hitler attached to the identification card he wore on his uniform. (Headquarters personnel had switched from civilian clothes to uniforms with the coming of war.) When no one challenged him for that, he tried a picture of actress Mae West and got by for another half day.[65]

Commander Milton Miles (having been promoted to that rank) was at work on other pursuits. The morning coffee sessions had continued to develop plans for sending an intelligence mission to China. And, going beyond a purely intelligence-gathering role, the planners had in mind a guerrilla action that would strengthen the Chinese soldiers. For a Navy at war, virtually anything that would aid in preparing for combat could be placed under the "readiness" rubric. Lee continued as the patron of the affair. Then it got support from an officer with even more clout than two-star Admiral Lee—four-star Admiral Ernest King. The U.S. strategic plan called for defeating Germany while the Pacific and Japan were considered as secondary. In that area the strategy would be primarily defensive. But King wanted a more aggressive approach in the Pacific, and the Interior Control Board's China initiative suited his purposes well, in part because, as Miles had envisioned, Allied forces might land there on their way toward Japan.[66]

In early 1942 Miles was summoned to Admiral King's office. King was sending Miles to China "to find out what is going on out there." As Miles' memoirs recounted, Admiral King told him something along the lines of, "You are to go to China and set up some bases as soon as you can. The main idea is to prepare the China coast in any way you can for U.S. Navy landings in three or four years. In the meantime, do whatever you can to help the Navy and heckle the Japanese."[67] The process was later formalized with the establishment, by a treaty between the United States and China in 1942, of the Sino-American Cooperative Organization (SACO). When he went overseas after the war started, Miles was designated as commander, Naval Group China.

While Miles was in China—and he stayed there the rest of the war—Jeff Metzel was his Washington contact. Metzel, who often stayed at the Navy Department for days at a time, took care of his Readiness Section business during the day and tended to the reports and requests from Miles at night. (Even after Lee left for sea in the summer of 1942, he maintained a keen interest in Miles' activities.) Metzel maintained a frantic pace; he constantly threw off intellectual sparks on a variety of topics. One of his 1919 Naval Academy classmates said that Metzel "had a new idea on how to win the war about three or four times a day, and about every ten days he had an excellent idea."[68] Willis Lee had an affinity for these "brilliant screwballs." He was able to stimulate their thinking and then send them off to perform the services at which they were valuable.

In the area of readiness, submarines were, to a degree, included in Lee's purview. Lieutenant Commander John R. Waterman, who had previously commanded the submarine S-45, was tasked with addressing submarine engineering problems. A number of complaints came to his desk about a shortage of pure water to refill the storage batteries that enabled submarines to operate underwater. The upshot was that a number of submarines had to cut their patrols short—not because they were out of torpedoes but because battery water was exhausted. Waterman told Lee that an excellent new device, the Kleinschmidt evaporator, was available but held up in the Bureau of Ships (BuShips) for further testing. He alerted Lee to the problem, and immediately Lee directed, "Tomorrow start installing every one that is complete." That was the solution and made the submarines self-sufficient with regard to their supplies of distilled water.[69]

Early in the war another submarine-related difficulty was that torpedo exploders were defective. A number of courageous submarine skippers took their boats in close and hit their targets—only to have the torpedoes bounce off enemy ships without exploding. Some were equipped with magnetic exploders that were supposed to go off when passing under the keel of a ship and be activated by the target's magnetic signature. The program was highly classified in the Bureau of Ordnance and, as experience demonstrated, not adequately tested. It was only in the middle of the war, when the Pacific Fleet type commander for submarines, Vice Admiral Charles Lockwood, ordered empirical tests, that the problem was effectively identified and solved.[70] This long after the fact, it is difficult to say whether the Readiness Division under Admiral Lee should have taken a more active role in identifying the problem, especially with all the other balls it was juggling.

Pete McDowell continued his own gadfly missions on behalf of the boss. Lee gave him plenty of freedom and then covered for him if he had to. McDowell was the admiral's alter ego, attending conferences on his behalf. If a meeting seemed to be drifting in the wrong direction, he would make a quick call to Lee, who would come in, get a quick briefing, and present his views. As McDowell recalled, the tenor of these meetings often changed quickly as the result of Lee's intervention.

In the course of his travels, McDowell talked to Lieutenant Commander Arleigh Burke, a Naval Academy classmate of his who was stationed at the Naval Gun Factory in Washington. Burke told him that the York Safe and Lock Company was not making good breech mechanisms for 40-mm guns and that the Navy should get them from the Pontiac Division of General Motors instead. McDowell passed the information on to Admiral Lee, who told him to make the recommendation to Commander Ernest E. Herrmann at the Bureau of Ordnance. Soon, Captain Theodore D. Ruddock Jr., of BuOrd's production division, called back and wanted to know where McDowell had gotten his assertions about York's breech mechanisms. Despite a lot of prodding, McDowell wouldn't tell, because he didn't want to get Burke in trouble.

Before long, Admiral Lee received a letter from the Bureau of Ordnance, putting McDowell on report for "unwarranted interference" and going around collecting "misinformation about the breech mechanism." Lee asked McDowell what he proposed to do, and McDowell said he'd lie to protect Burke. He would say that he didn't really know much about the subject and didn't recall where he had heard it. Lee responded, "I don't think you're going to have to do that." He asked his secretary to bring him all the copies of the letter, and across the face of the original, he wrote a note to Admiral Blandy: "Dear Spike, In this matter, Pete performed strictly in accordance with my orders. Regards, Ching." It was typical of the way Lee operated and was the reason his subordinates held him in high esteem. He took the heat for them.[71]

Throughout his time on the fleet staff, Lee was frequently concerned with providing ships with adequate antiaircraft weapons. In the spring of 1942, for example, correspondence came to him from the skipper of the recently commissioned battleship *South Dakota*, one of his future flagships. Captain Thomas Gatch asked that an additional thirty-five .50-caliber machine guns be added to the ship's allowance, in addition to the eight already on board. In his endorsement, Admiral Lee noted that the ship already had seven quadruple 1.1-inch mounts and thirty-five 20-mm guns. He quickly put the kibosh on the skipper's request, saying that the addition of the machine guns was "neither necessary nor desirable." The .50s did not have sufficient hitting power or range. Even so, the armament that Lee enumerated was still pitifully inadequate, especially since the 1.1s were prone to jamming. Of the latter, Lieutenant Commander Eller reported that the 1.1 had been developed by the Bureau of Ordnance, a very fine gun but with unforgiving tolerances, so that once it was afloat with sailors and salt air, it was always giving trouble. Most in the fleet didn't like it. Later in the year, the *South Dakota* gained a sizable number of 40-mm weapons and put them to good use.[72]

After the attack on Pearl Harbor, Commander Holloway pleaded with Lee to be released from his job in gunnery readiness so he could go to sea. Even though Holloway was a valued and experienced team member, Lee reluctantly agreed to let him go in the spring of 1942 so that Holloway could take command of newly commissioned Destroyer Squadron Ten. Holloway later recalled that Lee acquiesced, even though it was a critical time on the CominCh staff and Lee "wanted to get to sea as badly as I did." Under Holloway's leadership, DesRon Ten played an important role in the Allied invasion of North Africa in November 1942.[73]

On 12 May 1942, the newly formed Joint Committee on New Weapons and Equipment held its first meeting. The committee, which reported to the Joint Chiefs of Staff, was chaired by Dr. Vannevar Bush, a noted civilian scientist who was president of the Carnegie Institution of Washington. Rear Admiral Lee was the Navy member. He was already using civilian scientists in the quest for new devices that would contribute to the fleet's ability to do its job. One such was Dr. Edwin Land, then in his early 30s and later the inventor of the Polaroid camera. Lee appointed Land and McDowell as a "committee" of two to work on new weapons, with Land serving as chairman. Then, if someone challenged McDowell's actions or requests, he could blithely respond, "You'll have to talk to my chairman."[74]

As before, getting AA weapons onto ships was a prime consideration. McDowell got the blueprints for all types of combatant ships in the fleet. Then he cut out circles of paper to represent the proportional sizes of various gun mounts—20-mm, 40-mm, and 5-inch. He put them down on blueprints to see how many would fit on each type of ship. Then he drafted a letter that authorized the procurement of the necessary number of mounts. He showed the letter to the appropriate officer in the Bureau of Ships and asked him to sign. The man balked, saying that the mounts would disrupt the seaworthiness of the ships. McDowell pointed out that the letter authorized procurement only and not installation. Reluctantly, the officer signed, and McDowell removed a period and got the letter changed from procurement to "procurement and installation." The letter went up the chain of command, got the requisite approval from the Secretary of the Navy, and was implemented. Thereafter, whenever a combatant went into a shipyard, light antiaircraft guns were added everywhere there was room—and sometimes in places where there had been no room. For some of the ships, topside equipment was removed to make way for the guns.[75]

"Uncle Ching's boys" were not alone in the production of new ideas. One cruiser skipper sent in a letter recommending that the ship's airplane catapults be used to launch torpedoes. McDowell suggested to Admiral Lee that they should send a reply that thanked the captain for his idea but told him that it was totally impractical because there weren't even enough torpedoes to provide full supplies to submarines and destroyers—let alone cruisers. Lee smiled and suggested an alternate course of action. He said such a reply would only disappoint the cruiser captain and serve to dampen his morale. Instead, said the admiral, McDowell should draft a response saying that it was a good idea. He should recommend it for action and then send it on up the chain of command. But it would have to make a lot of stops, for the catapults were under the cognizance of the Bureau of Aeronautics, the ship's deck under the Bureau of Ships, the catapult powder charge under the Bureau of Ordnance, new use for the catapult under the General

Board, and the possibility of a patent under the Secretary of the Navy. Such a response would take months to get around, said Lee, and there would be a new endorsement perhaps once a quarter. The captain would be happy, and he would be long gone before the letter finished making its rounds. That's what McDowell did, and that's what happened to the letter.[76]

Lee had handled the same sort of situation somewhat differently in late 1940 when a captain in the Army Air Corps Reserve submitted an idea for using sea sleds as a means of attacking enemy submarines. It was duly forwarded to the Navy by Secretary of War Henry Stimson and then sent to Fleet Training for evaluation. After he had perused the suggestion, Lee wrote, "Holloway tell him no possibility—the old bed-bug letter WAL." Thereupon Holloway drafted a two-page letter for Secretary of the Navy Frank Knox to send to Stimson, explaining in logical, detailed terms why the sea sled idea was impractical.[77] (In hotel circles, a bed-bug letter is a polite response to a complainer. The answer says that the hotel management is surprised by the complaint because the establishment has no bed bugs. A problem comes when the note saying, "Send the bed-bug letter" is inadvertently attached to the outgoing letter.)

Lee had other means of getting his light touch into the flood of paper. As each new demand piled on top of the last one, priorities climbed higher and higher. Previously, action matters had been stamped "routine" or "priority." Now everything was "urgent." Lee responded by devising his own rubber stamp, "Frantic." There was one thing he didn't have any answer for, because he was used to a service exclusively composed of men. As more and more male sailors went to sea, women came into the Navy and took over secretarial jobs as yeomen. Admiral King ruled that the enlisted women should be addressed by their last names, just as the men were. It happened that Admiral Lee's secretary was an attractive yeoman second class named Dorothy Angel. Lee was embarrassed when a visitor came in and he had to call out, "Angel, bring me the file on such-and-such."[78]

Lee had worked long hours before the war, but his schedule became even more crowded as the war progressed. He was frequently at the office seven days a week. Perhaps it was just as well that he was not interested in the social whirl. There was an occasional cocktail party in the Kalorama Road apartment, but mostly the Lees kept to themselves. When they did go out, it was often to an obligatory affair or a party in the home of close friends, such as Commander Milton Miles and his wife Wilma, who had a big home in Chevy Chase, Maryland. Mrs. Miles recalled of the Lees, "He treated her like a little doll. She was small and gentle. He could almost wear her for a watch fob. He was protective and sweet toward her." They were not outwardly demonstrative of affection for each other, because, as Wilma explained, "That just wasn't the style then."[79]

After Commander Miles took off for China, his wife hosted a small party by herself one evening. As a means of starting conversation, she devised a game in which each guest would relate his or her most embarrassing moment or tell a whopping lie. Uncle Ching told of an experience he supposedly had as a midshipman. He and his roommate left their ship during a summer cruise to Norway and proceeded to the local church. Unfamiliar with the language, they decided to watch the man in the pew in front of them and copy his actions. At one point, the man stood up, so the pair obediently followed suit. To their surprise, they were the only three on their feet. As they were leaving at the end of the service, they spoke to the minister, who happened to understand English. They explained their predicament, and he laughed when he told them what happened. There was a new baby in the congregation, said the imaginary minister, and he had asked the father to stand up.[80]

The real world of 1942 was still at work, though, and that meant still more requirements of the "urgent" and "frantic" variety. Again, following his philosophy of moving for a workable solution rather than a perfect one, Lee urged production of the new proximity antiaircraft fuze for 5-inch guns, even though Commander William S. "Deak" Parsons wanted it held up until it was one hundred percent satisfactory. (In 1945, as a captain, Parsons was the "weaponeer" on board the B-29 *Enola Gay* that dropped an atomic bomb on Hiroshima, Japan.) Lee and McDowell also concocted a letter to BuOrd and BuShips, saying they wanted at least one radar on board every combatant ship in the Navy. Admiral Lee added the prodding final sentence, "If you can't produce them in this country, buy British."[81]

As head of the Readiness Division, Lee was responsible for seeing that weapons and ammunition were procured and delivered to each ship to meet the requirements of upcoming operations. Security by then had tightened to the point that it caused problems even for Admiral Lee. His staff had a great deal of difficulty getting advance word on the names of ships to be involved in a given operation. Sometimes, there were only a few hours to work with BuOrd and the logistics section of CominCh to meet deadlines for such things as the delivery of high-capacity projectiles to ships scheduled to be involved in shore bombardments. Truck convoys carried the new 20-mm and 40-mm guns to ships, and BuOrd had radio communications with truck convoys so destinations could be changed en route to meet emergency installation needs.[82]

One enterprise that called for massive preparations because of its scope was Operation Torch, the planned invasion of North Africa in the autumn of 1942. Some of the preparations came under the aegis of a new subdivision of Readiness Division called Special Weapons. Again, Commander McDowell was running with the bit in his teeth, fully aware that Captain Schuyler wasn't going to be pleased with the infringement on BuOrd turf. McDowell had reserve officers reading research reports and making recommendations for ideas that could be turned into hardware in one, two, or three years. They worked on landing craft, new types of amphibious ships, and getting tanks to the beach. They came up with airborne radar sets that could provide an overview of landing craft on their way to the beach and then send the picture to the bridge of the flagship by television. Still other Special Weapons projects were Hedgehog rockets for antisubmarine work and infrared viewing devices. An inflatable rubber soldier figure was another innovation; it was intended to draw fire away from real soldiers during amphibious landings. The inflatable figure had weighted feet and could be booby-trapped. On one occasion McDowell brought one of these "men" into Lee's office and introduced it to the admiral by saying, "Sir, I want you to meet my relief."

Lee replied, in his droll way, "Pete, I can see the improvement immediately."[83]

It was time for Lee's relief. He had been on the job in Main Navy for more than three years. Hundreds more ships inhabited the fleet than when he had last been on sea duty in 1939. The biggest and most impressive of the new gunnery ships were the 35,000-ton fast battleships of the *North Carolina* and *South Dakota* classes. A war was on, and Lee wanted to go to sea. He had proved his genius in gunnery and had earned the approbation of Admirals Stark and King. He may have asked for command of a battleship division. In any case, King undoubtedly approved Lee for the job, for flag officer assignments during the war routinely required the initials "EJK." Lee was officially detached from Washington duty on 10 August.

His wife Mabelle often wrote notes, shopping lists, and dates on the back of her calendar. Her sister Margaret saw a note on the 1942 calendar: "Lee left apartment August 14th." That summed up Mabelle's sense of loneliness. She disposed of the furnishings in their Kalorama Road apartment as she prepared to return to Rock Island, Illinois, to spend the ensuing years with her sisters and young nephew Don Siders. There was no telling how long her husband would be gone. Rear Admiral Willis Augustus Lee Jr., fifty-four years old, was on his way to rejoin the fleet he loved so well.[84]

■ 9 ■

BATTLESHIP DIVISION COMMANDER

August–October 1942

I n August of 1942, the city of Washington was enduring its customary summer heat. The whirring blades of fans provided scant relief in those days before air-conditioning. Residents who were fortunate could escape to cooler climes farther north. Recently promoted Rear Admiral Lee would be heading to the South Pacific instead.

The strategic situation in the Pacific had changed dramatically during the preceding six months. In the weeks following the successful attack on Pearl Harbor, the tentacles of the Japanese octopus had expanded farther and farther to ensnare new conquests. They were virtually untrammeled by U.S. efforts that were limited to submarine attacks and hit-and-run raids on Japanese-held territory. Included in the latter was an 18 April bombing of Tokyo and other targets in the home islands. The strikes were led by Lieutenant Colonel James Doolittle, whose Army Air Forces B-25 Mitchell bombers were launched from the aircraft carrier *Hornet*. The *Enterprise* was also involved in the mission, though she launched no Army planes herself.

That spring codebreakers working in a basement room in the Pearl Harbor Navy Yard divined Japanese intentions from intercepted radio messages. That intelligence put U.S. warships into position for the Battle of the Coral Sea in early

May. The carrier *Lexington*, destroyer *Sims*, and oiler *Neosho* were lost. The carrier *Yorktown* was damaged, but the Americans drew blood as well. In a battle fought entirely by carrier planes with the enemy task forces not in sight of each other, U.S. pilots sank the light carrier *Shoho* and damaged the heavy carrier *Shokaku*. Much more importantly, by waging a successful defense, the Navy prevented the Japanese from occupying Port Moresby on the south coast of New Guinea. The Japanese had planned to use it as a stepping-stone to Australia.

Still more defense came in June when the octopus attempted to stretch far to the east—an invasion of U.S.-held Midway Island in the mid-Pacific. It was part of a strategy for an early negotiated peace. By capturing Midway and using it as a springboard for taking Hawaii, Japan could perhaps threaten the U.S. West Coast and, in any event, deprive the U.S. Navy of Pearl Harbor as a significant logistic support base and staging area.

Admiral Isoroku Yamamoto, commander in chief of the Japanese Combined Fleet, was a risk-taker. He had gambled big with the December strike on Pearl Harbor and won—at least temporarily. As Japanese planning moved into the spring, Yamamoto entertained the Midway gamble as a way to keep pressure on the Americans. This time his roll of the dice came up snake eyes. The codebreakers, who inspired confidence by their Coral Sea predictions, were able to decipher sufficient Japanese messages to predict Midway as an upcoming target. Admiral Chester Nimitz, commander in chief of the Pacific Fleet, had sufficient faith in his intelligence officers that he supported an ambush of the attacking forces. He sent the carriers *Yorktown*, *Hornet*, and *Enterprise* to lie in wait. On 4 June, American dive-bombers knocked out the heavy carriers *Akagi*, *Kaga*, *Hiryu*, and *Soryu*. All were veterans of the attack on Pearl Harbor. The other two carriers from that raid, the *Shokaku* and *Zuikaku*, were not available to take part. The former was damaged in the Coral Sea engagement, and the latter suffered losses of airplanes and crews to the extent that she had to return to Japan to recover. The American triumph was, to use the words of author Walter Lord, an "incredible victory."

Now it was the Americans' turn to seize the initiative. Admiral Ernest J. King, Chief of Naval Operations and commander in chief, U.S. Fleet, brashly proposed an invasion of the islands of Guadalcanal and Tulagi in the Solomons chain in the South Pacific. The overall U.S. strategy put the conquest of the Germans in Europe at the forefront. The Pacific was decreed to be a defensive holding action.

King's biographer, Thomas Buell, wrote that King was not satisfied with that role for the Navy and was concerned that the Japanese, unless challenged vigorously, would be able to regroup and resume their offensive. He sought to prevent that. On 30 June, he and the Army chief of staff, General George C. Marshall, agreed to move the boundary line dividing the Pacific Fleet's area of responsibility from that of General Douglas MacArthur to the west so that it would encompass the Solomons. On 2 July King and Marshall met to settle on near-term Pacific strategy. King then ordered the invasion of Tulagi and Guadalcanal for 1 August, a date later delayed by nearly a week.[1]

In the meantime, the Allies were kept informed about Japanese operations in the area by reports from an alert coastwatcher named Martin Clemens. Clemens, a twenty-seven-year-old native of Scotland, served in the British Colonial Service as director of the Solomon Islands Protectorate. On 8 June the Japanese arrived to begin their occupation of Guadalcanal. The Japanese intent, which King and Pacific Fleet Commander in Chief Chester Nimitz already knew through radio intelligence, was to build an airstrip on Guadalcanal. It could provide the enemy with a wide radius for air attacks. A Japanese convoy comprising construction equipment and personnel arrived at the island on 6 July to begin laying out the aviation facility.[2]

On 7 August, the Navy sent ashore an assault team comprised of members of the First Marine Division. The team established footholds on Guadalcanal and Tulagi. As part of the occupation, the Marines captured the airstrip. The Americans renamed it Henderson Field in honor of Marine Corps Major Lofton R. Henderson, who was killed while leading a dive-bomber squadron in the Battle of Midway. The issue around Guadalcanal was in doubt right away. On the night of 8–9 August a Japanese cruiser force commanded by Vice Admiral Gunichi Mikawa mounted a devastating surface attack that sank four heavy cruisers: the American *Astoria*, *Vincennes*, and *Quincy*, plus the Australian *Canberra*. The night action of confused firing was a melee known as the First Battle of Savo Island, which is near Guadalcanal. The Japanese force received some damage during and after the massacre. U.S. guns inflicted hits on the heavy cruisers *Chokai*, *Aoba*, and *Kinugasa*. The American submarine *S-44* torpedoed and sank the heavy cruiser *Kako* on 10 August as the Japanese strike force was returning to the island of Rabaul.

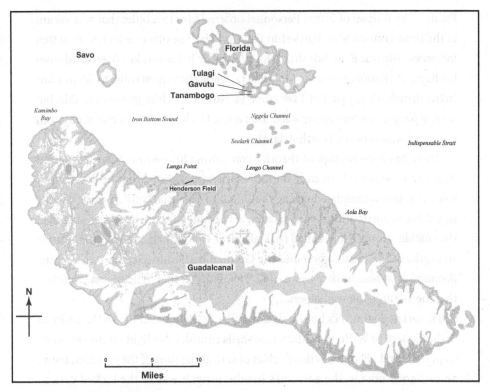

Map 1. Guadalcanal, 1942

While this naval disaster was taking place, the Marines initially encountered little resistance ashore. That changed on 19 August when a Japanese convoy of nine destroyers delivered nearly one thousand trained army troops to the island. The commander of the infantry regiment was Colonel Kiyonao Ichiki. His mission was to recapture Henderson Field. Fierce fighting followed the Japanese landing. U.S. Marines killed Ichiki and hundreds of his men, but a desperate struggle for control of the island persisted for the next few months. The Japanese continued to pour more troops into Guadalcanal.

■ ■ ■

It was toward this hotbed that Willis Lee would be heading. He was designated to take the first division of the new twenty-seven-knot fast battleships to the

Pacific. The Bureau of Naval Personnel ordered him to a billet that was vacant at the time: commander, Battleship Division Six. The officer who had held that job previously was Rear Admiral John W. Wilcox Jr. He was lost overboard from his flagship *Washington* on 27 March 1942, while she was en route to Scapa Flow in the British Isles as part of Task Force 39. No one saw him go over the side, but several people saw him in the water afterward. His body was not recovered from the frigid waters of the North Atlantic.

There has been no lack of theories concerning his demise. Some suspected that a wave washed him over the side; others speculated that he committed suicide as he contemplated taking the ship into potential conflict alongside the Royal Navy. Ensign John Cadwalader, a *Washington* crew member, disputed the suicide rumor. He recalled that Admiral Wilcox had assessed the relative strengths of the *Washington* and the German battleship *Tirpitz*—sister of the *Bismarck* that was sunk a year earlier. He observed that Wilcox was confident that the *Washington* was superior.[3]

Historian Arthur Nicholson discovered a newly opened file in the archives of the College of William & Mary that sheds considerable light on the situation. Captain John L. Hall Jr., Wilcox's chief of staff at the time of the incident, found an unsigned note in the admiral's handwriting; it was in the locked desk in Wilcox's cabin. The note could be read to suggest that America would be better off without him. On the orders of Rear Admiral Robert C. Giffen, who had succeeded Wilcox as commander of the task force, the note was not submitted to the board of investigation on board the *Washington*.[4]

A sidelight to this substitution of Lee for Wilcox is that both were named in a secret selection board convened at the behest of President Roosevelt after the Navy's lackluster performance in the early months of 1942. FDR directed Secretary of the Navy Frank Knox to put together a group of nine senior admirals. Their task was to pick the forty "most competent" of the Navy's 120 active-duty flag officers and report back. The number of votes received by individuals ranged from nine to five in coming up with the top forty. Surprisingly, neither Chester Nimitz nor Raymond Spruance made the cut. Wilcox and Lee each received five votes. Historian Richard Frank lauded Lee as the star of the surface officers in the five-vote category and called him "clearly one of the finest officers of that generation." Knox turned over the results of the board to Roosevelt on 9 March. Eighteen days later Wilcox was dead.[5]

■ ■ ■

The *South Dakota* served as Lee's flagship. She was the lead ship in a new class of fast battleships, shorter and better armored than the *North Carolina* and *Washington*. She carried a main battery of nine 16-inch/45-caliber guns. Her secondary battery differed from the other ships in her class in that she had only sixteen—rather than twenty—5-inch/38-caliber dual-purpose guns for use against both air and surface targets. One twin mount was omitted from each side of the *South Dakota* so that she could provide accommodations for a force commander and his staff. Lee's initial staff required far less space. After the death of Admiral Wilcox, members of his staff departed for other duties, so Lee had to start from scratch.

Lieutenant Ray Thompson was a member of the *South Dakota*'s commissioning crew. The ship went through sea trials and shakedown training in the Chesapeake Bay, safely protected from U-boat threats. Later she had further training in the Atlantic before going into dry dock at the Philadelphia Navy Yard, across the river from Camden, New Jersey, where she was built. Around noon on 14 August, Thompson heard "a rumor that an admiral had sneaked aboard with his suitcase."[6] The crew of the ship had not been aware of Lee's imminent arrival, and the suggestion that he had sneaked on board fit his low-key character; he went on board in civilian clothes rather than in uniform.

The ship got under way down the Delaware River the following day and fueled. Thompson was in his sea detail station, high in sky control forward. He was checking out some circuits when he received a call from the ship's gunnery officer, Lieutenant Commander Paul Johnson. Thompson learned that he was the subject of dispatch orders that detached him from the crew. The lieutenant was baffled, but, sure enough, the orders directed him to report to the staff of the newly arrived admiral as his flag lieutenant. He made himself presentable and went to see Lee, who was ensconced in the flag quarters. He mentioned the orders, and Lee quipped, "You're the only one on the staff. Do whatever a staff's supposed to do." Lee showed him the op order, which directed the ship to proceed to Tongatabu, which very few on board had even heard of. Thompson went to flag plot and pulled out the appropriate charts. He learned that the person who selected him for the staff was Lee's old friend Commander Bill Jennings. Jennings had gone to the Bureau of Naval Personnel to find an officer with postgraduate education in ordnance and fire control. Thompson fit those specifications and was immediately available.[7]

Ensign Paul Backus and several of his new shipmates were available to serve as members of the *South Dakota*'s commissioning crew because their previous ship, the battleship *Oklahoma*, had capsized and sunk during the attack on Pearl Harbor. His roommate was killed that day, and Backus was haunted by survivor's guilt. He pondered plaintively on his fate: "Why them and not me?"[8] The voyage was held up for a day while crew members, aided by personnel from the Navy yard and the Bureau of Ships, made repairs to a main engine. On the morning of 16 August, the *South Dakota* began the long voyage to Tongatabu; she was accompanied by three destroyers, the *Livermore*, *Kearny*, and *Rowan*. On 21 August, the *South Dakota* went through the Panama Canal and steamed into the Pacific. There she picked up three different destroyers; the *Lansdowne*, *Lardner*, and *Meade* of Destroyer Division 24 joined the battleship.[9]

During the course of the Panama Canal passage, the admiral wrote a letter to his wife in Illinois. She spent much of the ensuing three years there, where she lived with her sisters and her nephew, Don Siders. She probably enjoyed more companionship there than she had while living with her workaholic husband in Washington. Lee's missive to his wife read,

> Dear Chubby,
>
> It seems like more than a week since I saw you—I *do* miss you.
>
> Arrived OK, and am delighted with the ship and people on it. My quarters look bigger than our apartment.
>
> Aside from leaving you it has been a relief to get away from the office. Have had quite a peaceful time with plenty of fresh air and sunshine. Cold is much better and I think I am already taking on weight.
>
> Did Bill J. [Jennings] fix up your ticket and trunk checks for you? He said he would stop back at Apt. and see that you got straightened out on them. Did you see Miles and Bobby?

Suppose you are back in R.I. [Rock Island] now, and if you are give my love to Peg, Ada, Donny and Gert—saving the major portion for yourself. Will write again soon

With love
Lee

An admiral's flag lieutenant often takes care of personal chores in addition to handling signals. But Lee wanted someone who could aid him in the substance of the tactical challenges ahead, thus the intervention by Jennings. As Backus remembered, Thompson was "an acknowledged hot shot in the weapons field." (He had finished fifth of 432 in the final standings for the Naval Academy class of 1933.) Backus and his cohorts were disappointed when he was detached from ship's company to join the staff, but Thompson soon warmed to the task and his relationship with Lee.[10] Since the aide's job came as a surprise to Thompson, he did not already have a set of aiguillettes, the gold-colored cords that go around an aide's shoulder and are sometimes known as "loafer's loops."

Lieutenant Commander William R. Smedberg III was the skipper of the *Lansdowne,* one of the escorting destroyers that joined on the Pacific side of the canal. He had been with Lee on Admiral Stark's cruiser staff in the late 1930s. Back then, Smedberg was hoping for a billet as a destroyer executive officer as a stepping-stone to commanding a destroyer, so he initially declined when Stark offered to take him to Washington in 1939. Lee pulled him aside and said, "You're crazy, Smeddy. You can't possibly go to any job in the Navy where you'll learn as much about the Navy and enhance your career as much as going as aide to the Chief of Naval Operations." So Smedberg accepted and got a destroyer command after all, without having been an exec. He still had his aiguillettes from the job as CNO's aide and sent an extra set over to Lee's flagship by light line for Lieutenant Thompson's use. As it happened, Thompson seldom wore them because Lee wasn't given to formalities. Smedberg's career prospered; he eventually served as a vice admiral.[11]

Lieutenant (j.g.) Norman C. Hoffman served as one of the flagship's officers of the deck under way. Like Backus, he was a refugee from the *Oklahoma.* He stood his watches on the navigation bridge, while Lee was on the flag bridge one deck below. To the junior officer Lee appeared "quiet, relaxed, and friendly," but he acknowledged there was little for the admiral to do during a transit in company with three destroyers. The *South Dakota*'s chaplain, Lieutenant Commander James Claypool, a Naval Reservist on active duty, was an officer who did have some insight into how the admiral was spending his time. Years later he recalled, "My chief responsibility so far as he was concerned was to keep him supplied with all the new mystery books that came into the library. He liked to read late at night and at all hours of the night. . . . I reckon he went through as many as two volumes in a twenty four hour period."[12]

One incident during the transit demonstrated Lee's forgiving nature in the area of discipline. Marine Private Herb Preston served as an orderly for Lee and the *South Dakota*'s skipper, Captain Thomas Gatch. At one meal the admiral ate only a small piece of white meat from a chicken, and the steward put the rest of the bird back in the refrigerator. Preston and the other orderlies did not generally get food this good in the enlisted mess, so they made a practice of raiding the refrigerator at night after the admiral's steward had gone off duty. That night they polished off the rest of the fowl and threw the carcass over the side. The steward questioned them about it the following morning, but they acted innocent, as if they knew nothing of the missing bird. The steward wanted the admiral to punish the orderlies, but Lee said, "I guess the orderlies were hungrier than I was," and he let it go at that. The steward retaliated by putting a big lock on the refrigerator door, and that ended the nocturnal food forays.[13]

After the trek southward, which included crossing the equator, the men of the *South Dakota* got the first peek at their destination as coconut palms began to rise above the horizon. Soon the land on which the trees stood came into view. On 4 September, the dark gray battleship made her way into Nuku'alofa anchorage at Tongatabu, one of the Tonga Islands. The Tongas, a sovereign Polynesian state, are also known as the Friendly Islands. That name was welcoming because so much Pacific territory was in unfriendly Japanese hands that summer. That same day Lee wrote wistfully to Mabelle, "Except that I miss you, this is a welcome relief from the office in Washington." He also lamented that the movie *It Started with Eve* was the only good one on board.

The ship was soon ordered into action from the headquarters of the commander, South Pacific Force (ComSoPac), Vice Admiral Robert Ghormley, in Nouméa, New Caledonia. Lee was designated Commander Task Group 2.9. On

6 September he was to lead a force comprising the *South Dakota*, antiaircraft light cruiser *Juneau*, and escorting destroyers to rendezvous on the eighth with Rear Admiral Leigh Noyes' Task Force 18 in the carrier *Wasp*. That afternoon, only two days after her arrival, the *South Dakota* got under way at 1300 to steam out of the anchorage. Even though she was following the specified course while doing twenty knots, at 1420 she hit an uncharted submerged 35-foot coral pinnacle in Lahai Passage and did extensive damage to her bottom. Lieutenant Thompson compared the sensation to running up on a cement ramp and then suddenly being released when the coral broke. Ensign Backus, the turret two officer, likened the impact to that of being hit by a torpedo. Ensign John C. Hill II was on the bridge as part of the navigation team going into and out of Tongatabu. He recalled that the *South Dakota* had taken on fuel while there, with the result that she had a deeper draft and thus struck the reef that had not been a threat on the same track when the ship had entered.[14]

Following the grounding, divers from the repair ship *Vestal* went into the water to survey the situation and discovered a 150-foot-long underwater gash in the battleship's hull; it was some eighteen inches deep. Fuel and boiler feed-water tanks in the ship's bottom were contaminated with salt water. The ship suffered a number of dents and holes; the largest of the latter was an opening two square feet in the outer skin. Fuel leaked, and one condenser that brought in seawater to be turned into fresh water was clogged. In his message report to Ghormley, Lee estimated that the damaged battleship could maintain twenty knots. In his homespun language, Lee added, "Tobacco juice estimate about two weeks in dock."[15]

Artificers from the *Vestal* provided temporary repairs to the hull, but the ship needed far more work than that. After Ghormley recommended to Admiral Nimitz that she be sent to Pearl Harbor Navy Yard for repairs, he got approval and issued the order. On 12 September, the *South Dakota* joined Task Force 11, including the aircraft carrier *Saratoga*, which had been torpedoed in the Battle of the Eastern Solomons in late August. The cruiser *New Orleans* and five destroyers escorted the two heavy ships on their long voyage.[16] The time off proved a blessing for the battleship. During the yard period, workmen removed balky 1.1-inch guns and added quadruple mounts of 40-mm antiaircraft guns and single 20-mm guns. These would stand her in good stead in late October.

After the *South Dakota*'s departure from Tongatabu, Lee and his staff of one—Thompson—spent two days on board the transport *Hunter Liggett*, which was in the same harbor. One of the transport's grim tasks the previous month was to recover survivors from the three cruisers that had been sunk near Savo Island and deliver them to Nouméa for medical treatment. On 14 September the USS *Washington* steamed into the anchorage. She thus joined her sister ship *North Carolina* to restore the number of operational battleships in the theater to two. Lee embarked in the *Washington* that same day and moved into her flag quarters. The *South Dakota*'s accident thus put him on board a different flagship, which he came to like.

A photo of Lee's arrival on board the *Washington* shows him at the top of the starboard accommodation ladder, saluting the American flag on the fantail. Navy tradition calls for enlisted men, known as side boys, to stand by and salute as a senior officer passes through their two rows. The photo shows the sailors in crisply pressed white uniforms. Lee donned his service dress khaki uniform for the occasion. His appearance was not nearly so sharp as that of the side boys. Both his trousers and blouse (which is the Navy's term for a jacket) were wrinkled, the lower left pocket of his blouse bulged with objects, and he wore no service ribbons. Typical Lee.

Once the *Washington* was in the forward area and faced potential combat, her officers and crew got some welcome-to-the-real-world suggestions from visiting survivors of the cruiser disaster off Savo Island in early August. Officers described the fires that ravaged their sinking ships. Ensign Hal Berc observed that some of the remedies included chopping up linoleum from the wardroom deck, removing curtains from the entrances to officers' staterooms, and even pushing a grand piano over the side.[17] Another precaution was to strip flammable paint off bulkheads and overheads. This the *Washington*'s crew did, with considerable manual labor involved. When the ship was ready to face a surface battle two months later, the crew was directed to throw into the sea what little paint remained on board. At that point in November, one enlisted man remarked, "I wish we had done this months ago, before I had spent so many hours spreading so much of this around the ship."[18]

On 15 September, while escorting Marine-filled transports en route to Guadalcanal, the *North Carolina* was torpedoed and put out of action for repairs. Her departure again left the *Washington* as the only operational U.S. battleship in the South Pacific. In that same action the aircraft carrier *Wasp* was also torpedoed and badly damaged. Lieutenant Commander Smedberg's *Lansdowne* hit her with three torpedoes to supply the coup de grâce and prevent the carrier from falling into enemy hands.

Lieutenant Edward Maslanka, a member of the *Washington*'s communications department, observed Lee's immediate impact. When Admiral Wilcox was on the ship's bridge in early 1942, the enlisted personnel there were "scared to death of him," said Maslanka. When he walked from one place to the other, the sailors moved rapidly out of the way, backing themselves up against bulkheads to get as far away as possible. Lee, on the other hand, was quiet, low-key, and not at all intimidating. Though friendly, he was not particularly outgoing. When he walked on the bridge, he might walk around a sailor rather than expecting the other man to clear a path.[19]

Lee smoked, in Maslanka's estimation, 95 percent of his waking hours, chain-smoking from one cigarette to another. Even at night, when the *Washington* was steaming at darkened ship in a task force, Lee smoked, usually taking care to cup the cigarette inside his palm to prevent the glow of the cigarette from being seen by someone off the ship. Because of his communications duties, on a number of occasions Lieutenant Maslanka had to go into Lee's cabin to deliver messages. Even when the clock was well past midnight, Lee was often wide awake. While lying in bed, he was reading a detective novel and smoking at the same time.[20]

Lieutenant John Cadwalader of the gunnery department added that Lee "never stopped drinking black coffee."[21] An enlisted man named Ray Baker also recorded his observations of Lee. He invoked a familiar description of the admiral when he wrote, "He was a quiet, genteel man who, I'm sure, never raised his voice. Some of us who came from a farm thought of him as a farmer who all of a sudden found himself on the bridge of a ship instead of behind a plow. But we knew what a sharp and brilliant man he was. He loved to read Western stories and many an hour he spent in his chair on the flag bridge with a paperback Western story in his hand."[22]

One of the things Lee did after arriving on board his new flagship was send his Marine orderly for Lieutenant Chad Knowlton, a reservist who was serving as the ship's electronic maintenance officer. He'd had a background in amateur radio before being commissioned in 1940 and called to active duty the following year. He did repairs on all of the ship's radars, so Lee sought him out for information on their capabilities, derived from his experiences in standing radar watches.[23] Lee sought to pass on his knowledge of the intersection of radar and gunnery by pooling what he knew with inputs from others. He gathered together officers in those specialties with the objective of enhancing the shooting of the fast battleships. Lieutenant Commander Edwin Hooper, the ship's fire control officer and assistant gunnery officer, was one of the officers who attended these informal sessions. Another was Lieutenant Lloyd Mustin from the antiaircraft light cruiser *Atlanta*, which had been involved in the Guadalcanal campaign from the start. He shared a technique for improving rapid reaction to incoming enemy planes. Mustin imparted another lesson as well: he gave those in attendance a sense of the rigors of combat against a determined enemy.[24]

Hooper was a bright individual who had been involved in the study of fire control at MIT. He and Lee, not surprisingly, frequently discussed gunnery. In fact, said Hooper, he had more frequent conversations with Lee than did the gunnery officer, Commander Harvey Walsh, because he had a deeper technical background than did Walsh. Hooper recalled later that he had trouble keeping up with Lee, though Lee didn't notice. They were concerned about the calibration of the gun batteries so that projectiles would fall where intended. One of Lee's concerns was that the pressure and density corrections for 16-inch/45-caliber powder were wrong. The result was that the guns were shooting at longer ranges than specified in the Bureau of Ordnance range tables. Lee had Thompson conduct an experiment to determine the specific heat of the powder that fired the big guns. Hooper said Lee later demonstrated to the Bureau of Ordnance that its figures were wrong, though it took some convincing.[25]

Soon after Lee's arrival on board the *Washington*, the size of his staff doubled—from one to two. Lieutenant Commander Richard D. Zern became the flag secretary and proved to be a wise choice. The great strength he brought was that he was a stickler in his ability to handle the Navy's unavoidable paperwork. Thompson said of him, "He just loved paperwork, and he did a good job of it." An officer who joined the staff later recalled Zern as a "loveable character, with all his quirks and eccentricities." Thompson, by comparison, was intense, absorbed in the problems of the moment, and a demanding finger-snapper in relation to enlisted men.[26]

Lee tasked Zern with beefing up the staff. Lieutenant Robert G. Merritt, an affable and professionally competent Naval Academy graduate, transferred from ship's company to become assistant communication officer. To avoid robbing the *Washington*'s crew of too many academy men, Zern picked reservist William Bentinck-Smith as another addition to the staff. Bentinck-Smith was a green ensign who had joined the ship in Brooklyn that summer after her sojourn in the Atlantic. The young man received on-the-job training as a communications watch officer. He was an observant Harvard alum whose frequent contact with Lee enabled him to describe the admiral well many years later.[27]

Bentinck-Smith saw Lee as informal, someone who would have been more comfortable in old clothes and rocking on a porch than in a clean Navy uniform and wearing shoes highly polished by a steward. The admiral was unruffled, rarely angry and then only with good cause. The young officer said, "He had a penetratingly clear mind which got to the crux of any issue and swept away irrelevant detail. . . . This calm, intelligent, hard-working, quiet man inspired his subordinates and made them proud to serve under him and share the perils of a very desperate time."[28]

Lieutenant Commander Edwin S. Schanze, who had been the communications officer when the ship was commissioned on 15 May 1941, served as the *Washington*'s navigator from early November onward. At that time the *Washington* and her sister *North Carolina* were among the relatively few ships in the Navy equipped with radar. Initially she had an air-search version, officially dubbed CXAM, with what was known informally as a "bedspring" antenna because of its design. As Schanze recalled, it provided "some little help" for navigation and detection purposes but had no value for the control of gunfire.[29]

In July 1942, after the *Washington* returned from a deployment to serve with the British Fleet, the ship underwent an overhaul at the New York Navy Yard in Brooklyn. During that time, an SG surface-search radar was installed, as were several fire control radars. The Bureau of Ships directed that the antenna be placed on the forward side of the superstructure, just below the sky control station on the foremast. Lieutenant Commander Hooper, the ship's fire control officer, saw this as a mistake because it did not permit radar coverage of a 60-degree arc aft of the ship, 30 degrees on each quarter. Hooper raised his concerns with Commander Harvey Walsh, the gunnery officer, and Captain Glenn Davis, the skipper. Hooper got permission to telephone the Chief of the Bureau of Ships and request a change order that would put the antenna atop the foremast. He was not able to reach the chief and talked to an assistant instead. The upshot was that there was no change. Hooper, who had taken special instruction in radar fire control, well understood the situation. He would have an eyewitness view of the unfortunate consequences that came a few months later.[30]

When the *Washington* was not in action, Lee had a "passion for shooting at Japanese glass floats." These were used to hold up fishing nets, and Lee often indulged in firing his .45 automatic pistol at items in the water. Nor was he selfish about it. When he wanted to pop away while passing through a community of the glass balls, Lee issued an invitation on the ship's announcing system for others to join him in the unofficial target practice. Those who did were mostly members of the ship's Marine detachment.[31] The Marines on board had a direct connection with Lee, because they were detailed to serve as his orderlies. They stood outside his quarters to monitor visitors and sometimes to accompany him as he traveled to different parts of the ship. First Lieutenant Jonas M. Platt, one of the officers with the detachment, made an observation on the feedback he received from his enlisted men. He never heard complaints about Lee's treatment of the Marines, whereas he had certainly heard complaints about his predecessor as division commander, Rear Admiral Wilcox. As Platt put it, "It was sheer pleasure to have an admiral like Lee aboard after Wilcox."[32]

Lee had a common touch in dealing with enlisted men. Electrician's Mate Stanley J. Krawczyk took care of topside lights, which included staterooms, chart house, pilothouse, and the cabins of the captain and admiral. As part of his duties, he went into Lee's flag cabin every day to check the lights—always after getting the go-ahead from the Marine orderly manning the door. One morning he entered and saw Lee working at his desk. The young enlisted man discovered an overhead bulb had burned out. Since he was five feet six he couldn't reach the socket. Rather than bother the admiral, he said he would come back with a ladder sometime when Lee was out. Krawczyk told the rest of the story about Lee: "Just then he got up from his desk, told me wait a minute, reached up and changed lamps. I thanked him and left with a feeling of warmth for this man who I believe was just dying to do something with his hands, even for one day."[33]

Signalman Henry C. Price had daily contact with the admiral. Because of the nature of his job, he spent a lot of time on the bridge. He recalled that whenever a visual message arrived, Lee wanted a copy before it went to the communications department. As watch supervisor, Price hand-delivered messages to Lee. Sometimes Lee asked him to read a Morse code message being sent by flashing light from another ship. Once, when the signalman took him a copy of a message that had just arrived, Lee read it and said, "That will be all, thank you, son. Oh, by the way, you had better knock off that saluting, or you might break your arm someday." Price wrote years later that he nevertheless continued to salute.

Lieutenant Albert T. Church Jr. was one of the *Washington*'s junior officers during that period. Years later Church recalled that the ship, and indeed warships in general, were in a period of transition as they dealt with the new phenomenon of radar and how it could be used to best advantage. The *Washington*'s radars came under the purview of the gunnery department because they were used in conjunction with the firing of the guns. Church was the radar officer, and he later acquired the added job of acting communications officer. Because of Lee's avid interest in the radars, he had a lot of contact with Church. Though there were no official orders as such, he became a de facto member of the admiral's staff. Ensign Robert Gooding, whom Church recalled as a "technical wizard," worked with him. Gooding served as the radar material officer to keep the equipment running well.[34] In the 1970s, as a vice admiral, Gooding served as commander, Naval Sea Systems Command.

The radar screens for the air-search and surface-search sets were in a compartment just aft of the flag bridge and flag plot, both of which were one deck below the ship's navigation bridge, the site for control of the rudder and engines. This radar room was in a space that was designated in the ship's plans as the admiral's sea cabin. Now it had a more pressing use, and its proximity to flag plot meant that the space was so convenient for Lee that the *Washington* remained his favorite flagship throughout a considerable amount of the war. The space contained a dead-reckoning tracer (DRT) that kept a record of the ship's movements, plotting tables, and it received direct inputs from the fire control radars. Church later described it as "an embryo CIC," for actual combat information centers were just in the beginning process of becoming standard in the fleet.[35]

Schanze observed that Lee "virtually supervised the installation of the new radar equipment as it came aboard." While at sea, Lee spent a lot of time in the compartment with the radars. Schanze added, "He felt that it was important to have the valuable information of CIC right at his elbow and I know that he opposed the design of new battleships where CIC was below the armor belt."[36]

Lieutenant Church experienced Lee's teaching technique. One evening, about dusk, Lee and Church were watching the air-search screen as it tracked the movements of a Japanese Betty bomber. The admiral posed a question, "Which way is he going to turn?"

Church replied, "Oh, Admiral, I don't know."

Lee said, "He is going to turn to the east." The young officer characterized Lee's question and answer as a very nice way of saying, "You stupid oaf, you've been watching this scope all this time and you haven't drawn any conclusions as to a pattern?" Church said that lesson stood him in good stead during later air interceptions.[37] Schanze witnessed such an occasion when Lee took a group of ships into the Coral Sea. The Japanese sent planes out to search for his force. Through Lee's familiarity with the enemy tendencies and what the radar told him, he maneuvered his ships to keep them at least sixty miles away from the Japanese. As Schanze put it, "After several hours of search the Japanese planes retired without having completed their mission."[38] The flagship was not always able to avoid being seen by Japanese scouts. Lieutenant Thompson observed, though, that the planes were careful to stay out of range of the antiaircraft guns.[39]

Within the next several months, combat information centers were added to surface combatants at an increasing pace. In the autumn of 1942, however, setups such as the one in the *Washington* were still a novelty, and Lee was addicted. He spent hours sitting by the screen, watching and smoking. At times he dozed off with a burning cigarette in his hand. The cylinder of ash at the lit end gradually lengthened until someone gently removed it from his fingers. The glowing screen attracted other men as well; they came into the radar space from flag plot when radar detected a contact.

The staff members crowded around the screen and sometimes obstructed Lee's view of it. He directed Al Church to set up a transparent circular plotting board in the flag plot area and have it manned by a seaman who was equipped with a set of earphones. Lee said, "I don't care whether he can plot or not, but any time he gets a contact, have him make a mark on there. Then my staff will go to that table, and I can come around and get into CIC and see the screen." The plotting board for the air-search CXAM was vertical and that for the surface picture was horizontal.[40] (Men in combat information centers in various ships soon developed the ability to write backward from behind vertical plots. The tracks of targets could then be viewed in the correct way by those on the other side of the plotting board. I observed this skill in person years later while standing watches in the *New Jersey*'s CIC, which was deep inside the ship.)

Captain Davis, the flagship's skipper, also appreciated Lee's teaching techniques. The two had not served together previously but soon developed a professional bond. As Davis wrote years later, "Adm. Lee had the faculty of making those around him *think*. He would pose a professional question to start a discussion and then sit back and listen except for interjections to point out fallacies or agreements. In this way he was able to really know his officers and their approaches and reactions to problems and unforeseen situations. At the same time he gave them much of his knowledge without lecturing. He was a great leader."[41]

During this learning process on board the *Washington*, the struggle for control of Guadalcanal was tenuous, even desperate. The Japanese continued to feed in reinforcements. On 24–25 August the fleets of the warring nations had mounted an encounter that came to be known as the Battle of the Eastern Solomons. The carrier *Enterprise*, veteran of the Doolittle Raid and the Battle of Midway, was heavily damaged by a direct bomb hit. The Japanese lost the light carrier *Ryujo* and dozens of skilled aviators. The Japanese continued their attempts to reinforce Guadalcanal, where the beleaguered Marines were fighting with their Japanese counterparts and being shelled in nighttime bombardments by ventures known as the "Tokyo Express." Rations were slim, and the commander of the First Marine Division, Major General Archer A. Vandegrift, felt he and his men were receiving short shrift in terms of support from the Navy.

In Hawaii Admiral Nimitz was concerned about the condition of Vice Admiral Robert L. Ghormley, who was Commander, South Pacific Force. Ghormley was attempting to exert command from his flagship *Argonne* at Nouméa, but he was worn out. He had not made the effort to visit Guadalcanal in order to get a firsthand impression of what the Marines were up against. Nimitz decided to

see Ghormley in person to assess conditions; his seaplane landed at Nouméa on
28 September. Among other things, he learned the disappointing information
that Lee's *Washington* was still based at Tongatabu, some eighteen hundred
miles from the action at Guadalcanal.[42] In a later communication, Nimitz told
Ghormley that the *Washington* was "so far removed from the critical area that
she might as well have been in Pearl or San Francisco, insofar as taking advantage
of favorable opportunities is concerned." In the same letter Nimitz wrote, "In
closing let me again urge you to take such calculated risks as may be warranted
in order to continue the attrition which we are now inflicting on the enemy's
sea and air forces."[43]

Throughout the autumn of 1942, one of the components of the high-speed
Tokyo Express that sought to reinforce Guadalcanal was the seaplane tender
Nisshin. Based in Kavieng, New Ireland, and Shortland in the Solomons, she
operated floatplanes and ferried troops to the contested island. On 8 October
she and her escorting destroyers headed toward Guadalcanal and were attacked
by SBD dive-bombers and TBF Avengers of the Cactus Air Force. ("Cactus" was
the code name for Guadalcanal.) The Navy sent in ships to stave off a return
engagement by the *Nisshin*. Rear Admiral Norman Scott's Task Group 64.2,
Rear Admiral George Murray's Task Force 17 (built around the carrier *Hornet*),
and Lee's Task Group 17.8 were poised for a preventive mission the following day.
In addition to flagship *Washington*, Lee had a light cruiser and two destroyers.

That same day Rear Admiral Kelly Turner set out from Nouméa in a formation
of seven ships to deliver an Army infantry regiment and a ground detachment
for the 1st Marine Air Wing. On 11 October the *Nisshin* and another seaplane
tender, the *Chitose*, set out from Shortland with escorts, and the Japanese also
sent a force of cruisers and destroyers to bombard Guadalcanal's Lunga airfield
after midnight on the twelfth. In response Admiral Ghormley dispatched the
various task forces and directed Lee's group to protect Turner's convoy.

The response to this attack was a successful surface action—rare in this period.
The action the night of 11–12 October was dubbed the Battle of Cape Esperance,
named for the northernmost part of Guadalcanal. The results represented a
considerable improvement on the one-sided 8–9 August sinking of four heavy
cruisers. In that instance, U.S. naval forces were caught unprepared and unaware.
In *Neptune's Inferno*, James Hornfischer's superb account of the role of the U.S.

Navy in the Guadalcanal campaign, the author praised the tactical commander, Rear Admiral Norman Scott, for his preparation of the forces under his command. In the last two weeks of September, Scott had his cruisers and destroyers drill incessantly in maneuvers that involved gunnery practice and the use of radar. He conducted night-fighting exercises, because the Japanese would come only at night. They did so because American planes controlled the skies during daylight hours.[44]

During the nocturnal confrontation that took place on 11–12 October, the Japanese augmented the supply and reinforcement convoy of seaplane tenders with a separate group of three heavy cruisers and two destroyers to bombard and disrupt the Americans ashore. Scott countered with heavy cruisers *San Francisco* and *Salt Lake City*, light cruisers *Boise* and *Helena*, and five destroyers. Despite Scott's tactical training of his ships, the fog of war descended, and the Americans paid a heavy price while driving off the bombardment force. In the exchange of gunfire against the Japanese, Scott's formation sank the cruiser *Furutaka*, badly damaged cruiser *Aoba*, and sank the destroyer *Fubuki*. The Americans lost the destroyer *Duncan*, and the *Farenholt* suffered damage. The *Boise* and *Salt Lake City* also took damaging hits. The gun duel prevented the planned heavy bombardment of Guadalcanal, but the Japanese supply formation slipped through unmolested to deliver its cargo of troops and material.[45]

Shortly afterward, on 15 October, while the *Enterprise* was being repaired from her Eastern Solomons damage, Vice Admiral William Halsey and members of his staff took off on a flying trip to the South Pacific. The plan was that he would return to command a task force, once again rejoining the *Enterprise* when she returned to action. When the touring party was at Canton Island, Halsey received a dispatch from Admiral Ghormley, who suggested that he and his men bypass Guadalcanal itself because of the tactical situation and proceed directly to Nouméa. Halsey replied that unless otherwise directed he planned to keep his original itinerary and sent a copy to Admiral Nimitz. Nimitz responded by telling him to proceed to Suva and then Nouméa.

When Halsey's PB2Y Coronado seaplane landed at Nouméa on the eighteenth, Admiral Ghormley's flag lieutenant came aboard and gave Halsey a sealed envelope marked "Secret." It contained a message from Admiral Nimitz: "You will take command of the South Pacific Area and South Pacific Forces." In his memoir is

Halsey's reported reaction, "Jesus Christ and General Jackson! This is the hottest potato they ever handed me!" Nimitz had concluded that the Navy's fighting in the area needed an aggressive commander, and Halsey was the man.[46] In the wake of the lackluster and hesitant leadership supplied by Admiral Ghormley, morale in the South Pacific Theater shot skyward with news of Halsey's arrival.

There was at least one skeptic. After Halsey took command, he visited the *Washington* and Admiral Lee. Lee had called on Halsey ashore in Nouméa, and the new area commander was returning the call, a customary practice for naval officers in that era. Halsey went informally around the ship, and during the course of the visit came to the makeshift radar area, where Al Church was standing by with the machine lit off and running. Lee pointed out the SG radar screen. As the lieutenant observed, "At that time, battles were being won or lost by judicious or misuse of the SG radar, and Halsey said, 'I've heard of that.'" The lieutenant observed that Lee didn't change expression but presumed the admiral had the same reaction he did: "My God, here's the commander, and he's just *heard* of this?" Years later, Church observed, "I'm not trying to detract from the great leader Halsey was, but this was just an incident where my confidence was so fully in Admiral Lee and somewhat shaken in Admiral Halsey."[47]

Historian Richard Frank put Church's reaction into perspective. Radar, he wrote, was so new to the fleet that few officers had an opportunity to learn much about it from firsthand experience. It didn't start reaching U.S. warships in numbers until after the attack on Pearl Harbor, so senior officers hadn't really acquired knowledge of its benefits and shortcomings. Frank wrote, "I would guess that this may well have been the first time Halsey set eyes on a display from an SG radar. . . . All of this still goes to show how really exceptional Lee was in grasping the new technology and mastering it."[48]

During the autumn of 1942, the *Washington* was in a standby period as events continued to unfold on Guadalcanal. The surface actions involved cruisers and destroyers because the waters around the contested island were narrow and not that well suited for blue-water battleships. The *Washington* had escaped her exile at Tongatabu on 7 October, probably as a result of Nimitz's chiding of Ghormley. She steamed north to the vicinity of the New Hebrides, where she was based at the island of Espiritu Santo, now Vanuatu, only six hundred–some miles from Guadalcanal. As usual, Lee focused on gunnery and convened an informal "gun club" among the gunnery and fire control officers in the flagship.[49] Even though Lee's forces were not yet directly involved in Guadalcanal, he and his flag lieutenant Ray Thompson kept up to date through Ultra messages derived from intercepted Japanese transmissions. Thompson recalled that it was probably Lieutenant Commander Zern who decoded the Ultras for Lee.[50]

In this period, Lee's flagship joined in escorting convoys and prepared for potential operations by exercising with other warships. Among them was the antiaircraft light cruiser *Atlanta*, the first of a new type of ship in the U.S. fleet. She was armed with sixteen dual-purpose 5-inch guns and thus able to put out a high volume of fire. Her assistant gunnery officer was Lieutenant Lloyd M. Mustin, who joined Lee's staff two years later.

Long afterward, Mustin recalled that when the two ships were together, Lee would direct that the *Atlanta* steam to a position thirty-five thousand or so yards away—definitely long-range gunnery for a battleship. The *Washington* employed offset fire—that is, shot at a prescribed angle astern of the cruiser. Mustin went to the *Atlanta*'s fantail and set up a homemade device that could measure where the battleship's projectiles landed in relation to their desired spots. He then reported the results to the firing ship, and they were excellent. In his visual memory, Mustin recalled that the *Washington* was mostly over the horizon, except perhaps for the top of her mast. Even so, he said,

When she would fire, you'd see this enormous blast of familiar yellowish brown muzzle smoke from the guns. After a predictable lapse of time, crash would be the salvo landing in our wake. The first sound that you would hear would come after that. It would be the familiar crack of the projectiles in the air at supersonic speed, and then finally the last thing you'd hear would be the sound of the guns firing from over the horizon, because the projectiles traveled all the way at speeds greater than sound so they were there not only before the sound of the gun firing but before the sound of their traveling through the air reached us. The point of the whole thing was that these salvo patterns would be very tight and very small.... The second thing was that they came right down on the wake. They didn't come down over or short. They came down right on, meaning that the *Washington*'s battery was beautifully aligned and beautifully calibrated.

Those 2,700-pound armor-piercing projectiles were going to be very bad news for anybody they were ever aimed at.[51]

Bad news for the Marines on Guadalcanal came soon after the Cape Esperance tangle. Admiral Isoroku Yamamoto, commander in chief of the Japanese Combined Fleet, concluded that sterner measures were needed. He upped the stakes by sending to Guadalcanal a heavy bombardment group built around the battleships *Kongo* and *Haruna*. On the night of 13–14 October, shortly before Halsey's arrival on scene, the two dreadnoughts pummeled Lunga Point and environs with nearly one thousand 14-inch projectiles.

At sea Lee's *Washington* and accompanying ships were in the general vicinity but not close enough to engage. They were returning to the new base at Espiritu Santo after escorting a convoy of transports loaded with Army troops to an area near San Cristobal Island, southeast of Guadalcanal in the Solomons. The Tokyo Express continued to unleash nighttime doses of terror. On the night of 14–15 October came another bombardment. No Japanese troops landed that night, but their transports were anchored fifteen miles away. On the fifteenth planes from the Cactus Air Force plastered them.[52]

When Ghormley was still in command, he ordered the deployment of Task Force 64, now under Lee's command, to the waters around Guadalcanal, an area that had come to be known as "torpedo junction" because of the submarine peril. Accompanying the *Washington* when she got under way at dusk on 17 October were the other ships of the task force: cruisers *San Francisco*, *Helena*, and *Chester*. They were directed to support resupply operations for the troops on Guadalcanal. While the ships were under way, Lee received a radio message from Admiral Nimitz's headquarters that reported the order for Halsey to take over the South Pacific Area. Lieutenant Commander Hooper, the ship's fire control officer, offered what was undoubtedly a widespread reaction following the lassitude that had emanated from Nouméa up to then. He recalled, "We were absolutely elated when we heard the news. It was a shot of adrenaline for the whole command; things had been getting pretty wishy-washy down there."[53]

On 20 October 1942, a detachment composed of the cruisers *San Francisco*, *Helena*, and *Chester*—along with six destroyers—split off to bombard Japanese positions near Cape Esperance. That night, when the *Chester* was about halfway between Espiritu Santo and San Cristobal, a torpedo from the Japanese submarine *I-176* rammed into her number-one engine room after tearing a large hole in the skin of the ship. The attack killed eleven crewmen and injured twelve. It also damaged the ship to such an extent that she needed significant repair work. As a result, she headed back to the United States. She did not get back into combat action for nearly a year.[54]

A Naval Reserve ensign named Guilliaem "Guil" Aertsen III was the signal officer on board the *Chester* at the time of the incident. He did not return to the States with his ship but was instead transferred at Espiritu Santo to Lee's staff to serve as aide and flag lieutenant.[55] His arrival freed Lieutenant Ray Thompson to focus on his duties in the gunnery and fire control area. When Aertsen arrived, he recalled years later, Lee quizzed him about the events of the torpedoing—the sights, sounds, and impressions. The ever-curious admiral wanted to get a sense of what it was like when a ship was hit by an underwater missile. (The second of the submarine's two torpedoes missed the cruiser, but the first inflicted substantial damage.)

Unlike many officers who served in flag lieutenant roles in that era, Aertsen was not a Naval Academy graduate, but he was sharp and had a couple of years of shipboard experience under his belt. He was a Harvard graduate who was commissioned through the V-7 program that produced junior officers sometimes known scornfully as "Ninety-Day Wonders." He had taken his training on board the decommissioned pre-dreadnought battleship *Illinois*, which had been part of the Great White Fleet that steamed around the world in 1907–1909. For years afterward she was moored in New York's North River, to the west of Manhattan. There she served as a barracks, floating armory, and training school.[56]

Years later Aertsen explained how he came into the role as flag lieutenant: "At the time Lee had a need down in the South Pacific for a young guy on his operations to serve as his aide and assistant operations, a bit of everything. I happened to be available and had been blessed with the kind of training that he needed that guy to have." Lee didn't have to explain things to him, because the young ensign had been operating in the area and knew communications, navigation, and what happens on the bridge of a ship, because that had been his role on board the *Chester*.

Aertsen said, "I brought that discipline with me because I'd been trained properly . . . so that each one knew what his responsibility was. And if I did for this man what he wanted done, that's what he expected. The chemistry between us happened to work." The aide's commissioning source was not an issue with Lee, only his ability to get the job done. Aertsen observed that Lee, unlike many of his contemporaries, did not wear a Naval Academy class ring—or even a wedding ring. The two men meshed so well that Aertsen remained with Lee throughout his entire tour in the Pacific and beyond. Aertsen became something of a surrogate son of the childless Lee. As Aertsen put it, "I think he got a kick out of having a little puppy around."[57]

Dick Zern continued as the flag secretary and handled the paperwork. Every once in a while, Aertsen explained, Lee would give Zern a diatribe about the paper, but Zern would "take it and roll with the punches and come back for more. He got it done. I think once in a while Lee was right. Zern would turn up just at the wrong time." Lee did write letters to the Bureau of Ordnance about the things that were important to him—all kinds of things about guns. And, interestingly, he kept in frequent touch with his friend Milton "Mary" Miles, who had gone to China at Lee's behest to set up and run SACO, known more formally as the Sino-American Cooperative Organization.[58]

Still another significant air-sea action occurred the last week of October. With the *Enterprise* having returned from repairs at Pearl Harbor, the U.S. aircraft carrier force in the South Pacific doubled as she joined up with sister ship *Hornet*. That twosome did not remain the case for long. The Japanese came in force: four aircraft carriers, five battleships, fourteen cruisers, and forty-four destroyers. Rear Admiral Thomas C. Kinkaid, now in command of the *Enterprise* task force, was a Naval Academy classmate of Lee. He was a cruiser-destroyer officer. Along with Rear Admiral Frank Jack Fletcher and Rear Admiral Raymond Spruance, Kinkaid was an exception in that year of 1942 in being a surface officer rather than a naval aviator in command of a carrier task force. Kinkaid was ordered to take his ships north of the Santa Cruz Islands, east of Guadalcanal, and cut off the approaching Japanese.

Lee and his *Washington* group, which also included three cruisers and seven destroyers, was directed to patrol off Guadalcanal's southern coast. Admiral Yamamoto's plan was contingent on capture of Henderson Field to enable the

Japanese pilots to land there. Meanwhile, the Japanese heavy ships were to take on Lee's surface force. Since the airfield remained in American hands, the Japanese carrier planes were to fly bombing strikes, and the attack on Lee's force was called off.[59] Lee's force patrolled in the vicinity of the Slot, a waterway that divided the Solomons northward from Guadalcanal. Had the Tokyo Express run that night, Lee's ships would have provided an unwelcome surprise, but the engagement did not take place. Instead, they steamed away to the Coral Sea; as they did so, they passed near Guadalcanal's Cape Esperance, site of a U.S. victory two weeks before.

At 0127 on 25 October, when the *Washington* was eleven miles from Savo Island, an Army B-17 bomber showed up on the ship's radar screen and sent a plain-language radio transmission that men on board the *Washington* overheard. It reported the position, course, and speed of Lee's ships. Lieutenant Commander Hooper knew the airplane was "friendly," but he later explained that, "It was one time I felt tempted to shoot down one of our own!" One result of this trip, Hooper said, was that it enabled radar operators to learn how to sort out the blips that represented ships from clutter produced by the nearby mountains of Savo and Guadalcanal. That skill would prove useful in battle a few weeks later.[60] Lee's Task Force 64, composed of battleships, cruisers, and destroyers, took up a position between the islands of Rennell and San Cristobal, out of range of Japanese carrier planes but also not in position to support the carrier task forces.[61]

With carrier action imminent, Admiral Halsey recalled that he sent a message to his forces: "Attack Repeat Attack." Historian Richard Frank's documentary research discovered that the ComSoPac war diary recorded the message as simply "Strike."[62] The attacks against the American carriers were relentless. In the Battle of Santa Cruz Islands on 26 October, the *Enterprise* maneuvered adroitly and survived because of the antiaircraft protection rendered by the *South Dakota*. The 40-mm guns added during the Pearl Harbor repair period paid a huge dividend. The battleship's gunners shot down numerous enemy aircraft. The claim went as high as thirty-two but in all likelihood was less because some of the planes that plummeted toward the sea may have been double-counted or hit by other ships. In any event, the number was impressive, and the *South Dakota's* efforts enabled the *Enterprise* to survive.

During the engagement, a Japanese bomb hit the top of the battleship's turret one and sent shards of metal flying. One hit the skipper, Captain Thomas Gatch, in the carotid artery. Two alert quartermasters were able to stem the flow of blood and save him. Two officers with him on the bridge ducked below a metal shield and avoided injury. Gatch's explanation for not seeking shelter: "The captain of a United States battleship considered it beneath his dignity to flop for a damned Japanese bomb."[63]

While that battle was taking place, Lee's Task Force 64 and the *Washington* were elsewhere. They were operating some 130 miles south of Guadalcanal, ready for a possible arrival of Japanese ships, but the Tokyo Express wasn't running, so the task force subsequently returned to Nouméa. The upshot, however, was that the *Hornet* operated without a battleship escort at Santa Cruz. She did not have the benefit of the antiaircraft protection that the *Enterprise* received. The *Hornet* was hit repeatedly by attacks from torpedo planes and dive-bombers. Attempts to rescue and tow her were fruitless, so Halsey ordered her crew to abandon ship and that she be sunk because Japanese surface ships were in the area.

Neither an effort at scuttling nor gunfire from U.S. destroyers succeeded. Two Japanese destroyers finished her with deadly torpedo attacks. The *Hornet* sank at 0135 on 27 October. The ship had been commissioned on 20 October 1941 and had a busy record after that. She launched Lieutenant Colonel Jimmy Doolittle's raid on Tokyo in April 1942, took part in the Battle of Midway in June, and now had been part of the Guadalcanal campaign. Her period of commissioned service amounted to one year and one week. The experience from the Santa Cruz engagement reinforced the lesson that surface ships steaming in company with carriers could provide generous and necessary antiaircraft protection. That pairing would be the template for U.S. carrier operations throughout the remainder of the Pacific War.

▪ 10 ▪

NIGHT ACTION OFF SAVO ISLAND
November 1942

In 1942 Lieutenant Commander Edwin T. Layton was the Pacific Fleet intelligence officer. He had served in the same role for Admiral Husband E. Kimmel, commander in chief, Pacific Fleet (CinCPac), in the months leading up to the 1941 Japanese attack on Pearl Harbor. Admiral Chester Nimitz, as the new leader, had wisely retained a number of Kimmel's staff members. Layton, who was fluent in the Japanese language, had a close relationship with another Japanese linguist, Commander Joseph Rochefort. Rochefort led the team that deciphered intercepted Japanese radio messages. Their intelligence work paid off in a big way at the Coral Sea encounter and with the tide-turning victory in the June 1942 Battle of Midway.[1]

Years later, Layton recalled that information from the intercepted Japanese messages was forwarded to Lee on board the *Washington*. Nimitz's staff sent a daily Ultra intelligence summary to flag officer task force commanders in what was known as a two-star system. Task force commanders in the rank of captain did not have the crypto keys that would enable them to read the two-star messages. The dispatches were serially numbered and served to provide task force commanders with all current strategic and tactical information not contained in regular operational dispatches or summaries.[2]

When codebreaking revealed that Japanese task force action was imminent and likely to threaten U.S. forces, a special Ultra message was sent to those with the two-star system so they could take steps accordingly. Messages regarding the expected movements of the Tokyo Express forays to reinforce or bombard Guadalcanal were in the special category. In messages such as the ones to Lee, Admiral Nimitz almost always added a personal note such as, "Good luck and good hunting." Layton recounted that Nimitz had an especially high regard for Lee as a war-fighter, which would explain why Lee remained in the war zone for nearly three years without relief so he could command the battle line when appropriate circumstances arose. In Layton's commentary on Lee's involvement in the upcoming Guadalcanal clash, he quoted Nimitz: "Now we'll see a real fighter show those Japs how we *can* fight." Layton added, "It was obvious to me that Nimitz felt *far* more confidence that Lee would 'do the job' on the Japs—than he had had of others (*unnamed!!*)."[3]

As mentioned in the previous chapter, William Bentinck-Smith, a Naval Reserve ensign, was a recent addition to the admiral's staff at that point. He was a Harvard man and acquainted with Dr. Samuel Eliot Morison, who subsequently wrote a fifteen-volume series on U.S. naval operations in the war. Of the Guadalcanal volume, Bentinck-Smith said, "Though factually rich it somehow fails to contain the mood of desperate necessity characteristic of the units of the U.S. Fleet in the South Pacific in the late summer and early fall of 1942. It was a rude shock for a very green Ensign, after only eight weeks of wholly inadequate basic training to find himself heading for the war zone on the USS *Washington* (BB 56) to join that shockingly thinly spread Naval force attempting to gain control of the Solomons."[4]

■ ■ ■

The Japanese in March established a base on Shortland Island. It is part of the Shortlands archipelago in the northwestern area of the Solomons chain. Guadalcanal, the second-largest island in the Solomons, is about 340 miles southeast of Shortland. San Cristobal serves as the southern anchor of the chain. In mid-November the Japanese put together a group of eleven transports filled with seven thousand soldiers, artillery pieces, ammunition, and stores to support the soldiers once they reached Guadalcanal. They set out southward. Riding shotgun

Willis A. Lee Sr. and Susan Arnold Lee were the parents of the lad who became known as "Mose" in his Kentucky hometown of Owenton. *Courtesy Donald Siders*

Lee posed for this portrait during his midshipman years, 1904–1908. When he wasn't wearing glasses, his vision was sorely deficient. *Courtesy Donald Siders*

Lee (*right*) is pictured with other members of the Naval Academy rifle team. *M. E. Warren*

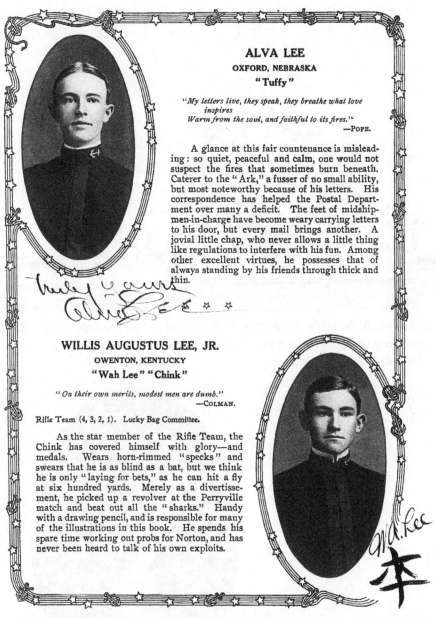

ALVA LEE

OXFORD, NEBRASKA

"Tuffy"

*"My letters live, they speak, they breathe what love
inspires
Warm from the soul, and faithful to its fires."*
—POPE.

A glance at this fair countenance is misleading: so quiet, peaceful and calm, one would not suspect the fires that sometimes burn beneath. Caterer to the "Ark," a fusser of no small ability, but most noteworthy because of his letters. His correspondence has helped the Postal Department over many a deficit. The feet of midshipmen-in-charge have become weary carrying letters to his door, but every mail brings another. A jovial little chap, who never allows a little thing like regulations to interfere with his fun. Among other excellent virtues, he possesses that of always standing by his friends through thick and thin.

WILLIS AUGUSTUS LEE, JR.

OWENTON, KENTUCKY

"Wah Lee" "Chink"

"On their own merits, modest men are dumb."
—COLMAN.

Rifle Team (4, 3, 2, 1). Lucky Bag Committee.

As the star member of the Rifle Team, the Chink has covered himself with glory—and medals. Wears horn-rimmed "specks" and swears that he is as blind as a bat, but we think he is only "laying for bets," as he can hit a fly at six hundred yards. Merely as a divertissement, he picked up a revolver at the Perryville match and beat out all the "sharks." Handy with a drawing pencil, and is responsible for many of the illustrations in this book. He spends his spare time working out probs for Norton, and has never been heard to talk of his own exploits.

This page from the 1908 *Lucky Bag*, the Naval Academy yearbook, shows Lee's signatures in English and Chinese. *Courtesy Mrs. Thomas Kinkaid*

Lee served in the tall-stack, shallow-draft gunboat *Helena* from 1910 to 1913. Her trips along the Yangtze River provided him with a wide-ranging introduction to China. *Courtesy Donald Siders*

Lee married Mabelle Elspeth Allen, affectionately known as "Chubby," in Chicago on 14 July 1919. *Courtesy Donald Siders*

Secretary of the Navy Josephus Daniels (*center*) congratulates Lieutenant Commander Lee and Commander Carl Osburn for their shooting at the 1920 Olympic Games in Antwerp, Belgium. Lee's eight medals sit in front of him. *NARA 19-N-3525*

The four-stack destroyer *William B. Preston* looks a bit bedraggled during her tour with the U.S. Asiatic Fleet in the mid-1920s. *Courtesy Donald Siders*

Skipper Lee kneels at center with a plaque won by the strapping members of the *William B. Preston*'s race boat team. *Courtesy Donald Siders*

Lee spent many hours of his naval career with a pair of binoculars suspended from a strap around his neck. Here he is on the bridge of the light cruiser *Concord*, which he commanded from 1936 to 1938. *Courtesy Donald Siders*

A 1937 issue of *Our Navy* magazine contained a photo feature on the *Concord*. Included in the issue was this picture of Captain Lee and his executive officer, Commander Eugene T. Oates, posing front and center. Arrayed beside them in the first row are the ship's department heads. The enlisted crew crowds the superstructure. *Courtesy Captain Fitzhugh L. Palmer*

The commander and staff of the type command, Cruisers Battle Force, were nicknamed "Snow White and the Seven Dwarfs" after a popular animated film in the late 1930s. *Front row, left to right*: Charles Wellborn Jr., Willis A. Lee Jr., Harold R. Stark, and Ellsworth Ross. *Back row*: Horace Butterfield, William F. Jennings, Harold D. Krick, and William R. Smedberg III. *Courtesy William R. Smedberg III*

Lieutenant Commander Milton "Mary" Miles took these photos of Captain and Mrs. Lee when they visited his home around 1940. Surprisingly, Lee's civilian necktie is "two-blocked," that is, cinched all the way up. Lee later sent Miles to China on a special mission. *Courtesy Wilma Miles*

Rear Admiral Lee reports on board his new flagship, the USS *Washington*, at Tongatabu on 14 September 1942. *Courtesy Glenn B. Davis*

Lee enjoys the view from his chair on the flag bridge of the *Washington*. *Courtesy Glenn B. Davis*

When he went to war in 1942, Lee's staff was a small one. Here Lee poses with his flag lieutenant, Raymond W. Thompson Jr. (*left*), and flag secretary, Richard Zern (*right*). *Courtesy Raymond W. Thompson Jr.*

Lee, ever-present cigarette in hand, sits in his chair on board the *Washington*. Standing is Captain Glenn B. Davis, who was the ship's commanding officer during the 14–15 November 1942 night battle near Savo Island. *Courtesy Glenn B. Davis*

Dwight Shepler's magnificent watercolor depicts the night action off Savo Island. The flagship *Washington* is in the lead, trailed by the *South Dakota*. Both ships are shown firing at the Japanese to starboard. Savo Island looms in the background. *Navy Art Collection*

Lee addresses the crew of the *Washington* in February 1943, just after receiving the Navy Cross from Admiral William F. Halsey Jr. *Courtesy Raymond Baker*

While the *Washington* was out of service for repair of collision damage, Lee was briefly embarked in the *New Jersey* in May 1944. He is shown here in the flag cabin. This is the photo of Lee that appeared in the ship's postwar cruise book and inspired the author to write the admiral's biography. *Courtesy Donald Siders*

TO ALL AND SUNDRY WHEREVER YE MAY BE,

KNOW YE
By These
Presents That

Lieut. Oscar E. Gray Jr., U.S.N.

having well and faithfully served as a
Hunting ship in the Pacific is by

gunner on a Jap
virtue thereof a
fully qualified and
honored member of the

ACME GUN CLUB

Given under my hand,

Capt., USN, Comdg.
USS NEW JERSEY

V.Adm., USN
COMBATPAC

When the Pacific Fleet battleships were not operating, they spent time in various atoll anchorages. Once ashore, officers and men were able to imbibe alcoholic beverages. As the type commander, Lee was head of the unofficial Acme Gun Club. Here the turret is expelling a cap from a bottle of Acme beer. The membership card is duly signed by Vice Admiral Lee. *Courtesy Oscar Gray*

Guilliaem Aertsen III served as Lee's flag lieutenant from late 1942 until August 1945. Aertsen's recollections of his daily contact with the admiral provided much of the source material for this book. This photo is from 1945. *Courtesy Bea Wetherill*

Lee is at the center of this photo of the Battleship Squadron Two staff officers on board the *South Dakota*. By this time, late in the war, the group was far larger than Lee's 1942 staff. *Courtesy Donald Siders*

Top-ranking officers in the Pacific War pose together on board the heavy cruiser *Indianapolis* in February 1945. *From left to right*: Admiral Raymond A. Spruance, Vice Admiral Marc A. Mitscher, Fleet Admiral Chester W. Nimitz, and Vice Admiral Willis A. Lee Jr. Lee, who specialized in unkempt, is wearing a nonregulation belt. *Naval Historical Foundation NH 49705*

In the summer of 1945, while he was in Washington before heading to Maine, Lee went to dinner with his gunnery officer Lloyd Mustin, at left, and his wife Mabelle's niece Lila Mae Hanna. Lee looks uncharacteristically tidy in a gray uniform he evidently bought after returning to the United States. The grays were the brainchild of Chief of Naval Operations Ernest J. King, but were not popular in the fleet. *Courtesy Donald Siders*

Niece Elizabeth V. Palmer, the daughter of Lee's sister Lucy, served as sponsor of the destroyer leader *Willis A. Lee*. Here she christens the ship at the Bethlehem Steel shipyard at Quincy, Massachusetts, on 26 January 1952. The christening was followed immediately by the launching. *U.S. Navy*

The USS *Willis A. Lee* steams at sea in November 1960. *NARA 80-G-1054374*

Lee's nephew Donald Siders (*left*) and author Paul Stillwell visit the admiral's grave at Arlington National Cemetery on 25 August 2005, the sixtieth anniversary of Lee's death. *Photo by Joseph Stillwell*

for the convoy was a heavy surface force under Rear Admiral Hiroaki Abe, commander, Battleship Division Eleven, embarked in the *Hiei*. Also in the party were the *Hiei*'s sister *Kirishima*, nine destroyers, and the light cruiser *Nagara*. In addition to shepherding the transports, the Japanese heavy ships were to bombard Guadalcanal and thus carried high-explosive projectiles rather than the armor-piercing variety that would be more effective against American warships.[5]

Vice Admiral William F. Halsey Jr., as commander, South Pacific Force, dispatched two surface forces to escort a convoy of American transports headed for Guadalcanal. The transports, which set out from Nouméa on 8 November, arrived at Guadalcanal four days later. They were loaded with contents comparable to those in the Japanese ships—food, ammunition, and men to reinforce the beleaguered Marine force. The second mission for the thirteen-ship escort group of cruisers and destroyers was to counter an expected Tokyo Express bombardment of Guadalcanal.

Rear Admiral Daniel J. Callaghan was the commander of U.S. Task Group 67.4. He had been chief of staff to the previous commander, South Pacific, Vice Admiral Robert Ghormley. When Admiral Halsey took over, he brought his own chief of staff, Captain Miles Browning, and Callaghan was displaced. Halsey put Callaghan in command of the combatant task group even though, as historian Richard Frank expressed it, "His two weeks of sea time as a rear admiral were unlittered with any battle experience except an air attack that very day." He certainly had scant appreciation for the value that radar could play in battle. However, by a quirk of being fifteen days senior to Rear Admiral Norman Scott, who had been the victor at Cape Esperance in October, Callaghan was in command as the ships approached battle the night of 12 October.[6]

The thirteen American ships were strung out in a column with destroyers ahead and astern of a combination of light and heavy cruisers. Callaghan's flagship, the *San Francisco*, did not have an adequate radar for the assignment. Five ships were equipped with the capable new SG surface-search radar, the cruisers *Helena*, *Juneau*, and *Portland*, and the destroyers *Fletcher* and *O'Bannon*. But they were not assigned the best positions in the column to provide early warning of an enemy force. Ironically, tail-end Charlie was the *Fletcher*, which would have been much better positioned up ahead. Callaghan had intended for his ships to reverse course, but they never got the chance.

The ships of both nations first sighted each other at 0142 on Friday the thirteenth. The American radars could have enabled the ships to open fire and surprise the oncoming enemy. The opportunity to open fire first was lost because of Callaghan's lack of radar awareness. Historian Trent Hone observed, "Callaghan used what radar information he had to successfully adopt a collision course with Abe and force a melee."[7] The ensuing tangle between the enemies was chaotic, and even that might qualify as a understatement. In his magisterial work on Guadalcanal, historian Frank painstakingly researched and described the fates of the Japanese and American ships. Ships on both sides were often firing at such close ranges that John Paul Jones would have seemed at home. The upshot of the close-quarters struggle was that the Japanese bombardment was forestalled but at a heavy cost to the American task group.

During the night action, U.S. forces lost the cruiser *Atlanta* and the destroyers *Barton*, *Monssen*, *Cushing*, and *Laffey*. Later on 13 November, Japanese submarine *I-26* torpedoed and sank the antiaircraft light cruiser *Juneau* with the loss of nearly all hands. Evidence demonstrated that some of the damage to the *Juneau's* sister *Atlanta* was the result of 8-inch projectiles fired by the *San Francisco*. In addition to the lost and damaged ships, both Callaghan and his subordinate, Rear Admiral Norman Scott, were killed in the battle. On the Japanese side, the losses included the battleship *Hiei*, which was damaged at night and then pummeled to death by American aircraft from Guadalcanal during daylight on the thirteenth. The Japanese also lost destroyers *Akatsuki* and *Yudachi* as the result of the nighttime tangle; destroyers *Amatsukaze* and *Ikazuchi* suffered more than slight damage. Rear Admiral Abe, whose bombardment mission had failed, lost both his flagship and his job. He retired from the Japanese navy forthwith.[8]

The remaining Japanese ships, including the eleven transports, turned back north to reconvene under new leadership. An intelligence report from Pacific Fleet headquarters to Halsey in midafternoon of 13 November indicated that the Japanese were going to send another surface force to attack Guadalcanal that night. In the late afternoon the eleven plucky transports again set out from Shortland, accompanied by a dozen gunnery ships comprising cruisers and destroyers. Rear Admiral Thomas Kinkaid, who was a surface officer rather than an aviator, was commander, Task Force 16 on board the *Enterprise*. Lee's battleships, *Washington* and *South Dakota*, constituted part of the task force; it was the first time they had operated together. Halsey directed Kinkaid to move the force north to a line south of Rennell and San Cristobal islands, latitude 11°40' south. There Lee's ships would be in position to take the offensive and strike the Japanese. Even though the narrow waters between Savo Island and Guadalcanal were ill-suited to such large combatants, Halsey wanted Kinkaid to detach Lee's battleships and four destroyers for a run to Guadalcanal to counter the expected attack. However, Kinkaid had not directed his ships as far north as Halsey expected. In fact, they had been steaming south to facilitate air operations, so late in the afternoon, when the order came to dispatch Lee's projected force, his heavy ships were much too far away to intercept that night's Tokyo Express bombardment force. Halsey was shocked and disappointed when he received that news.[9]

Historian John Lundstrom, who has written an extremely thorough study of U.S. fighter actions in the Guadalcanal campaign, offered this analysis: "In retrospect Halsey should have been more specific as to where he desired Kinkaid to be. As for Kinkaid's motives, the reports mention continuous flight operations that unexpectedly slowed the *Enterprise*'s northward speed of advance, but it seems clear that Kinkaid deliberately kept far to the south. Three weeks before [at Santa Cruz] he had suffered greatly from a head-long assault into the teeth of the Japanese forces; now he felt good reason to be more cautious."[10]

That night the Japanese ships delivered a pasting to Guadalcanal, an event that might well have been deterred had Lee's force had been there. The following day, aircraft from Guadalcanal and the *Enterprise* had open season on the Japanese. The planes sank the cruiser *Kinugasa* and six of the eleven troopships; one transport took survivors back to Shortland. Only four survived to plod on toward Guadalcanal. Also heading for Guadalcanal was a three-pronged force that included the *Hiei*'s sister, battleship *Kirishima*, two heavy cruisers, two light cruisers, and nine destroyers. The mission, as it had been on 12–13 November, was to land the transports and to blast American emplacements on the island of Guadalcanal. The bombardment group, led by Vice Admiral Nobutake Kondo, deputy commander in chief of the Combined Fleet, also included heavy cruisers *Atago* and *Takao*. The screening ships and sweeping ships, which came at Savo Island in two groups, were commanded by a bevy of flag officers: Rear Admiral Tamotsu Takama, Rear Admiral Shintaro Hashimoto, and Rear Admiral Raizo Tanaka. Their numbers included the light cruisers *Nagara* and *Sendai* and destroyers *Shirayuki, Teruzuki, Samidare, Hatsuyuki, Inazuma, Uranami, Shikinami,* and *Ayanami.*

The task of taking on this new collection of Japanese warships fell to Lee's Task Force 64, which had steamed to a position about one hundred miles to the south and west of Guadalcanal by the evening of the fourteenth. As Captain Glenn Davis, skipper of the flagship *Washington* explained, "After Callaghan and Scott were thrown out of the action, we were the only thing left. . . . I don't think Halsey would have thrown us in if he had anything else he thought he could use."[11] As it approached Guadalcanal to forestall yet another run by the Tokyo Express, Task Force 64 was definitely a pickup team. In the column ahead of the *Washington* and *South Dakota* were four destroyers: the *Walke, Preston, Benham,* and *Gwin.* They happened to be four that had the most fuel in their tanks. They were not members of a division that had operated together. There was no division commander on board to direct their actions. These were 1,500-ton ships built in the 1930s and not equipped with the latest SG radars that were on board the two battleships. Of the destroyers only the *Walke* had fire control radar.[12]

Trent Hone pointed out that in addition to the task force having no experience operating together, Lee had only enough time to develop a specific battle plan but not enough to issue a formal operation order. Lee communicated the plan to the other ships by visual signals. As in the battle two nights earlier, the ships steamed in column. The battleships followed about five thousand yards behind the tin cans. The destroyers were, in a sense, the bait that would attract attention and thus enable the gunners in the battleships to fix on their targets. In addition to being strangers to each other, the ships did not have a common doctrine for fighting, especially in confined waters. The prewar expectation was that in a night action, destroyers would wait until larger ships had damaged the enemy vessels and only then fire their torpedoes at the biggest targets. Doctrine hardly specified actions to take in a confused melee, and the destroyers were to suffer mightily.[13]

Another handicap involved the mounting of the *Washington*'s SG surface-search radar antenna. As Commander Harvey Walsh, the gunnery officer and later executive officer, pointed out, it was mounted just above the masthead light on the forward side of the foremast high in the superstructure. The unfortunate result of this location was that the radar had a blind spot aft that extended about

30 degrees on each quarter. That blind spot was to have unfortunate consequences in the slugfest that followed.[14]

Lieutenant Lloyd Mustin of the *Atlanta* had operated with the *Washington* previously and observed the problem. When the ships were steaming together at night, the *Washington* would occasionally make a radical turn so that her SG could scan the area astern and pick up the *Atlanta*'s blip. Then she would return to base course. In his oral history years later, Mustin railed at the placement of the antennas on board the fast battleships: "Somewhere along the line, somebody who didn't know very much about radar and less about tactics apparently decided that this was a good convenient place to locate this radar. In the meantime, when people who knew something about tactics found out about it, they evidently felt that it was too late to change."[15]

The bedspring air-search radar, which bore the designation CXAM, offered a significant shortcoming. When the *Washington* went into battle, the CXAM was linked to an A scope that had a horizontal line of electrons that provided vertical presentations of the target blips at various bearings as the antenna rotated. Lieutenant James Ross said the height of a blip gave an indication of the size of the target but not type. As he expressed it, "You couldn't tell the difference between a carrier and a battleship but you could between a battleship and a destroyer when they got out to 10 or 15,000 yards range. The whole operation was a sort of an educated guessing game but at that time it was a marvelous device that helped eliminate those nasty surprises that came in out of the night."[16]

The brand-new SG, on the other hand, was an almost-miraculous gift and a tremendous step up as far as shipboard radar was concerned in late 1942. The SG featured a plan position indicator (PPI) scope. Rather than showing an electronic straight line as did the A scope, the circular scope presented a geographical view, as if God were somehow looking down on the scene. The *Washington* was in the center of the picture, and arrayed around her were the blips of other ships that showed up at the correct ranges and bearings. Ship movements could be plotted in terms of course and speed.

■ ■ ■

On the evening of 14 November, Captain Glenn Davis met with the *Washington*'s officers in the wardroom to give them a preview of the upcoming battle. Among those with whom he spoke was the ship's chief engineer, Lieutenant Commander John A. "Red" Strother. The skipper directed him to make sure that the electrical circuit breakers designed to prevent overloads be secured closed because they had been known to open as the result of shock from gunfire. Opening would mean a power shutdown, a problem that would severely plague the *South Dakota* during the battle.[17] The *Washington* had a brand-new navigator, Lieutenant Commander Ed Schanze, which posed a particular challenge in facing the enemy. His predecessor, Commander William M. Hobby Jr., had recently been detached without the Bureau of Personnel providing a relief. Hobby went to the light cruiser *Juneau* as executive officer. He and nearly all of his new shipmates were killed when the *Juneau* was torpedoed and sunk in the wake of the disastrous surface action of 13 November.[18] Schanze had moved up from duty as communications officer. Davis designated Lieutenant Commander Ray Hunter, the main battery officer, to serve as the officer of the deck (OOD) during the coming action.[19]

Ensign Hal Berc lingered in the wardroom after virtually everyone else had left. He saw Davis and Schanze standing before a chart mounted on a bulkhead. He heard the captain saying to Schanze something along the lines of, "This is a tricky action, and these are tricky waters. If you feel you can't handle it, tell me now."

Schanze replied, "I can handle it." Subsequent events, albeit harrowing, demonstrated that he could and did.[20]

As Lee's thrown-together task force steamed to the vicinity of Savo Island that evening, the admiral's vantage point was on the navigation bridge. The flag bridge was smaller and did not yet have a radar repeater. There was a radar screen in the makeshift combat information center but that would have involved a fair amount of running back and forth. Instead, he was outside where he could see the action. After the battle, Lee observed that it was unfortunate that he did not have a direct radar picture himself. He had to rely on oral reports from phone talkers in order to supplement what he was seeing through his binoculars. His after-action report stated, "In spite of all these remarkable aids however, a great deal of the confusion and uncertainty characteristic of all previous night actions were still present. The OTC [officer in tactical command, Lee] was never completely and correctly informed as to the immediate situation."[21]

With the admiral on the bridge were Captain Davis, Lieutenant Commander Ray Thompson, Lieutenant Commander Dick Zern, and Lieutenant Al

Church—all equipped with binoculars as they sought to correlate visual sightings with radar information. Church at the time was the ship's acting communications officer and ex-officio CIC officer. Logically he would have been providing information from CIC, but he was also the relief officer of the deck. Had Ray Hunter required a replacement as OOD, Church was close at hand. In his communications role Church had previously been unsuccessful in getting motor patrol torpedo (PT) boat radio frequencies from South Pacific Force headquarters. By accident, the day before the battle he ran into Lieutenant Commander Clifton Maddox, a former shipmate. Maddox was then head of a PT squadron based at Tulagi and supplied the needed information.[22]

As the force steamed toward its collision with the Japanese, Lee sought to get the latest intelligence on the enemy. Those on the bridge overheard radio communication among a group of PTs that indicated they were tracking the task force. Lee told Zern to tell the PTs, "This is Lee." A PT answered, "Who's Lee?" Since his force had no assigned call sign for the operation, Lee seized the voice radio handset. He identified himself by name as he spoke to "Cactus," the call sign for Guadalcanal. The response he received was hardly welcome: "We do not recognize you."

Lee's next words over the radio have been rendered in a number of variations over the years. Historian Morison visited the ship in April, five months after the battle, and put together what he considered the most accurate reconstruction, which included inputs from Lee and Thompson. In the reconstructed version Lee said, "Cactus, this is Lee. Tell your big boss [Major General Archer Vandegrift, whom he knew] Ching Lee is here and wants the latest information." The *Washington*'s radio receivers picked up more PT chatter: "There go two big ones, but I don't know whose they are." To that Lee replied, "Refer your big boss about Ching Lee; Chinese, catchee? Call off your boys." The response from the island was, "The boss has no additional information." Ensign Bentinck-Smith remembered that it was Zern who suggested, "Chinese, catchee" to make those who overheard the transmission think it was some kind of code.[23] The Japanese intelligence was sketchy as well; the Tokyo Express running that night did not know precisely what it was up against.

Nearly forty years after the event, the commander of the PT boats provided his own recollection of the voice radio dialogue that took place that night. It differed somewhat from accounts of those on board the battleship. At the time

Lieutenant Hugh Robinson was commander of Motor Torpedo Squadron Three, which was based on the nearby island of Tulagi. Normal operations included patrols in the waters between Guadalcanal, Tulagi/Florida, and Savo Island. Their primary mission was to intercept Japanese ships that sought to reinforce and resupply forces on Guadalcanal. Nightly instructions came from Tulagi after being relayed from Guadalcanal. In the early evening of 14 November, Robinson's force received intelligence on the approach of Japanese transports and bombardment ships headed for Guadalcanal. The PT boat crews also received information that Lee's battleship task force was approaching the area, but there was some question whether it would arrive in time to engage the enemy.

Robinson was ordered to get under way at dusk with all operational boats and proceed to the area west of Savo to engage the approaching Japanese. The squadron comprised eight boats, but four had been damaged, so only the other four were available for that night's mission. As the boats headed for a position near Savo, a plain language message came through on the voice tactical circuit: "Peter Tare, Peter Tare, this is Ching Lee, Chinese, Ching Lee, catchee?" ("Peter" and "Tare" were at the time the phonetic alphabet designations for the letters PT.)

As officer in tactical command, Robinson replied, "Lee, this is Peter Tare. I recognize you."

"Peter Tare, this is Lee. Stand clear, we are coming through."

Robinson answered enthusiastically, "Roger, wilco [will comply], and out." He realized that Lee's force had indeed arrived in time to engage and did not want the PTs to interfere. The boats then turned on full power and returned to Tulagi. He described what happened next: "Several of us trotted up to the top of the hill on Tulagi where we arrived just in time to see Admiral Lee's ships take under fire the Japanese . . . group which had just steamed into the area from the northwest. It was a clear night and we had a fantastic view of the ensuing battle."[24]

On board the *South Dakota*, the skipper, Captain Thomas Gatch, was on the bridge. A sling supported his left arm, which was still essentially useless as the result of the bomb fragment that hit him on 26 October. He was incapacitated for a while, but Lee wanted his expertise and drive available for this battle. As he had explained to the skipper when the subject came up earlier, "Go ahead and take her out—I don't expect you'll have to strangle the Japs."[25] As she followed the *Washington* that night, the *South Dakota* was buttoned up for watertight integrity, and the water and ventilation systems were shut off to prevent the spread of flooding and fire. Crew members had a sense of anticipation inside their honeycomb of steel compartments. The ship's chaplain, Commander James Claypool, recounted later that men buttoned collars, rolled down sleeves, and tucked pant legs into socks—all to prevent flash burns. The officers, including the chaplain, carried small containers of injectable morphine in their pockets in case they were needed to alleviate pain.[26]

The night was clear, "drowsily warm, and a quarter moon provided some illumination." In the vicinity of Guadalcanal, the chaplain's assistant, Yeoman James Buck, served as a topside lookout. He described the nocturnal aroma from the island as smelling like gardenias.[27] Others also perceived the odor from ashore to be the almost cloying smell of gardenias. Some months afterward, Seaman First Class Tom Page of the *South Dakota* explained, "The association of gardenias with the action that followed five minutes later is so vivid that I never want to smell another gardenia as long as I live."[28] Morison reported a different impression: "A rich, sweet odor like honeysuckle floated out from the land over the calm waters, a pleasant change from the normally fecal smells exuded by the Guadalcanal jungle."[29] (In speaking with one of his research assistants, Roger Pineau, Morison used an earthier term to describe the odor.) Supply Corps Lieutenant Commander Albert Kohlhas Jr. was charged with maintaining a plot of the *Washington*'s movements. In emphasizing the calmness of the water, Kohlhas recalled, "The stars were so bright they reflected a path in the water."[30]

After having approached from the southwest, the six-ship task force steamed to a point north of Savo Island, turned east, then to the southeast. Finally, the lead ship in the column, the *Walke*, put on right rudder at 2252 to head west into Iron Bottom Sound—so named for the ships that had sunk there—and thus to complete the circumnavigation of Savo. The other five ships turned to starboard in her wake. That night Lieutenant (j.g.) Edward Maslanka was serving as the *Washington*'s assistant signal officer. He saw Lee and Glenn Davis together on the navigation bridge as they figured out where the Japanese ships were.[31] When they were confident that they knew, based on radar detection, Lee gave the order to Davis for the *Washington* to commence firing.

The 16-inch guns of the *Washington* began belching flames and projectiles of a nine-gun salvo at 2317. The target was a cluster of Japanese warships east of

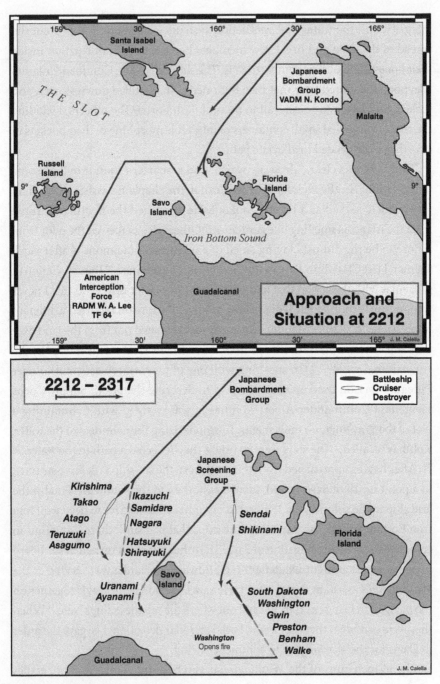

Map 2. Night Battle, 14–15 November 1942

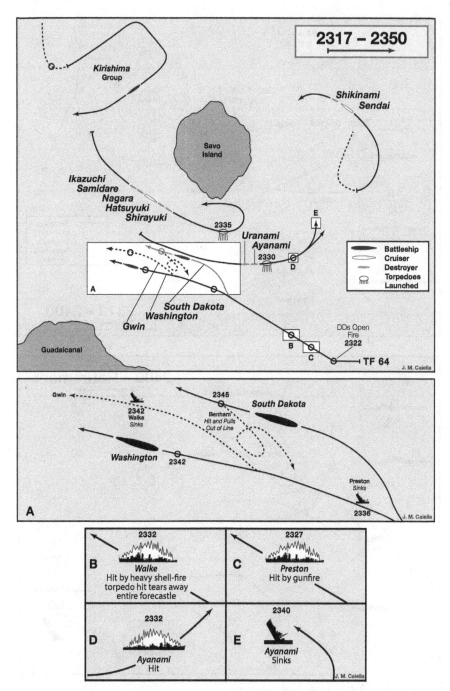

Map 3. Night Battle, 14–15 November 1942

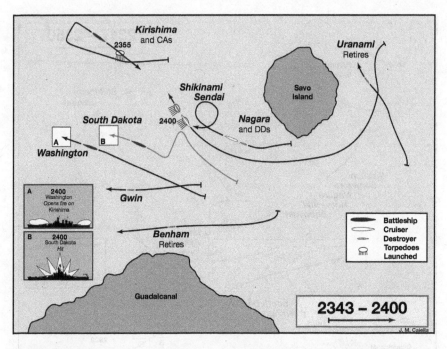

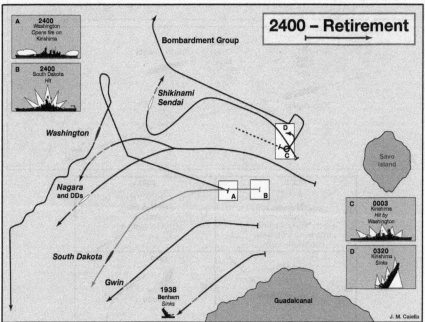

Map 4. Night Battle, 14–15 November 1942

Savo Island and almost due north of the American battleships. The range to the Japanese was around 18,500 yards. The immediate effect of the salvo was to knock off Lee's always-necessary spectacles. Soon Church and Lee were feeling around for them on the deck of the bridge; Lee recovered them himself. Maslanka was at that point descending a ladder from the signal bridge to the navigation bridge. When the big guns erupted, the concussion was such that it knocked him a few steps down to the bottom of the ladder.[32] In a Mark 37 director for 5-inch guns on the starboard side, Lieutenant (j.g.) George Matton reacted when the forward turrets fired. He recalled, "This was the first time I had seen a night firing of a 16" gun and the brightness was blinding."[33] The target for the first shots from the *Washington* was the cruiser *Sendai*, which was not hit. The cruiser doubled back, followed by more *Washington* projectiles that also did not hit.

The guns sent out yellow-orange flashes as the barrels erupted. The air was filled with the acrid sulfurous smell of burned gunpowder, doubtless overwhelming the aroma of honeysuckle and gardenia that had wafted past earlier. Shortly before that, Gatch had sent word to Lee that the *South Dakota* had spotted Japanese ships. Lee's response was, "Go ahead and fire when you're ready." (Even though the *Massachusetts* had fired the first in-anger main-battery battleship rounds a week or so earlier during the invasion of Casablanca, Morocco, she had been firing at a stationary, in-port target, the French battleship *Jean Bart*.) For a while, Gatch thought his ship would be the first battleship to fire her biggest guns in a real open-water engagement since the Spanish-American War in 1898. His hopes were dashed when he saw the *Washington*'s main battery open up. The *South Dakota*'s big guns began firing a minute and a half later.[34]

In each of the battleships, the compartment that tied together the process of aiming and firing the 16-inch guns was the main battery plotting room. It was far down inside the ship, protected within the cocoon of the armored box. The main-battery range keeper was essentially an analog computer that assembled information from several sources, particularly the gun directors high in the superstructure. They provided optical inputs from the range finders and electronic ones from fire control radars. These radars were a key advantage over the methods used by the Japanese, who relied on optics alone. The range keeper incorporated each ship's course, speed, and gyro horizon while continuously monitoring movements of the enemy ships. Additional inputs, which Ensign Erling Hustvedt handled in the *South Dakota*, included muzzle velocity of the projectiles (based on the number of powder bags in the charge), magazine temperatures, barrel erosion, and wind. The range keeper, with supervision of the man operating it, provided solutions that sent orders to the turrets in terms of desired ranges and bearings. Crew members could then fire the big guns either automatically from the plotting room or by local control in the turrets. The latter involved matching pointers with signals sent from the plotting room.[35]

Captain Davis remembered that night vividly. As enemy projectiles appeared during their inbound flights, Lee said to the skipper, "Stand by, Glenn. Here they come." Of the imperturbable Lee, Davis observed that the admiral was "[n]o more excited than at a peacetime target practice." Lee's admonition to Davis was audible to other men on the bridge. He recalled the sense of relief that fell over the cohort when the Japanese rounds did not hit the *Washington*. Soon afterward more of the Japanese force came within range in separate groups. Davis used a well-worn phrase in recalling that "all hell broke loose. Projectile tracers from both sides were crisscrossing the sky."[36] Lieutenant Church, on the bridge, characterized the airborne projectiles as a "red snowball fight, flying back and forth." In this instance, the *Washington*'s armor-piercing "snowballs" weighed twenty-seven hundred pounds apiece.

Lieutenant (j.g.) Robert Macklin's battle station was the starboard director for the forward 1.1-inch guns. He was positioned just above the flag bridge, and because the 1.1s would have no role in this battle, he was able to focus on being an eyewitness. He saw the *Washington* being fired upon by the fast battleship *Kirishima*, sister of the deceased *Hiei*. His description makes it seem as if time almost stood still, moving forward in fragments: "You could see a salvo of . . . white hot shells as they left the enemy turret; they seemed to float slowly toward us, picking up speed as they came and turning bright red as they came closer. . . . One salvo passed close aboard our stern, and as I watched it, the glow of the shells illuminated our huge battle flag which I hadn't realized had been hoisted. It was like re-living the first stanza of the Star Spangled Banner and an unforgettable thrill for me." He later saw at least one of the *Washington*'s 16-inch salvos strike home on the *Kirishima*.[37]

American radar was the difference maker in the battle. Lieutenant Bob Merritt was in the makeshift CIC and provided information via sound-powered telephone to the men in flag plot and on the bridge. Lieutenant James Ross was on the main battery control circuit. Since radars came under the gunnery department, he was primarily supplying information to the gunners and only secondarily to the bridge. As he recalled years later, Ross was trying to describe to the gunnery officer what he could determine from the surface contacts and thus to coach the main battery directors onto the leading and largest targets.[38]

The *Washington* remained almost completely unscathed during the engagement, but the destroyers up front were not nearly so fortunate. They began firing at the enemy at 2322, but they soon began absorbing even heavier punishment than they dished out. Quite soon the destroyers became the sacrificial lambs for Task Force 64. Gunfire hit the *Preston* five minutes after she had started shooting, and she sank at 2337. In his fine book *Neptune's Inferno*, author James Hornfischer cited officers on board the *South Dakota* who reported that at least part of the *Preston*'s damage came from the guns of the *Washington*.[39]

When the tin cans' batteries first started shooting, Chief Fire Controlman R. P. Spearman of the *Walke* reported, "We opened up at a range of around 14,000 yards, but the ranges came down very fast. I don't remember what it was when we ended up, but I know it was pointblank." Around 2332 the *Walke*, at the head of the column, was hit by gunfire, and at 2338 a torpedo tore off her bow. The Japanese clobbered the *Gwin* at 2337 and torpedoed the *Benham* a minute later. The *Walke* sank at 2345, and at 2348 Lee ordered the *Benham* and *Gwin* to retire in order to escape the relentless punishment. The *Walke*'s depth charges went off underwater and killed a number of men who had survived the sinking of the ship.[40]

Fate spared Ensign Bob Reed of the *Preston* from the death that claimed so many of his shipmates. He had an excellent vantage point during the battle, because the destroyer's skipper relieved the engineer from his normal battle station and put him up on deck to photograph the action. He faced aft toward the *Washington* and *South Dakota*. The result was that he absorbed a series of visual images that stayed with him, even though the camera did not. He saw the 16-inch salvos leave the *Washington*; they arced upward and then descended on their targets. The back ends of the projectiles glowed cherry red as they left barrels, disappeared for a time into low clouds, and then reappeared as they approached the Japanese ships. As his ship went down, he was able to float off into the water, unlike those trapped inside the destroyer.[41]

Lieutenant (j.g.) Silvic DeChristofaro was in the *Washington*'s secondary battery plotting room that night. He wore headphones and received a report that when the *Walke* was hit, she had gone up "like a match." A member of the crew in a director topside described the scene as the battleship passed by; he could hear the cries of the destroyer crewmen who suddenly found themselves in the water. During regular watches (while not in battle) DeChristofaro served as officer of the deck and had frequent contact with Lee. He remembered Lee as "obsessed with a desire to engage the Japanese in battle." That night's engagement fulfilled the obsession.[42]

Lieutenant John M. Gore was also in secondary plot that night. He had been with the ship during her previous venture with Britain's Royal Navy before reporting to the Pacific. In both places the ship had seemingly been "up on the step," close to action, but it hadn't happened yet. Now it had. Years later he conveyed the mood that enveloped him and others in the compartment when the *Washington*'s guns roared: "I don't think fear entered into the picture at all, but a kind of exhilaration. Everyone looked up, caught the eyes of various shipmates and broke into a broad smile."[43] Lieutenant Bill Fargo was another officer in that plotting room. As with the others, he experienced the battle vicariously through reports from phone talkers topside. He later wrote, "One memory is of one director officer describing hits on a Japanese ship as a gigantic hand, slapping big pieces off the ship which was burning."[44]

Though the destroyers were so soon out of the fight, they played a key role in the battle nonetheless. The funeral pyres of the ships that sank, along with the fires on board the other two damaged ships lit up the night sky. The *Washington*, with Captain Davis on the bridge and Lieutenant Commander Ray Hunter as officer of the deck, adroitly steered to port to move past the destroyers. At 2335, in response to the conning officer's order, the *Washington* changed course from 300° to 282°. Hunter said years later, "I think my greatest contribution to the war effort was when this destroyer immediately ahead of us—I saw a salvo hit it, and I think a torpedo hit it about the same time, and it blew immediately. And I gave an order to the helmsman, 'Come left.' And those were the exact words I used, 'Come left, come left.'" Hunter recalled that he had the conn throughout the battle—he issued orders on the courses to be steered. He said the decision to turn to port came to him in an instant. Davis said years later that it was he who directed Hunter to order the turn. As President John Kennedy once said, "Success has many fathers, but failure is an orphan." In this case, the action was a success, no matter who initiated it, in view of what happened next.[45]

Two minutes earlier, the *South Dakota* had experienced a temporary but crucial loss of electrical power because of the shock effect from firing her big guns. Her crew was disoriented as she steamed along. To avoid running into the destroyers, the conning officer turned the ship to starboard, which put her between the fires and the guns of the Japanese bombardment ships—*Kirishima*, *Atago*, and *Takao*. Enemy searchlights lit her up as well, and she became the next target in the shooting gallery. She was riddled with a variety of projectiles that caused heavy personnel losses. The barrage also knocked out her radar and radio equipment, so she was unable to communicate with the *Washington*. As the flagship roared past the destroyers, her crewmen threw life rafts overboard to benefit the men in the water. Many survived the night and were rescued the next day.[46] Japanese projectiles rained in and made a shambles of the *South Dakota*'s superstructure, creating multiple fires. After the battle, Captain Gatch recalled, "I'd been dying for a cigarette and now I thought I could have one, so I drew my lighter. One of the men shouted, 'Cap'n, Sir! You'll give away our position!' I just looked up at the flames near the top of the mast and finished my smoke."[47]

At 2332, the *Washington* unleashed her 5-inch guns on the already-wounded destroyer *Ayanami* and created fatal damage. Some of her crew subsequently transferred to the destroyer *Uranami*, and others escaped by boat to Guadalcanal. The *Uranami* then polished her off with a torpedo, and the *Ayanami* sank shortly after 0200, adding still more metal to Iron Bottom Sound.

At 2338, Lee directed the two remaining U.S. destroyers to leave the formation, in part to protect them and in part because they were no longer capable of offensive action. They peeled off to the southwest, toward Guadalcanal and beyond. Throughout this time, the *Washington*'s fire control radars had been tracking a large target, which proved to be the biggest fish in the barrel, the Japanese flagship *Kirishima*. She had been designed by a British engineer and built at the Mitsubishi shipyard in Nagasaki as the third of four *Kongo*-class battle cruisers. She went into service in 1915 and was thus not nearly as modern as the *Washington* and *South Dakota*. In the 1920s and 1930s she underwent modernizations that made her a full-fledged battleship. Her top speed of thirty knots put her among the fastest capital ships in the world. Lee held off firing for a while, because he was concerned that she might be the *South Dakota*. He was concerned about the radar blind spot aft of the *Washington* that resulted from the ill-conceived mounting of her SG radar antenna. Lieutenant Commander Ed Hooper in the main battery plotting room told Lee that he had an accurate track on the Japanese dreadnought, but the admiral wanted to be certain. All doubt was removed when the enemy ship was illuminated by star shells, and her own searchlights revealed her as well.[48]

Hooper later used silhouettes of the *Kirishima* and *South Dakota* and conceded that the aspect the *South Dakota* presented was "amazingly close" to that of the Japanese ship when viewed visually, as Davis and Lee were doing. He explained, "For some time after that I was critical of Admiral Lee in my own mind. Yet, as time passed as I analyzed the situation and considered the factors he had in his mind, I came to the conclusion that he was correct. Of course, I, as a rather young officer, wanted to sink all the Japanese ships I could and saw this as my objective."[49]

At midnight, as the new day of Sunday began, the *Washington* opened up on the *Kirishima* with her main battery at the range of eighty-four hundred yards, truly a close encounter when naval behemoths were firing. The *Washington* unleashed seventy-five radar-controlled 16-inch rounds at the *Kirishima*. Of the 16-inch projectiles, Lee's action report assessed the hits at "about eight." A recent study claims that as many as twenty struck home. The rounds from her 5-inch guns hit maybe as many as eighteen times.[50] These figures are from the conclusions of Robert Lundgren, an individual who has done a great deal of study of the naval aspects of the Guadalcanal campaign. None of the *Kirishima*'s damage came from the *South Dakota*'s firing; the *Washington*'s projectiles inflicted all of the deadly blows. Within seven minutes of being on the receiving end of 16-inch gunfire, she was out of the fight. Some of the big hits were below the Japanese dreadnought's waterline, thus acting essentially as torpedoes, which let water into her hull. The *Kirishima*'s rudder was jammed, limiting her to steering in clockwise circles. She was uncontrollable, and fires raged topside.[51] The damage was so extensive that she sank around 0320, about eleven miles west of Savo Island.

Lieutenant Commander Hank Seely was the topside spotter on board the *Washington*. He was in the main battery director, Spot I, high in the superstructure. When his ship was firing, his sound-powered phone reported that the big guns had made hits on an enemy target. About that same time came reports that the *South Dakota* was being hit. Seely asked the personnel in the main battery plotting room, far down inside the ship's armored box, "Are you sure we're on the right target?" Lieutenant (j.g.) Frank Sanger Jr. was in the plotting room and heard the report. Years later he recalled a sense of anguish that *Washington* had shot her accompanying battleship. But that emotion lasted only a short time until the men in the plotting room established that they were not firing at the *South Dakota*.[52]

Until the heated battles off Guadalcanal that mid-November, the Japanese Navy had not lost a battleship. Sister ships *Hiei* and *Kirishima* had been part of the Tokyo Express that riddled the American task force the night of 12–13 November. The *Hiei* was so badly damaged in that surface clash that she was easy prey for Guadalcanal-based aircraft on the thirteenth. Now the Japanese had lost two dreadnoughts in a three-day span. At 0015, soon after the *Washington* finished plastering the *Kirishima*, the battered *South Dakota* turned to course 235°. She was no longer capable of aiding the fight, so she began her withdrawal from the scene. The *Washington* was now fighting alone.

Because of his ship's topside damage, Captain Gatch was unable to communicate. As Morison explained dramatically, "Admiral Lee tried without success to raise *South Dakota* by radio; he could only hope that she was retiring, not sinking."[53] In his post-battle report, submitted three months later, Lee said that the other battleship had been reduced from an asset to a liability and that Gatch's decision to withdraw was "to the great relief of the Task Force Commander."[54] From this point onward, the *Washington* effectively constituted the entirety of the U.S. fighting force. Neither the destroyers nor the *South Dakota* were capable of combatting the enemy.

The Mark 37 directors that controlled the *Washington*'s secondary battery were arrayed in a diamond pattern. Number one was in the forward part of the superstructure, two on the port side, three on the starboard side, and four aft. Thus three of the four were able to point to starboard, in the direction of the enemy. Lieutenant (j.g.) Leo R. Schwabe was in charge of the number-four director on board the *Washington*; Lieutenant (j.g.) Martin L. Olson had the director on the unengaged port side. Lieutenant (j.g.) Matton had the forward director. In addition to shooting at Japanese warships, the 5-inch guns were responsible for firing star shells during the engagement. These were flares suspended from parachutes; after being fired in a parabolic arc, they drifted slowly down to provide illumination over the enemy ships. The directions came from the plotting room in the form of range and bearing.

Captain Jonas Platt was in charge of the Mark 37 director on the starboard side and got plenty of action. Schwabe praised the starboard mounts for the fast-paced rate and volume of fire. Schwabe also recalled that his director controlled one of Platt's mounts.[55] Platt, the commanding officer of the ship's Marine detachment, was outside to see what was happening and watched as the first incoming salvo from the *Kirishima* landed in the *Washington*'s wake. It sent up a splash well above him. As he explained later, "I decided it was time to climb back into the director." The radar operator inside the director reported that he could see on his screen the enemy shells coming toward the ship. Platt's crew directed 5-inch fire at enemy searchlights and blinded their probing beams. Some Japanese searchlights were operated by remote control and some were manned. Platt said of the situation, "If it was a manned searchlight, we really discouraged the hell out of the guys running the light."[56]

One of the battle reports subsequently stated that the star shells blinded the Japanese optical range finders and presumably the Americans' as well. But the *Washington* was relying on radar fire control. The Japanese did not have radar, either for search or fire control. "So," as Schwabe put it, "messed up communications proved a blessing." The *Washington* was barely hit by Japanese gunfire during the battle, but often the misses were not by much. Chet Smith in the number-two antiaircraft director, had his back to the action and later said he heard many shells whistling past.[57] Ensign Robert Bennett was assigned to the 1.1-inch gun mounts at the stern of the ship. He reported afterward that he was terrified by the star shells "and the enormous din of the main and secondary batteries." He huddled virtually unprotected behind the steel shielding of a gun mount.[58]

Soon after the *Washington*'s main battery fired, George Matton's director began pumping out 5-inch projectiles; the targets were enemy searchlights and gun flashes. The mounts were in automatic control, through the plotting room to the guns. One of the mounts began to fire high, so Lieutenant H. J. Campbell in sky control shifted the guns to Jonas Platt in director three, and for a while Matton was a spectator. The view from his elevated perspective: "Gunfire was everywhere." When his guns continued to fire erratically, he shifted them to local control. He compared the sensation to aiming a fire hose and watching the tracers fly out to strike home on the enemy. The image of the hits, he wrote, was akin to seeing sparks flying from a welder's torch. (Years later, Matton, as a four-stripe naval aviator in Hawaii, entertained a rear admiral of the Japanese Maritime Self-Defense Force during a joint exercise. In the course of the visit, his guest revealed that he had been a floatplane pilot on board the *Kirishima* during the night battle.[59])

Fire Controlman First Class P. J. "Dutch" Stahnke was topside. He had essentially a front-row observation platform from his battle station in the forward main battery director high in the superstructure. He recalled years later about himself and his shipmates who were connected by sound-powered telephones: "All of us who were tied to General Quarters and fighting the ship, it didn't take long for those of us 'seeing' the battles through the telescopes, periscopes, and rangefinder to realize that we were fighting with a man who had unlimited tactical ability." He added, "After the first engagement with the Admiral commanding, I can speak for not only myself but many of the Ship's Company in that he gave us the confidence to win against all odds."[60]

Lieutenant Robert Simpson was in one of the engine rooms of the *Washington* during the battle "with all hatches thoroughly battened down." Simpson and his engineers were fully expecting one or more Japanese torpedoes to come into their space during every minute of the battle. Unlike those who were topside and could see what was going on, those below had to rely on sporadic reports from those above. Their own task was to coax every last tenth of a knot out of the ship's turbine engines, because the ship was steaming flat out during the entire episode and the crew didn't want anything to happen that would reduce the speed. Simpson concluded, "It is an understatement to say we were all relieved when 'secure' was sounded."[61] The rated speed for the *Washington* was officially twenty-seven knots. Simpson recalled that the ship's "flat-out" speed was around twenty-eight.[62] During one stretch that night, an officer on the bridge asked for even more speed. The reply from the engine room was that there was no more to add. A machinist's mate on watch then heard one of his fellow sailors suggest, "Oh yeah, everybody lean forward!" The resulting laughter helped dispel tension.[63]

■ ■ ■

On board the *South Dakota*, before she retired from the fray, the situation had gone from bad to worse in a hurry following the power outage, even though she regained electricity after a few minutes. Turret three's 16-inch salvo at 2342 set afire the floatplanes on catapults aft. A subsequent salvo blew them overboard. Hindsight suggested that the planes should have been put ashore before the engagement, which was what the *Washington* had done with her planes. As Commander Harvey Walsh, the *Washington*'s gunnery officer, observed, Lee "rightly considered them 'sitting ducks' in the air for Jap Zeroes and a fire hazard aboard during night actions which all our surface actions were at that time. Their presence aboard meant the choice of limiting the arc of fire of turret three or of destroying our own planes by gun blast or jettisoning."[64]

The antiaircraft guns that had compiled an impressive score while protecting the *Enterprise* a few weeks earlier had no place in this night action. Of necessity their crews were out in the open and exposed during air combat. A reserve officer, Lieutenant (j.g.) Sargent Shriver, was in charge of a group of 20-mm guns on the starboard side of the main deck. On this night, he looked out for his men. Shriver, of course, became much better known later as the brother-in-law of President John F. Kennedy. During the Kennedy administration he became the first director of the Peace Corps. He later served as U.S. ambassador to France and in 1972 was candidate for vice president on the ticket headed by fellow World War II veteran George McGovern.

On this night, though, all that was well in the future. A few months after the battle, he spoke of his gun crew: "We had nothing to do, so I told the crew to lie down and hug the deck and try to keep out of the way of any shells. After a while, I got curious, so I got up on my haunches to see what was going on. Then I tried to 'seek cover' again, but I couldn't get back down. Someone was 'seeking cover' underneath me!"[65] Some of the shrapnel that was flying around that night hit one of Shriver's arms, which began bleeding. He recalled, "I thought sure I must have lost my arm or something. I started waving it around to see whether it worked, and of course it worked out all right. But it's funny how you can be shocked just by being hit." It turned out to be a flesh wound, not serious.[66]

Lieutenant (j.g.) Paul Backus was the *South Dakota*'s turret two officer. On 26 October at Santa Cruz the ship had protected the *Enterprise* with antiaircraft fire that knocked down a number of planes. As mentioned, a Japanese bomb had exploded atop turret one, and a fragment flew up to the bridge and nearly killed the skipper, Captain Gatch. What's more—and this was problematic for Backus during the November battle—two of his turret's guns had been badly gouged by bomb fragments, and the other gun was in dubious condition as well. After the damage incurred at Santa Cruz, the ship sent messages to the Bureau of Ordnance in Washington to ask whether it was safe to fire the guns. The ship received no satisfactory answers, so Backus asked the gunnery officer, Lieutenant Commander Paul Johnson, whether he could shoot in the night engagement. His answer to Backus was, "Paul, you are going to have to make a decision; if things get real tough, shoot those guns."

The *South Dakota*'s action report said that turret two fired during the battle. Moreover, when the turret was trained all the way aft and fired, it caused blast damage on the main deck and superstructure.[67] So a presumption is that at least one gun did fire. When the ship eventually got to the New York Navy Yard for extensive repairs, the damaged 16-inch guns were removed, and the Bureau of Ordnance directed that one be tested.[68] Lieutenant John Wilson was the inspection officer at the naval ordnance plant in Pocatello, Idaho. He had the barrel magnafluxed and concluded that a 2-foot longitudinal crack was too deep for firing the gun. But BuOrd directed that it be tested anyway. It was fired with a reduced charge of powder. As Wilson recalled years later, "Pieces of it went all over the Idaho desert and all that was left was just a stub that looked like a Civil War mortar. I'm glad that the South Dakota boys didn't try to fire it."[69]

Inside the armored turret, Backus and his crew were somewhat insulated from the sounds of battle outside. Lieutenant (j.g.) Charlie Francis was the junior officer in turret two. The officers were in a booth aft of the guns. Because it was a high turret, it might have to take over control of the main battery if the regular fire control directors were unavailable. As part of his function, Francis was looking through a periscope in the turret to keep an eye on what was happening outside. At one point he turned away with, as Backus remembered, "eyes as big as saucers," and said, "It's right out there; I can touch it." He was referring to the *Kirishima*.[70]

Lieutenant Norman Hoffman had a similar experience in turret three, seeing the enemy battleship at point-blank range through the periscope and range finder—both while the *South Dakota* was firing and being hit.[71] A 14-inch hit on the turret jammed it from rotating. Hoffman and a chief petty officer climbed down through the overhang hatch at the rear of the turret to survey the problem. They discovered that the light metal covering the roller path was the culprit, so they used a blowtorch to burn it off and free the turret to move again.[72]

Once the shooting had stopped, Backus was to be officer of the deck and went to the bridge, which he found to be a shambles. A salvo of 8-inch fire had gone through the chartroom aft of the bridge. The assistant navigator, Lieutenant (j.g.) Dwight Moody, had been at the chart table. Though Moody escaped unscathed, an enlisted man who was right next to him taking depth readings from the Fathometer was cut in two. The Sky I director that controlled the forward 5-inch mounts on the starboard side was knocked out by gunfire. When Backus was finally able to get to his stateroom after being relieved from the bridge, he found the body of a dead Marine in his bunk. While the Marine was stationed in Sky III, which controlled the after 5-inch mounts to starboard, a radar antenna on the director was hit by gunfire. The shrapnel entered the Marine's back and neck. He was taken out of the director and put in the bunk temporarily but had not yet been removed.[73]

As was customary, the *South Dakota*'s wardroom doubled as a treatment center for tending the wounded. Adding to the unpleasantness of the situation, men opened watertight doors to bring in the injured, and water from fire hoses flowed into the space to a depth above ankles. Chaplain Claypool was in the dressing station to provide comfort for the injured. He was helping to transfer a wounded young man from a stretcher to a cot when he felt something wet and warm on his arm and leg—the sailor's blood. The chaplain changed uniforms three times during that gory night.[74]

■ ■ ■

During the closing phase of the battle, the *Washington* was on her own, the only effective American warship still able to deal with the enemy. At Lee's direction, the flagship initially steamed to the northwest, as explained in his action report, to close with the "enemy transports and other suitable targets."[75] His likely aim was to delay the arrival of the enemy transports, but they were farther away than were

Japanese combatants that could inflict harm. Lookouts spotted torpedo tracks in the water, but no torpedoes hit. With the flair that Admiral Morison often sprinkled into his prose, he wrote, "Through moonless darkness keen lookouts spotted the torpedo tracks and Captain Davis's clever maneuvering dodged their embarrassing caresses as nimbly as a young girl eluding a sailor on a park bench."[76] The flagship was headed for New Georgia, an island that was partially surrounded by coral reefs. As Lieutenant Chad Knowlton remembered years later, this was problematic because the navigation charts on board were about as old as Captain James Cook's exploratory visit to the area. Lee told Knowlton the *Washington* had to turn left to avoid the reefs.[77]

The Japanese departed at that point, having apparently exhausted their torpedoes. Admiral Kondo began withdrawing his ships, concerned that if they lingered too long, they would be targets for American aircraft with the coming of daylight. Knowlton tracked the Japanese on radar to a range of 18,000 yards as they escaped to the north.[78]

Admiral Lee assessed the situation. His destroyers were out of the fight. The *South Dakota* was no longer an effective combatant. Satisfied that Task Force 64 had thwarted the Japanese plans, Admiral Lee turned to his flag captain and said, "Glenn, let's get the hell out of here." In recalling that moment years afterward, Davis said, "No further urging was required."[79] Lee began the *Washington*'s retirement at 0033 and headed southward. By doing so, he could protect the retiring *South Dakota*. The flagship emerged from the heavyweight slugging match with only the slightest of wounds. A Japanese projectile had created a 5-inch hole in the CXAM radar's bedspring antenna, which was mounted high on the foremast tower.[80]

Lieutenant John Cadwalader was up in the foremast with the lookouts. One of them shouted "Breakers," which indicated a line of surf pounding up against a shoreline. The *Washington* had turned toward Lamon Island in the Russells in order to evade enemy torpedoes. Lee reported that four or five torpedoes had come "uncomfortably close."[81] As the ship approached Lamon, Cadwalader passed the word down to the conning officer, who put on hard rudder to avoid running aground. The next time Cadwalader talked with Captain Davis, the skipper said to him, "My God, what a monument we'd have been." During the battle, Cadwalader was on a little platform outside the superstructure. When the *Washington* first unleashed her big guns, the shock nearly flattened him. As for the incoming fire, he said, "The 14-inch shells from the *Kirishima* sounded like a subway train coming at you."[82]

When Admiral Lee directed the ship to leave, Davis turned to Schanze and asked for a course. Schanze said, "South." Davis told him to bring the ship around to a course in that general direction. Lee nodded in approval but never interposed himself into the situation. It was the captain's ship to run. Davis added, "I presume he felt confident. Otherwise, . . . I guess he'd have taken it away from me sooner if he wanted and felt he should."[83] As the flagship retired following the action, the plan was to rendezvous with the *South Dakota* at a prearranged point about one hundred miles south of Guadalcanal. Schanze used a sextant to get a star fix and, with the permission of Lee and Davis, set course for the rendezvous. After eating breakfast and double-checking in the chartroom, he discovered that the course would put the ship about twenty miles from the desired spot. He explained later in a letter: "It is true that I had had no sleep for at least 48 hours and there was no danger since the Coral Sea was wide open in front of us." Lee was then on the wing of the bridge, and the navigator asked him to have a look at the chart and show him the error. Lee replied, "That's alright. Set the course for whatever you like to get to the rendezvous.'" Schanze said that if he had made such an error in the peacetime 1930s, he might have lost his job.[84]

In the wake of the battle, Lee conferred with Lieutenant Commander Hooper about Japanese 24-inch torpedoes. Lee had seen their effectiveness in the battle and was grateful that the *Washington* had not been hit, though some sailors in the engineering spaces heard a thud they thought might have been a dud torpedo. Lee, with his scientific mind, concluded that the Japanese Long Lance torpedoes had longer range and higher speeds than U.S. intelligence had attributed to them. He did calculations of skin friction and drag and concluded that the weapons could well have the capabilities he attributed to them. Hooper said he believed that Lee's conjecture was verified later when captured Japanese torpedoes were tested.[85]

Once the immediate threat was over and the *South Dakota* was headed south, Ensign Warren Calhoun from turret two was assigned to supervise the cleanup in the perforated foremast area that had been riddled by Japanese projectiles. He didn't use a light that night because the ship was still in enemy territory and might have attracted attention from lurking Japanese vessels, so he had to do the job by feel. When he reached out his hand in the darkness, he might find a severed limb or something similarly grotesque. His division officer, Lieutenant (j.g.) Backus, said he had "difficulties later on in the Navy" and wondered whether it was related to that experience—what we now call post-traumatic stress disorder.[86]

Enlisted men were also part of the working party, and human entrails were among the things they encountered. One man affected by the experience was either a leading seaman or a boatswain's mate at the time. A few years after the war, as a chief boatswain's mate, he sought out Backus, who was then serving in the light cruiser *Huntington*. The enlisted man said he was "having problems with nightmares. He would wake up in the night, and he'd have his wife by the throat against the wall or something like that." He had seen medical people, but they had been unable to help him with the nightmares that plagued his subconscious. Backus got in touch with the Philadelphia Naval Hospital and arranged for the man to be treated by hypnosis. That treatment revealed that the man was still suffering from the effects of the cleanup detail in 1942, and that proved the key to recovery—no more nightmares.[87]

The following morning, as the *South Dakota* steamed toward Nouméa, crew members went out on deck. There they saw corpses of their shipmates, some of them mutilated during the night's bombardment. It fell to survivors to identify those who had been killed. Dog tags provided the relevant information in only ten cases. Other names were matched to bodies by names sewn into their uniforms, by watches or rings, or by personal effects left behind in lockers of those who had not been accounted for as among the living. The ship then sent the personal possessions and locker contents to the families of the deceased. Chaplain Claypool presided over the burials at sea. The ship's sailmakers, whose job it was to do canvas work on board, created shrouds into which 5-inch projectiles were inserted along with the bodies to ensure that they would sink once sent on their final journeys into the deep. Both sailmakers suffered mental anguish as the result of carrying out their gruesome task. One had to be hospitalized; the chaplain described him as a "broken man."[88] The human price for the *South Dakota*'s ordeal that night amounted to thirty-eight men killed or missing and sixty wounded.[89]

On board the *Washington* that night, as the ship was steaming away, Lee was imperturbable. He had just fought the biggest battle of his life. After a while, the adrenaline rush had probably subsided. When Lieutenant Commander

Ray Thompson went to Lee's cabin, the admiral was still awake, calmly reading a mystery novel, as if this were any other night of his life.[90] Ensign William Bentinck-Smith of Lee's staff recalled his reaction the following morning, before the rendezvous with the *South Dakota*: "No one topside could ever forget the noise and confusion, the loss of our escorting destroyers, and the utter loneliness and ignorance which gripped us all when the *Washington* finally withdrew. To face daylight with an empty ocean surrounding us and no real knowledge of what had happened—even to fear that we had suffered a serious defeat, on top of the disaster-filled action of two nights previous—made the later intelligence from Guadalcanal about our victory almost hysterically joyous. . . . [Victory] was not immediately clear to the participants, and there were aspects of that period which left no room for certain satisfaction. The margin of victory was thin indeed. Sheer chance played a big part."[91]

Admiral Lee was succinct in explaining the factor that made a difference in the outcome of the clash that night near Savo Island: "We entered this action confident that we could out shoot the enemy. From the instant they retired after our opening salvos, we knew we had the Indian sign on the Japs. We, however, realized then, and it should not be forgotten now, that our margin of superiority was due almost entirely to our possession of radar. Certainly we have no edge on the Japs in experience, skill, training or permanence of personnel."[92]

After it was light on 15 November, the two battleships headed for the planned meeting. Navigator Schanze recalled his sense of relief when he first sighted the top of the *South Dakota*'s foremast. The rest of the ship was still hull down over the horizon. The two ships gradually steamed closer, joined up, and then proceeded together to Nouméa. Schanze observed that it was the first time in the war that battleships had operated without a destroyer screen. Of the four destroyers that took part in the battle, none was still with the battleships.[93] Before Lee directed the destroyers to depart the scene, the *Benham* was taking on water. The following day the *Gwin* took aboard *Benham*'s crew as they abandoned their ship while she was breaking up. The *Gwin* then had the task of sinking the *Benham* with her 5-inch guns before proceeding to the island of Espiritu Santo in the New Hebrides. The *Gwin* was the only one of the four destroyers that survived the vicious shootout.

Once she arrived at Nouméa, the *South Dakota* licked her wounds and obtained temporary repairs before making the long voyage to the New York Navy Yard to be put back together. The Bureau of Ships created a diagram that displayed graphically the horrendous punishment the ship had taken. The pounding comprised twenty-six separate hits—by projectiles from 14-inch, 8-inch, 6-inch, and 5-inch guns. The radar antenna atop the foremast was completely destroyed. Several of the Japanese projectiles tore through the superstructure without detonating. One 14-inch projectile passed through both sides of a vertical coaming that surrounded a hatch in the deck. It detonated on impact with the turret three barbette and blew a 3-foot by 10-foot hole in the main deck. The explosion gouged the gun sleeves on the right and center guns of the aft turret. On the morning after the encounter, Lieutenant Backus went on deck and measured two 14-inch half-moon cutouts of the hatch coaming, both at the same height. They indicated that the *Kirishima*'s guns had been firing at a flat trajectory. The guns were typically elevated for greater range; in this case there had been no need, because the ships were so close to each other.[94]

The *Washington* had pulled away to the northwest at the end of the battle, in order to draw the enemy away from the wounded *South Dakota*. The crew of the latter did not know that at the time, so rumors started that the *Washington* had abandoned them. The upshot was a good deal of resentment between the crews and even some fights among men on liberty when the ships got back to Nouméa. Ensign Hal Berc of the *Washington* observed that some of his enlisted shipmates were badly injured when they returned following altercations with their *South Dakota* counterparts. As Paul Backus of the *South Dakota* put it, it was "all through this big misunderstanding." He also recalled that Admiral Lee conferred with the skippers of the two battleships to determine a remedy. The crew of the *South Dakota* mustered on the fantail and received a report on the real reason for the *Washington*'s diversionary move. There was no further trouble.[95]

A more lighthearted outcome of the battle had to do with the *South Dakota*'s turret three. In honor of the salvo it had delivered that blew the floatplanes off the fantail, someone jokingly painted silhouettes of "lame ducks" on the base of the turret. This was comparable to painting symbols to represent enemy planes shot down. In this case, the message was that the *South Dakota*'s pilots—at least temporarily—had no wings.[96]

The *Washington*'s high-speed steaming, before, during, and after the battle, exacted a steep price on the boilers below decks. As the ship made the trip from the Guadalcanal area to Nouméa, Lieutenant (j.g.) Robert Harris observed that the boiler bricks intended to provide insulation had turned molten. The liquid was gently sloshing back and forth inside every boiler as the ship rolled during the transit. Once the ship reached Nouméa, Harris' men spent the first forty-eight hours rebricking all eight boilers. This was while shipmates were ashore on liberty. Once the task was completed, the boiler gang went to a recreation island in the harbor and "disposed of double the normal ration of cases of beer." They had to make up for lost time.[97]

Task Force 64 that night had prevented the bombardment of Henderson Field and—for the most part—the Japanese attempt to land troops and supplies on Guadalcanal. The four troopships that did make it were mauled by U.S. forces the following day. The final outcome was not immediately apparent. Late in November, an American cruiser force made a hash of things in an encounter that came to be known as the Battle of Tassafaronga, but that was anticlimactic. Lee's victory had been the straw that broke the camel's back. The Japanese fairly soon conceded that Guadalcanal was a lost cause and withdrew their forces. A year after the attack on Pearl Harbor, the initiative was on the American side. Admiral Halsey sent a dispatch to Admiral Nimitz in Hawaii: "I think we proved in Lee's night action that the duty of the battleships is far from a thing of the past."[98]

Two days later Lee sent a laconic "after-action" report to his wife:

Dear Chubby
    Am well and having interesting time. Received two of your letters and one from [Mabelle's niece] Lila. Tell Lila Ill get around to answering her some day.
    I miss [you] and am sorry I wont be able to see you Christmas. Dont let newspaper stories worry you. I will take good care of me.
    Above is my address. You can send "V-mail" letters—get blanks and instructions at Post Office—possibly quicker than regular air mail coming this way.
    Give my love to family and remember that I love you.
    Lee[99]

▪ 11 ▪

WATCHFUL WAITING
December 1942–October 1943

A few weeks after the battle, the *Washington* received a timely visitor who recorded events in the Guadalcanal campaign for posterity. A Naval Reserve officer, Lieutenant Dwight Shepler was a gifted artist. His close-up painting of the *South Dakota*'s antiaircraft action in the Battle of Santa Cruz Islands in October 1942 is a classic of the genre. The same may be said of his depiction of the night action on 14–15 November: in the foreground the flagship *Washington* fires away at the enemy to starboard; in the background, splashes bracket the *South Dakota* while the Japanese ships and Savo Island loom in the distance. Shepler talked to a variety of shipboard personnel to gain their visual impressions of the Savo action. Lieutenant (j.g.) Robert Macklin was among those and recalled that "we all hung over his shoulder as he painted, showering him with unwanted information and arguing with him and with each other about how it really was." The painting appeared on the dust jacket of Samuel Eliot Morison's account of the Guadalcanal campaign. Morison dedicated that volume "To The memory of Willis Augustus Lee."[1]

While on board, Shepler also drew pencil sketches of Lee and the flagship skipper, Captain Glenn Davis. To Ensign William Bentinck-Smith, who was in his twenties while Lee was in his fifties, the admiral appeared to be an old man.

He thought that photos from the period made Lee "look younger than he really looked—and even Dwight Shepler's portrait depicts a man younger than he really appeared." To the ensign, Lee looked careworn and tired. He noted, "All of us sensed that Lee was driving himself too hard, but that was his way."[2]

Around the same time in December, Admiral Lee visited Admiral Halsey when the flagship was in Nouméa. Shortly before departure in a boat, Lieutenant Ed Maslanka gave Lieutenant Commander Ray Thompson the news that Admiral Halsey was promoted to four stars. Thompson replied, "You'd better be right." The group then proceeded to the meeting, and during the course of it, Admiral Lee congratulated Halsey on his promotion. Halsey, caught by surprise, asked what he was talking about, and Lee told him of the message. Halsey then sent his communicators to look through the files and finally came up with the message, which they had not yet decoded. Thompson and Lee were quite pleased with the meeting when they got back to the *Washington* and described the visit.[3]

Halsey and Lee got together on other occasions as well. They had quite different personalities but respected each other professionally. Halsey boasted that he would ride the emperor's white horse in Tokyo; Lee shunned the spotlight. Lieutenant Guil Aertsen went along on some visits and observed that at times Halsey was able to relax and let his hair down.[4] A few weeks after the night action, Lee met up with Rear Admiral Thomas Kinkaid, a Naval Academy classmate. Lee's ships had been attached to Kinkaid's *Enterprise* task force prior to being released to approach Guadalcanal.

In doing a rehash after the engagement, Lee told Kinkaid with great satisfaction that the American salvos were landing on the enemy ships from the beginning of the exchange of gunfire and that no enemy projectiles seemed to be landing near the *Washington*. Kinkaid wrote years later of Lee, "He was feeling pretty good about the whole situation but, when his own gun-fire permitted, he heard strange noises overhead as though they were in the rigging. It did not take him long to realize that the *Washington* was, indeed, under fire, that enemy salvos were passing overhead and that a down correction in the enemy's range would land them on the *Washington*. That changed the complexion of the situation but the *Washington* came through with little or no damage."[5]

Back in the United States, Mabelle Lee, who was living with her sisters in Rock Island, Illinois, had shown none of her husband's hesitation about publicity. She proudly posed for a newspaper picture that showed her holding a portrait photo of her husband. The accompanying article reported that she was particularly gratified by a statement issued by Major General Archer Vandegrift, commander of the First Marine Division: "The battered helmets of the fighting forces on Guadalcanal are lifted in deepest tribute to Rear Admirals Callaghan, Scott, Lee and Kinkaid and to their forces, who against seemingly hopeless odds, did, with magnificent courage, attack and drive back the first hostile stroke and make later successes possible."[6]

The assignment of Commander William F. Jennings to Lee's battleship division staff in December 1942 was significant. Jennings had been with him on the cruiser staff in the late 1930s and in the readiness section of the CominCh staff in Washington. In late 1942, Lee asked for him specifically because they had served so well together previously.[7] Each was accustomed to the working style of the other, so they knew what to expect. Jennings, as chief of staff, was adroit at coordinating the work of the staff members and handling the administrative matters that Lee preferred to avoid. The division of labor enabled Lee to focus on his area of strength—the operation of the ships under his command. The personal bond continued until Lee was forced to relinquish Jennings' services in the summer of 1944.

Because of their close association, it is worth quoting Jennings' recollections at length:

As a seaman he had no peer and as a gunner and tactician there was none from whom I could have learned more. He had an awe-inspiring fund of knowledge on a score of subjects but his outstanding characteristic was his bed rock of down-to-earth common sense. I never once saw him display any sign of strain or excitement and never in all of our association heard him raise his voice in anger. I was once asked how the Admiral could stand the strain of front-line areas for months without showing signs of strain or fatigue and I replied that his abilities and the extent of his knowledge were so great that it never occurred to him to worry over what might happen or was happening because he knew within himself that he was capable of dealing with any situation that might possibly eventuate. Also, that this self-confidence had plenty of justification as it was also the firm belief of every individual under his command. He had an ingrained dislike of pomp or show and many are the stories illustrating his simplicity which endeared him to all ranks. He had also an aversion to any personal publicity and while we furnished the correspondents with all that they needed to know, the Adm., like Adm. [Raymond] Spruance, deprecated all reference to himself. We had a mutual affection and esteem for each other and indeed, he treated me as a younger brother while my feeling for him fell little short of hero-worship. At the same time there was no relaxation in the high standard of performance which he demanded and the highest guardon [reward] I ever received was his statement in my final fitness report to the effect that there was no officer in the Navy whom he would rather have as his Chief-of-Staff.[8]

Admiral Halsey, by now with four stars, honored Lee in a ceremony on 15 February 1943. While the *Washington* was in Dumbéa Bay at Nouméa, the South Pacific commander went aboard to present a Navy Cross to the task force commander. Lieutenant John Gore observed the scene on the ship's fantail. He said that Halsey delivered a "typical blood-and-guts" type speech and then pinned the medal on Lee. The latter had a diffident expression, and a photo of the ceremony shows him with his head bowed as Halsey awarded the medal. Lee, with his down-home appearance, stepped to the microphone and said to the crew of the flagship, "You won it; I wear it."[9] Commander Jennings said that the award of the medal was "much to the satisfaction of everyone, except perhaps the Boss."[10]

In early 1943, the period after Guadalcanal was secured, Admiral Halsey proposed sending the *Washington* to Australia for installation of 40-mm guns. Richard Frank concluded that the real reason was to provide liberty for the crew. Alas, Admiral Ernest King was the killjoy. Frank explained, "Pretty obviously King did not want to put ships within the reach of [the Southwest Pacific commander, General Douglas] MacArthur on any basis." Lieutenant Commander Bill Dawson, the aviation officer on Lee's staff, recalled that during a rest period he three times made arrangements for the admiral to fly to Australia or New Zealand. One time they were even boarding a plane when Halsey's courier put a stop to the planned travel.[11]

There were occasions when Dawson took Lee for flights in the *Washington*'s OS2U floatplanes. Characteristically, Lee took great interest in the mechanical aspects of the aircraft and flight. Dawson recalled years later that the admiral had "an inordinate interest in aviation," because he knew what an important role it played in waging the war in the Pacific. While on board ship, Dawson observed that Lee was not a person to sit quietly doing nothing. On occasion Lee would send for him in the middle of the night. When the flier arrived, he would find the admiral in his cabin, feet up on the desk, clad in pajamas and robe while checking out ordnance tables with a slide rule.[12]

■ ■ ■

For years, Lee had focused his efforts on improving antiaircraft gunnery. Back in the United States a project was under way that would provide a dramatic upgrade in capability. A brilliant young scientist from Iowa was at work on a solution. James Van Allen had sought an appointment to the Naval Academy but did not succeed because of flat feet, a slight problem with eyesight, and his inability to swim. Instead, he went to civilian institutions and earned a PhD from the University of Iowa in 1939 in the field of nuclear physics. With war in the offing, Van Allen went to work with Dr. Merle Tuve at the National Defense Research Council. In April 1942 he was in on the ground floor at the establishment of the Johns Hopkins University's Applied Physics Laboratory in Silver Spring, Maryland.[13]

Van Allen's aim was to help develop a rugged vacuum-tube fuze as part of a projectile for a 5-inch/38-caliber shipboard gun. The fuze would send out a radio signal, sense the nearness of an enemy aircraft, and receive a response that would explode the warhead. The task required a great deal of miniaturization and repeated refinements. It was a proximity fuze, so designed that it had only to come near an aircraft to detonate. To disguise the capability of the new device, it became known as a variable-time, or VT, fuze. The type of antiaircraft fuze then in use had the detonation time set in mechanically, with the hope that the projectile would explode close enough to the airplane to damage or destroy it. By autumn of 1942, proximity fuzes were being produced in defense plants and tested. In early November 1942 Van Allen and two fellow researchers, Neil Dilley and Robert Peterson, received commissions as lieutenants (junior grade) in the Naval Reserve. Their task was to introduce the new projectiles into the Pacific Fleet. At Mare Island Navy Yard, a load of three thousand projectiles went into the hold of a troopship and headed west to Nouméa, New Caledonia, with Van Allen as chaperone.[14]

Lieutenant Van Allen and his cargo reached Nouméa a few weeks after the Savo Island night battle. Soon he was assigned as assistant gunnery officer on Lee's staff on board the *Washington*. In a letter to the author years later, Van Allen wrote that Lee "was my most favorite person of all of those that I had contact with during my World War II service as a naval reserve officer." Of an initial meeting with Lee, Van Allen described the device and the admiral's reaction during the meeting: "He was intensely interested and displayed the most complete, intelligent, and enthusiastic understanding of their properties of anyone that I had encountered."[15]

A second meeting took place a day or so later, and Lee asked to see the interior of the fuze so he could understand how it worked. Van Allen recalled that doing so aboard ship was forbidden, but he assured Lee that he was familiar with the ammunition, and it would be safe to cut one open. Van Allen and a gunner's mate went to a below-decks workshop and removed the fuze from a projectile, removed the detonator, and then used a hacksaw to cut a cross section through the fuze so Lee could see the innards. With Lee's interest in mechanical devices, one can well imagine the grin on his face when he saw what activated the new weapon. Van Allen then explained each element, to Lee's "intense interest and delight." During the session, Captain Davis came to Lee's cabin to tell Lee that his barge was alongside the ship, ready to take him to see Admiral Halsey. Lieutenant (j.g.) Van Allen was gratified when Lee answered, in effect, "Don't bother me. I am learning something." Years later, by then a renowned scientist, Van Allen recalled that Lee immediately focused on the importance of the new fuze. It eliminated the "range error" inherent in the previous mechanical time fuze and was thus five to ten times more effective than its predecessor.[16]

Lieutenant Commander Ray Hunter, who was officer of the deck during the night battle, became the air defense officer and thus was a principal participant when the *Washington* went to sea to test the new projectiles. She fired a number of rounds, and Lee was pleased by the results. Hunter later recalled a night when a lone Japanese aircraft was some distance away on a reconnaissance mission. The screening ships unleashed a barrage of perhaps a dozen VT rounds that found the target. Hunter saw the body of the plane and its engines engulfed in flames.[17]

Van Allen cautioned Lee on the restrictions involving the fuze-equipped rounds. The guns with the projectiles needed a clear field of fire, thus could not shoot over other ships in formation. Moreover, at least initially, they could not be used for shore bombardment, lest a dud be recovered by the enemy and used to replicate the design or develop countermeasures. Van Allen's next task was to deliver the projectiles to a variety of ships and brief their commanding officers and gunnery officers on the properties and restrictions of the new projectile and how to use it. He wrote later that he was met with a "wide range of understanding and lack of understanding." Lee's interest resulted in a large increase in orders for the proximity fuze and its general issue to combatant ships in the Pacific. Van Allen explained that Lee's personal influence was, in large part, responsible for the highly successful use of the radio-proximity fuze in antiaircraft defense of the Pacific Fleet.[18]

■ ■ ■

In February 1943, the Japanese evacuated their forces from the island of Guadalcanal. It had been a long, costly campaign and one of great strategic importance. With the derailment of the Tokyo Express in the 14–15 November night battle, it was time for the strategists in Washington and Hawaii to make plans for what would come next. In the meantime, the *Washington* remained in the South Pacific, based at Nouméa. Lee and the fast battleships had no immediate role, though they did steam at times with the *Saratoga* and *Enterprise* task groups. Captain Davis, the flagship skipper, acknowledged years later that there was no real action in this period because the Japanese chose to stay away from the area.[19]

Lieutenant Commander Samuel Eliot Morison visited the *Washington* that spring. He was a well-recognized Harvard historian who was commissioned as a Naval Reserve officer in order to gather material for his subsequent writing of a series of books on U.S. naval operations during the war. His visit to the flagship was fortuitous because it occurred only a few months after the November night battle when the memories of the participants were still fresh. At Lee's invitation he boarded the ship at Nouméa on 4 April. As Morison wrote in his diary, "The younger men were very cordial & the staff table in wardroom most entertaining—but Admiral Lee seemed shy of talking to me and Captain Davis was either suspicious or resentful of my coming aboard without his permission."

Morison remained on board for nearly two weeks and was able to observe the ship's operations at sea.[20]

With apparent freedom to mix and mingle, the visitor talked with a number of officers whom he considered congenial and heard their recollections of the night action. Morison, who was an accomplished sailor, got a chance to do some navigating, which he enjoyed. He was also trying to get access to records. He wrote that the documents were hard to come by and "no place to read 'em when I get 'em except flag office where light is poor & air foul. But it's a privilege to be on such a noble BB." The ship steamed in the Coral Sea in case the Japanese showed up; antiaircraft drills were part of the program.[21]

Gradually Lee loosened up. On 13 April Morison and Lee got around to discussing the November night battle, especially the maneuvers the battleships made to avoid the burning destroyers in their path. He speculated that one "hit" the *South Dakota* incurred was probably the result of exploding depth charges from the destroyer *Walke*. Morison observed gunnery practice on 14 April from a high perch known as sky forward. He noted that when the *Washington* fired at a target 15,000 yards away, it took twenty-two seconds for the projectile to travel and twenty-seven to thirty seconds for the splash to subside.[22]

The next day Lieutenant Commander Ed Hooper told Morison that after the encounter with the Japanese heavies on 15 November, Lee had an opportunity to steam on and attack the transports that had landed at Guadalcanal. According to Hooper, "a great many deplored" the admiral's refusal to fire on them. Hooper believed the admiral was too cautious in not attacking, but Hooper was mistaken. The transports were farther away. Lee concluded that the ships were combatants, part of Admiral Kondo's striking force. They posed a threat that transports did not; a track of one of them at twenty-nine knots bore out his judgment. Lee did concede that early in the battle he had "naively" used the U.S. destroyers to counter enemy destroyers. Obviously, that did not work. In sum, Lee told Morison that he had fulfilled his mission of countering the Japanese heavy force.[23]

Captain Thomas Gatch of the *South Dakota* had been seriously wounded during the Santa Cruz battle, and temporary command of the ship went to his executive officer, Commander Archibald Uehlinger. Gatch was sent ashore and in 1943 was promoted to rear admiral when he became the Navy's top lawyer, the judge advocate general. Glenn Davis, some months after he also became a rear admiral, had a meeting with Lee, and the subject of the *South Dakota*'s September 1942 grounding at Tongatabu came up. An investigation took place shortly after the incident, and Davis inquired about it. It was probably with a twinkle in his eye that Lee told his former flag captain, "That's still in my safe. I never forwarded it. I guess I can send in that investigation now." Lee was not the vindictive type; instead, he was inclined to be forgiving. By waiting until Gatch was promoted and no longer in a seagoing billet, the report could do no harm to his career. Ray Thompson had earlier asked Lee about the grounding report, and Lee also told him that he was sitting on it for a while.[24]

An insight into the relationship Lee had with the crew of the flagship *Washington* came from Lorenzo Russo, a young quartermaster who stood his watches on the bridge. One night while the ship was steaming in formation, Russo was staring out into the darkness feeling "half homesick I guess." Lee walked up behind him and stood alongside. Soon Lee asked the quartermaster his name and where he was from, and, as Russo remembered, "That kind of made me feel real good again." Lee never forgot his name after that. Russo also enjoyed hearing from the "older salts" on board; they recalled the time Lee commanded a four-stack destroyer on the China Station.[25]

Another incident that endeared Lee to the crew occurred one Sunday afternoon while the ship was anchored at Nouméa. Russo and his shipmates were engaged in a poker game on the wing of the bridge. (It was an unusually overt venue, since gambling was against regulations, and sailors generally opted for more clandestine locales for their wagering.) In this instance, a blanket lay on the deck, and a fair amount of money was on the blanket. Lee approached, trailed by his Marine orderly. Russo and his cohorts all started to leap to attention, but the admiral quickly raised his arms and said, "Continue with your game, boys. Don't mind me." Lee then stepped over the blanket, taking care not to step on the money or cards.[26] Radarman Third Class Patrick Gormley observed that Lee didn't strut his rank, just the opposite: "I remember sailors lying around or sleeping, yet it was plain to see he would step around them so carefully."[27]

Once, as the evening was getting dark, Lee, the tobacco addict, lit up a cigarette on the wing of the bridge. This was a definite no-no during war at sea. The rationale was that the tip of a cigarette might be seen by the crew of a prowling submarine and thus endanger the battleship. Russo saw the bright orange glow before he recognized the person at the other end of the cigarette. He hollered, "Put out that cigarette." Lee quickly did so.[28]

There was another light-related incident. Generally, the combat information center was kept at a low light level so as not to overwhelm the phosphorescent pips on radar screens. Even so, there was a light-lock arrangement that plunged the space into complete darkness so that no light would leak to the outside when a watertight door was opened to enable someone to enter or leave. One night the lights remained out longer than usual while someone fumbled with the door. Lieutenant (j.g.) E. F. Kendall reacted by yelling, "Shut the god-damned door!" As he did so, the door closed, the dim lights went back on, and there was Lee. The junior officer quickly added, "Admiral, sir!" Lee politely overlooked Kendall's reaction.[29]

On 16 April, Lee got a new figurative hat while still remaining as commander, Battleship Division Six. His concurrent new billet was as commander, Battleships Pacific Fleet. Coincidentally, the officer he relieved was Vice Admiral Herbert Fairfax Leary, who had held the job since September 1942. Leary was also his predecessor as director of Fleet Training in Washington. Ironically, shortly after the attack on Pearl Harbor, Leary said to a friend, "This is an airpower war. There's no place for an old battleship horse like me."[30] Once Lee relieved him, Leary spent the rest of the war in billets ashore.

In his new role as type commander, Admiral Lee was responsible for evolving doctrine and procedures. He also had a say in the assignments of ship captains and battleship division commanders. He had a wide knowledge of senior surface officers, because great store was placed on service reputations. He also had the opportunity to observe how the subordinates performed during operations. He was able to influence assignments and exercise veto power if necessary, though the Bureau of Naval Personnel had the final say. Occasionally he would suggest the sidelines for those who weren't up to snuff, observed Lee's aide Guil Aertsen: "I know he was . . . very swift in his exercise of power in getting a guy dumped on the beach if he showed signs of incompetence once he was out there, either as an executive officer or a captain." This was not something that happened often because the deadwood in the front ranks at the time of Pearl Harbor had already been eliminated. Even so, conditions could change. Aertsen cited the case of one unnamed officer who had been excellent as a battleship skipper and division commander but finally succumbed to exhaustion and was no longer as capable as before. Lee assessed the situation and arranged for a quiet transfer.[31]

On 27 April, Captain Davis turned over command of the flagship to Captain James Maher. Davis was immediately promoted to rear admiral and became commander, Battleship Division Eight, subordinate to Lee's command. The *Washington*, accompanied by three destroyers, finally departed Nouméa on 29 April. The following day, after a refueling stop at Efate in the New Hebrides, she headed for the Hawaiian Islands. En route she joined up with Task Force 16, including the carrier *Enterprise*, and the ships reached Pearl Harbor on 8 May. For the next three weeks the *Washington* joined other ships to form Task Force 60. They engaged in battle maneuvers, including gunnery practice, to prepare for future operations.[32]

First Lieutenant Shuichiro Kato, a Japanese army officer who had surrendered to the Americans during the Guadalcanal struggle, was a passenger on the journey to Hawaii. His new custodian was Captain Jonas Platt, head of the *Washington*'s Marine detachment. Befitting Kato's status as an officer, he bunked in a stateroom in flag country. He had a Marine guard twenty-four hours a day. He was essentially treated as a pet, provided with cigarettes, chocolate, and American magazines. The latter he could not read, but he enjoyed the pictures. The prisoner was polite and passive, for his new existence was surely preferable to being shot at. One *Washington* enlisted man complained that the POW got better treatment than the sailor did.[33] At Pearl Harbor, Kato was delivered to Army military policemen who were likely not as hospitable as the battleship's crew had been.

In May the flagship entered the Pearl Harbor Navy Yard for repairs and over-haul. She had been deployed since the previous summer, and it was time for upkeep and modernization. Relocation of the SG radar antenna to the top of the forward superstructure was included in the yard work, thus giving it 360-degree coverage of its surroundings—something that had been sorely missing in the Guadalcanal night action.[34]

With his new additional billet as commander of battleships, Pacific (ComBat-Pac), Lee (accompanied by his aide, Guil Aertsen) had flown on ahead before the ship reached Hawaii. There Lee met up with the staff that took care of admin-istrative matters. In particular the type command was involved in dispatching personnel to the various battleships. For a time, some officers were concerned that the seagoing staff would break up. The remainder of the staff moved to the *Massachusetts* for temporary duty with the commander of Battleship Division Eight, Admiral Davis. In early June the staff's senior officers flew to Hawaii to resume duty with Lee. To rejoin the group that went ahead early, the junior officers and the enlisted personnel of the flag allowance went from Nouméa to Pearl Harbor on board the plodding Liberty ship *Elihu Thomson*.[35]

While in Hawaii, Lee hosted a party for some of his staff members at the Halekulani, a grand hotel on Waikiki Beach in Honolulu. It was a welcome break for relaxation after some of the side operations in which the *Washington* participated. As Guil Aertsen described, "It was a good wet party, and everybody was having a good time." The downside was that some of the officers were talking shop, saying things not intended for alien ears. All of a sudden, a beachboy-type individual came in and joined the group. Being the resourceful aide that he was, Aertsen began putting together a mickey for the interloper, but Lee interceded and said, "No, Guil, don't do that; he'll never forgive you." Lee saw what the unwelcome visitor was drinking and advised, "Look, put straight gin in that ginger ale bottle, and he'll fix himself up." The visitor mixed his own drink, and in time the beachboy's ability to make any sense of classified information disappeared.[36]

On another occasion, Lee's enlisted driver went to the Pearl Harbor officers' club and said he was there to pick up a bottle of I. W. Harper whiskey for the admiral. What he didn't tell the man behind the bar was that he, not the admiral, intended to drink it himself. Captain Jennings, the straight-laced chief of staff, learned of the chicanery and questioned the man in Lee's presence. His purpose was evidently to see the man be disciplined for his action. Instead, Lee said, "No, any time you need it, just go ahead and ask." Aertsen remembered that Jennings was frustrated as hell and added, "Jennings was very military, very rank conscious, very punctual, very this, this, this, and this." Yet the two functioned well as a team because Jennings took care of the details that Lee didn't want to be bothered with. Both Jennings and, presumably, the driver felt a great deal of loyalty to the old man. As Aertsen described the relationship between the men with opposite personalities, Lee was the one with the imagination, and Jennings was the one who implemented Lee's ideas.[37]

Ensign William Bentinck-Smith did not have such a positive impression of the chief of staff. Once he overheard Aertsen ask a seaman, "Would you please go down to my cabin and get the signal book on my bunk?" Jennings exploded, "Don't ever say please when you give an order to an enlisted man!" Another day Jennings asked a question of a junior officer. The young man replied, "I'm sorry, I don't know, sir." Jennings retorted, "A naval officer never says he does not know!"[38]

A welcome addition during the shipyard period beefed up the *Washington*'s antiaircraft capability considerably. In place of the touchy 1.1-inch guns came the installation of fifteen quadruple 40-mm mounts. They would prove useful in the carrier task force operations that lay ahead. The main battery fire control radar setup was improved with the addition of a system known as a servo that directly relayed information from plotting rooms to directors, which now were equipped with the Mark 8 fire control radar. That avoided the use of a phone connection. Hooper explained that with "this high-resolution radar, you could see the fall of shots and do the correcting right down there." In addition, Hooper used "midnight requisitioning" to obtain a radar repeater for the fire control tower. It was a productive time in the yard.[39]

Once the upgrades were finished, the *Washington* diversified her ammunition load with the addition of high-explosive projectiles that had point-detonating fuzes that would explode on impact with shore targets. Lieutenant Commander Ed Hooper supervised the servo work and the installation of more radar repeaters. The combat information center was relocated down inside the ship, where there was more room than in the jury-rigged setup in the former flag sea cabin. The Navy yard replaced the CXAM air-search radar with the newer SK, which had improved displays. Lee preferred the CXAM's ability to detect contacts at greater range than the new equipment, which operated at a higher frequency. But he did not oppose the change, figuring it was the ship's business, and the *Washington* would not necessarily remain his flagship.[40]

Once the yard period was completed, the *Washington* headed back to war. The immediate destination was Havannah Harbor in the island of Efate. When she entered port, Captain Platt was topside, near turret one, with his Marines. He was decked out in dress uniform so that the *Washington* could render and receive passing honors from other ships in the harbor. The ship's sailors were in whites. As the ship approached her assigned anchorage, skipper James Maher gave orders in what Platt later recalled as a "stentorian" voice, "Back down full. Let go the starboard anchor."

The forecastle crew followed the order by releasing a metal device known as a pelican hook because of its shape. That freed the anchor, and the chain kept going and going, creating a deafening clatter as fathom after fathom tumbled downward. The chain gathered so much momentum that the brakes on the forecastle could not stop it. The noise and movement finally ceased when the rear end ripped loose from its fastening in the chain locker and followed the predecessor links overboard and into the harbor. Platt got his Marines out of the way so the bitter of the end of the chain didn't act as a scythe in their direction as it departed. Fortunately, it bucked vertically rather than horizontally. The port anchor was then permitted to descend much more cautiously to hold the ship in place. Once the incident was over, Platt accompanied Maher to an officers' club ashore. Lee and members of his staff were already there. As Platt recalled, Lee gently teased the skipper by saying, "Nice anchoring, Jim."[41]

Later in 1943, the Central Pacific island-hopping amphibious campaign would begin in earnest with the aircraft carriers forming the principal striking force. The bulk of the naval combat that year took place in the upper Solomons, where the waters were too narrow for battleship operations. Indeed, there was little sea room around Guadalcanal, but the 14–15 November slugfest had been a case of dire emergency. The surface ships that carried the workload farther north were light cruisers and destroyers. Captain Arleigh Burke, commander of Destroyer Squadron 23, made his reputation there as an aggressive, even instinctive fighter. The Japanese also avoided sending heavy combatants into those same restricted waters. The fast battleships did provide a benefit by staying put until the Central Pacific offensive began. They did not proactively seek surface combat, but their presence in the general vicinity essentially constituted a fleet in being. That is, by remaining in the area, they may well have deterred offensive action by Japanese battleships. Some, including battleship scholar Malcolm Muir and Vice Admiral Ed Hooper, believed that the fast battleships could have made a more productive contribution to the war if they had been used more actively in 1943.[42] The decisions on where and when to deploy the ships, of course, were up to Halsey and his staff, not Lee. That said, Lee was not the assertive type; we can only guess whether he proposed more active employment.

In that summer of 1943, after being with the fleet for eight months, Lieutenant James Van Allen went back to the Applied Physics Lab to read reports on the use of the proximity fuze in combat. He discovered that many duds resulted because the internal batteries had expired during the long sea transits to the combat area, sometimes in overheated stowage. He then returned to the forward area to meet with Lee and Commander Lloyd Mustin, who would later join Lee's staff. The solution was to set up stations at the ammunition depots at various islands and atolls where new batteries, flown in by air, could be inserted into the projectile fuzes.

Van Allen remained on active duty until he transferred to the inactive reserve as a lieutenant commander in 1946. From there, he went on to international renown. In 1959, at the dawn of the space age, a satellite with one of his devices on board discovered a phenomenon of intense radiation encircling the globe, now known as the Van Allen Radiation Belt. He was *Time* magazine's man of the year in 1960. Of his wartime service, Van Allen later reflected, "Among other things that I learned in the navy by close observation of my peers and superiors was how to make a sound decision when the basis for a decision was diffuse, inadequate, and bewildering. This lesson has served me well."[43]

From time to time, newspaper correspondents visited Lee's flagship. He let them observe operations but, of course, prevented their access to classified information. Staff members were permitted to brief the visitors and give them the overall picture without getting into details. Lee himself considered the visitors to be a distraction. Commander Edwin Schanze, who was navigator and later executive officer during Lee's time on board the *Washington*, remembered, "I can state that Lee disliked publicity. It was clear throughout the war that Lee felt that his mission was to defeat the Japanese and he had a particular dislike for dramatic news stories involving himself and the ships under his command."[44]

■ ■ ■

Even though he was type commander for all Pacific Fleet battleships, Lee was not about to set up shop in Pearl Harbor, where the administrative portion of the staff was situated. That did not suit him, and it is unlikely it would have suited Admiral Nimitz. Lee set up a mini-staff that stayed under way often and took part in a variety of missions. One member of the inner group, Lieutenant Commander Bill Dawson, recalled, "He had his flag in anything and everything. . . . Admiral Lee had an obsession with just staying in the forward area." He had had one bite of the apple with the night surface action in November 1942 and wanted more from the orchard. His intent was to make sure that he would be the man available to command in a surface action, whenever it would take place.[45]

The seagoing admiral did not leave things to chance in that regard. On 14 August 1943 he sent a letter to Vice Admiral Richard S. Edwards, who was deputy CominCh on Admiral Ernest King's staff; he expressed his desire to remain at sea. In his "Dear Chink" response, Edwards teased Lee by writing, "I must say I deplore your pusillanimous attitude with regard to life in the front line trenches in Washington. You buzzards who have been basking in the sunshine of tropical islands can not expect to go on living a life of luxury forever. . . . Subject to the foregoing I concur in the opinion that the battleships are going to do a very important job and that you are the man to see that they do it." The upshot was that Lee was gone from the United States from August 1942 until June 1945. (Hawaii was then still a territory.)

In September came a truly odd assignment for a battleship commander. As commander, Task Force 11, Lee and his reassembled staff were on board the armed cargo ship *Hercules*, which was so infested with bedbugs that it was impossible to sleep below decks.[46] The mission was far from glamorous and did not require the skills Lee possessed. Perhaps he went along because it would provide an interesting change of pace. The objective was to occupy Baker Island, an atoll barely north of the equator and about halfway between Hawaii and Australia. The small task force, which landed on 1 September, included the dock landing ship *Ashland* to carry landing craft loaded with bulldozers. The light aircraft carriers *Princeton* and *Belleau Wood* were along to provide air cover, and four destroyers made up the escort. A transport and another cargo ship composed the rest of the task force.

The purpose was to build a landing strip that would enable aircraft to conduct photo reconnaissance for the upcoming invasions of the Marshall Islands. The first plane to land on the island was an Avenger from the *Princeton*, which did so on 7 September. The airstrip was completed by 11 September and that day an Army Air Forces fighter squadron landed to set up shop. On 15 September a bomber strip was completed. Nearby was Howland Island; its airstrip was intended as a stopover point for aviatrix Amelia Earhart during her ill-fated attempt to fly around the world in 1937. As Samuel Eliot Morison puckishly said of Howland, "Early in the war it had been bombed by American planes so that the Japanese could not use it, and by the Japanese so that the Americans could not use it; but both sides were poor marksmen and the strip was soon put into condition for use for emergency landings."[47] William Jennings, by now a captain, signed the thirteen-page report of the operation on Lee's behalf, because Lee had already departed.[48]

During that year of 1943, Lee did more hopscotching of ships. After the Baker operation, he wound up boarding the *Indiana* as a temporary flagship. Her skipper was Captain William Fechteler, who some years later served as Chief of Naval Operations; their friendship went way back. During the continuing lull before the Gilbert Islands operation, the *Indiana* and Lee were in Pearl Harbor. Commander Freddie Withington was the ship's executive officer. Years later he still had vivid memories of a party he attended there. He recalled that some girls were present. The event took place in a nice house, and, said Withington, "Everybody had a good time and got thoroughly pickled, including Admiral Lee. And he ended up spending the night alone, asleep outside the house. The rest of us—at least we found some beds. He was the life of the party." Withington concluded that both Fechteler and Lee were outstanding when it came to relaxing.[49]

■ ■ ■

In the late summer, Rear Admiral Davis, former skipper in the *Washington*, was embarked on board the *Massachusetts*, a near-sister of the *South Dakota*. One day Lee, as commander of all the fast battleships, paid a visit to Davis' flagship. A junior officer named Joseph Bryan III (who later served as the coauthor and actual writer of *Admiral Halsey's Story*) had also come on board that day. Bryan arrived by highline from the oiler *Tappahannock* along with many bags of incoming mail. Soon afterward, remembered Bryan, Father Joseph Moody, the ship's chaplain, made an announcement, "We have just taken aboard forty-six bags of mail and one staff lieutenant [Bryan]. Let us all give fervent thanks that we did not take aboard one bag of mail and forty-six staff lieutenants."

This was Bryan's first experience on board a battleship, and he was literally lost at sea. He had scarcely reported to the executive officer and been shown to his battle station when another announcement over the 1MC circuit said, "Rear admiral, arriving." Bryan was sent to the quarterdeck to escort Lee to the bridge. As he recalled years later, "I found the quarterdeck all right, but on my way back to the bridge, I got helplessly lost and made a number of detours, including one through the crew's head." Lee demonstrated his patience with the junior officer, going through the roundabout route before expressing his only reaction, "Been aboard long, son?"

Bryan replied, "Two hours, sir." Lee did not report him to the admiral or chief of staff, for which Bryan was grateful.[50]

While Lee's ragtag force was involved in the Baker operation, the fast carriers were building up experience and doctrinal know-how for the coming Central Pacific campaign. Rear Admiral Charles Pownall led the strike force during an air raid against Marcus Island, which had last been hit by a Halsey attack in early 1942. Pownall's Task Force 15 comprised the carriers *Yorktown*, *Essex*, and *Independence*, battleship *Indiana*, two cruisers, and ten destroyers. Pownall and his staff put the three carriers at the center of the formation, where they were surrounded by the antiaircraft ships. It was a disposition that served as a model for many operations to come.

Because of concern about the welfare of his aviators, Pownall got in touch with Vice Admiral Charles Lockwood, commander of Pacific Fleet submarines, and asked that submarines be posted in the vicinity of strike areas to recover downed aviators. Pownall's force hit the Gilberts on 18–19 September. Rear Admiral Alfred E. Montgomery commanded a similar attack against Wake Island on 6 October. Heavy ships provided antiaircraft protection, and again submarines proved their worth as rescuers of downed fliers. This practice was also carried into the future. Damage to the enemy in these various hit-and-run attacks was limited, but the raids provided valuable experience. As Admiral Morison observed, "Battle is the best battle practice."[51]

The date 11 November was still celebrated in that era as Armistice Day, marking the anniversary of the end of World War I in 1918. On that day in 1943, Lee wrote a letter to his wife. Among other things, he reported that he was receiving *Time* and *Life* magazines, generally several weeks to months after publication. He also wrote, "See that 'Old Nameless' has now been named. Didnt think much of the book."[52]

On 18 December 1942, the *South Dakota* had limped to the New York Navy Yard for repair of the damage suffered in the Savo Island action. Sidney Shalett, a reporter for *The New York Times*, wrote a hurry-up book that glorified the ship's activities in the South Pacific. That was the book Lee didn't care for. For security reasons, her name was not revealed at the time of publication, so she acquired the sobriquets of "Battleship X," "Old Nameless," and, less delicately, "The Big Bastard." Captain Gatch of the *South Dakota* made substantial contributions to the book. He also published a first-person account of the ship's exploits titled, "The Battle Wagon Fights Back," in *The Saturday Evening Post* issue of 1 May 1943. Now, months later, the *South Dakota* was publicly identified as the mysterious battleship.

A week after Lee wrote to his wife, he received a letter from Gatch—by now a rear admiral. Gatch said several of his *South Dakota* shipmates had asked whether the ship would be awarded a presidential citation now that her name had been announced. He said that the recommendation for such an award should come from the task force commander, namely, Lee. He added, "Such citations have been given rather freely of late. It occurs to me that perhaps the way the South Dakota carried on despite the punishment she took in the night action might be deemed worthy of the honor."[53] The *South Dakota* did subsequently receive a lesser award, the Navy Unit Commendation, for Santa Cruz and Savo Island.

Lee had put things in perspective earlier when his Marine orderly brought him a magazine article touting the achievements of "Battleship X." The admiral responded, "Son, we've got to do something for the morale of the people back home, but we know who won the battle."[54]

▪ 12 ▪

CENTRAL PACIFIC CAMPAIGN
Autumn 1943–Summer 1944

After whiling away nearly a year following the Savo Island engagement near Guadalcanal, Lee's battleships got back into combat in the autumn of 1943 while supporting the invasion of the Gilbert Islands. This was the start of the island-hopping campaign that would eventually lead to Japan. The battleships were to be valued not so much for their big guns, but for their smaller ones; they would provide antiaircraft protection while operating as part of carrier task groups. This validated Lee's push in the prewar period to get as many antiaircraft guns to sea as possible.[1]

In the early phases of the Central Pacific campaign, the primary opposition to American forces came once the troops were ashore. Vice Admiral Raymond Spruance, Commander, Central Pacific Force, had directed that both old battleships and new would join to form a battle line under Lee to deal with a challenge from the Japanese Navy. As it happened, on 24 November the submarine *I-175* torpedoed and sank the escort carrier *Liscome Bay* during the Gilberts operation, but there was no real challenge to the U.S. fleet from large surface combatants. In part that situation came about because a shortage of refining capacity forced the Japanese to husband their fuel carefully. During part of the war, they got crude oil in Borneo and burned it in warships. However, there were two main drawbacks—added fire hazard from fumes and damage to ships' boilers.

Although his ships had been blended into the fast carrier task groups during the campaign to invade the Gilberts, Admiral Lee got a rare opportunity to exercise tactical command on 8 December 1943. The operation was an air-sea attack on the flyspeck island of Nauru, northeast of the Solomons. It had a phosphate operation and airstrips and was sufficiently well defended by the Japanese that U.S. forces bypassed it rather than invading. It did, however, provide an opportunity for all six of the fast battleships in theater to participate as a unit and test their abilities at shore bombardment. The ships involved were the *North Carolina, Washington, South Dakota, Indiana, Massachusetts,* and *Alabama.*[2]

Captain Jonas Platt of the ship's Marine detachment was impressed by his observations on board Lee's flagship. He recalled it as a "clear, jewel-like morning." He had a great vantage from his post in a secondary battery director. Years afterward his mind's eye visualized seeing the battleships approach the beach while steaming parallel to each other. On signal, the ships turned simultaneously to form a column parallel to the shore.[3] At 0700, on Lee's signal, transmitted by flags, all six ships unleashed nine-gun salvos toward the coast. Fifty-four 16-inch projectiles were in the air simultaneously. The opening range was thirty thousand yards, and the ships moved gradually closer during forty minutes of firing, bringing the accompanying destroyers into position to fire as well. When the results were added, the American ships had fired 810 16-inch projectiles and 3,400 of 5-inch. Later the carriers *Bunker Hill* and *Monterey* strafed and bombed the island as well.[4] Rear Admiral Frederick Sherman had long service in carriers during the war and admired Lee. Even so, he resented the fact that a surface admiral should command combined air and surface forces during the operation. Lee was the senior of the two.[5]

As it happened, the old battleships, which had taken little part in the early phases of the war because of the shortage of fuel, became proficient at shore bombardment as their primary mission. They had much more opportunity to develop their craft because they, unlike the fast battleships, were not tied to carrier screens. Another boost came with the advent of high-explosive battleship ammunition. Up until then, battleship barbettes had been filled with armor-piercing ammunition, which had little utility against shore targets. The new projectiles had point-detonating fuzes that exploded upon contact with the ground. Though the *Washington* got the high-explosive type at Pearl Harbor, it was not yet available to all of Lee's ships. An officer in the *Indiana* remarked of the Nauru bombardment, "It was great for morale, but I'm sure we did no harm."[6] Commander Freddie Withington, exec of the *Indiana*, observed that the bombardment made a few holes in the ground but did little damage. A Japanese projectile hit the destroyer *Boyd* and killed ten crew members. Withington felt the event was more favorable for the Japanese than the Americans.[7]

During the early months of the Central Pacific offensive, Rear Admiral Charles A. "Baldy" Pownall commanded the fast carriers that supported the landings. Air strikes hit Marcus Island and the Gilberts. A later attack on 4 December was against Kwajalein in the Marshalls as the fleet prepared for a landing there in early 1944. It was successful in damaging and destroying Japanese aircraft, but senior naval aviators faulted Pownall as overly cautious in being unwilling to launch a second strike and thus to destroy many more aircraft that remained untouched. His decision not to send a follow-up attack on Kwajalein resulted directly in a torpedo hit on the carrier *Lexington*.[8] Pownall's hesitance was rooted in a desire to protect his aviators and ships.

On 27 December Pownall received notification that he was to be relieved as commander of the fast carrier force. The explanation was that the aviation armada needed a more aggressive commander. The new man was Rear Admiral Marc A. "Pete" Mitscher, who was originally a classmate of Lee at the Naval Academy but eventually graduated two years later. He was immediately available and he reported to his new job on 5 January 1944, when he relieved Admiral Pownall. The change in carrier commanders was a watershed event in improving the effectiveness of the fast carriers in the Pacific War.[9]

Lee had a special relationship with his aviation counterpart. The new arrangement involved an inversion of the relative seniority of the two officers; Lee had become a rear admiral earlier. However, because the task force was built around aircraft carriers, Mitscher had overall tactical command and Lee was subordinate. But that was not an obstacle because of Lee's personality and the nature of the job that had to be accomplished. The only times Lee exercised independent tactical command came when his ships separated from the carriers for shore bombardment or maneuvering exercises. A third possibility would present itself if heavy Japanese surface ships opposed the task force; in that case, Lee's ships would separate to take on the enemy combatants. During normal operations, Lee was largely a passenger in his flagship, though he was responsible for readiness training and for evaluating the performance of division commanders and the commanding officers of ships under him. Also, as the type commander, his staff dealt with administrative matters. He remained cognizant on the tactical picture to fulfill his responsibility for the ships that comprised the carrier screens.

Much of the two admirals' interaction in the combat area was through messages between ships, but they did take the opportunity to get together and chat in person during shore periods preceding operations. As Lee's aide Guil Aertsen explained of the pair, "There was a lot of attraction between [Mitscher] and Lee, because each one had qualities that the other lacked, and each admired it in the other guy. . . . And I think that's why they had this mutual respect."[10] Admiral Halsey summed it up best when he said, "Putting Ching Lee and Pete Mitscher together was the smartest thing the Navy ever did. You had the best surface tactics and the best air tactics the world has ever known."[11]

Lieutenant Commander Bill Dawson, who was the aviator on Lee's staff, observed that Lee had a complete appreciation of what aviation was contributing to the war. He recalled, "I don't think he felt any resentment that the . . . relatively young aviator admirals [Mitscher's two-star subordinates] were running the task groups, because, for the most part, the airplanes were doing most of the work. But he was always prepared and ready to take charge and run the surface forces."[12]

■ ■ ■

The coterie of fast battleships in the war zone received a major upgrade on 22 January 1944 when the first two thirty-three-knot behemoths, *Iowa* and *New Jersey*, arrived at Funafuti Atoll in the Ellice Islands. They had a six-knot speed advantage over the ships of the two preceding classes. Also in the anchorage were the sisters *Washington* and *North Carolina*, along with aircraft carriers, supply ships, tankers, and transports. Seaman Rafael Maza of the *New Jersey* was awestruck by the sight: "When we went there and we anchored, I never, never in my life had seen so many ships together."[13]

The new dreadnoughts brought with them an embarked flag officer, Rear Admiral Olaf Hustvedt, commander of Battleship Division Seven, on board the *Iowa*. He and the skippers of his two new ships paid a call on Rear Admiral Frederick Sherman, the air admiral on board the carrier *Bunker Hill*. They entered the conference with an attitude that they, the battleship people, had expected to win the war by showing up. Sherman soon set them straight: "I don't care whether or not you can shoot your 16-inch guns, but you'd better know how to use your anti-aircraft batteries."[14]

As the battleships steamed with the aircraft carriers on a regular basis, Lee's aide, Guil Aertsen, observed that the doctrine for placement of screening ships in formation had evolved since early in the war. At that time he was a junior officer in the cruiser *Chester*. In the circular formations in the periods shortly before and shortly after the attack on Pearl Harbor, the escorting ships were too close to the carriers, he recalled. The escorts in those days didn't have nearly the amount of antiaircraft gun power that they achieved later. They were still equipped with jam-prone 1.1-inch guns and had not yet acquired 20-mm and 40-mm guns in significant numbers. They had to be close to be useful, but the downside was that maneuvering was more difficult when ships were in close quarters. As Aertsen put it, "Everybody was in everybody's way." Another factor was the improvement in destroyers' sound gear. They could be farther away from the main body and still have sufficiently effective sonars to keep submarines from finding open pathways through the formations. As so often happens, changes in doctrine resulted from changes in weaponry and technology.[15]

Standard practice then, as now, required aircraft carriers to turn into the wind in order to land and launch planes. That inevitably required maneuvering to chase the wind. Aertsen found it highly desirable for the carriers to provide sufficient advance warning on their upcoming movements in order to enable the escorts to adjust. The escorts also had to be aware of the differing turning circles of the various classes of carriers, because standard practice required that the small boys keep out of the way of the bigger ones. During World War II, almost all of the carrier operations were in daytime, so the escorts were able to keep watch on what the carriers were doing.[16]

Always present in Admiral Lee's mind was the need to be ready to respond if called upon to engage Japanese surface ships. He had to find means of safely extricating the big ships from the carrier screens to haul off for other duty. That meant keeping a steady finger on the pulse of operations. The philosophy Lee imparted to his staff was that each ship was responsible for her own destiny. As Aertsen explained it, "You don't just sit on your hands and wait for an admiral in a carrier someplace to let you know you're standing into immediate danger." At all times under way, at least one member of Lee's staff was on watch in flag plot. If situations developed that called for action when Lee was asleep, recalled Aertsen, his orders to the staff officers were, "Do something. Don't wake me out of a sound sleep and wait around for me to try and wise up and then come up with some genius operation. Do something. If do nothing is a positive decision, then do nothing, but don't do it by default." All of this depended on training, knowledge of the operation orders, and adjusting to changing situations as necessary. And, of course, Lee spent a lot of his waking hours in flag plot, monitoring events in person.[17]

On 30 January 1944, the day before the invasion of Kwajalein Atoll in the Marshall Islands, Lee commanded Task Unit 58.1.3 during a bombardment of the southern part of the atoll. His command comprised the *Washington*, *Massachusetts*, and *Indiana*, which were accompanied by a division of destroyers. The battleships launched their Kingfisher floatplanes to spot the fall of shot, though Lee's after-action report said that these aircraft did not have sufficient endurance to observe the entire operation. He recommended that carrier planes be used in future missions. All told, the battleships fired 1,029 rounds of 16-inch high-explosive shells. The combined task unit sent out 8,215 rounds of 5-inch projectiles. In summing up, Lee's assessment was, "The bombardment appeared to be most effective and undoubtedly inflicted heavy damage on enemy personnel and installations."[18] On the day of the first amphibious landings, the chore fell to old battleships and heavy cruisers. As in the Gilberts, Lee had been designated to command the battle line if Japanese ships came out to contest the invasion, but again the Japanese did not.

Early on the morning watch of 1 February, the *Washington* and *Indiana* were steaming together at nineteen knots on course 340° while surrounded by a circular screen of destroyers. Their mission was to support the southern attack force for the invasion that was to begin just a few hours later. The *Indiana* was directed to maneuver independently to refuel some of the destroyers in the screen. At 0415 she came right to course 150° to head for a refueling rendezvous. The officers on watch on her bridge had evidently not been aware that another maneuver had been ordered, a change of course for the entire formation as part of a zigzag antisubmarine plan. Soon the *Indiana* officers spotted the *Washington*'s bow at a range of fifteen hundred yards, and both ships braced for collision. The *Washington*'s conning officer ordered emergency back full and put the rudder hard left, but it was too late. At 0428 the *Washington*'s bow rammed into the starboard quarter of the *Indiana*, just forward of the aircraft catapult. The hulls came together and sliced off more than two hundred feet of the *Indiana*'s armor belt. The *Washington*'s bow was smashed in and crumpled downward. From the *Washington*, three officers were killed and two officers and an enlisted man lost at sea.[19] Lieutenant (j.g.) Robert R. Kyser, the senior communications watch officer on Lee's staff, was one of those who died.[20]

In the aftermath of the smashup, Lee sent his Marine orderly to summon Lieutenant Commander Bill Dawson. The admiral didn't reveal the purpose of the summons, but the aviator surmised that it was to make sure he was all right. Dawson's stateroom was on the ship's starboard side, just abreast of the forward end of turret one. Dawson had heard the *crack-crack-crack* sound of the ramming but didn't realize the source of the noise. The strange odors and smoke he encountered on his way upward seemed not to register. When he did get up to see the admiral, Lee told him that as soon as damage estimates were arrived at for the two ships, he was to fly one of the ship's floatplanes ashore to make arrangements for emergency repairs.[21]

One of the nonmaterial casualties of the event was the killing of Captain James M. Steele's chances for further promotion. The *Indiana*'s skipper had taken over command only a few weeks earlier, on 13 January. He came to that job after Captain Forrest Sherman relieved him as war plans officer for Admiral Chester Nimitz, CinCPac. The typical practice of the era was for a promising captain to get his ticket punched with a big-ship command in order to be eligible for selection for rear admiral. A court of inquiry assessed the *Indiana* at fault because Steele did not properly communicate his intentions to other ships and did not appreciate the difficulties of maneuvering heavy ships at high speed in darkness. He had, after all, been on board less than a month. He would not remain much longer; he was relieved of command on 17 March when the *Indiana* was at Pearl Harbor Navy Yard for repairs.[22] Commander Freddie Withington had been the ship's executive officer and left shortly before the collision for other duty. He observed years later that it was unfortunate that both the skipper and new exec were inexperienced in running the ship. Withington stated bluntly, "The collision was entirely the fault of the new captain of the *Indiana*."[23]

Rear Admiral Glenn Davis, former *Washington* skipper, was on board the *Indiana* as division commander. He was in his bunk when the collision occurred. He had left word to be alerted if the ship was going to maneuver, but someone dropped the ball. He described the fast battleships at that point as "high-priced tankers." In discussing the situation with Lee afterward, he heard Lee say, "You know why I picked the *Indiana* [for the refueling assignment]? Because you were on it."

Davis replied, "I let you down on that one. I was in my bunk."[24] But, of course, there was nothing Davis could have done about it.

As the proverb goes, clouds can have silver linings. One who benefited from the accident was Major Jonas M. Platt, the commanding officer of the *Washington*'s Marine detachment. He had been part of the crew since 1941 and been on board during her venture with the British Home Fleet in early 1942. Notably, he had made a valuable contribution while commanding a portion of the ship's starboard 5-inch battery during the November 1942 night battle. During his time in the crew, he had made several requests to leave the ship so he could join a Marine ground combat unit. With the damaged *Washington* pulled out of action, his services were no longer needed. When the ship was at Pearl Harbor, he was released to the Fleet Marine Force. Subsequently, as a member of the First Marine Division, Platt participated in assault landings on Peleliu and Okinawa.[25] He eventually retired as a major general.

The *Washington* limped into Majuro, where she was fitted with a temporary bow. At Pearl Harbor the temporary bow was strengthened for the transit to the West Coast. At the Puget Sound Navy Yard in Bremerton, Washington, a prefabricated permanent bow was waiting at the end of the dry dock, ready to be installed. Some in the *Washington*'s crew groaned because they had hoped to be out of action for a longer period.[26] In any event, the ship was offline, as far as Admiral Lee was concerned, until the end of May. In the meantime, he and his staff embarked in the *North Carolina*, the *Washington*'s sister, as operations moved forward.

■ ■ ■

In mid-February 1944, U.S. naval personnel experienced a considerable degree of trepidation as they contemplated an attack on Truk Atoll in the Caroline Islands. It had a foreboding reputation as a tough nut to crack, a haven for major ships of the Japanese navy. The ships and aircraft there could pose a threat to imminent landings at Eniwetok in the Marshalls. It was to be a combined air-and-surface strike led by the new commander of the Central Pacific Force, Admiral Raymond Spruance. The carrier planes had the lead because the atoll provided protection to the Japanese ships inside.

In preparation for the attack, remembered aide Guil Aertsen, Lee and Mitscher were involved in planning together. One concern was the accuracy of the intelligence. Another was the safety of downed American pilots. A strong reason for the willingness of carrier pilots to run the risks they did was a conviction that Mitscher would do all he could to ensure their safe recovery. In some cases, the scout planes from the battleships were used to pick up downed aviators. As Aertsen put it, "Marc Mitscher's forces were peculiarly successful because his fliers knew that he was going to leave no stone unturned to get them back."[27]

As he exercised tactical command of the overall force, Spruance embarked in one of Lee's newly arrived battleships, the *New Jersey*, though Lee was not present for the operation. As Spruance's biographer Tom Buell wrote, Spruance's normal practice was to leave the operation of the ships to subordinates such as Mitscher. In this case, he held the baton for himself. Spruance was a long-time battleship man, having commanded the *Mississippi* in the late 1930s. His expectation was that Mitscher's attacks would flush out an anticipated slew of surface ships that his force could attack once they sought to escape from the atoll.

The carrier planes struck Truk on the morning of 16 February and found many targets. The Japanese did indeed seek to escape to open water. To counter them, Spruance had the *New Jersey* and *Iowa*, plus the cruisers *Minneapolis* and *New Orleans*, and four destroyers. They began to circle the atoll in column formation in which the tin cans were ahead of the American heavies. It resembled the approach Lee had used in the November 1942 night battle. Spruance rejected advice from his chief of staff, Captain Carl Moore, to change to a circular disposition that would be more effective against air attack. Buell reported, "Moore began to suspect that Spruance's motive for his independent expedition was sightseeing rather than ship hunting." Mitscher's planes would have been sufficient to take out fleeing Japanese ships. Another objective was probably to provide an in-your-face example to the Japanese of American naval superiority. Biographer Buell indicated that taking tactical command when his staff was much better suited to dealing with big-picture strategic situations was a failing on Spruance's part. Enemy destroyers got close enough to fire torpedoes that "missed the battleships through luck alone." It was not Spruance's finest hour.[28]

■ ■ ■

The *Lexington* arrived at the Majuro Atoll anchorage in the captured Marshall Islands on 8 March. She reached there from the Puget Sound Navy Yard, where she had received repairs to fix damage inflicted by a Japanese torpedo the previous December. Rear Admiral Mitscher and his Task Force 58 staff embarked in the carrier to prepare for action. Alan C. Byers, a civilian technical observer from the radiation laboratory at the Massachusetts Institute of Technology, was on board the new flagship. His primary mission was to coordinate evaluations of new radars. When Lee learned of Byers' proximity, he dispatched his barge to bring him to the *North Carolina*. Byers found the admiral to be enthusiastic about all aspects of radar and was keen to learn of new developments. He was interested in the SP height finder but decided it was not for battleships because it would involve sacrificing another type of radar, and there was not much prospect of doing fighter-direction work. That was best left to the aircraft carriers. Lee did seek a radar that could measure miss distances while tracking targets when his ships were performing the antiaircraft function. Lee was concerned about the effects that atmospheric variations would have on radar performance. The admiral also had other ideas for performing various functions, so Byers was later able to send him classified reports from MIT on project progress.[29]

On 18 March the *Iowa* and *New Jersey* had an opportunity as the newest fast battleships to get some live-fire practice in shore bombardment. This was the first time Lee was able to see the U.S. Navy's biggest battleships in action. He was on board the *Iowa*, ostensibly as an observer. The target was Mille Atoll in the Marshall Islands; it was nearest the Gilberts. It had been bypassed but still had stubborn Japanese occupants; air and submarine reconnaissance missions revealed that it had a large airfield and was well defended. The U.S. mission was a combination air-surface attack. Planes from the carrier *Lexington* bombed the island also. Lee was in overall command of the Mille surface striking group, which included the destroyers *Hull* and *Dewey*. The division commander, Rear Admiral Hustvedt, commanded the battleship component. Lieutenant Paul Backus, who had been through the Savo Island battle on board the *South Dakota*, was sent to the *Iowa* as an observer. The idea was that this combat veteran could impart some of the knowledge he had acquired in the past year and a half. Speaking of that day's outing, Backus said years later, "This was the cruise on which I was the most scared during the war, because I had nothing to do but observe."[30]

The bombardment lasted three hours in the morning and two in the afternoon. The two battleships began firing 1,900-pound 16-inch high-explosive rounds into the island.[31] They fired their turrets in turn at the objective, then gradually moved closer in. After this had gone on for hours, the U.S. dreadnoughts moved in to a range of 15,000 yards in order to give the 5-inch secondary battery some live-fire practice. The stubborn Japanese returned fire.[32]

Two Japanese projectiles hit the *Iowa* and caused damage to the face plate of a turret and to the port side of the hull. The damage raised the logical question—if your guns can far outrange the enemy's, why get in close enough to be hit? That was an early lesson for the new ships. Captain John McCrea, skipper of the *Iowa*, had an explanation. In his memoir he said that intelligence reports indicated the Japanese guns were 4.7 inches in diameter and that his ship would be safely out of range. When rounds came close to the ship, it was evident that the intelligence reports were wrong. The projectiles were larger. McCrea said he notified Lee and Hustvedt that he was altering course to seaward. McCrea's recollection was that he took the action on his own, though he had two flag officers on board.[33]

In his subsequent oral history, Hustvedt remembered, "I should like to record here my appreciation of the fact that Admiral Lee, although he was a very interested observer of the operation . . . never at any time interposed anything which could be interpreted as an interference with the plan which I had issued in my operation order nor with the movements as they were executed by the forces under my command."[34] Lieutenant Frank Pinney, assistant gunnery officer in the *Iowa*, had a different perception. He wrote later that Lee told Captain McCrea to move the ship out of range and save ammunition for more worthwhile targets.[35]

What really happened? That's a problem when memories are recorded long after the fact. In any case, Lieutenant Harry Reynolds of the *New Jersey*'s engineering department, summed up the situation in rhyme: "We looked silly at Mille."[36]

On 22 March—21 March in the United States, where President Roosevelt signed the official letter—Lee was promoted to vice admiral, as was his friend Marc Mitscher. Aide Guil Aertsen observed that Lee was "obviously pleased." As usual, little tasks fell to Aertsen where the admiral was concerned. He got the ship's metalsmith to take three sets of two-star insignia and turn them into two sets of three-star insignia for Lee's collar tabs. Aertsen was involved in pinning on the new collar devices. The admiral himself didn't make a big deal about it, but it conferred a couple of benefits—a raise in pay and a validation of the role of the fast battleships in the wide-ranging campaign against the Japanese. There was another wrinkle involved. Lee had been senior to Mitscher as a rear admiral, so there was potentially some slight awkwardness in the rank-inversion setup when Lee was subordinate tactically to Mitscher. From now on they were on the same level of seniority.[37]

In that same month, Mitscher acquired a new chief of staff in the person of Commodore Arleigh Burke, who had distinguished himself as a destroyer squadron commander in the Solomons campaign. This was part of a new policy on the part of Admiral Ernest King, who dictated that aviation admirals should have surface chiefs of staff and vice versa. Mitscher had long relied on Captain Truman Hedding, an aviator, but now Hedding had to go. Mitscher was initially not happy with the new arrival, but gradually he warmed up, and fairly soon Burke gained his respect. Mitscher came to rely on him so much that Burke became, in his own description, Mitscher's "hatchet man." He said that when Mitscher felt that a two-star task group commander "was lacking in aggressiveness, or lacking in courage, or lacking in skill, or lacking in leadership—any quality at all that he felt that he was not a good commander, we'd talk about it." Then Burke would fly over to the task group commander's flagship and tell him it was time to go home. Other aviation rear admirals had been riding carriers as observers, and they would be the replacements for the ones who were relieved. Burke remembered that some surface officers also demonstrated the qualities that Mitscher would not permit in his carrier admirals. Burke asked if he could relieve those individuals as well. Mitscher's response was, "No, that's not my job."

Burke said, "Admiral, you're the head of this whole force."

Mitscher replied, "I know, I know, I know, I've got the same authority. I know that, but I don't have the feel of battleship admirals and surface admirals."

Burke responded, "I have."

Mitscher's rejoinder, "Yes, but you don't have the authority. But I'll tell you what you can do, though. You go over and see Ching and talk to him about it."

Burke did talk to Lee, who said he wouldn't go along with Burke's recommendations. Lee said, "They're not under my command. They're under Admiral Mitscher's command." Burke got irritated at him. Lee agreed with the evaluations of the junior admirals by Burke, who didn't think they were as good as they should be—not as willing to go into battle. (Arleigh Burke's recollection on this point differed from that of aide Guil Aertsen, who said that Lee did not hesitate of get rid of subordinates who were not performing up to expectations.) The upshot was that Lee believed it was Mitscher's call, and Mitscher wasn't willing to invade Lee's turf. As Burke put it, "Mitscher had a very high regard for Lee, probably liked Lee better than any other of his flag officers. He would ask Lee for advice lots of times on a personal message . . . and I know [Lee] had the same high regard for Mitscher. They were very careful of each other's toes." Burke observed that Lee completely accepted his subordination to Admiral Mitscher, and that the two exchanged jokes in their private exchanges.[38]

■ ■ ■

Two lieutenant commanders, Ray Thompson and Bill Dawson, were regular watchstanders in flag plot while the flagship was under way. They both graduated from the Naval Academy in the class of 1933, twenty-five years after Lee. Dawson remembered years later that Admiral Lee took a fatherly interest in them. Lieutenant (j.g.) William Bentinck-Smith, a communications watch officer, was another staff officer who served Lee. Years later he recounted that one of his duties on "seemingly innumerable occasions" was to wake up the admiral to deliver a message deemed important. He explained that whenever he did wake Lee, the admiral was always tolerant and never complained about being aroused unnecessarily. A typical reaction: "He would grunt a bit, seem to shake himself awake, sit on the edge of the bunk in his pajamas, light the light, wiggle his feet into an old pair of slippers and then fumble for his glasses." Usually he would light up a cigarette as he thought about the latest message, considered a potential response, and then went through the file of decoded dispatches that had arrived since he went to bed. In such moments, the young officer felt a sympathetic kinship for a man who appeared prematurely aging and weary but was still alert and wise.[39]

On 14 April 1944, the title of Central Pacific Force, commanded by Admiral Spruance, was abolished. In its place came the new designation, Fifth Fleet. Admiral Halsey's command, formerly South Pacific Force, became the Third Fleet. Both were under the aegis of Admiral Nimitz, CinCPac, in Hawaii. As the war progressed, the nomenclature shifted whenever Halsey and Spruance shifted command between them—even though the ships essentially stayed the same, except for the inevitable arrivals and departures. The system was characterized as involving the same horses but with different riders at various times.[40]

In late April, the target for invasion was Hollandia, New Guinea, as part of General Douglas MacArthur's campaign on that island. Admiral Nimitz emphasized that the primary objective was to destroy ships of the Japanese fleet if they came out to fight. To that end, Lee, on board the *North Carolina*, was designated as commander, Task Group 58.1, a force that comprised six fast battleships, thirteen cruisers, and twenty-two destroyers. Mitscher's carrier groups would provide air attacks from some distance away. The invasion was executed on schedule on 22 April, but the Japanese fleet refused to take the bait; no surface battle ensued. As the month closed down, the ships headed back to the Marshall Islands. En route, the carrier force put Truk out of business as an operating base.

On 1 May Lee and his fast battleships received an opportunity to operate independently from the carriers and unleash their big guns. The target in this case was the tree-clad island of Ponape, the largest of the Caroline Islands. It had a harbor, a seaplane base, one airfield already completed, and another under construction. Instead of the usual pose of standing by for possible action, this was a real action with Admiral Lee in tactical command. His battle line force, which was supported by destroyers, comprised the new battleships *Iowa* and *New Jersey*, and older ones, *North Carolina*, *South Dakota*, *Massachusetts*, and *Alabama*. The *Washington* was still back on the West Coast for post-collision damage repair. Lee was on board the *North Carolina*. Rear Admiral Joseph J. "Jocko" Clark's Task Group 58.2 stood off to provide air protection if needed.

It was something of a reversion to the prewar practice of carriers in a support role for the battle line. The 16-inch projectiles rained ashore for seventy minutes until Lee concluded that there were no further targets that merited destruction. Token opposition came from Japanese antiaircraft guns that ceased firing when the curtain of steel arrived from offshore. The benefit from the operation was that the battleships were able to steam together and fire against live targets.[41] Six weeks later, in the Marianas, Lee concluded that the practice was not sufficient to try to engage heavy ships that were likely to fire back.

While Lee and his staff were in the *North Carolina*, gearing up for the invasion of the Marianas and awaiting the return of the *Washington* from repairs, they received a visitor from Pearl Harbor—Commander Harold Hopkins, a Royal Navy officer assigned to U.S. Pacific Fleet headquarters for liaison. Hopkins had been an observer for a number of operations, including the assault on Tarawa in the Gilberts. Rear Admiral Charles McMorris, Admiral Nimitz's chief of staff, decided that it was time for Hopkins to get some exposure to Pacific Fleet battleships and thus sent him to visit Lee.

Twenty years afterward, Hopkins published a memoir of his wartime experiences with the Americans and included some enjoyable vignettes about his time in the *North Carolina*. When he met Lee himself, the Royal Navy man offered this assessment, "From the moment I set eyes on Admiral Lee I knew I was going to like him. Stocky, and with a determined jaw, he *looked* a fine seaman, which he was." Hopkins' recollections, some of which may have been a bit on the fanciful side, purport to repeat dialogue involving the respective seashell collections that Jennings and Lee had gathered during their forays ashore. Jennings supposedly bragged that he had the finest shells in the ship, but then Hopkins said the admiral kept after him until he admitted that Lee's were even better.[42]

The seashell experience had a postscript. Lee collected three large wooden boxes of shells and coral and sent them to his wife. As it happened, they arrived on her birthday. After all the miles the boxes had traveled, Mabelle's sister compared the timing to making a hole in one. Lee's accompanying note read, "We made chowder from the clams instead of eating them on the half shell."[43]

Commander Hopkins had a chance to observe the atmosphere in the flagship. He noted the pleasure sailors had in reminiscing nostalgically when they saw pretty women in the movies and the even greater pleasure when they heard they were going to have a shipyard period that would permit some liberty in an American city rather than a tropical atoll. At the end of his stay in the *North Carolina*, the British visitor concluded, "I was extremely pleased to have served in Admiral Lee's flagship and to have had the opportunity of getting to know this most distinguished officer. He was, without doubt, one of the most effective battle leaders in the Pacific Fleet, with a particularly brilliant record in the early desperate days when everything had to be risked."[44]

■ ■ ■

On the afternoon of 14 May, the *North Carolina* was due to get under way from her anchorage at Majuro Atoll. Shortly before her departure, Lee and his ComBatPac staff shifted to the *New Jersey*, a slightly younger sister and near-twin of the *Iowa*. The principal difference was that the *Iowa* was configured as a fleet flagship and had one more level on her conning tower. The shift was part of the continuing process of musical battleships as Lee went from one to another while awaiting the return of the *Washington*. Also in port was the aircraft carrier *Lexington*, Admiral Mitscher's flagship. It is likely that Lee and Mitscher put their heads together on a number of occasions during the period as they planned for the upcoming invasion of the Marianas, a month away. It was their regular practice to do so in order to discuss tactics and potential contingencies.[45]

On 19 May the *New Jersey* went to sea with a number of officers from other ships on board as observers. Over the next three days, the ship unlimbered her main battery, secondary battery, and machine guns and responded to a simulated air attack by carrier planes. Not only did the visiting observers have an opportunity to view the shooting, but Lee himself also got an opportunity to evaluate the underway performance of yet another ship under his command. The ship was back at Majuro on the twenty-first. On 30 May, a covey of ships steamed into the atoll. Among them was a welcome sight for Lee: the *Washington* was back. That afternoon Lee transferred back to his former home along with ten staff officers and nineteen enlisted men of the flag allowance. The majority of the enlisted men were radiomen because of the importance of communications for a fleet in wartime. There were also two yeomen to handle paperwork, a signalman for visual communication, and two steward's mates to handle the care and feeding of members of the flag mess.[46]

■ ■ ■

Lee had been a pioneer in developing the idea of a combat information center to coordinate the receipt and coordination of information from radar and radio. It was at his direction in 1942 that the former admiral's sea cabin in the *Washington* had been converted into a makeshift CIC. Doctrine was continuing to evolve as the result of combat experience. As mentioned earlier, during the night battle of 12–13 November 1942, the officer in tactical command, Rear Admiral Dan Callaghan, had paid a lethal price for not having an appreciation for the value of information that radars could provide. Thus the new destroyer *Fletcher*, equipped with the latest SG surface-search radar, was tail-end Charlie of the thirteen ships in the column formation that subsequently collided with calamity.

Lieutenant Joseph. C. Wylie Jr., one of the *Fletcher*'s officers during that battle, became a de facto CIC expert. In 1943, Wylie was part of a team on the staff of Rear Admiral Mahlon Tisdale, the type commander for Pacific Fleet destroyers. Lieutenant Commander Caleb Laning was another team member. The group worked on physical layouts for CICs in order to optimize the various warfare challenges—air, surface, and subsurface. They designed it to be the electronic intelligence heart of the ship, not just a series of individual plots. In 1943 Tisdale issued a manual titled *CIC Handbook for Destroyers*. The destroyer plan called for each destroyer's executive officer to have his battle station as the evaluator who would coordinate the information flow while the skipper was on the bridge in charge of the ship's movements. Wylie then returned to the battlefront as an evangelist on this new way of making war.[47]

As historian Trent Hone explained in *Learning War*, his excellent book on Navy doctrinal development, Lee took a necessarily different approach in setting up procedures for battleship combat information centers, which he did in a tentative doctrine publication issued in June 1944. Obviously, the missions were different for the types of ships. Battleships were not equipped with sonars and thus left the antisubmarine mission to escorting ships. The big ships' missions focused on air and surface gunnery, and CICs played a major role in that. Thus, as mentioned previously, Lee decreed that the CIC function should be part of the gunnery department. In a battleship, the executive officer had a specified battle station in secondary conn, prepared to take command of the ship's movements if the primary conning station on the navigation bridge was disabled. Battleships' evaluators were chosen from among officers who demonstrated capability and experience.[48] A somewhat parallel function in an aircraft carrier was that of fighter direction officer (FDO). His mission was to keep track of incoming air raids and vector planes from the combat air patrol to intercept and destroy. The FDOs were to become extremely important in the battle for the Marianas. The battle kicked off on 15 June with the invasion of the island of Saipan. U.S. ships sent ashore a combination of soldiers and Marines.

With the American approach to the Marianas, the prospect of an invasion so close to the Japanese homeland was too grave to go unchallenged. Vice Admiral Jisaburo Ozawa's force at Tawi-Tawi in the Philippines and Vice Admiral Matome Ugaki's at Batjan in the Dutch East Indies both fueled with unrefined oil. They sortied on 13 June and headed for a rendezvous east of the Philippines.[49]

That same day Lee and a coterie of seven fast battleships, joined by a number of destroyers, left the carrier groups to deliver the first surface-ship bombardment of the islands of Saipan and Tinian. Saipan was to be the first of the Marianas to be invaded by U.S. forces; Tinian would come later. Tinian would prove to be the base for Army Air Forces B-29s launched for heavy bombing of the Japanese home islands. The old battleships were not scheduled to arrive for shore bombardment until the following day, so Lee's ships got first crack. Their crack was a dud. As Samuel Eliot Morison assessed the event, "Sad to relate, the bombardment of 13 June was a failure." The new battleships had not had sufficient practice in the slow, deliberate process of focusing on individual targets. Nor were the floatplanes of Lee's ships experienced in distinguishing targets, observing fall of shot, and sending appropriate corrections to the firing ships. The fast battleships' methods, Morison noted, differed considerably from the type of fire used against other ships. Thus most of the 16-inch and 5-inch projectiles went wild. A sailor with a sense of humor summarized the 13 June operation as a "Navy-sponsored farm project that simultaneously plows the fields, prunes the trees, harvests the crops, and adds iron to the soil."[50]

On the afternoon of 17 June, with the Japanese fleet approaching in an attempt to stymie the attempts by Americans to strengthen their foothold on Saipan, Admiral Spruance sent out his battle plan in a message to Lee and Mitscher: "Our air will first knock out enemy carriers then will attack enemy battleships and cruisers to slow or disable them. Battle line will destroy enemy fleet if enemy elects to fight or by sinking slowed or crippled ships if enemy retreats. Action against the enemy will be pushed vigorously by all hands to ensure complete destruction of his fleet. Destroyers running short of fuel may be returned to Saipan if necessary for refueling"[51] Spruance then specified that Mitscher would be in tactical command for the operation. He and Lee were to seek the best methods for engaging the Japanese under advantageous conditions.

At 0400 on 18 June, Mitscher and Lee received a scouting report from the submarine *Cavalla* that showed the Japanese fleet headed east toward Saipan at nineteen knots. As Mitscher's chief of staff, Commodore Arleigh Burke tried to urge Lee's forces into a surface action against the Japanese. Burke was aggressive and experienced in surface tactics. He believed that Lee's ships were well trained and battle hardened and that Lee would be eager to take on the Japanese fleet. On Mitscher's behalf, he sent a dispatch to the battleship commander: "Do you seek night engagement? It may be we can make air contact late this afternoon and attack tonight. Otherwise we should retire eastward tonight."[52]

Lee demurred in an emphatic message that left no doubt as to his preference: "Do not, repeat, not believe we should seek night engagement. Possible advantages of radar more than offset by difficulties of communications and lack of training in fleet tactics at night. Would press pursuit of damaged or fleeing enemy, however, at any time." Historian Clark Reynolds reported that both Mitscher in command of Task Force 58 and many officers on Nimitz's staff in Hawaii were "most disappointed," because Nimitz had emphasized the importance of destroying the Japanese fleet.[53]

Admiral Lee doubtless recalled the confused close-quarters action off Guadalcanal and that the Japanese were skilled at night operations. As his aide Guil Aertsen put it, "You have to recognize that if you're going to be the father protector for the carrier task force, and the air arm is going to be the one that really does the job, you don't have the time to train yourself and your ships to a level of sharpness that surface ships, operating on their own, would require." From Aertsen's perception, Lee knew that he was performing a valuable function in protecting the carriers, though he "was not happy in playing second dog." He did, however, recognize the realities of the situation and the obligation they conferred.[54]

In a sound recording he made ten months after the battle, Commodore Burke summarized the exchange of messages in rather prosaic language. He did, however, add a further possibility that might have occurred: "We could choose the time of attack. We could fight either during the night or the next morning." He added, "We also received a dispatch from ComFifth Fleet which stated that Task Force 58 must cover Saipan and our forces engaged in that operation and that he felt that the main enemy attack would come from the westward but it might be diverted to come in from the southwestward. Well, we thought so too."[55]

In an interview with this author thirty-two years after the battle, Burke was much less restrained than in his sound recording of 1945. He complained that Lee was not one to volunteer opinions and suggestions. He did not view it as a defect in Lee but instead as Lee's complete understanding of the responsibility of command.[56] Burke said of Lee's decision not to engage, "I was amazed that Admiral Lee did not want to do that." He did concede that Lee was concerned about being involved in a melee, and that such an engagement could take place only at night. (This contradicted his view in the 1945 recording that the battle could have taken place in the daytime.) Burke did say that he was not criticizing but tying the decision to Lee's sense of caution and the fact that being linked to carriers had not provided many opportunities to exercise independent command responsibility. He added, though, "You never can outguess another man."[57]

Dr. Allan Millett, distinguished professor of history at The Ohio State University, considered that Lee's explanation was really an excuse for having cold feet, not being willing to take the sort of risks that aviators and submariners did routinely during the war. Lee had remained in the battle area so he would be in position to engage the Japanese surface fleet, but in this instance declined when the opportunity was presented.[58]

Admiral Spruance was cautious about letting his ships stray too far from Saipan, lest they leave the beachheads vulnerable to a Japanese attack from a separate force that could slip in behind. Burke's suggestion that Lee might take on the enemy heavy combatants in the morning was at odds with the Japanese preference for night action. The idea that the American fleet could have chosen the time for the engagement is unlikely. The Japanese had the option to advance or retreat as it suited their purposes. As Clark Reynolds wrote, Lee had a healthy respect for night torpedo attacks by destroyers and submarines. He also said that Spruance had "naïve assumptions" even after the Gilberts and Truk, that a surface action was possible during daylight with carrier aircraft present. Spruance's handling of the *New Jersey* at Truk in February had nearly come a cropper. Reynolds, who well appreciated the power of naval aviation by this point in the war, added, "Being a formalist like Lee, leaving nothing to chance, Spruance then quickly supported Lee's decision and agreed to the alternative, a night retirement toward Saipan. Little did these battleship-weaned tacticians realize that *only at night* could a pure surface action take place in the presence of fast carrier forces."[59]

Among those who criticized Lee's decision not to engage the Japanese heavies was historian Malcolm Muir, who reported that some officers on board Lee's ships expressed surprise at their commander's decision. Lieutenant Frank Pinney was assistant gunnery officer of the *Iowa* during the Marianas campaign. Years later he wrote to Muir: "I recall the stated reason for not sending the fast battleships to look for the Japs in the Philippine Sea battle was lack of practice in night engagements. As far as my gunnery department was concerned, all our engagements, except for shore bombardments had been night shoots against Jap planes, and the main battery under full radar control couldn't have cared less whether it was day or night. I believe the other gunnery officers felt the same way."[60]

On the afternoon of 18 June Mitscher arranged his various carrier task groups to be prepared for the following day's actions. Burke, acting for Mitscher, deployed the battleships to the west of the carrier formations, that is, closer to the Japanese. Burke said he wished he had received more input from Lee regarding the deployment. Burke's reasoning was that it would "suck in the planes against a hell of a hard antiaircraft target." Task Force 58 would also provide air cover for Lee's heavy ships.

One result of that positioning came the following day when the *Alabama* provided the first radar detection of the approaching Japanese planes at a range of about 190 miles. Lee asked the *Iowa* to confirm the contact, which she did at 130 miles. Following the engagement, Lee saluted both ships: "To *Iowa*, well done. To *Alabama*, very well done."[61] Burke recalled that he probably asked Lee if he had an opinion regarding positioning the battleships to the west, and Lee didn't offer one. Afterward, Lee conceded that putting them there was a good idea.

On 19 June Lee had set up the antiaircraft screen in a circular formation with the *Indiana* in the center as guide. There were six more battleships and a covey

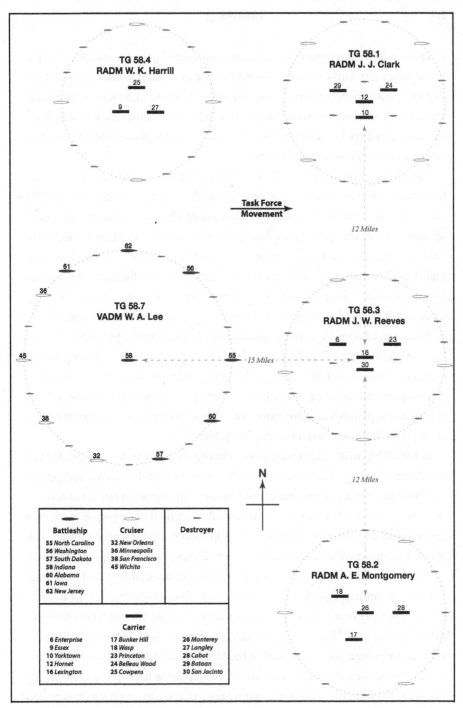

Map 5. Battle of the Philippine Sea, 19 June 1944

of cruisers and destroyers. It was a day that would gain the nickname "The Great Marianas Turkey Shoot" because of the one-sided results of the action. The Japanese lost more than 350 aircraft to the shooting of American pilots and antiaircraft gunners on board ships. An onslaught of Japanese carrier planes came toward Task Force 58 off Saipan. The U.S. fighter planes had a field day in sending enemy pilots to the afterlife.

Lieutenant Noble C. Harris Jr., who had recently joined Lee's staff as a communications and electronic countermeasures officer, got a close look at one of the attackers. Years later the memory was still vivid of a Japanese plane that flew right alongside the *Washington* with a dead pilot in its cockpit.[62] Captain Jennings, the chief of staff, remained glued to the PPI scope in the flag area during the battle and thus didn't get a chance to see the excitement outside firsthand. Lieutenant James Ross, who was on an antiaircraft defense station topside, said that Jennings missed quite a show, noting it was "the most spectacular event I ever saw."[63]

Lieutenant James Van Allen, who had briefed Lee on the proximity fuze in late 1942, rejoined the ComBatPac staff at Lee's request in 1944. He got a personal exposure to the combat use of projectiles with proximity fuzes. Even though the *Washington* had only a peripheral role in the battle, her gunners knocked down two Japanese planes that came close. As he remembered, "One exploded at such close range that it showered the ship with debris."[64]

A battleship that did get hammered during the air attack was Lee's former and future flagship, the *South Dakota*. She took a direct hit from a 500-pound bomb dropped by a Japanese Judy dive-bomber. The explosion put out of action a 40-mm quad mount and two 20-mm guns; it also killed twenty-seven crewmen and wounded another twenty-one. The ship fired on sixteen of the twenty-five planes that attacked the formation of which she was a part. Her guns shot down five of the sixteen. Despite the bomb hit, she kept on shooting and steaming. Later in the morning, gunfire from the *Alabama* discouraged two enemy torpedo planes that were headed toward what historian Samuel Eliot Morison sardonically referred to as "Japan's favorite target, *South Dakota*."[65] Early on June 20, after having wiped out a good deal of the Japanese air capability the day before, Task Force 58 steamed westward toward the Japanese fleet. Lee and his heavy surface ships were twenty-five miles out ahead of the carrier groups and poised for action, which they did not get. Mitscher sent out a long-range mission to attack the Japanese fleet. The enemy ships were so far away that the U.S. planes did only limited damage. They returned to Task Force 58 that night. Some planes landed on board carriers, some ditched in the sea, and some did not make it at all.

Of all the actions that Admiral Lee took during World War II, his decision not to engage the Japanese surface fleet in the Marianas campaign remains the most controversial and the one for which he has been criticized. The night action off Savo Island in 1942 had taken place out of desperate necessity, and it had been a narrow victory, especially because no Japanese torpedoes struck the flagship *Washington*. When the time came to take on the Japanese heavies, Lee expected that he could do so in a situation that provided his battle line with a clear tactical advantage—an element missing off Saipan. He remained in the war zone for so long because of the expectation that the opportunity was bound to come for his ships to display their prowess. The following chapter explains why they did not have that opportunity.

• 13 •

THE BATTLE OF LEYTE GULF
Summer—Autumn 1944

For many years, the Gun Club had run the Navy. For its members the traditional path to the top jobs involved service in destroyers, cruisers, and, of
course, battleships. Until the shock of Pearl Harbor in 1941, the battle line was
considered the "backbone of the fleet." Things changed fairly rapidly thereafter
with the ascendance of carriers, submarines, and the amphibious forces—the
types of ships needed to fight a war in the vast reaches of the Pacific Ocean. Of all
the flag officers who epitomized the Gun Club in 1944, Vice Admiral Willis Lee
was at the top. Battleship officers even carried wallet cards that proclaimed them
as fully qualified and honored members of the "Acme Gun Club," so named for
a brand of beer served at island outposts when the fleet was at anchor. Each card
carried a facsimile signature of the battleship's captain and that of Admiral Lee.
The illustration, perhaps reflecting Lee's propensity for humor, showed a battleship turret with a beer bottle as a barrel and a bottle cap being blasted upward.

The dominance of the Gun Club waned as the war progressed and battleships
found themselves relegated to a secondary role. Clark Reynolds put it bluntly in
his classic volume, *The Fast Carriers*. He wrote, "By the summer of 1944 the Gun
Club had lost control of the Navy, but the aviators had not quite taken over."[1] One
dramatic consequence of the change came at the direction of Admiral Ernest J.

King, the Chief of Naval Operations. King's edict of senior aviators having surface chiefs of staff and vice versa was what sent Commodore Arleigh Burke to Marc Mitscher's staff earlier in the year. Inevitably, the directive meant Lee had to take on an aviator. That came as a real blow, because Lee had relied on Captain Bill Jennings for years, and their personas meshed well. Jennings was not an aggressive type; he went along with what Lee wanted. Aide Guil Aertsen joked that, "If Lee sneezed, Jennings would have been the first one to say, 'God bless you.'"

In August, Jennings departed, and in his place came Commodore Thomas P. Jeter, who until then had been commanding officer of the carrier *Bunker Hill*. Jeter graduated from the Naval Academy ten years after Lee. In the 1920s he qualified as a naval aviator and served in aircraft squadrons. In 1924 he was in the Bureau of Aeronautics and had additional duty as a White House aide when Calvin Coolidge was president. That same year he received the bronze medal in fencing at the Paris Olympics. In the 1930s he commanded a fighter squadron and was operations officer on the staff of the commander of the Aircraft Squadrons Battle Force. He was also a graduate of the Naval War College.[2]

Jeter had no desire to be cooped up in a battleship, and Lee was certainly not welcoming. Commander Lloyd Mustin had encountered him when Jeter was executive officer of the *Enterprise* early in the war. His perception was that the Jeter of 1944 was bitter and viewed the assignment as a sidetracking of his career. He had not been selected for rear admiral and thus not chosen to command a carrier division/task group.[3] As Aertsen observed of Lee, "He couldn't see any reason why he needed an aviator under his wing. . . . He could see plenty of reasons why a surface man like Arleigh Burke certainly ought to be there with Mitscher, because he's commanding ships. Lee certainly wasn't about to go and be in command of a carrier group, so why that aviator?" Be that as it may, Lee was stuck with aviators as chiefs of staff for the rest of his time in the Pacific.[4]

The new man had served on Admiral Ernest King's staff in Washington prior to his aircraft carrier command. Jeter was very meticulous and got upset when a senior didn't follow his recommendations, which Lee was not inclined to do. That produced built-in friction, especially since the new subordinate had been anti-battleship since he was a lieutenant (j.g.). In Jeter's view, Lee was hostile to aviators, though intriguingly, one-star Jeter felt sorry for three-star Lee because—except in rare instances—Lee didn't command anything.[5]

The consequence of this substitution was that the familiar routines changed, because Jeter inevitably had his own ways of doing things. He was nominally in charge of the staff, though one staffer called him a "negative presence" and felt Jeter did not really coordinate efforts and tell people what to do and when to do it. A change, after so many months of doing things a certain way, was bound to cause some upset. That upset was magnified because Jeter and Lee were clearly not on the same wavelength. So Lee was not as comfortable in using the new chief of staff as a sounding board for ideas, a function that Jennings had served ably. As Aertsen put it, there would have been potential for irritation, "even if Jeter was a saint."[6]

The whole episode involved a degree of chicanery on Lee's part, a finagling of the system. His position had been that he did not need another aviator on board because he already had on his staff Commander Bill Dawson, whom he liked and trusted. The upshot was that Lee was able to delay Jeter's arrival for a few months by his resistance. Finally, he was given no choice. As Dawson explained in an interview years later, he departed without a relief, because Jeter's arrival checked off the aviator box. When Dawson finally got his orders, they directed him to report as executive officer of the escort carrier *Gilbert Islands*. Lee said to Dawson, "That ought to make you happy, get you back into real aviation." He then handed Dawson a sheaf that contained several earlier messages he had not previously shown to Dawson. One of them asked, "When can Commander Dawson be released?" The earlier messages had not contained such an appealing billet as exec of a small carrier. All told, Lee had delayed his departure for five months—until he had no choice—and Dawson got a better assignment than he might have previously.[7]

Another new staff member, Lieutenant Commander Edward "Ned" Mathews, had joined when the *Washington* was at Eniwetok in the Marshalls. Lee and Jennings had known him when they were in the Readiness Section of CominCh in 1942. Mathews worked for the Office of Naval Intelligence on recognition diagrams of U.S. and Japanese ships, using the illustrating skill that made him a contributor to *Life* magazine and later an architect. Mathews also organized technical information and characteristics on various ships. As fellow Kentuckians, Lee and Mathews developed a friendship. In the summer of 1944, Lee sent for Mathews, a reservist, to join his staff as assistant intelligence officer.[8] Lieutenant William

Bentinck-Smith described Mathews as "a very lively, bright, witty, energetic fellow, full of ideas, and strung as taut as a good violin."[9] As a midshipman and later in his career, Lee drew cartoons and sketches. Mathews was also adept at such things. During periods when the flagship was at sea, Mathews stood duty watches in the flag plot. To pass the time during periods of tedium, the lieutenant commander wrote doggerel verse and drew sketches that were a source of entertainment for the boss. Mathews added, "In fact he would often appropriate the sketches if I left them lying around."[10]

■ ■ ■

One of the reasons Lee hesitated to go after the Japanese fleet in June was the concern that the battle line had not had a chance to maneuver together and thus was probably rusty in surface tactics—comparable to a football team that had been playing only defense and hadn't had a chance to work on its offensive plays. In August Admiral Halsey embarked in the flagship *New Jersey* as he took over the command of the Third Fleet. Since he didn't want another missed opportunity, he directed that the battleships practice. They did so after leaving Manus Island on 5 September.

Lee, on board the *Washington*, was designated commander of Task Group 38.5 and had tactical command for several days of operations. Halsey sent some officers from his staff to confer with Lee on plans. Six of the fast battleships maneuvered in company, including Halsey's flagship *New Jersey*. The other ships that underwent the September training were the *Alabama, North Carolina, Massachusetts,* and *South Dakota.* The fast battleships' role in a fleet action involved racing out ahead of the carriers to pick off cripples that had been damaged by carrier aircraft. The tactical exercises included rotating the formation axis, changing cruising dispositions, and varying speeds. Lieutenant Carl Solberg, an air intelligence officer on Halsey's staff, observed that the massing of the dreadnoughts jump-started morale: "The men on *New Jersey* drilled with shining eyes. Their time was at hand."[11]

Among Lee's duties was serving as the assistant commander of the Third Fleet, able to step in and direct fleet operations when Admiral Halsey was away or if incapacitated. A brief interlude began on 28 September when the fleet flagship was anchored at Saipan Harbor. Halsey and a dozen of his staff members, including

Rear Admiral Robert B. Carney, the chief of staff, left on a trip. The admiral's command plane, a PB2Y-3 Coronado, took the group on an eleven-hundred-mile flight to Hollandia, New Guinea. There they spent a day conferring with General Douglas MacArthur's staff about the upcoming invasion of the island of Leyte in the Philippines. The following day they toured the Palau islands, including Peliliu and Angaur, which had recently been invaded at great cost to U.S. forces. On 1 October Halsey and his group arrived at Ulithi Atoll in the Western Caroline Islands.[12] The Navy had occupied Ulithi and nearby islands earlier in September. With its vast anchorage, Ulithi served as the Third Fleet base for the next several months. The nearby island of Mog Mog became a rest and recreation site for the officers and enlisted men of the fleet. A substantial appeal was the opportunity to consume alcoholic beverages—an option not available on board ship.

The same day that Halsey and his people left, Lee and four members of his staff rode a boat over to go on board the *New Jersey*. They were to be temporary settlers in the Third Fleet domain, available to take action if something unexpected arose. On 29 September, the day Halsey was meeting with MacArthur's people, the collection of ships departed Saipan to move to the new "homeport" of Ulithi. With Lee as the task force commander, the ships formed a special cruising disposition with the battleship *Indiana* as guide.[13] The division of labor called for one of Lee's staff members to be paired with one of Halsey's for each watch period in flag plot—a strategic watch and a fleet watch. Lieutenant Guil Aertsen drew as his opposite number Naval Reserve Commander Harold Stassen, the Third Fleet flag secretary. Stassen, who was then thirty-seven years old, had been the youthful governor of Minnesota from 1939 to 1943. He had been reelected in 1942 but then stepped down a year later to accept a reserve commission with the Navy.[14]

Aertsen recalled the experience of watch-standing with the former governor:

> He was exceedingly careful to point out to me that those things which Lee was doing on behalf of Halsey [were] his affair, and those things which Lee was doing on behalf of the maneuver of the fleet, that was my affair. "In other words," said Stassen, "if President Roosevelt or Eleanor wants to talk to the commander of the Third Fleet, [I] will be the one to handle that. But that if we're going to maneuver these ships that are around, go ahead and do that. Don't bother me with that kind of stuff." Of course, he was the administrator, and an excellent one he was. And he was a bright

guy, so Halsey did have able people there. And they liked to be awful sure you knew where your pigeonhole was. That staff was pigeonhole-oriented.[15]

The *New Jersey* and accompanying ships arrived at Ulithi on 1 October. Dozens of anchor chains rolled down out of hawsepipes as the Third Fleet took up residence in its new base of operations. In the late afternoon Halsey's entourage came back aboard, and Lee and his people returned to the *Washington*.[16]

■ ■ ■

One of the keys to U.S. success in the Pacific War was the ability of codebreakers to decipher the contents of Japanese radio messages and thus divine their intentions for upcoming operations. The biggest successes from reading the enemy's messages were at the Coral Sea in May 1942 and at Midway the following month. In 1943, codebreakers had advance word of the itinerary of Admiral Isoroku Yamamoto, commander in chief of the Combined Fleet, during a visit to the Solomon Islands. Army Air Forces fighters shot down Yamamoto's plane and killed the admiral who had been a key architect of the attack on Pearl Harbor. American submarines sank many Japanese merchant ships because they had been tipped off on the routes of convoys. Unfortunately, the American codebreakers were not able to provide advance word on the overall scheme for Leyte Gulf. Years after the war, one of Halsey's intelligence officers wrote, "When Third Fleet went to sea the admiral continued to receive daily ULTRA dispatches from Nimitz's basement eavesdroppers filled with invaluable if sketchy clues as to enemy moves. But it must be emphasized that never during the battle for Leyte was it possible to read the command messages of the Imperial Fleet."[17]

The Japanese effort to disrupt the American landings on Leyte was a three-pronged effort. The Sho ("To Conquer") plan called for a force of battleships, cruisers, and destroyers under Vice Admiral Takao Kurita to thread its way through the Philippine archipelago via the Palawan Passage, the Sibuyan Sea, and the San Bernardino Strait to attack the American landing force on the east side of the Philippines. A northern force, under Vice Admiral Jisaburo Ozawa, comprising aircraft carriers, converted battleships, and smaller ships, would operate to the north as a decoy force to draw the Third Fleet away from San Bernardino Strait. The carriers had so few effective planes on board that the plan made this largely a suicide mission. Two more groups of surface ships were to

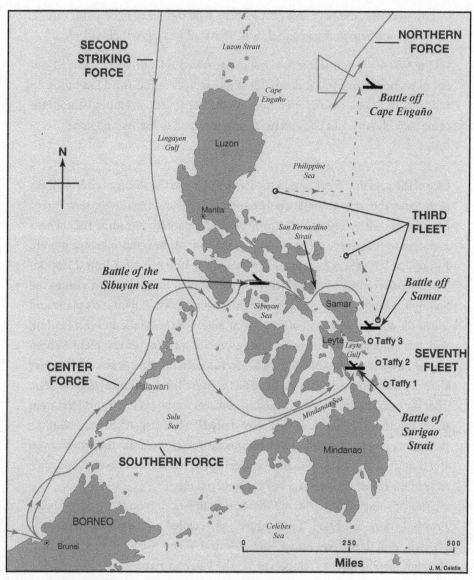

SECOND
STRIKING
FORCE

Luzon Strait

NORTHERN
FORCE

*Cape
Engaño*

Battle off
Cape Engaño

N

*Lingayen
Gulf*

Luzon

*Philippine
Sea*

Manila

THIRD
FLEET

*San Bernardino
Strait*

Battle of the
Sibuyan Sea

Battle off
Samar

Samar

*Sibuyan
Sea*

Leyte *Leyte
Gulf* o Taffy 3

CENTER
FORCE

Palawan

o Taffy 2 SEVENTH
FLEET

o Taffy 1

Mindanao Sea

Battle of
Surigao
Strait

*Sulu
Sea*

Mindanao

SOUTHERN FORCE

BORNEO

Brunei

*Celebes
Sea*

0   250   500

Miles

J. M. Caiella

Map 6. Battle of Leyte Gulf, 24–25 October 1944

approach from the south. Vice Admirals Shoji Nishimura and Kiyohide Shima commanded those groups.

Things did not go well for the center force. At the outset, the U.S. submarine *Darter* sank Kurita's flagship, the heavy cruiser *Atago*, on 23 October. The admiral was forced to seek a new flagship, in this case the super battleship *Yamato*. The *Yamato* and her sister, the *Musashi*, were behemoths, displacing some 72,000 tons apiece and each mounting nine 18.1-inch guns. They had been on the sidelines during the early part of the war. U.S. intelligence had only vague knowledge of the specifics of their capability.

Things got worse for the Japanese on 24 October as the force transited eastward across the Sibuyan Sea. Planes from Mitscher's Task Force 38 pummeled the ships relentlessly during daytime attacks. The American planes also went after Japanese aircraft that flew from land bases. The scope was not as vast as at the Marianas, but the results were again one-sided. Commander David McCampbell was air group commander for the carrier *Essex* and supposedly consigned to coordination duties. But some of the land-based planes constituted too much of an immediate threat, so he jumped into his F6F Hellcat fighter, which was only partially fueled. He had a day for the record books, shooting down a total of nine enemy planes in one flight, a feat for which he later received the Medal of Honor.

The U.S. carrier planes mortally wounded the *Musashi* that afternoon with an overwhelming combination of armor-piercing bombs and torpedoes. The *Yamato* was also hit but survived. At 1530, Kurita turned his force west to get away from the pounding his ships were taking and to get some room to maneuver. At 1715, by which time the aerial attacks had ceased, Kurita reversed course, and his ships again headed east to carry out their mission in Leyte Gulf. Years later, Kurita's chief of staff, Rear Admiral Tomiji Koyanagi, wrote of a fascinating alternative scenario. He said that if the U.S. planes had maintained surveillance, Admiral Halsey could have ignored Ozawa's carrier force and set up his ships outside San Bernardino Strait for an ambush. Wrote Koyanagi, "If he had done so, a night engagement against our exhausted forces would undoubtedly have been disastrous for us."[18]

Meanwhile, the southern arm, under Nishimura and Shima, steamed through the Sulu Sea with the objective of breaking through Surigao Strait into the gulf. In this case, lying in wait was a layered force of U.S. PT boats, destroyers, cruisers, and battleships under commander, Task Group 77.2, Rear Admiral Jesse Old-endorf. The night battle was disastrous for the Japanese. The American heavy ships had the tactical advantage of crossing the Japanese T, that is, the Japanese ships were in column formation so that only their forward guns could bear. The Americans were in a perpendicular column so that all their turrets turned broadside could fire at the Japanese. Among the losses were the battleships *Fuso* and *Yamashiro*; the only survivor of the ambush was the destroyer *Shigure*.

Oldendorf's battleships (nearly all Pearl Harbor survivors), cruisers, and destroyers were attached to the U.S. Seventh Fleet, commanded by Vice Admiral Thomas C. Kinkaid. Their intended main role was to support the assault force on Leyte. The fact that they were available when the southern prong showed up was fortuitous and eliminated the Nishimura and Shima ships from any further role in the conflict. The lack of an overall U.S. command structure for the battle was far from fortuitous. Halsey's Third Fleet was an independent entity. The amphibious force was detailed to handle the landings, while Halsey maintained command of Third Fleet, including Task Force 38, the carriers and associated ships. His assigned mission was to protect the landing force, but Admiral Nimitz had given him the additional option of going after the Japanese carriers if they appeared. The aggressive Halsey chose to make attacking the de-fanged carriers his principal mission.

At 1512, before the Japanese turned west in the Sibuyan Sea, Halsey sent out by radio message a battle plan that aimed to set up Task Force 34 under Lee with four fast battleships, seven cruisers, and nineteen destroyers. Though Kinkaid was not an addressee on the message, his communicators intercepted it, thus leading to Kinkaid's assumption that Lee's force would be ready to take on Kurita's remaining ships. What he didn't know was that Halsey's message was a contingency plan for an uncertain future time, not an order to execute. Halsey informed Kinkaid that he was taking the carrier force north, but his message was so vaguely worded as to be unclear about the role of Lee's force. In fact, Halsey took almost the entire Task Force 38, including Lee's ships, to the north in order to avoid dividing his assets. The exception was Vice Admiral John S. McCain's Task Group 38.1, which Halsey had dispatched to Ulithi for replenishment and a chance for crew members to relax from the grind of combat.

Rear Admiral Gerald Bogan, commander, Task Group 38.2, was embarked in the *Essex*-class carrier *Intrepid*. His group was a mixed bag. In addition to his flagship, he had two CVLs, light carriers built on cruiser hulls, the *Independence* and the *Cabot*. Most of the U.S. carriers were capable of flight operations only in daylight. The *Independence* had Night Air Group Forty-One on board. Planes from that ship went out on reconnaissance patrol on the night of 24–25 October. They maintained surveillance on Kurita's ships until 2300, when they had reached the end of their range. Bogan talked with Captain Edward Ewen, the skipper of the *Independence*. He relayed reports from the aircraft that indicated that the Japanese center force ships were steaming on course 060° and that Japanese navigation lights were burning en route to San Bernardino Strait, showing the way for Kurita's ships to head there.[19]

Twenty-five years later, Bogan recalled it simply: "I thought that Admiral Halsey was making a hell of a mistake." Bogan sent a message to the *New Jersey*: "Recommend Form Leo [which was Task Force Thirty-Four]. Leave my group in support and let the other two groups handle the northern force." When Bogan reported that the navigation lights were burning, a member of Halsey's staff said, "Yes, yes, we have that information." The idea was to send Lee's surface force to guard San Bernardino Strait, with Bogan's group along to provide air cover. A member of Halsey's staff brushed him off, and Bogan concluded it would be useless to say any more. It would have been a superb plan, allowing Halsey to have his cake and eat it too, but Halsey (or his staff) did not agree.[20]

Lee's staff was concerned that the Ozawa force was a decoy, that Kurita's force was headed east, and that Task Force 34 should be left to guard the strait. Before darkness fell, Guil Aertsen recalled, Lee sent a flashing light message to Halsey to share his views about the coming battle. The only response from the *New Jersey* was the simple word, "Roger," indicating that the message had been received.[21] After dark, once the *Independence* reconnaissance reports arrived on board the *Washington*, Lee sent a voice message to Halsey's flagship and pushed his belief that Kurita was coming. No response came from the *New Jersey*. As Aertsen put it, "I do know this much—that Lee would get very pissed that he knew damn well that a lot of the times all these staffs would filter more than perhaps they should have."[22]

Author Evan Thomas' illuminating book on Leyte Gulf paints a fascinating picture of the atmosphere on board the *New Jersey* that evening. He asserts that for some time Halsey's doctor, Captain Carnes Weeks, had been routinely giving the admiral shots of whiskey to help him sleep while under the strain of combat. Flu was also a factor. According to Thomas' research, Halsey took the whiskey and went to bed around 2000 without knowledge of the report from the *Independence* that Kurita's force was again headed east. In flag plot the fleet intelligence officer, Captain Marion C. "Mike" Cheek, argued with Captain Horace D. "Doug" Moulton, staff air operations officer. After seeing the report from the *Independence* Cheek told Moulton of the impending threat from Kurita's force, but Moulton brushed him off, declining to countermand the order to head north. Halsey slept on, presumably with no knowledge of the force heading toward San Bernardino Strait.[23]

Lee's voice message was his last attempt to alert Halsey, and Halsey's staff apparently also failed in that regard. As Aertsen said of Lee, he was respected because of his sound opinions and the fact that he generally proffered those opinions only after being asked. Aertsen added, "Lee was generally fairly quiet, respected the other guy for what he was. If he felt that there was factual input to the decision-making process, he'd give it. The only time he really sounded off in no uncertain terms that I fully remember was that chase [by Halsey]. He was hot about that. And he wasn't wrong. The rest of the time, for obvious reasons, he wasn't a heckler, as such." As Aertsen put it, Lee would assert himself only "when the chips were really down and the handwriting was on the wall that something was awfully damn wrong, as at Leyte Gulf. Then he'd sound off and he'd make a noise, and he had spoken his piece. That was it, though. He didn't push it anymore."

Another witness to the events of that night was Lieutenant William Bentinck-Smith, assistant communications officer on the staff. His battle station was in flag plot. His observation was that "Lee certainly told Halsey as clearly as he could without openly quarreling with Halsey's decision that he questioned the wisdom of sending Task Force 34, with its battleships, after the Northern Force. I never heard Lee discuss this matter more than perfunctorily with his aides. He was very curt, quiet, and controlled about it, though those in flag plot . . . could tell that he was deeply disturbed."[24]

Commander Ray Thompson, the staff gunnery officer, added another slant: "We told Admiral Lee to tell Admiral Halsey to leave something out there watching the strait, because they were bound to come out and everyone seemed to know that. But the reaction was, if you tell Halsey to do something, that's the one thing he won't do. . . . In my opinion it was the greatest tactical blunder of the war."[25]

Mitscher, though still officially in tactical command, had become the same sort of passenger as Lee. Commodore Burke, his chief of staff, took the *Independence* reports and woke up Mitscher to suggest that he urge Lee's force be activated. Mitscher asked if Halsey had the spotting report. Assured that he did, Mitscher said, "If he wants my advice he'll ask for it." As Burke recalled, Mitscher concluded that any suggestions he made would be distractions for Halsey.[26] Thus, presumably, Halsey assumed that Kinkaid's ships were guarding the strait, and Kinkaid assumed that Lee's were. In some cases, two wrongs can make a right. In this case two wrongs led to disaster for the Americans.

Meanwhile, Halsey and the entire Task Force 38 were under way northward through the night—with the exception of McCain's Task Group 38.1. Years later, Burke argued that he exercised tactical command of Task Force 38 on Mitscher's behalf, though a number of his orders were countermanded by Third Fleet. About 0200 on 25 October, Halsey (or his staff) ordered the *Independence* planes to look for the ships of Ozawa's northern force. Mitscher protested on the grounds that the planes would be detected by Japanese radar and would lead the northern force to change course to get farther away. Bogan said that Halsey ordered the search anyway, meaning there would be a delay in Lee's ships being able to get at the Japanese while American planes were in the air.[27]

At the time, Captain James S. Russell was on board the carrier *Franklin* as chief of staff to Rear Admiral Ralph E. Davison, who commanded the four carriers of Task Group 38.2. He listened to the voice radio traffic between the flagships of Admiral Mitscher and Admiral Halsey. Russell detected the voice of Commodore Burke, Mitscher's chief of staff, who said, "I recommend you form Leo." That was the call sign for the battle line. After a period of silence, a response came through the air from the *New Jersey*: "Form Leo."[28]

So even as Japanese ships were being chewed up in Surigao Strait, at 0240 Halsey finally ordered the formation of Task Force 34, which was to move out ten miles ahead of the carriers. It was a time-consuming task to withdraw the heavy ships from the carrier formations. As Clark Reynolds wrote, "Lee liked this close maneuvering at night even less than did Mitscher, and he ordered all his battleships to change to a different fixed course and slow to 15 knots, thus drawing them out of formation in a painfully slow but safe manner."[29] Captain Russell watched this process on a plan position indicator (PPI) radarscope on board the *Franklin*. He essentially had a bird's-eye view of the formation shedding battleships, cruisers, and destroyers. To him the changing image "looked like an amoeba."[30]

While the amoeba was reshaping itself, Lee's aviator chief of staff, Commodore Thomas Jeter, grew impatient. Jeter deemed Lee to be overly timid, even nervous, though the latter adjective was seldom applied to Lee. He urged the battleship commander to speed up the process, but Lee maintained the slower and safer approach at fifteen knots.[31] Once the ships were extricated, they moved out ahead and slowly built up to twenty knots. They were the *Iowa*, *New Jersey*, *Massachusetts*, *South Dakota*, Lee's flagship *Washington*, and *Alabama*.[32] This middle-of-the-night reorientation was a contrast to Spruance's approach in June, when he sent the battleships forward of the carriers early in the process.

To Russell's great surprise, Task Force 34 continued northward, out ahead of the carrier groups. Admiral Davison turned to his chief of staff, Russell, and said, "Jim, we're playing a helluva trick on the transports in Leyte Gulf."

Russell asked, "Do you wish to say anything to Mitscher?"

The admiral responded, "No, they have far more intelligence than we do, but this doesn't look right to me." His reaction was essentially the same as Mitscher's had been when asked to assert himself with Halsey.[33]

Lieutenant Commander Ned Mathews was on his watch station in *Washington*'s sky control, high above the main deck, on the morning of 25 October. At the first glimmer of dawn, he remembered, the battleships fanned out to form a line abreast as they prepared to engage. Their forward turrets would be able to shoot on a wide front.[34]

That same morning, with Lee's ships heading north, three small task units were operating to the east of San Bernardino Strait. They were part of Kinkaid's Seventh Fleet. The northernmost was Task Unit 77.4.3, known as Taffy 3. It was under the command of Rear Admiral Clifton A. F. Sprague, embarked in the escort carrier *Fanshaw Bay*. Taffy 3 comprised six small escort carriers, three destroyers, and four destroyer escorts. Their role was to provide support to the landing forces on Leyte. As the men on board the ships looked to the west, toothpick-like shapes appeared on the horizon. They were the topmasts of Admiral Kurita's force. At 0658, even before their hulls were above the horizon, the Japanese ships opened fire, dropping large-caliber rounds in amongst the ships of Taffy 3. The small ships battled gamely and put up heroic resistance, but at considerable cost in terms of lost ships and lost lives.

As would be expected, news of this battle off the island of Samar soon reached Admiral Kinkaid. It came as a considerable surprise, because he expected Lee's battleships were there, not the light force that bore the brunt of Kurita's attack. Within a few minutes, shortly after 0700, Kinkaid sent a message to Halsey about the events in progress. He also posed a question that came as a surprise to Halsey: "Is TF 34 guarding San Bernardino Strait?" A later message to Halsey said, "Urgently need fast BBs Leyte Gulf at once." At 0900 Kinkaid's message to Halsey said, "Our CVEs being attacked by 4 BBs, 8 cruisers, plus others. Request Lee cover Leyte at top speed. Request fast carriers make immediate strike."

Lieutenant Noble Harris was on staff communication duty in the *Washington* that morning. Years later he recalled, "I think the saddest thing that ever happened as far as Admiral Lee and the staff and everything concerned was when we kept getting these messages." He remembered one in particular that was on paper tape after having just come out of the decoding machine: "I showed that to Admiral Lee, and he just sort of grunted and maybe a couple of tears came to his eyes or something like that. It was sort of a dramatic thing, that here we were, way the hell and gone from where we should have been."[35]

Typically, the admiral did not make a great show of emotion, for he was not a demonstrative individual. Moreover, Lee was in a powerless position. As Harris remembered, the admiral shrugged his shoulders and said something along the lines of, "I can't do anything about that" or "I can't respond to that."[36]

The final plea from Kinkaid was a desperate one, sent in plain language rather than taking time to encode it: "Where is Lee? Send Lee."[37]

Kinkaid's messages also attracted the attention of Admiral Nimitz in Hawaii. His normal approach, as fleet commander in chief, was to leave the tactical decisions to the commanders on scene, presumably because they had a better knowledge of the situation than he. As did Kinkaid, Nimitz had concluded that Halsey had left Task Force 34 at San Bernardino Strait, but clearly something was amiss.

At Nimitz's direction, his war plans officer, Rear Admiral Forrest Sherman, drafted a message to Halsey that read, "Where is, rpt, where is Task Force Thirty

Four?" However, in those days of Morse code, it was standard practice to put nonsense padding at the beginning and end of messages to foil possible enemy decryption. The decoder on board the *New Jersey* quickly stripped away the beginning, "Turkey trots to water," but left "The world wonders" at the end.

This is one of the most-often quoted naval messages of the war because of its considerable consequences. For nearly three-quarters of a century, the world wondered who added the final padding and why it was so stated that it could be construed as part of the body of the message rather than as a nonsensical insert. The answer came from a combination of efforts on the part of noted author Rich Frank and archivist Chris McDougal. Frank got the answer while doing research at the National Museum of the Pacific War, formerly the Admiral Nimitz Museum, in Fredericksburg, Texas.

Frank was reading through the unpublished memoir of Elmer R. Oettinger Jr. in the museum's collection. As a lieutenant, Oettinger was a communications security officer on Nimitz's Pacific Fleet staff in 1944. Ensign John Donald Kaster was another communications watch officer on the staff, though McDougal, a dedicated researcher on the museum staff, had to do considerable digging to confirm the name. Kaster had been an enlisted radioman who served in the crew of the heavy cruiser *Northampton* when she was sunk near Guadalcanal in 1942. He was credited with keeping classified material out of Japanese hands, and that action helped him become an officer. He was commissioned in early 1944 and, in Oettinger's view, had not been properly trained in handling the padding for sensitive messages and thus posed a risk that the substance of messages might be misinterpreted. That lack of training and awareness changed the course of history as it manifested itself in the poorly worded message transmitted from Hawaii to the vicinity of the Philippines.[38]

Even though the message contained the letters "RR" to indicate a break before the final padding, the communicators on board the *New Jersey* included "The world wonders" in the version delivered to Halsey. He took the unintended second sentence as a sarcastic jibe and flew into a rage. Concluding that he had to do something, Halsey detached Lee's force to head south, along with Bogan's Task Group 58.2. That combination was what Bogan had suggested the night before, only to be rebuffed. Included in Lee's force was Halsey's flagship *New Jersey*. It had to be irksome for Halsey to leave the scene of the carrier action for which he had so yearned. It was probably irksome for Lee as well, once his ships had come so close to those of the Japanese. Ozawa's force included two old battleships, the *Ise* and *Hyuga*, that had been retrofitted with flight decks aft. They still retained their big guns forward and had powerful antiaircraft batteries. In the Leyte action Mitscher's carrier planes sank the large carrier *Zuikaku*, the last surviving carrier from the six that hit Pearl Harbor in 1941. Also sunk were the light carriers *Chitose*, *Chiyoda*, and *Zuiho* and the destroyer *Akizuki*. The damaged light cruiser *Tama* sought to retire, but the U.S. submarine *Jallao* sank her. The aerial bombing damaged other ships as well, but the old "hermaphrodite" battleships survived the battle.

Commander McCampbell, the *Essex* air group commander who had shot down nine planes the day before, coordinated the attack from overhead that day. At one point during the morning he saw, from his Hellcat fighter far above, both the Japanese and American fleets steaming toward each other. He estimated that the enemy fleets got within about thirty miles of each other. And then, in response to Halsey's signal, Lee's big ships turned south at 1115 to head for San Bernardino Strait. At the time, McCampbell wondered why they had reversed course. Only later did he learn of the message from Nimitz to Halsey.[39]

Heading south with Lee, in addition to his flagship *Washington*, were the two thirty-three-knot ships, *Iowa* and *New Jersey*, and three more of the twenty-seven-knot battleships, *South Dakota*, *Massachusetts*, and *Alabama*; supporting cruisers and destroyers; and Bogan's Task Group 58.2, which was to provide air cover. Halsey had blundered yet again in sending all the battleships south, just as he had earlier in taking them all north. Had two of Lee's ships continued on toward the Japanese instead of turning around, it is likely they would have sunk the *Ise* and *Hyuga*.[40] The force was delayed for two hours while fueling destroyers. In addition, Bogan's carriers had to turn into the wind to launch and recover planes. The result was that the battleships and carriers got farther and farther apart. In Russell's recollection, Lee sent word to Bogan via tactical radio transmissions that were relayed by two destroyers with line-of-sight communications. He recalled Lee's message as, "Close up on me."[41]

Russell said years later, "Well, this infuriated Bogan. And it's alleged that Bogan made a remark over the voice radio which has never been recorded in history to my knowledge, and this is, 'You are running away from me. I suggest you retire to the protection of the carrier's guns.'" Lee wanted to get his ships south as quickly as he could, and Bogan would much rather have had his planes attacking the Japanese targets to the north. As Russell put it in colorful fashion, "Gerry Bogan was furious because he knew there was pie and cake up to the north, because there was Ozawa's force with no air opposition and just all sitting ducks." As it happened, the carrier planes did have a field day because there was no fighter opposition from Ozawa's ships.[42]

As the American ships sped south, shortly before noon on 25 October, Kurita ordered his center force to turn around and steam north, and thus leave the American transports unmolested. Around 1925, his ships prepared to enter San Bernardino Strait and head west. In the late afternoon, Halsey sent the two fastest battleships, *Iowa* and *New Jersey*, ahead of the rest of Task Force 34, steaming in company with three cruisers and eight destroyers. Rear Admiral Oscar Badger commanded this Task Group 34.5, leaving Lee's slower ships behind. Badger's group did not arrive at the strait until around 0100 on 26 October. By then the Japanese heavy ships were long gone.

Writers have put forth a number of possible explanations for Kurita's decision to give up the fight: severe fatigue after his ships underwent three days of attacks; the mistaken belief that the plucky escort carriers and destroyers constituted Halsey's force of big carriers; the belief that the American transports had already disgorged their troops and cargoes to the shore; heavy fuel consumption during high-speed maneuvering; the desire to preserve his fleet; and a reluctance to sacrifice still more men and ships. Kurita's chief of staff, Koyanagi, said the overall plan was flawed and would have constituted a suicide order for Kurita. He did offer a tantalizing tidbit: "Giving up pursuit [of the escort carriers and destroyers] when we did amounted to losing a prize already in hand. If we had known the types and number of enemy ships, and their speed, Admiral Kurita would never have suspended the pursuit, and we would have annihilated the enemy."[43]

After the war, Captain Russell, who had been on board the *Franklin* during the battle, was detailed as one of the interviewers of Japanese participants. In his oral history thirty years after the fact, he relayed the essence of Kurita's explanation, "In the first place, you sank my flagship [*Atago*]. . . . You knew we were coming. Certainly you would have left none of your transport in Leyte Gulf. You were certainly not that rash. I had sunk four of your *Essex*-class carriers, possibly six." (This was Kurita's perception, based on Japanese reports, of the damage done not to the big carriers but to the CVEs.) Kurita continued: "Having dealt that blow and knowing there was a big battle raging to the north, I went to join them. However, when I got opposite the Straits of San Bernardino, I found out that my fuel was limited, my destroyers would have run out of fuel by the time we could join the battle, so I gave the order to retire."[44]

Monday-morning quarterbacking was inevitable. Clark Reynolds opined, "If TF 34 had been detached a few hours earlier, after Kinkaid's first urgent request for help, and had left the destroyers behind, since their fueling caused a delay of over two hours and a half, a powerful battle line of six modern battleships under the command of Admiral Lee, the most experienced battle squadron commander in the Navy, would have arrived off San Bernardino Strait in time to have clashed with Kurita's Center Force. . . . There is every reason to believe that Lee would have crossed Kurita's T and completed the destruction of Center Force."[45]

A few years later, Admiral Kinkaid added a bitter postscript in commenting on an account of the battle written by newspaperman (and Naval Academy graduate) Hanson W. Baldwin. Kinkaid's comments were essentially parallel to those of Reynolds. He wrote of the benefits in terms of Lee's force being in a more advantageous position if it had been sent south when Halsey received Kinkaid's first call for support. He added, "The net result of all this was that the six strongest battleships in the world—except the *Yamato* and *Musashi*—steamed about 300 miles north and 300 miles south during 'the greatest naval battle of the Second World War and the largest engagement ever fought on the high seas'—and did not fire a single shot. I can well imagine the feelings of my [Naval Academy] classmate, Lee."[46]

Lee's aide, Lieutenant Aertsen, did not have to imagine them. He summarized the difference between the Marianas tactical situation and that at Leyte Gulf. In June, as Lee explained to him, the enemy was retreating and did not constitute a threat. In October the Japanese were approaching and were indeed a threat. In June, Japanese torpedoes might have posed a threat. At Leyte, the Japanese ships would have had to thread their way through a bottleneck and could have been picked off by U.S. gunnery before steaming close enough to launch torpedoes. Even so, remembered Aertsen, Lee did not brood in the aftermath about what might have been or what should have been. It was a fait accompli over which he had had no control, and there was no way to change the outcome retroactively.[47]

In Washington, Admiral Ernest King was angry and disappointed that Halsey had not left Lee's ships to guard San Bernardino Strait. He added, "That the San Bernardino detachment of the Japanese Fleet ... did not completely destroy all the escort carriers and their accompanying screen is nothing short of a dispensation from the Lord Almighty."[48]

Sometime after the battle, Admiral Bogan talked with Admiral Halsey, who tried to justify taking sixty-eight American ships to attack the Japanese force of seventeen—and a decoy force at that. Halsey told him, "I thought it was Kinkaid's responsibility to guard the strait, not mine." Bogan felt great frustration at being so close for the U.S. fleet to deliver a knockout blow to the Japanese surface navy. In Bogan's oral history, interviewer Etta-Belle Kitchen asked, "How did that make you feel, when you know something in your own mind is right and it doesn't happen, doesn't get accomplished?"

Bogan's answer came as a true surprise to the interviewer: "It's hard for me to put myself in your place, but I felt that some girl had said yes, and I wasn't ready."[49] The supreme irony in all of this was that Halsey had designated Lee as his choice to take command of the Third Fleet if either Halsey or his flagship were disabled. But when Halsey could have benefited greatly from Lee's input, he or his staff chose to ignore it.

The outcome of the battle generated many hypotheticals, including one that has tantalized battleship enthusiasts for decades—what would have been the outcome of a gunnery duel between the ultimate Japanese battleship and the ultimate U.S. battleship? Scholars Thomas Hone and Norman Friedman took on that challenge in a 1983 professional note in the journal, U.S. Naval Institute Proceedings. They concluded that Lee would have attempted to get in hits at long range because the U.S. ships had the superior Mark 8 fire control radar while the Japanese used optics. The Yamato's heavy armor provided little protection beyond 35,000 yards. Thus the U.S. ships would have fired from over the horizon and won.[50] Vice Admiral Lloyd Mustin (Lee's gunnery, radar, and combat information center officer during the war) submitted a subsequent letter to the editor in which he argued that the capability of the Mark 8 radar to distinguish targets at a distance was even better than Hone and Friedman believed, because he had seen the results at sea. In sum, Mustin concurred that, with Lee at the helm, the outcome would have been the same, a U.S. victory.[51]

■ ■ ■

The end of the line for Admiral Lee's association with his favorite flagship, *Washington*, came on 21 November when she was anchored in the sprawling lagoon of Ulithi Atoll. He had first embarked in the ship in September 1942 after the *South Dakota* scraped a gash in her hull at Tongatabu. Since then he had been on board for the Guadalcanal campaign, the Gilbert Islands, the Marshall Islands, the collision with the *Indiana*, the Marianas, and the frustration of Leyte Gulf. Now he and his Battleships Pacific Fleet staff transferred back to that initial flagship, *South Dakota*. Early in his tour on board the *Washington* he had two staff officers; now he had nearly two dozen. Commander Edwin Schanze, who by late 1944 was executive officer of the *Washington*, said that Lee did not want to leave, adding, "I understand it was only because of a diplomatic directive from Nimitz that he made the change."[52] Lieutenant William Bentinck-Smith of Lee's staff recalled that the admiral did not have a high regard for the *South Dakota* during his time on board.[53]

The *South Dakota* had been built with extra accommodations to serve as a force flagship. She had flag quarters and offices, requisite communications gear, and one more conning tower level than those of her three near-sisters that followed: the *Indiana*, *Massachusetts*, and *Alabama*. Originally the ship was designed to accommodate 114 officers and 2,240 enlisted men. During the war the quarters were modified for occupancy by 160 officers and 2,113 enlisted. The head of the ships histories section of the Naval History Division explained, "As a flagship, she could accommodate more officers than any of her sister ships; her enlisted complement was slightly smaller to compensate. During the war years, her accommodations were altered to provide for the increasing size of wartime staffs." Lee's staff had certainly increased.[54]

The heavily armored conning tower contained the helm and lee helm for steering the ship and communicating orders to the engines. When the officer of the deck was outside on the bridge, he gave orders through slits in the armor. In the extra level built into the *South Dakota* was the flag conning tower, one deck below. Abaft of it was the flag plot, a larger space that had two or three inches of armor, compared with seventeen inches in the tower itself. The flag bridge was outboard of flag plot. Lee had previously arranged for a radar repeater to be installed in flag plot. Soon after he returned, he got a second one so that he would be able to monitor both the air and surface pictures.[55]

In connection with the transfer, Lee relinquished one of his command hats, that of commander, Battleship Division Six, which he had held since the summer of 1942. He remained as ComBatPac, but now Rear Admiral Ross Cooley took over the BatDiv 6 portion with his new flag embarked in the *Washington*.[56] He and Lee went way back. They had been shipmates in the *Concord* in the 1930s and when Cooley commanded the *Washington* from April to November of 1944; so for Cooley it was essentially a matter of moving from one cabin to another in the same ship. As for Lee and the return to the *South Dakota*, baseball great and malaprop philosopher Yogi Berra coined an expression in another context that applied to Lee's situation as well: "It's déjà vu all over again."

▪ 14 ▪

CLOSING IN ON JAPAN,
November 1944–June 1945

T hough the officers and men on board the *South Dakota* could not know it in November 1944, the end of the war was less than a year away. In the meantime, a significant change to Lee's staff came on 23 November when the flagship was steaming in company with Rear Admiral Frederick Sherman's Task Group 38.3. Commander Lloyd M. Mustin rode in a two-step highline transfer from his previous ship, the light cruiser *Miami*, to the *South Dakota*. The intermediary was a destroyer. He became the new gunnery, radar, and fire control officer.

Mustin relieved Commander Ray Thompson, another fire control specialist, whom Lee had plucked from the crew of the *South Dakota* in the summer of 1942. In late 1944, Thompson requested a relief because of a family problem back home, so Admiral Lee agreed to send him. Thompson, who was Lee's lone staff member in the beginning, joked that by the time he left there were so many staffers that they got in each other's way. Thompson and Mustin had known each other since the early 1930s when they were both on the Naval Academy swimming team. During a visit ashore between operations, Thompson had mentioned his desire to leave. Mustin leaped at the opportunity, because he had a qualified relief on board the cruiser and was vulnerable to being sent to Washington for shore duty. He desired to stay at sea, where the action was.[1]

Mustin brought with him a seabag full of relevant experience. He was one of the four lieutenants who went to study with Dr. Stark Draper at MIT in the late 1930s. In 1942 he was on board the antiaircraft cruiser *Atlanta* when she was fatally wounded in the disastrous night battle near Guadalcanal on 12–13 November—the one that preceded Lee's duel with the Japanese two nights later. Before serving in the *Miami* as gunnery officer, he was assistant gunnery officer in the antiaircraft cruiser *San Diego*. He and Lee shared many of the same professional interests and enjoyed mutual respect. Years later Mustin said of Lee, "He had well-developed ideas and plans for dealing with whatever matter was at hand, or might come to hand unexpectedly."[2]

Soon afterward came another change, one that matched the reality of the use of battleships in the Pacific. Commodore Thomas Jeter, Lee's chief of staff, recommended in the autumn that the old battleships be separated from the ComBatPac type command, but Lee would have nothing to do with it.[3] A directive from Washington, however, imposed the altered organization, which made sense, given the way the war was going. On 15 December, Lee's new command was dubbed Battleship Squadron Two operationally, and now he functioned as type commander for only the fast battleships. Each of the fast battleship divisions was under a two-star admiral. The old battleships, which had been operating separately all along, now made up Battleship Squadron One. Vice Admiral Jesse Oldendorf, the victor at Surigao Strait in the Philippines in October, commanded that new organization. He was now type commander for those ships. Lee's administrative command remained in Pearl Harbor, though now it dealt with fewer ships. Among the staff in Hawaii was a personnel officer who occasionally visited the flagship to discuss various issues and get broad guidance. When there were specifics to deal with, Lee and the personnel officer communicated by radio message.[4]

In adjusting to the change in flagships, Lee's aide Guil Aertsen found his new quarters cramped. At 680 feet, the *South Dakota* was shorter than the 729-foot *Washington*. Worse than that, his new stateroom was near an uptake that took hot gases from the firerooms up to the single smokestack. To protect his feet against the heat radiating from the deck, Aertsen filched a rubber mat in the shape of the island of Palau. It had been used as an intelligence tool during attacks earlier in the year but was no longer needed for that purpose. The terrain map, by then a standard ingredient of the island-hopping campaign, was an indirect outgrowth of Lee's efforts in Fleet Training in 1940 to improve the quality of Navy photography.[5]

Aertsen had observed Lee's ever-larger staff and compared it with the early Guadalcanal days when "[y]ou could put his staff in a taxi cab."[6] Items of interest filtered up through the chain of command and were generally dealt with at the appropriate level, and the officers worked as a team. When the admiral had a topic on which he wanted to bore into the details, he dealt with the appropriate staff member directly. That was often the case in his relations with Commander Mustin on matters related to gunnery. As usual, Lee eschewed the paperwork aspect as much as possible. And sometimes Lee just wanted to be alone to think things out.

Aertsen generally served as the doorkeeper. As he recalled,

> One of the biggest jobs I had to do was govern access to him, depending on what he was doing at the time—if he wasn't feeling well, or he had a problem on his mind, you limited access. If there wasn't much going on, you opened the door wide . . . because he very much enjoyed the privilege of knowing how the man on the job was doing his work, because then, when the chips were down, he would know how to evaluate the results of the work that came to him.[7]

As for his daily routine, Lee liked to be up before dawn, because that was a time for general quarters and extra alertness for possible submarine attack. He monitored the events of the day, had meetings as appropriate. After sunset, he might sit around and think about current situations and pending operations. Occasionally he would join in watching shipboard movies, but those were generally shown only when the flagship was in port. In the evenings, Lee retired to his cabin in flag quarters and turned in, not necessarily to sleep.[8]

Lieutenant Noble Harris observed, as had many others, the admiral's dislike of dealing with paperwork, especially that which he considered unnecessary. At one point the command received a directive from Admiral Nimitz's headquarters. It specified that a certain action was supposed to be taken within twenty-four hours and a compliance report submitted right away. It fell within Harris' purview in electronics, and by his description he was excited to get a response out quickly. Lee's response was much more casual: "Well, just put it in my drawer over there,

and we'll think about it a little bit." More messages came in, demanding compliance with the original directive. Still more time passed, and another dispatch
arrived. It cited the previous exchanges and said to cancel the action in question.
Lee sort of chuckled and said, "See, we didn't have to answer it." Lee probably
figured the correspondence came from someone on the CinCPac staff who was
trying to make points, and he wasn't willing to let it become his problem.[9]

On the other hand, correspondence made a difference when the topic was something that did matter to Lee. The Bureau of Ordnance reported that it intended to
distribute the Mark 13 main battery fire-control radar to the battleships, because
it offered substantial improvement over the Mark 8. The Mark 8 had performed
well during the Battle of Surigao Strait in October when Admiral Oldendorf's
old battleships had done some remarkably accurate shooting. Lee nixed the
BuOrd proposal and was blunt about it, because he didn't want to have his ships
withdrawn from the combat theater in order to have the replacements made.[10]

Back in the autumn of 1943, a representative from Western Electric Company
had installed a modification to the Mark 8 sets on board the *North Carolina* and
Washington. It was dubbed Mod 1, with the result that they could be operated from
the ships' main battery plotting rooms. The two ships reported positively on the
effectiveness of the change, and Lee subsequently added his endorsement. That
led to the modification becoming the standard for all Mark 8 installations. But
the Mark 13 replacements were coming anyway. In February 1945 the Mark 13 was
installed in the *Iowa* and *Alabama* while both were in West Coast shipyards for
regular overhauls. When the two ships made tests at sea they reported improved
target definition at maximum ranges, while range accuracy was comparable to
that in the Mark 8.[11]

■ ■ ■

On 2 December 1944, the *South Dakota* anchored at Ulithi after a series of operations with the fast carriers. During one of those, on 25 November, a kamikaze
had pierced the antiaircraft screen and inflicted serious damage on the carrier
Essex. The strike killed twenty-five men and injured another forty-four. Clearly
the kamikaze menace posed a major threat to fleet operations. During that
period at Ulithi, on 8 December, Lee ordered tests of a countermeasure to be
employed by the battleships—shining searchlights into the eyes of enemy pilots

in an attempt to blind and distract them while they approached U.S. ships. It didn't work. The kamikaze problem would continue to vex the U.S. Navy for the remainder of the war.[12]

By then Vice Admiral John S. "Slew" McCain commanded Task Force 38. He had relieved Admiral Mitscher on 30 October, less than a week after the completion of the Battle of Leyte Gulf. Mitscher had commanded the fast carrier task force since the Marshall Islands operation early in the year. He was due for a rest. One could well argue that Lee was due also, but the Japanese heavy surface ships had not yet been vanquished. The relationship between Lee and Mitscher went back many years. They worked harmoniously throughout that year of 1944. Marine Corps Major Arthur MacArthur was landing force and shore bombardment officer on the staff. He observed that when Lee and Mitscher conferred by radio message they used channel thirteen, a top-secret circuit that was restricted to vice admirals and above.[13] Commander Mustin reported that the same level of mutual rapport did not exist between Lee and McCain. As he put it years later, "[Lee] sometimes spoke of McCain in a suggesting sort of a way that he just never used about Mitscher, just never used it."[14] It's worth pointing out that Mitscher had been a naval aviator since 1916. McCain earned his wings in 1936, when he was fifty-two years old. In the parlance of the time, McCain was a Johnny-come-lately to aviation.

Admiral Halsey's relentless attacks against the Japanese in the Philippines continued in mid-December with carrier strikes against the island of Luzon. On the sixteenth Halsey ordered Third Fleet ships to refuel northeast of Samar, despite threatening weather and heightening seas. In so doing, Halsey blundered into disaster by taking his warships and fleet auxiliaries into the heart of a typhoon. Shortly after noon on 17 December, Commander Carl Stillman, executive officer of the *South Dakota*, instituted a heavy weather bill for the ship.[15] At 1240 the destroyer *Hull* came alongside the battleship to starboard and delivered mail for the crew of the ship and for the embarked flag personnel. At 1300 the fueling exercises were canceled because of the rough weather. At 1341 the *Hull* cast off from the *South Dakota*'s starboard quarter. The small ship, which had been commissioned in 1935, had not long to live.[16]

On the morning of 18 December, Commander Lloyd Mustin had the 0400–0800 watch on the flag bridge. The barometer was dropping rapidly, and he could tell by the actions of the wind and waves that the refueling scheduled for that day was not feasible. The whirling winds were turning counterclockwise and heading in a northerly and westerly direction, which put them on the starboard bows of the task force ships. Mustin opined that the course would take the ships right into the heart of the storm. Admiral Lee appeared about 0600 and agreed with Mustin's conclusions that the present course would make the situation even worse, especially since ships ride better with rough seas astern rather than ahead. His reaction to the situation was reinforced by seeing images of the storm on the surface-search SG radar; by this time the air-search radar was unable to rotate.

Lieutenant David Gray of Lee's staff was in the flag plot of the *South Dakota* during the storm. As he recalled years later, the admiral was glued to the radar-scope and called the men in the space to gather around and see what he was seeing. Lee told his audience, it was "the first time man has seen the eye of a typhoon on radar." The men on watch plotted the course and were horrified by Halsey's action in taking the fleet into the storm's dangerous quadrant. Gray recalled thumbing through a copy of *Knight's Modern Seamanship* and came to the page that described the way to avoid the danger. He then suggested to Lee that the admiral send a message to Halsey, calling his attention to the page that applied. Lee sadly shook his head and said, "We can't send that kind of message to a four-star admiral." As at Leyte Gulf, Halsey blundered on.[17]

Instead, Lee informed Admiral Frederick Sherman, commander of Task Group 38.3, of his recommendation to reverse course, if feasible, in order to avoid the worst of the storm and put the ships on a course on which they would ride better. Sherman went along with the suggestion, and the ships executed the turn. Even so, conditions were ferocious. At best, the visibility was short range, maybe only two thousand yards from the next ship in formation. Mustin recalled, "Much of the time you couldn't see that, especially if you weren't physically able to look in that direction because of the 100-mile-an-hour winds just blasting the top right off the waves. It was raining horizontally, and a good portion of the rain was saltwater coming right off the wave crests. Nevertheless, the waves were giant, and it was a pretty awesome thing."[18] The ship's deck log reported that the barometer finally bottomed out at 29.29 inches at 1430.

The carriers, with their high freeboard, were taking a beating. Even the battle-ships, which usually plowed through heavy weather, were not immune. Aertsen recalled that green water was coming over turret two, some forty feet above the normal waterline. "Green water," as opposed to mere sea spray, is a solid wave from the greater metropolitan ocean. He likened the sensation to a train approaching a station and then coming to a grinding halt. The bow sort of shuddered, as if to throw off the weight of the water that engulfed it.[19] The damage was not only to the ship herself but to the floatplanes astern that were not strong enough to endure the beating they took from wind and waves.

On board the *South Dakota*, Ensign John Mullen Jr. observed the ship roll 22 degrees to one side and 22 degrees to the other. Sometime later, when things had calmed, he remembered, "I thought the [gunnery] director would roll off its pedestal!"[20] Commander Mustin recalled the rolling much less vividly, three to four degrees while steaming straight and from ten to twelve degrees during the turn to reverse course. By comparison, rolls on the much bigger *New Jersey*, Halsey's flagship and a member of the *Iowa* class, were estimated at 20 to 25 degrees.

Reconstruction afterward by the ship's navigation team estimated that the *South Dakota* had come within twenty miles of the center of the tropical cyclone. Destroyers were particularly vulnerable during the storm, especially those that had pumped ballast water overboard to make room for the expected fuel oil coming into their tanks. Buoyancy and stability were at risk. Three of them capsized and sank—the *Spence, Monaghan*, and the mail-delivery ship *Hull*. (Fewer than one hundred men survived from the three ships.) For two days, the storm prevented flight operations in support of General Douglas MacArthur's Army forces ashore. On the nineteenth Lee's flagship finally took a drink of fuel from the oiler *Marias*, but weather still impeded flight ops, and the *South Dakota* finally came to rest at Ulithi on Christmas Eve.[21] A few years later, Navy veteran Herman Wouk made the December storm the centerpiece of his Pulitzer Prize–winning novel *The Caine Mutiny*.

Commander Tom Buell, biographer of two admirals, Spruance and King, proffered an opinion on why the fleet was endangered by the typhoon (and would be again six months later on Halsey's watch). Buell wrote, "My own view is that Halsey was out of his league by then and was a tired old man, as evidenced by photos of the time. I think that Carney [Halsey's chief of staff] was also fatigued, although the fatigue of both Carney and Halsey worsened by 1945. But King and Nimitz were stuck with Halsey because he was a national hero and insisted on staying at sea, despite his demonstrated shortcomings."[22] Historian Richard Frank added two more to the list of fatigued senior officers: Vice Admiral John McCain and Lee himself. Lee had been in the forward area a long time and typically slept little.

■ ■ ■

Meanwhile, Sino-American Cooperative Organization (SACO) operatives continued their role ashore in China. Lee had helped set up now–Captain Milton "Mary" Miles in the outfit, and it provided useful information to U.S. naval forces. Commander Mustin observed that Lee, in his role as second in command of the Third Fleet, received regular reports from Miles' unit, and surely Lee maintained a strong interest because of his earlier personal relationship with Miles. Commander Walter Ebert was Miles' assistant chief of staff and naval liaison officer in China. He recalled that he initiated many dispatches to submarines, either directly or through ComSubPac, about the locations of Japanese ships operating near the China coast. He later sent information to Admiral Halsey during his strikes against Hong Kong and Indochina early in 1945. The SACO weather stations also provided much useful information to Pacific Fleet units because weather conditions moved from the China landmass toward the Pacific Ocean.[23]

With Lee at sea during the war, Captain Jeff Metzel was the Washington contact for SACO; he was in the readiness division that was previously Lee's bailiwick. Yeoman Lillian Gilroy observed that Metzel did his division work during normal working hours—if, indeed, they could be considered normal during wartime. After hours Metzel did his unofficial duties: recruiting personnel and shipping material for the crew in China. Gilroy recalled that early in the war she typed the original SACO agreement, which was signed by President Roosevelt and by Generalissimo Chiang Kai-shek. She also worked with Colonel Sin-ju Hsiao in Washington in getting documents translated into Chinese and reproduced in proper form.[24]

■ ■ ■

The *South Dakota* sortied from Ulithi on 30 December 1944 as part of Rear Admiral Arthur Radford's Task Group 38.1, flagship *Yorktown*. On New Year's Eve, Admiral Halsey sent out a message by voice radio to ships of the Third Fleet: "Well done in 1944. A happy and prosperous 1945. Keep the bastards dying." One response was, "Thank you, wilco and out for the *South Dakota*."[25]

One of the U.S. Navy's long-held traditions is that a ship's first deck log entry of a new year is written in rhyme. Lieutenant John C. Hill II was the officer of the deck charged with that duty when Lee was on board. As an ensign and only recently graduated from the Naval Academy, he had joined the commissioning crew of the *South Dakota* in 1942. (Originally, his father, Captain Harry Hill, had been slated to command the *South Dakota*, so son John felt greatly relieved when his father was switched to the cruiser *Wichita* instead.) John Hill had been with the *South Dakota* throughout the war and after enduring numerous engagements with the enemy now turned poetic. He ended his log entry with the following:

As with this watch the year came in—
We helped it to arrive!
So hope we the war will end
In 1945!

Lieutenant Hill's hopes would eventually be fulfilled, but there was still a lot of steaming and fighting to be done.[26]

After a couple of days of exercises at sea, the force attacked targets on Formosa (as it was then called) on 3 January. On 6 January carrier planes attacked Luzon, the main island of the Philippines, in conjunction with the Allied invasion of Lingayen Gulf. Next on Halsey's operational plan was a venture into the China Sea in order to go after objectives in that area. The goal was to destroy Japanese shipping and thus further weaken the supply line to Japan. Two targets in particular on Halsey's wish list were the flight-deck battleships *Ise* and *Hyuga*. They had escaped Lee's guns at Leyte Gulf because Halsey had sent Task Force 34 south after he got what he perceived to be Nimitz's stinging message. On 9 January carrier planes blasted Formosa and the task force proceeded at night through the Bashi Channel that separated that island from Luzon.

Commander Mustin felt that the venture was precarious and amounted to going out on a limb in search of a rich hunting ground. He was in flag plot as the task force proceeded through the channel. American radar picked up Japanese air traffic, which brought a response from U.S. night fighters. Mustin remembered the experience of watching on radar as the fighter director coached an American plane to intercept the target. The audio came from listening to the communication between the fighter director and pilot, which included a requirement for visual identification of the Japanese plane to ensure no American planes would be shot down by mistake.[27]

All told, Mustin and other members of the staff were silent witnesses as three Japanese planes dispatched from the Philippines were identified and shot down, one after another. The upshot was that the American force was able to get into the China Sea undetected. A number of the strikes were in Indochina, between Hanoi and Saigon, place-names that would become much more familiar two decades later during the Vietnam War. The force did not bag the *Ise* and *Hyuga*, which had sheltered temporarily at Lingga Roads near Singapore, though their fighting days were essentially ended. The carrier planes did sink a captured French cruiser and a Japanese light cruiser as well as further constricting the supply lines. Meanwhile, American submarines were taking a toll as well. On 16 January the carrier planes attacked Hong Kong, which the British had surrendered to Japan early in the war. The fleet then encountered heavy weather as it returned to the Philippines to provide protection for the Lingayen Gulf operation.[28] On 24–25 January, Lee withdrew from the carrier force and formed Task Force 34 for two days of gunnery exercises and tactical maneuvers.

Lieutenant Commander Bill McMillan served for a time as flag secretary for Lee's staff. He was struck by Lee's patience, saying he never experienced any exasperation on the admiral's part. Lee was willing to make allowances for the younger officer's shortcomings and to be encouraging. He saw another side of Lee's personality when the *South Dakota* was alongside a refueling ship. As he looked across the distance to the oil provider, Lee spotted a small dog on board. The admiral made a remark to the effect that it was too bad the battleship didn't have a mascot. As McMillan recalled, "Several days later he was ceremoniously presented by the crew a brightly painted wooden dog on wheels, which he happily towed about everywhere to the delight of all." McMillan saw Lee's humor under trying conditions while the ship was involved in providing antiaircraft protection to the fast carriers. The American ships were subjected to an intense night air attack. A nearby task group was shooting effectively at the Japanese aircraft, with the result that some of them began falling into the task group that included the *South Dakota*. Nerves were on edge, recalled McMillan. Admiral Lee lifted the handset for the voice radio and called the commander of the task group under attack. His message: "Stop throwing your dead cats in our yard."[29]

When Admiral Raymond Spruance relieved Admiral Halsey at midnight on 26–27 January, the ships that had comprised the Third Fleet were now redesignated as the Fifth Fleet. Vice Admiral Mitscher relieved Vice Admiral McCain; Task Force 38 now became Task Force 58. The modest Spruance chose as his fleet flagship the heavy cruiser *Indianapolis* rather than a battleship as Halsey had been riding. Spruance and Mitscher would be the leaders as the U.S. Navy carried the attack ever closer to Japan, including strikes on the home islands. On 16–17 February the fleet launched air attacks on Honshu, the main island of Japan. The strikes on the Tokyo area included the first U.S. Navy-launched planes to attack there since Lieutenant Colonel Jimmy Doolittle's famous air raid in April 1942. (Army B-29 bombers from the Marianas had been hitting Tokyo since November 1944.)

There was no time to rest, because the carrier task force then went to the Bonin Islands to support Marine amphibious landings at Iwo Jima on 19 February. The reasons for capturing Iwo Jima were several. It was a waypoint between the Marianas and Tokyo and thus could serve as an emergency landing point for B-29s that had engine trouble or battle damage during strikes. Further, Iwo's airstrip became a base for U.S. fighters to accompany the longer-range bombers on their flights from the Marianas and prevented Japanese fighters from using it. In addition, the island's capture prevented Japanese radar from detecting raids. The *South Dakota* provided antiaircraft gunnery to protect the fleet during the Iwo Jima mission. And the task force demonstrated the value of its speed and mobility by conducting further strikes on Tokyo and attacking Okinawa as well. The latter, part of the Ryukyu chain, was still another step ahead in the island-hopping campaign and strategically important because it is only a few hundred miles from the main islands of Japan. Mitscher's carriers hit it on 1 March. As part of the task force, the *South Dakota* returned to Ulithi on 5 March.[30]

Though Ulithi Atoll was considered a relatively safe haven for the U.S. warships, it turned out even that location could be fraught with peril. On 11 March, a kamikaze pilot flew his Frances attack plane fifteen hundred miles one way, went undetected, and hit the carrier *Randolph* while her crew was watching a movie in the hangar deck. The Japanese plane's bomb exploded, and the toll was 27 Americans killed and 105 wounded. The *South Dakota* was fewer than one thousand yards away at the time, essentially parallel to the carrier because of the winds and currents. Her crewmen were gathered on the fantail, also to watch a film. They heard the thunderous roar nearby as the bomb exploded. Ensign John Mullen of the *South Dakota* recalled that he heard a plane overhead but then resumed watching the movie. As he described the incident, "All of a sudden, the whole sky was lit up from a terrific explosion on the fantail of the *Randolph*. . . . Then came the sickening sound of the explosion. Then, smaller explosions, and the roar of flames."[31]

During periods in port at Ulithi, the crews of the *South Dakota* and many other ships enjoyed going ashore for recreation. Lee enjoyed it when the sailors were entertained by the likes of comedian Joe E. Brown, who had appeared in a good many movies. Another diversion came in the form of exhibition baseball games involving Bob Feller, who before the war was one of the top pitchers in the major leagues. During the war he was a chief petty officer and headed a gun crew on board the *Alabama*. What Lee did not like were the visits from people termed "Fancy Dans." As Aertsen put it, the admiral "put his foot down for any of these guys that were tooling around with a bunch of sexy girls, his point of view being that he didn't want to get these guys all worked up for no good reason when there wasn't anything they could do about it anyway."[32]

In early 1945, Captain Frederick Entwistle reported to the *South Dakota* for temporary duty on behalf of the Bureau of Ordnance. He was there to evaluate the effectiveness of the proximity fuze and radar in combat conditions. And he had still another mission on behalf of the Manhattan Project, which was developing the atomic bomb. As he put it years later, he was "generally viewing possibilities and probabilities" for the most effective target areas in Japan and also exploring potential storage areas for bomb components. Though he was confident that Lee understood the principles that made the weapon work, he could not discuss the bomb with him because Lee did not have the necessary clearance for the tightly held information.[33]

In mid-March the Fifth Fleet received reinforcements in the form of Royal Navy ships that constituted the British Pacific Fleet. Part of the reason for their deployment was to satisfy British political leaders that their nation's ships could help support an ally. Admirals Ernest King and Chester Nimitz resisted at first, but finally the ships were added. One of the factors was that Task Force 58 was minus a carrier because of the kamikaze attack on the *Randolph*. The added ships were designated as Task Force 57, commanded by British officers but under the overall command of the U.S. Navy. Essentially, the British task force was comparable to an American task group.

On the docket for coming weeks was the operation to capture Kerama Retto, a group of islands in the Ryukyus, and the subsequent invasion of Okinawa, practically knocking on the door of the home islands. Kerama Retto would serve as a support base and anchorage for the U.S. ships. In preparation for this operation Admiral Spruance designated Admiral Lee as commander of Task Force 59, which comprised eight fast battleships, eleven cruisers, and twenty-three destroyers. It was classified as a heavy striking force as it went out from Ulithi for two days of maneuvers, essentially comparable to the drills Lee had run with the surface ships in the summer of 1944, prior to the invasion of the Philippines. The difference this time was that the potential opposing force was considerably diminished in size and power by 1945. Even so, the super battleship *Yamato*, having survived the Battle of Leyte Gulf, still remained a potent threat. After the crews gained experience through the tactical maneuvers, Task Force 59 was dissolved, and the ships returned to their places in the carrier task groups.[34]

During the period of 18–21 March, the carrier force launched air attacks on targets in the home islands. On the morning of 19 March, while the fast carriers were operating under a low ceiling of haze, Japanese bombers and kamikazes struck at their oppressors. Japanese planes bombed the carriers *Franklin* and *Wasp*. The *Franklin* was grievously wounded and suffered heavy personnel casualties. The ship was out of the war and limped all the way back to the United States for repairs. She never fought again. Scholar Malcolm Muir made the point that she was the most seriously damaged ship of the period, and she was not under antiair protection from battleships at the time, because the Japanese pilots sought to attack the carriers farthest from the battleships. Muir wrote that only one fast carrier was lost to air attack while under fast battleship protection, the *Princeton* at Leyte Gulf. That bespeaks the value of Lee's ships in a role that was not conceived for them when they were designed and built. One possible explanation of why the Japanese turned to kamikazes was that pilots who intended to survive encountered such effective antiaircraft fire from the ships escorting carriers that they had difficulty carrying out their missions.[35]

Air attacks hit Okinawa as part of the softening-up process. The heavy ships were drawn out of the carrier groups to form Task Group 59.7, commanded by Admiral Lee. It was made up of eight fast battleships, Spruance's flagship, *Indianapolis*, and an assortment of destroyers and destroyer minesweepers. (As mentioned earlier, the *Iowa* and *Alabama* were in the United States at the time for overhauls.) Lloyd Mustin remembered that a plan to use the heavy ships for shore bombardment was a last-minute idea that developed as the ships were steaming northward to Okinawa. The gunnery bombardments of southern Okinawa constituted a diversion aimed at deceiving the defending Japanese on where the real landings would take place.[36]

The staff received a list of appropriate shore targets from aerial reconnaissance and other intelligence sources. During the night of 23–24 March, Mustin stayed up late to work with the staff Marine officer, Lieutenant Colonel Arthur MacArthur. They used grid coordinates to lay out the positions of targets to be hit. They also made up a bombardment plan that directed which ships would fire at which targets, how much ammunition, and sequence of firing. Then they disseminated the plan to the various ships. Mustin recalled it as a slow, laborious process that involved transferring the written plans by highline to accompanying destroyers, for further transfer to the ships that would be shooting.

Lee's four divisions of battleships opened up at 0930 on 24 March at a range of twenty-two thousand yards and proceeded to bombard the southern coast. They stayed at a distance because of a concern about mines offshore. The eight battleships unleashed a total of 1,375 16-inch projectiles during the day's shooting. During this operation, the *Missouri* and *Wisconsin* fired their main battery guns in anger for the first time since joining the war. Throughout the day, floatplanes from the battleships were over the island as spotters. Their inputs enabled the gunnery officers of the various ships to see how well their batteries were aligned in taking on the targets. Mustin, however, later said of the event, "As a matter of fact, the targets ashore were not really worth this effort. . . . Whether any substantial military effect was achieved by this bombardment, I don't recall ever hearing." He did concede that the Japanese might have concluded that the bombardment, accompanied by the minesweepers operating offshore, was a prelude to landings in that area.[37]

During that period leading up to the 1 April invasion, the carriers maintained their aerial assaults and continued their support once the troops were ashore. When the soldiers and Marines did go ashore, it was on landing beaches on the western side of the island. Perhaps the feint did have some effect.

Ever since his victory at Guadalcanal in November 1942, Lee had remained at sea much of the time so he could command the battle line in a surface engagement. By the spring of 1945 the only real remaining surface target was the biggest battleship in existence, the monstrous 72,000-ton *Yamato*.

On 6 April, the *Yamato*, accompanied by the light cruiser *Yahagi* and eight destroyers, steamed forth from Japan's Inland Sea and headed south on a suicide mission labeled Operation Ten-Go. Her sacrifice was perhaps to redeem what little fading honor still existed in the Japanese surface fleet. The plan called for her to steam to Okinawa, and there she was to provide gunfire support for Japanese troops on the island. As the *Yamato* made her way at sea, Lee's battleships were still involved in the carrier screens and too far away to engage. Rear Admiral Morton Deyo's older battleships were between the super ship and Okinawa and might have had a shot. Admiral Raymond Spruance, a former battleship skipper, would have preferred that. But the ultimate executioners were Marc Mitscher's carrier planes, undeterred by any air cover for the Japanese force. The attacking planes clearly had a far superior range advantage over the old battleships. On the afternoon of 7 April, hundreds of carrier planes approached the target. They were Corsair and Hellcat fighters, Helldiver bombers, and Avengers armed with torpedoes. The attack with bombs and torpedoes was merciless and decisive. American planes hit her with a combination of five bombs and ten torpedoes. The giant dreadnought exploded in a mushroom cloud and sank at 1423. She took with her to the bottom some 2,500 crew members and never got close to Okinawa. The carrier planes also sank the *Yahagi*, including 446 of her crew, and four of the eight destroyers. American losses in the engagement amounted to ten airplanes and twelve men.[38]

One of the prominent Japanese strongholds was known as Shuri Castle. It was east of the port of Naha in the southeastern area of Okinawa. It was the headquarters for Lieutenant General Mitsuru Ushijima, commander of the 32nd Army that sought to defend against the American invaders. The Shuri line comprised a series of underground tunnels and caves. On 19 April three U.S. Army divisions staged an attack against the line. American battleships, cruisers, and destroyers approached under cover of darkness to support the offensive. Their bombardment began at 0540. Lee's Task Group 58.7—comprising the *South Dakota, North Carolina,* and *Washington*—also arrived in darkness.

The *North Carolina* commenced the shelling at 0647. The *South Dakota* followed suit with her 16-inch guns at 0853, and they were joined by the 5-inchers at 1116. The *South Dakota*'s Kingfisher observation planes were overhead to direct the fire at preplanned targets of opportunity. American carrier planes joined in the onslaught. Even so, the Japanese remained mostly unharmed because they were underground. The *South Dakota*'s contribution to the fireworks included 227 16-inch projectiles and 114 rounds of 5-inch.[39]

As the Okinawa campaign continued to unfold, the American carriers were launching around one thousand aircraft a day to strike Japanese on the island. Even as the attacks by American planes continued unabated, the menace from Japanese kamikaze suicide attacks became ever more pronounced. As Guil Aertsen described it, "There was just no way of stopping the momentum of something like that it if was properly aimed at you. . . . We even shot the main batteries in the water and [tried] to knock them down with a splash. Part of the problem was that the American ships often didn't detect the suicide planes until they were close aboard, and there was precious little time to fire at them before impact."[40]

The kamikazes were also a huge concern for the staff gunnery officer, Commander Mustin. He observed that many of the Japanese pilots were not well trained; they were "bottom of the barrel," as he called them. Some Japanese pilots were experienced, but most of the best ones had already been lost. Those who took one-way trips to death were shepherded to the American ships by the more capable pilots who were not going to die during the mission. Once the kamikazes were in the vicinity of their targets, it was a matter of aiming directly at ships. This generally involved a no-deflection shot by the defenders, but the kamikazes often popped up at the last moment, giving gunners little time to respond. Sometimes they kept their presence hidden by approaching through clouds.

An additional menace came in the form of baka bombs; the nickname came from the Allies and was a translation of the Japanese word for "fool" or "idiot." The Japanese called them "cherry blossoms." Essentially they were guided missiles with 1,000-pound warheads. They were dropped from mother planes, and the guidance system was the human being inside; he used propulsion rockets at the aft end to steer. Even the 5-inch projectiles with proximity fuzes were not as effective as previously because they were not optimized for close-in targets such as these. As designed by the Bureau of Ordnance, they did not arm for explosion until a certain distance after being fired. The kamikazes were sometimes so close that the projectile fuzes could not work.[41] Historian Trent Hone explained, "The 5-inch gun was effective at bringing down kamikazes, and the proximity fuze was assessed to be twice as effective at that than conventional ammunition. Automatic weapons were handier and better for close range targets, so the 40mm accounted for more kills, but used lots of ammunition."[42]

Some battleships were hit by kamikazes, but the primary targets were aircraft carriers and the picket destroyers that had the mission of providing advance warning of the approaching killers. All told, the kamikazes sank dozens of ships, damaged many more, and killed nearly five thousand American naval personnel during the Okinawa campaign.[43]

As Admiral Lee contemplated the problem, his knowledge of radar was useful. Essentially, the air-search radars sent out a beam that measured about 15 degrees of arc. As Mustin pointed out, some of the energy was above the surface of the sea and some below. When these components went out in parallel, they sometimes reinforced each other, sometimes canceled each other. The general result was that radar could receive returns on incoming aircraft from some distance, but the closer they came to a ship, the higher their angle of approach and the difficulty of following them. There was no way for radar to detect planes directly overhead. The solution was to use a destroyer-type search radar antenna that had come from a repair ship at Ulithi. It was mounted atop the stub mainmast of the *South Dakota* to provide a zenith search. Determining the angle at which to tilt the antenna, recalled Mustin, was something less than scientific. Lee asked, "Well, how far back do you think we ought to tilt it. Is . . . thirty degrees a good number?"[44]

Mustin replied, "Yes, I think thirty degrees is a pretty good number. Let's try that." So the artificers from the flagship's machine shop did the necessary work to tilt the antenna backward. In summing up, Mustin said, "The idea worked more or less, but I don't think that we could claim a resounding success for it." The problem was that it was a new application, and the technicians who were looking at the radarscopes were slow in developing the operational experience to interpret what the images were telling them.[45]

Lee had been dealing with another gunnery challenge for several months. The carrier task groups, by their very nature, covered a good deal of ocean. When antiaircraft projectiles were fired at enemy planes, some destroyed their targets, and some headed back down toward the ocean to complete the arc. This could be hazardous for American ships. The 20-mm and 40-mm projectiles were equipped with self-destruct features that would blow them up after a certain period if they didn't encounter a target. Not so with the amazing proximity fuze. It was designed to explode when it came near something, whether it was a plane, a ship, or the surface of the water. This irked Lee because of the potential damage that could be incurred. He called upon the Bureau of Ordnance for a self-destruct mechanism in the proximity fuze and was essentially told that solving the problem was not on its immediate agenda. He responded by saying that such an answer was not acceptable and—by message while at sea—described a way to make the fuzes destroy a non-productive 5-inch round.[46]

Back in 1942, when he first went to war, Lee poached on the *South Dakota*'s crew to get Ray Thompson as his aide, and later, fire control officer. Now, nearly three years later, it was poaching time again. Mustin got Lieutenant (j.g.) Robert "Zeke" Foreman appropriated from the ship to the staff. He had served as the *South Dakota*'s fighter director officer and CIC watch officer. His skills were useful in trying to defang a fanatical enemy, because he had seen the kamikazes in action and knew U.S. tactics. When he first reported to the ship in 1943, he worked to tighten up CIC procedures. He told the crew to plot every air contact, both enemy and friendly. Crew members grumbled. One said, "We didn't do it that way at Santa Cruz."[47]

Foreman shot back, "And you got hit at Santa Cruz." During his initial service in the ship, CIC had been in the superstructure. When the ship went to Bremerton to be repaired after taking a bomb hit in the Marianas, the Bureau of Ships directed that a new CIC be established on the third deck, protected by armor. The ship's company mounted a protest because officers of the deck had been accustomed to ducking into the topside CIC to get updated information before going on watch; the protest was futile. And sometimes CIC would send someone out to the bridge to give advice on zigzag maneuvers. Now Lee talked with Foreman a lot about air control and kamikaze defense. Lee, for example, worked out data on radar reflections between low-flying planes and the surface of the water. Lee also talked with Foreman about what he had seen on radar screens down in CIC in order to compare it with what he had seen visually while topside. They discussed how to distinguish kamikazes with the use of identification friend or foe, or IFF (a radar add-on). Years later, Foreman recalled that even though Lee was well versed in theory, he was especially concerned about the pragmatic applications.[48]

In May 1945, the *South Dakota* continued to operate with the fast carriers in support of the Okinawa operation. On the afternoon of 6 May, the fleet once again demonstrated the ability to sustain extended operations at sea through underway replenishment. The ship was taking on 16-inch bags of smokeless powder from the ammunition ship *Wrangell*, which was alongside to starboard. While crewmen grappled to lower a tank containing bags of powder, the tank exploded in the entrance to a powder magazine on the first platform deck, near turret two. The blast led to the explosion of four more tanks. Flames and blast shot up through an ammunition-handling trunk and hatches. In particular, the flames went into a compartment used for stowing and clipping 20-mm ammunition. The fire seared the overhead and bulkheads and blistered paint on the other side of a bulkhead. The compartment contained more than 34,000 rounds of ammunition, all of which were thrown over the side into the sea as a safety precaution.[49]

Commander Carl Stillman was the ship's executive officer. He attributed the explosion to the use of metal tanks that were designed for full-charge bags of service ammunition powder; these were longer than those employed for reduced-charge bags. There were no spacers inside the tanks, thus allowing the smaller bags to slide inside the tanks. The charges were in bags of raw silk, which would burn without remnants. Apparently, the sliding bags produced an electrostatic charge in which metal inside the bags ignited fumes of the ether that was used inside the cans as a preservative. Stillman wrote that when one of the tanks was upended to get it over the sill at the entrance to the magazine, the bags slid and thus produced the charge. The executive officer recalled that "the Wrangell cast off its lines with alacrity."[50]

The instant result was the death of three men and fatal injuries to eight more; twenty-four crew members were injured but survived.[51] The potential consequences could have been far worse—a magazine explosion. When Lieutenant Foreman emerged from the forward junior officer bunkroom, near the affected magazines, he saw flames, smoke, and grains of powder that were jumping down the passageway.[52] The skipper of the *South Dakota* during the incident was Captain Charles B. "Swede" Momsen. He was the developer of the "Momsen lung," a rescue-breathing device to enable crew members to surface from sunken submarines. In this case the need was to rescue a surface ship from potential catastrophe. Initial actions included sprinkling selective magazine compartments deep in the ship with water.

In his biography of Momsen, noted crime writer Peter Maas took considerable literary license in crafting imagined dialogue that portrayed Admiral Lee as being nearly hysterical in conversation with Momsen. Maas had Lee asking whether the crew was carrying out the flooding order. In Maas' version of events, Momsen pointed skyward and said, "Anyway, we'll know soon enough. If they haven't, that's where we'll be in about thirty seconds."[53]

Aide Guil Aertsen was with the unruffled Lee at the time, which, of course, Maas was not. Aertsen's recollections differed markedly from Maas' dramatic rendering. Lee, Aertsen, and others were in flag plot, which was just aft of turret two. The space contained a big sofa, a plotting table, and a radarscope. In addition to the order to sprinkle magazine compartments, the captain had sent all crew members not engaged in running the ship or fighting the fire to the fantail so they would be some distance away if a big explosion erupted. Lee, Aertsen recalled, was given the same option but declined. His explanation: "You guys can go back if you want, but I'm going to stay here, because if that magazine goes, it won't make any difference. I'd rather be comfortable." One of Lee's staff members was a reservist, Lieutenant Dave Gray, who was a firefighter in civilian life. Aertsen described Gray as heading for the fire, "licking his chops." In any event, the fire was extinguished, and Lee remained comfortable.[54]

Though Aertsen deemed Lee to be essentially fatalistic, he didn't observe him to be foolhardy: "We didn't have any trouble getting him to stay under cover if we were under [air] attack . . . where there's no need to be out in the open. The ship's people were doing the fighting of that ship."

The aide did not perceive the admiral to be overtly religious. Neither did he consider him to be an atheist; after Lee had observed the wonders of nature, he expressed his belief that some higher power had been involved in producing them. Lee was not one who attended shipboard divine services; rather, he kept his beliefs in that regard to himself. Aertsen recalled, "We didn't get into any esoteric conversations on basic philosophy as to whether he believed in predestination."[55]

■ ■ ■

Since the summer and autumn of 1944, Commodore Tom Jeter had proven to be a mismatch as Lee's chief of staff. That changed on 10 May 1945, when Captain Joseph C. Cronin, another aviator, came aboard to relieve him. In the eyes of Lee's aide, Guil Aertsen, Cronin was a decided improvement. He was more willing than Jeter to adapt to the situation in which he found himself without shaking things up. It was a learning experience for the aviator and he was willing to fit in, to chat with Lee and the staff to pick up what he needed to know. He was likable and much quieter than the brash Jeter had been, which was a welcome change.[56]

One week after the near-catastrophic magazine incident, the *South Dakota* pulled out of Task Group 58.4 and headed for Apra Harbor, Guam, where she arrived on 14 May. What a contrast a year made. Eleven months earlier, the ship suffered major damage while supporting the invasion of nearby Saipan in the Marianas. The subsequent capture of Guam provided the Navy with a valuable logistic support base. On 15 May the ship entered the floating dry dock *ABSD-3*. Such was the forward movement of the Central Pacific campaign that Lee's flagship could get essentially shipyard-type repairs far from a shipyard. The damaged magazine was repaired, and more serious work was applied to the ship's propulsion system. High-speed operations with the aircraft carriers, and the resulting vibrations had damaged shafts, strut bearings, and all four propellers. The consequence was a shimmy at high speed that showed up when the ship was steaming with the carriers, and now it was repaired. The *South Dakota* had been under way continuously for fifty-five days, which had precluded boiler maintenance, which also was now accomplished. The time in port also provided a respite for the crew and the men who were part of the flag allowance. On 27 May the refurbished battleship emerged from the dry dock and again moored in Apra Harbor.[57]

An Army Air Forces repair ship with several helicopters on board was in port at the time. Lee wondered if one could land on board a battleship and asked Lieutenant Commander Bill McMillan to find out. The captain of the Army ship was most cooperative. On 28 May, sailors cleared the top of the forward turret and the helo landed there in the late afternoon. Lee, who had had some experience riding battleship floatplanes, boarded the Army craft and got a scenic tour of the harbor before returning. As McMillan recalled the admiral's reaction, "He was quite preoccupied for some time after this experience, and I felt sure he was considering the practicality of using helicopters for exchange of mail, personnel, etc throughout the Fleet. The Admiral said that this was obvious of course, but that he was really considering the time a helicopter could save him when going ashore at Ulithi."[58]

The following day a contingent of British warships arrived in the port. Included were top-of-the line battleship *King George V* and three destroyers. Lee hosted a visit from Vice Admiral Bernard Rawlings, who was second in command of the British Pacific Fleet. With the war in Europe having concluded earlier in the month, the Royal Navy ships augmented those of the Americans. Rawlings commanded Task Force 57.[59]

In recollection, Lee's aide Guil Aertsen described a visit on another occasion with the big boss, Admiral Bruce Fraser, overall commander of the British Pacific Fleet. The get-together took place on board Fraser's flagship, the battleship *Howe*. Aertsen observed that Fraser was a lord and "had a family tartan that went back to God knows what." But there was homespun, Kentucky-born Lee chatting amiably and showing no deference to British nobility. As Aertsen said, "He knew exactly how to stand up and speak his piece and be diplomatic about the thing. And he could say sweet nothings as well as it was necessary in the international way of doing things—in a very polite and able way." Lee was as formal as need be and commanded respect for his knowledge and experience. Aertsen summarized that Lee "had a lot of self-respect, and he knew he was good. But he was a very humble man, too, and I think that's part of the distinguished attributes. He had all of his competence, but he didn't bother to tell you."[60]

The flagship's stopover in Guam provided another benefit. Earlier in the year, Admiral Nimitz, as commander in chief, Pacific Fleet and Pacific Ocean Areas, had moved his headquarters from Pearl Harbor to Guam. The move put him closer to the scene of combat and in this case gave him the opportunity for face-to-face conversations with Admiral Lee on operational issues. Commander Mustin sometimes was present for the discussions. Mustin was impressed by Nimitz's acceptance of the validity of observations made by those who had experienced combat. He wanted to know, for example, what it was like to be on the receiving end of a kamikaze attack. Nimitz's approach was in contrast to the communications Lee had with offices in Washington. According to Mustin, they often responded with a "father knows best" approach when Lee suggested changes the officers there were recalcitrant about accepting.[61]

One of the topics that Lee explored was the idea that the combat information center on board a battleship, cruiser, or destroyer should be included in the gunnery department, as it had been in his flagships. His reasoning was that CIC provided information that was necessary for the effective use of the ship's armament and thus should have a direct link in the organizational structure. The Navy Department directed an experiment in which a few ships, including the battleship *Missouri*, were augmented by an operations department. The new department embraced communications and CIC. After the war, the change was made permanent in U.S. Navy ships. In the meantime, Mustin agreed with Admiral Lee's approach. In his oral history, many years later, Mustin observed of the *Missouri*, "She was the least efficient combat wise, the only one [of the fast battleships] that a kamikaze ever managed to hit because the others simply didn't permit any kamikaze that came toward one of those battleships. It was just torn to pieces in midair long before he got to where he thought he was going."[62]

On 29 May, the newly repaired *South Dakota* and destroyers *Hale* and *Stembel* departed Guam and undertook a couple of days of exercises that included antisubmarine drills and gunnery practice. On the afternoon of 1 June 1945 the flagship anchored in San Pedro Bay, Leyte. Admiral Lee's World War II combat service was over, having started in the summer of 1942. The primary threat, with plans on the table to invade Japan's home islands, was from kamikaze attacks. Lee had been selected to try to find effective countermeasures.

Mustin conjectured that Lee had probably learned during the visit to Guam that he would be leaving the battleship command. Lee was deeply disappointed. He had received his orders by the time the *South Dakota* got to the Philippines. He didn't want to leave, because he had brought the battleships this far and wanted to be in action until the end. However, remembered Mustin, the admiral realized that there was no use in arguing. He never proposed appealing the decision to Washington, though, as Mustin put it, this situation was "in quite vivid contrast to his quick response to other things from Washington that he didn't like."[63]

On 16 June, Lee turned over command of Battleship Squadron Two to Rear Admiral John F. Shafroth, who had been one of his division commanders. During the turnover, Lee told Shafroth, "Don't get yourself settled in that job, because

I'm coming back." Lee believed—or was led to believe—that he would return to the Western Pacific once the kamikaze problem was solved. Some of Lee's staff members thought, however, that they were leaving the war theater for good. Perhaps the idea that Lee could return to his battleships was a hollow promise—a carrot to get him to agree to the anti-kamikaze assignment.[64]

The reason that Lee had not been east of Hawaii since the summer of 1942 was the conviction on the part of the Navy's leaders that he was the best man to take on Japan's fleet in a surface action. But that possibility had essentially disappeared by June, especially after the sinking of the *Yamato* in April. Because of fuel shortages, the *Ise* and the *Hyuga*, the two half-baked battleship/aircraft carriers, were immobilized at Kure, Japan, where they served as stationary antiaircraft batteries. The *Nagato*, which had been the Combined Fleet flagship during the attack on Pearl Harbor, was limited to antiaircraft and coastal defense duties and posed no seagoing threat. She was the only unconverted Japanese battleship that survived the war.

Shafroth, a Naval Academy classmate of Lee, brought some staff officers with him; Mustin was unimpressed by them. Lieutenant Commander Edward Mathews, a Lee staff member who remained behind, later wrote that Shafroth and his people did a poor job tactically in executing the initial home-island shore bombardment. It took place on 14 July against targets at Kamaishi on the island of Honshu. Merchant ships and a small gunboat escaped the pounding unscathed. The battleships often overshot their targets; in one such case, they missed their target—a steel mill—but set nearby houses aflame. The smoke obscured the mill, which made spotting difficult, but eventually the big projectiles put it out of business. Unfortunately, Lee was no longer on hand to employ his operational expertise. He was needed elsewhere.[65]

▪ 15 ▪

WAR'S END AT LAST
June–August 1945

T here was little relief for anyone, from admiral to seaman, as the heat of
approaching summer radiated through the battleship *South Dakota* at San
Pedro Bay, Leyte Gulf, in the Philippines. Nor would there be much relief
for the Japanese farther north. Though the temperature was lower there, the war
would grow ever hotter as the U.S. Third Fleet prepared to sortie and resume the
relentless air and sea attacks that had begun earlier in the year against the Japanese
home islands. The fast carrier task force by this time had become a sustainable
entity, thanks to underway replenishment, and would not enter an anchorage
again for many weeks.

Halfway around the world, Commodore Arleigh A. Burke, an officer two grades
junior to Lee, had played a key role in having him ordered home to the United
States. Burke had already made himself something of a legend in the fighting of
the Pacific War. First were his destroyer exploits in the Solomons, then his superb
service as chief of staff to Vice Admiral Marc A. Mitscher, commander of the fast
carrier task force. Now Burke was commanding the Special Defense Section on
the staff of the commander in chief, U.S. Fleet (CominCh). Burke's section was
part of the Readiness Division within the staff. Lee himself was the first head of
the Readiness Division before he went to the Pacific in 1942.

Burke's task was to find a remedy for the Japanese kamikaze aircraft, which posed a horrific threat for the planned autumn invasion of Japan itself. Because the number of lives and ships that might be saved was potentially so great, Commodore Burke was assured that he would have a free hand in lining up the people and resources he needed. Burke coordinated the program from Washington, and part of his support came from a group of operations research specialists. The object of the overall effort was to devise possible solutions in the form of revised tactics, new equipment, new weapons, and so forth. The ships and airplanes assigned to Lee's force would run experiments to see what worked and what didn't. Commodore Burke selected Lee to command the operational tests because Lee was, in Burke's estimation, "the best analytical man in the Navy."

There were a few raised eyebrows over the choice, for it meant pulling an experienced combat commander out of the war zone. Rear Admiral Walter DeLany, the head of the Readiness Section of the fleet staff, challenged Burke's choice: "You can't order a vice admiral on that. It's a BuPers [Bureau of Naval Personnel] order."[1]

"They didn't tell me I had any restrictions," answered Burke. "If I had, I'd have gone away."

"You'll disrupt everything," complained DeLany. But Burke held out, and he got his man.

Early on the morning of 18 June, a PT boat came alongside the dark gray hull of the *South Dakota*, and for the last time in his life, Willis Lee took leave of a battleship. Going down the accommodation ladder ahead of him were the few members of his staff he was taking along: Captain John B. Taylor, operations; Commander Lloyd M. Mustin, gunnery, radar, and combat information center; Lieutenant Guilliaem Aertsen III, flag lieutenant; and Lieutenant (j.g.) Robert "Zeke" Foreman, fighter direction officer. The boat headed for the island of Samar, where the group climbed into a four-engine R4D Navy transport plane to begin the first leg of the long haul to the East Coast of the United States.

Lee had another conversation while he was on the island. One day when he was in an officers' club, he spotted Commander Ray Hunter; he walked over and put his hand on Hunter's shoulder. The admiral remembered Hunter as the *Washington*'s officer of the deck during the 1942 night battle off Savo Island. They spent nearly an hour chatting and catching up. It was a meeting that Hunter recalled warmly many years later.[2]

Zeke Foreman went on ahead to set up visits with people Lee wanted to see in the United States. The other four flew on to Hawaii, San Francisco, and Washington. It was a wearying journey in those days before jet passenger planes. Lee later told his wife that, except for a few nurses, the trip marked the first time he had seen white women since July 1943, when a ship with nurses on board passed within four hundred yards of his.[3] He was fibbing, because he had seen any number of Caucasian women when he was in Hawaii during the war.

While in Washington, where he spent a week or so, Lee met with Burke to find out how the experimental program would work and to discuss the things they hoped to accomplish. Lee also had meetings with various other people who were sponsoring new developments in antiair warfare. And Lee had a visit with the CominCh himself, Fleet Admiral Ernest J. King. Lee had served on King's U.S. Fleet staff in 1942, before he went to sea. Now was a time for talking about developing events in the Pacific and the hopes King had for solving the kamikaze problem. Guil Aertsen was along, and he observed that King was "relaxed" and "very warm," because both of them had come back from the combat area. King thanked Lee for what he had been accomplishing and added, "I don't have to tell you what this is about. You know more than I do."[4]

The trip to Washington also afforded Lee the opportunity to renew old acquaintances, because it was the first time he had been to the city in nearly three years. He went night-clubbing with Lila Mae Hanna, Mabelle's niece from Illinois; she was working in the capital during the war. He also took her to a party at the Chinese embassy. Their host was Sin-ju Hsiao, now a colonel. Hsiao was the attaché with whom Lee had developed close ties before the war and was involved in the process of sending Commander Milton E. Miles and his SACO group to China. Mrs. Miles, who lived near Washington, went to the party. She recalled that Lee took her aside, put his arm around her, and told her that her husband would be promoted to rear admiral on the basis of his service in China. She considered it an example of Lee's thoughtfulness regarding those who worked for him.[5] Still another aspect of the Washington visit was that Lee received a telephone call from David Lawrence, editor of *United States News*, which a few years later became

U.S. News & World Report. Not surprisingly, the publicity-averse admiral told Lawrence that he was too busy to participate in an interview.[6]

From Washington Lee called his wife in Illinois and asked her to meet him in Portland, Maine. He expected to be there when she arrived. Instead, on 4 July she got there ahead of him. The Navy plane with Lee on board circled the field, landed, and taxied to within a few feet of the waiting greeters. Lee got off first, followed by his staff members. Mabelle, who had missed her husband for nearly three years, was thrilled. Soon after, she wrote to her sisters, "Well, Lee looks grand and I was glad to see him and vica-versa [*sic*]. He is not so sun burnt—and no gray hairs. Sec. [of the Navy James V.] Forrestal told him that he was surprised to see him looking so well—and said the Japs surely didn't make a dent in him."[7] The letters she wrote to her sisters during the next two months bubbled with delight at being with her husband again.

On 2 July 1945, Vice Admiral Lee was officially designated as commander of Task Force 69, as the experimental unit was initially titled. It would operate within Maine's Casco Bay. Within a month, it was redesignated Composite Task Force, U.S. Atlantic Fleet. Initially, the staff was small, although it grew rapidly as reserve officers were added to the nucleus of regulars. As his chief of staff, Lee acquired Captain John B. McLean, a destroyer squadron commander in the battle of Okinawa and experienced in undergoing kamikaze attack.[8]

Lee had been given the same assurance as Burke—that he could pick the people he wanted, but it didn't always work out. He tried to get Commander Robert Pirie, an aviator, as his air operations officer, for aircraft would certainly be heavily involved in the experimental work. Nimitz's staff people in Hawaii had recommended Pirie, but as it turned out, he was not available, despite the earlier promise. Pirie had been on Rear Admiral Gerald Bogan's staff in Task Group 38.2. In January 1945 he reported to Washington and joined the staff of Fleet Admiral Ernest King as air operations officer.[9] Clearly, King had even more horsepower than did Lee. The pilot nominated for the project instead was Commander Edmund Konrad, who declined. He had had plenty of combat experience but wasn't interested in the experimental work. As Mustin remembered, Konrad wanted a quiet backwater job in which he could take it easy and still draw flight pay. Instead, Task Force 69 wound up with Commander Mustin himself, from Lee's former battleship staff, as both gunnery/radar and air operations officer.[10]

Casco Bay was useful as a naval base, because it was the place from which the escort ships departed to rendezvous at sea with transatlantic convoys in the war against Germany. It was almost a day's steaming closer to Europe than other East Coast ports. Because the escorts were destroyer types, the commander of Destroyer Force, Atlantic Fleet (ComDesLant) had his headquarters there. In the summer of 1945, that officer was Rear Admiral Oliver M. Read, and he was at the top of the rank pyramid in the area. But Lee had three stars to Read's two, thus displacing him at the pinnacle. There was irony involved, for few of the Navy's senior officers were less conscious of rank than Lee.

An early example of Lee's approach came when it was time to find a place for him to live. The DesLant staff was responsible for logistics in the area and had plans to put Lee up at a local country club that the Navy had taken over as an officers' club. But Lee would have none of it. He was more concerned about his aide, Lieutenant Guil Aertsen. Guil had been married during a brief leave period a year and a half earlier, so his time with his new bride had been practically nonexistent. Lee wanted a place for the Aertsens' honeymoon.

Such a place was the rooming house of Mrs. Frank B. Fish in Falmouth Foreside, a small community near Portland on the shore of Casco Bay. The house contained a large apartment on the third floor and a smaller one on the second. The DesLant people decided, after the country club was ruled out, that the top floor of Mrs. Fish's house would be ideal for the admiral and his wife. The Aertsens could then live on the second floor and "protect" the admiral upstairs. Lee looked it over, was satisfied with the place, and then announced, "Guil, now's your chance for your honeymoon. You take the upstairs, and Mrs. Lee and I will keep people from bothering you."[11]

Lee's initial flagship for Task Force 69 was the new radar picket destroyer *Dennis J. Buckley.* The role of picket ships in the Pacific was to provide advance warning of incoming enemy air raids. But even though he would go to sea in the destroyer from time to time in the ensuing weeks, Lee's principal command post was on land. The ship's gunnery officer, Lieutenant John J. O'Brien, wrote years later: "There was no need for the admiral to ride with us, and he spent his days ashore. We didn't see him but got some perverse satisfaction from flying his flag. COMDESLANT's flagship, a destroyer tender anchored permanently in Casco Bay, was obliged to salute us every time we steamed past on our way in or out.

The DESLANT staff, a little unfairly, was always regarded by destroyer crews as a notch below subhuman. Some of our individual and informal responses to their salutes were definitely not out of the Bluejackets Manual."[12]

Lee and his staff spent most of their time in a temporary wooden building on Great Diamond Island in Casco Bay. There they had offices from which Lee was able to talk with Burke by scrambler phone—both to find out what new things he wanted tested and to give him the results of tests already conducted. Also, the location ashore provided the opportunity for meetings, often over lunch, with people from the Navy Department in Washington and with representatives from contractors such as Raytheon and Pratt & Whitney.[13]

The task force initially included one other picket destroyer, the *Henry W. Tucker*. She and the *Dennis J. Buckley* had been altered for antiaircraft work by the removal of torpedo tubes, the enlargement of their combat information centers, and the addition of height-finding radars. The remainder of the force consisted of two destroyer escorts, some infantry landing craft, and the old gunnery training ship *Wyoming*. The latter was a former battleship that had been largely demilitarized as part of the 1930 London Treaty on the Limitation of Naval Armaments.

On 11 August the *Wyoming* replaced the *Dennis J. Buckley* as Lee's flagship, even though he was seldom on board. That meant no more saluting fun for the destroyer's crew. In her new role, the *Wyoming* served as a seagoing platform on which the experimenters could mount new guns, radars, fire control devices, and so forth in order to conduct their tests. Later the new heavy cruiser *Bremerton* was added to the task force. As for aircraft, three squadrons of aircraft carrier combat types were assigned to the force; they were based at the naval air station at nearby Brunswick, Maine. They were F6F Hellcat fighters and SB2C dive-bombers, and all the pilots had served a minimum of two combat tours in Pacific Fleet aircraft carriers.[14]

The experiments got under way immediately with a sense of urgency to them. If things were to be discovered that would help cut down the kamikaze threat, they would have to be implemented thousands of miles away and in rather short order. New tactics could be distributed to the fleet within a few weeks. But if some new piece of equipment—a radar, director, type of gun, or ammunition—was recommended, the problem was greater. There were logistical concerns involved in having it mass-produced and provided to a significant number of ships in time to be useful. In addition, ships' crews would have to be trained to operate the new equipment. Thus, an important concern included determination of how best to use the equipment already on board.

That meant constant firing tests against drone aircraft, towed target sleeves, and non-firing tests by ships singly and in groups against formations of aircraft simulating various attack tactics. The pilots took part in the experimentation with a great deal of enthusiasm. One of the destroyer skippers described the aviators as "a bunch of red-hot pilots," which indeed they were. In the words of a Lee staff member, they were "crazy and full of derring-do." One of the SB2C Helldivers made a run on the destroyer *Henry W. Tucker*. But the plane didn't pull up in time, and its propeller chewed up the ship's air-search radar. "We strive to make it realistic," Commander Mustin told the destroyer's commanding officer afterward. That skipper was Commander Bernard H. Meyer, who remembered the plane coming in low to simulate a kamikaze. Meyer expected the plane to crash and was prepared to rescue the pilot, but he returned to base safely. The ship had to go to the Boston Navy Yard for repairs. There were also tests on the use of new types of IFF, a radar device that enabled U.S. ships to pick out enemy planes that slipped in among American aircraft returning to their carriers. This included a type installed directly in the gun directors. Aluminum "chaff" was also used extensively; the Japanese were beginning to drop it from their aircraft to try to mask or confuse radar images.[15]

Other tests evaluated different ideas on linking up directors and guns. In repeated firing runs, during which ships had to get their 5-inch guns aimed effectively at a suddenly revealed attacking aircraft, the results demonstrated that the heavy Mark 37 director was better than the Mark 51 machine gun director, which was popular in many ships in the fleet for this situation. Techniques for fast-reaction use of the Mark 37, combined with its much better accuracy after it was on target, provided the firepower to knock down an approaching plane.[16]

The Mark 51 director, with its Mark 14 gunsight, was customarily used with the lighter 20-mm and 40-mm antiaircraft guns. The task force's tests showed that the Mark 51 was not sufficiently accurate for use with the 5-inch guns. Commander Mustin was thus demonstrating, through operational tests, a concept he had espoused when he was with Lee in the Pacific—that there were few enough

guns as it was without wasting some by putting them on anything but the best
directors. The tests confirmed that it usually took four bursts of proximity-fuze
5-inch projectiles in the vicinity of a plane to be confident of shooting it down.
The problem in such an arrangement was that the Mark 37 was best for getting
hits on a plane, but what was a ship to do when faced with more kamikazes than
she had heavy directors?[17]

One piece of gear put forth for testing was a radar with a moving-target indicator (MTI) feature. Surface-search radars could be used for tracking low-flying
raids coming in, but when the planes made their approaches over land, rather
than water, the radar would pick up the land and blank out the planes. The MTI
seemed to offer a solution, for it was designed to eliminate all radar returns
except moving targets. Thus, one could see only planes and no land. But what had
worked in the laboratories and test facilities ashore was only partially effective
on board ship. Commander Meyer of the *Goodrich* considered that the MTI
feature on the SG radar did well in tests against fighter planes while operating
in the Bay of Fundy. But that was only when the ship was anchored or lying to
but not when the ship was heading to or from land.[18] More than that, in order to
add a version of MTI, it was necessary to remove other operating features that
were important. Lee and Mustin told Burke that the answer to the MTI was not
only "No" but "Hell, no."[19] This evaluation caused a small storm and brought
Burke to Casco Bay.

Still another weapon tested was an extremely rapid-fire gun that could put
out 1,200 rounds-per-barrel each minute. The guns were 20-mm Hispano-Suizas,
four barrels to a mount. The volume of fire was such that the guns could surpass
the heavy machine guns, 20-mm and 40-mm, that had been mainstays during
the war for hitting close-in targets. These Hispano-Suiza guns were installed on
board the test ship *Wyoming* and given a good workout. Mustin described them
as "frighteningly effective" against drone targets. They did not stand up well to
the high rate of fire, and this meant they required a lot of maintenance, but, even
so, they showed promise. Their job was to be ready for a few critical seconds, and
the maintenance could come later. As it happened, though, the war ended—and
with it, the kamikaze threat—before any large-scale fleet installations could be
made of these new guns.[20]

An innovation that *was* adopted was the use of antiaircraft projectiles that produced different-colored bursts when they exploded. Previously, all flak bursts were black, meaning that if more than one ship was firing at a plane, there was no way of distinguishing among the bursts. In surface gunnery against ships, different colors of dyes were used in projectiles to enable individual ships to pick out their own splashes. Now the dyes were tried in antiaircraft projectiles as well, and the task force experiments showed them to be effective and useful. Lee's group gave Burke the go-ahead and urged sending the color-burst projectiles to the fleet.[21]

During the course of these tests, Commander Mustin went to sea seven days a week to observe results. Admiral Lee sometimes went out for a day on board a destroyer or the *Wyoming* to see the experiments, but for the most part he stayed around the office. Lee's group was a rapid-reaction outfit, able to be given a test assignment and provide a recommendation within a few days. Speed was essential as the planned invasion drew nearer. Years later, Mustin expressed admiration at the way Lee was able to grasp results of the experiments from oral briefings. He would then pass on the results to Burke. As Mustin put it, Lee was able to give Burke "the whole story, as though he had personally been there while every shot was fired. [It was], I guess, one more manifestation of the combination of a very quick mind with a basically very profound understanding of the technicalities that were involved. He was a top professional in the business of war at sea."[22] Aertsen had a colorful description for Lee's ability to go to the source and soak up information. He said the admiral was a "walking digestive system for all this."[23] Periodically Lieutenant Norman Zalkind of the staff served as a courier to deliver material to Commodore Burke in Washington. SB2Cs were involved in the dive-bombing tests, and they also served as airborne taxis on the courier flights. Zalkind explained, "I made the trip at least twice and believe me it was a nerve-racking flight."[24]

Though Lee's shipboard visits were infrequent, one in particular demonstrated something about Lee but also about the curious combination of wartime working conditions in a location far from the war zone. The admiral went aboard the *Dennis J. Buckley* to observe tests of a jury-rigged antiaircraft control that had been installed at the after Mark 51 director. It was a platform about ten or twelve feet above the deck and surrounded by a waist-high railing. It had telephone connections to all the gun control stations and selector switches so various batteries could be shifted to the appropriate control station.[25]

The ship's commanding officer was Commander Kinloch C. "Casey" Walpole, who had been a junior officer in the *Concord* when Lee commanded that cruiser in the late 1930s. Now, proud of having his own ship and receiving a visit from his former "old man," Walpole put out the word to his officers that they should wear coats and ties when Lee joined them for lunch in the wardroom.

But the informal Lee was the opposite, typically casual in dress at sea. John O'Brien, the ship's gunnery officer, recalled that he and his shipmates were ill at ease in their unaccustomed formal dress when Lee was informal. O'Brien added, "It was my impression that he was too big a man to be [discomfited] by such an inconsequential thing but that he was unhappy at being unable to rescue our regular Navy [commanding officer] from such a ridiculous gaffe. No word or expression on his face was needed to communicate this; we made as quick work of the meal as possible and got back to our exercises. [During the meal], I got the impression that he [Lee] would have liked some informal conversation with us about the experiments but was too refined a gentleman to break the stiff etiquette imposed by our C.O.'s demeanor."[26]

Something similar happened ashore, although it had a happier ending. Mary Aertsen, the young wife of Lee's flag lieutenant, was also trying to make a good impression on the boss. One evening she invited the Lees up to the top-floor apartment for dinner. Being new at domestic practices, she went to the local meat market and sought the butcher's advice on a suitable dish for the admiral. The butcher suggested fowl, so Mrs. Aertsen took home a bird—"legs, feet, feathers, insides, the works," as she recalled later. She painstakingly removed the feathers with her manicuring tweezers, but she was unaware that she had to relieve the bird of its giblets and other unsavory internal organs. After finally getting her chicken plucked, she shoved it in the oven, and the apartment was pervaded with a stench that "was something out of this world." Panicking, she called her husband to find out what brand of cigarettes Lee smoked so she could offer some sort of diversion. She learned that it was Pall Mall, so she bought a whole carton and placed packs around her living room. She also tested all the chairs to find out which was the most comfortable.[27]

In due course, Lieutenant Aertsen arrived with the Lees. Embarrassed by the odor and nervous anyway, Mary Aertsen grabbed the admiral, offered him a drink, shoved him into the most comfortable chair, and then pushed a package of cigarettes in his face with the question, "Admiral, will you have a Palmolive?"

Lee looked at his hands, front and back, pretending to see if they were dirty. Then he went over to his wife and, in a stage whisper, asked, "Do you think I need any soap?" Everyone had a good laugh, Mary relaxed, and soon she developed a close relationship with the Lees. It was a friendship that worked both ways, because the admiral and his wife were able to be at ease with the young couple. Guil said of Mabelle that "she was a lovely person but shy. It took a little while to bring her out. He was a shy guy, too, actually."[28]

From time to time, there were social occasions, either at an officers' club or on one of the islands in the bay. The latter were popular for clambakes. The Navy wives, used to the deprivation that ration-conscious civilians had endured throughout the war, were somewhat in awe when they saw the large quantities of butter, for example, that were issued through Navy supply channels. But they were not so awed by the admiral's presence to forget that they might be able to advance their husbands' careers with some buttering-up of their own. Alas, Lee was the wrong target for such attentions, because he liked to pick his own friends, and he did not take kindly to such tactics. With the Aertsens, though, he could be himself. He and Guil were so close after nearly three years in the Pacific that he treated Aertsen almost as a son. In addition, Guil was a reserve officer with no career aspirations.

Casco Bay, with its pine-clad islands and shores, was a vivid contrast to the Pacific anchorages of which Lee had seen so many. During his stay in Maine, the admiral often ate fresh lobster, a delicacy not available during his Pacific years. He also delighted in going onto beaches and digging for clams—about as much chance to work with his hands as he could get. One day, in a letter to her sisters, Mabelle described a party with Captain and Mrs. James Clay that included lobster and baked potatoes. Lee demurred on that one and also on an evening dinner party. The letter explained, "Lee says we have to rest between parties a bit or we will turn into a party or a lobster." She remarked that her husband often didn't get home from work until 6:00 or 7:00 in the evening.[29] When he was away from the office, he had a chance to relax by listening to the radio in the top-floor apartment and to read the back issues of *The Saturday Evening Post* that Mrs. Fish had been piling up since 1943. They were all new to him, because he had been out of touch since even before that.

The cool northern weather and the absence of action messages and general quarters alerts enabled him to sleep better than he had on board ship, although he never did need a great deal of sleep. He was still putting in long days at his Great Diamond Island office. As long as there was a job to be done, he was giving it the effort required. But his job no longer carried the pressure of combat command with people's lives at stake and action messages at 0300. Nevertheless, he still felt a wistful longing for the war he had been forced to leave behind. In early August, after Lee had returned from one of several trips he had made to Washington to confer with Arleigh Burke, Mabelle Lee wrote to her sisters in Illinois, "Lee will be here all this month but doesn't know how much longer. He is anxious to get back to his battleships—you'd think they were his toys and afraid someone will damage them while he's away."[30]

Mabelle herself was enjoying the best time she'd had in years. After more than twenty-five years as a Navy wife, she had grown accustomed to frequent loneliness and was sometimes bitter about it. Now she was with her husband again. In that respect, remembered Guil Aertsen, it was as if they were lovebirds, delighted to be with each other on sort of a second honeymoon. There were other delights as well—parties, movies, shopping. And she spent time going out with Mary Aertsen, visiting stores in Falmouth and Portland and exploring the Maine countryside. These were almost childlike pleasures associated with being the admiral's wife. In one letter she wrote, "Don't advertise that Lee's driver can take me places in Lee's navy car as it is not good publicity for the Navy—and tax payers might object." In mid-August, following the dropping of two atomic bombs on the Japanese home islands, Mabelle Lee was exultant. To her sisters and nephew she wrote, "I know you all are excited as we about the war news. Hope the surrender comes thru soon."[31]

Hostilities did end soon, but her husband was not among the merrymakers. Mary Aertsen described the night when the news of the war's end arrived: "Everyone else was celebrating, and the four of us [Lees and Aertsens] sat in silence. . . . Lee's head was down. His shoulders were slumped. He was in his shirtsleeves. . . . He looked tired, and old, and sad, because it was irreparable.

There was no way [he could be in the Pacific for the end of the war]. I remember we sat most of the night with him that night." Admiral Lee had not gotten back to his battleships, and now he would not be going. The war had been finished without him. His task force hadn't really found a breakthrough solution to solve the kamikaze menace. And now that didn't matter either. In the days that followed, he went through the motions at work, but there was little purpose in it.[32]

One night, lying in bed in the apartment above that of the Lees, Mary Aertsen heard the admiral pacing the floor below. Since she was trained as a nurse, she thought she might be able to help. "Why aren't you in bed?" she asked when she went down to see him.

"Well," he answered, "when I do go to bed, I'll sleep badly. I won't be in bed long. It doesn't take more than a couple of hours for me to have a good night's rest." And then, as they talked further, he unburdened himself to his listener. With both Germany and Japan defeated, to Mary he sounded depressed about his possible future in the postwar Navy. To her husband Guil, this was an entirely new side of him—much different from the world of ships and guns and radars. Up to then, Lee's focus had been on dealing with the mission at hand and concentrating on solving immediate problems. Now there was no immediate problem, nor did he have any idea of where he would land next. It was, as Guil described it, a vacuum, and Lee had not yet adjusted. He was pleased that the killing had stopped, but he had no alternate plan on how he would deal with what lay ahead. Certainly the Navy would be different as a result of the rapid rise of naval aviation.

As Guil explained the situation, there was no remaining hostile nation that had a navy of any merit. This made Lee wonder about the need for the U.S. Navy as it was then constituted. And then there was the obvious dreaded corollary: with no formidable foe on the horizon, what would be the need for a seasoned flag officer such as Lee himself? Guil added, "He was not unaware of the pressures to downgrade the military machine, mothball ships and cut the Defense budget and all that sort of let-down after a war. In short, the career to which he had so single mindedly dedicated his life suddenly seemed to have no future."[33]

There was soon to be a personal disappointment as well. With the war over, the Navy no longer had as much need as before for reserve officers such as Guil Aertsen. Having been overseas for almost the entire war, Aertsen had enough discharge points to get out right away. So he and Mary packed up their luggage, and she thoroughly scrubbed the apartment in which they had enjoyed their belated honeymoon during July and August. The Lees came up for a last visit, and Lee kidded Mary by running his finger over one of her freshly cleaned surfaces and producing some dirt. "You had that on your finger before," she protested. After they'd had their laugh, the Lees invited the Aertsens down for breakfast the next morning so the clean apartment could stay clean. "I'll be there," Mary responded instantly. "And one more thing, I'm going to step on that damn board tomorrow morning and wake you up so you'll be sure to get down there and cooking before we get down there."

"What are you talking about?" asked Lee. She explained that her husband had instructed her not to step on the third board from the bed, because it creaked and might disturb the Lees below.

Lee roared with laughter and said to Guil, "Well, you've got her well trained. Keep it up; that's all I can say."

At the appointed time on the following morning, the soon-to-be-discharged aide and his wife showed up to be served a breakfast cooked by the boss and his wife. The Lees worked well together on that morning of Saturday, 25 August, happy to be giving pleasure and to be doing something together. They fussed over the little details of how to arrange the eggs and sausage. When the meal was over and the Aertsens were about to drive away, the four of them expressed a good deal of warmth—friends without pretensions. They talked about getting together again now that the war was over. And, as a parting shot, Lee patted his cigarette pocket and said with a smile, "Palmolives."

Soon afterward, Lee walked away from Mrs. Fish's boarding house and headed for the boat landing. Now he did so alone, without Guil Aertsen. It was his normal practice to make the fifteen-minute walk from the house to the dock, rather than taking a staff car.[34] At the landing he ran into Chief Signalman James Gamage. Gamage had been on the signal bridge of the *Washington* during the November 1942 Battle of Guadalcanal and was now skipper of a water barge on Casco Bay.[35] The two exchanged greetings, and then Lee boarded his barge for the trip out to his office on Great Diamond Island.

Moments after the boat pulled away from the landing, Lee began choking. He slumped over in his seat in the cockpit, and the boat crew rushed in to try to support him. Lee attempted to speak but couldn't. The barge's coxswain headed for the nearest ships and came alongside the *Goodrich*, one of the destroyers in Lee's task force. Within twenty seconds, doctors from the *Goodrich* and *Henry W. Tucker* boarded the boat and found that the admiral was already dead of a coronary thrombosis. It had been only seven or eight minutes since the barge had left the landing.[36]

The man from Kentucky died deep in the land of the Yankees. The man of huge ships died in a boat. The splendid warrior died with the coming of peace.

▪ 16 ▪

EPILOGUE
1945–1949

The quiet of Saturday morning, 25 August 1945, was interrupted by the ringing of a telephone in a large gray stone house in the Kenwood section of Chevy Chase, Maryland. When Wilma "Billie" Miles answered, Captain Jeff Metzel was on the line from the Navy Department. Metzel and her husband had served together on the Interior Control Board before the war. Now Metzel passed on news that was as startling as it was sad—"Uncle Ching" was dead. The man who had come home from war safely was gone.[1]

Mrs. Miles soon put through a call to console Mabelle Lee in Falmouth Foreside. "Why, Billie dear, how are you?" Mrs. Lee answered sunnily, "And why are you calling?" Billie Miles instantly had a sinking sensation, for it was obvious that Mabelle had not yet been told of her husband's death. She back-pedaled awkwardly, saying she had heard that there had been a heart attack, but she didn't know how Lee was. Mrs. Lee pressed for details, but just then Mrs. Miles was spared any further embarrassment, for Mrs. Lee told her she saw a chaplain approaching the big rooming house where she and her husband had spent two happy months together.[2]

Admiral Lee had left their home earlier that morning, seemingly in fine health, and now came word from the Navy's official representative that he was dead.

Mrs. Lee went into a state of shock from which she never really recovered the rest of her life. In fact, because she was so evidently dazed by the news, the Navy people handling things tried to lessen the impact.[3] Norman Zalkind, then a public information officer on Lee's staff, recalled that directions were given to lay out Lee's body on a bed at the funeral home. He was clad in pajamas so that it would appear to Mrs. Lee that he was only sleeping, not dead.[4]

Admiral Jonas Ingram, commander in chief, Atlantic Fleet, was a longtime friend of Vice Admiral Lee. Ingram had graduated from the Naval Academy a year before Lee. Both were involved in the 1914 landing at Veracruz, Mexico, and they had been shipmates in the fleet flagship *Pennsylvania* in the early 1930s.

On 27 August, two days after Lee's passing, Ingram sent a personal message to Admiral Halsey: "I have been up here at Casco working with Ching Lee on his new assignment and was shocked beyond words at his sudden and unexpected passing. He just snapped out while sitting in his barge—without a struggle. He was apparently in the best of health. He was deeply disappointed that he did not ride in Tokio [*sic*] Bay w/you."[5] Ingram's assessment echoed some of the same thoughts Mrs. Lee expressed in her letters to her sisters—that he looked great, not even gray hair at age fifty-seven.

In the absence of a detailed medical report, one can speculate on causes for his early passing. Probably part of it was genetic. Both of his parents died of heart disease. His mother died of a heart attack in 1913 and his father of the same cause in 1931. Lee was a habitual chain-smoker and an insomniac. On board ship he got little exercise, and he had developed a paunch. During high-speed operations with the fast carriers, stress was a frequent companion. Then there was the psychological impact of doing experimental work—albeit important—in a backwater area. He was greatly disappointed that he had not been in the far Pacific when the war to which he had contributed so much came to a successful conclusion. He had counted on being there again when his kamikaze work was done, but that didn't happen. As soon as the Japanese surrendered, the mission disappeared. His contemporary, Vice Admiral John S. McCain, was on the deck of the *Missouri* for the surrender ceremony on 2 September. He died four days later, after the pressure was off.

Guil Aertsen remembered a sense of dejection on Lee's part, echoing what his wife Mary had heard during a heart-to-heart talk one night when the admiral could not sleep. As her husband put it, "I think what killed him was a recognition that his future was pretty much finished in his chosen career—that he didn't see too many bright lights ahead. The trend of the higher commands in the peacetime Navy would be oriented to the air part of the game rather than the surface part of the game. And the disciplines in which he was highly proficient were not the disciplines that would be in demand in the coming years." Aertsen also speculated that some of the disappointments of the war had buried themselves deep in the admiral's psyche and had festered there—the lack of action in the Battle of Leyte Gulf being the primary example.[6]

Who knows what might have lay ahead? Lee was an unlikely candidate for an administrative post such as Chief of Naval Operations because he would have disliked having to deal with Congress. Admiral James L. "Jimmy" Holloway Jr., who had served with Lee in the Navy Department in the 1930s and 1940s, said of the possibility of negotiating with politicians, "He was so brilliant he'd been impatient of what we then called Pedigreed Bunk." Instead, Holloway opined that Lee could have been in line for a fleet command. Arleigh Burke speculated that Lee probably would not have received command of a fleet at that point and would likely have retired fairly soon after the war if he had lived longer.[7] Lee's friend Admiral Marc Mitscher served as commander in chief, Atlantic Fleet from 26 September 1946 until his early death on 3 February 1947. McCain, Mitscher, and Lee had exhausted themselves in the winning of the war.[8]

Vice Admiral Glenn Davis, flagship captain during the Guadalcanal battle, remembered, "I have always regretted Admiral Lee's early death, because I think he would have gone places, but he was not a politician. Sometimes you don't get these high jobs if you're not politically minded in a way. . . . You would never accuse him of climbing up on anybody's shoulders or stepping over anybody."[9] Lee's approach was to do the job assigned and do so professionally, but he was not consumed by ambition as some of his fellow officers were.

When it came time for the funeral, Mabelle Lee's sisters, Margaret Allen and Ada Siders, caught a train to Washington. Arleigh Burke met them at the station and took them to stay at the home of Captain George Wright and his wife, Estelle. Lee had served with Wright years earlier. Billie Miles had gone to Maine and accompanied Mabelle on the flight to Washington.[10] At the funeral on 28 August, Secretary of the Navy James Forrestal said to Mabelle, "You had a gallant husband."[11] Lee was buried in the Arlington National Cemetery, near the Tomb of the Unknown Soldier and down a slope from it. His flag-draped coffin was atop a horse-drawn caisson, and the honor guard rendered the customary honors, including a gun salute and the playing of "Taps." Secretary Forrestal was the principal speaker. He lauded Lee's victory in the Guadalcanal battle, regretted his early death, and offered the conclusion that his naval service had caused his demise. Other high-ranking officers present were Fleet Admiral William Leahy, chief of staff to the president, and Fleet Admiral Ernest King, Chief of Naval Operations and commander in chief of the U.S. Fleet.[12]

In the years after her husband's death, Mabelle Lee returned to Rock Island, Illinois, to live with her sisters. It was a homecoming, because she had been living there when she met the future admiral and had gone back there during his overseas service, particularly during his long time away during World War II. Upon her return to Illinois, Mabelle stopped in Chicago to visit old friends Irma and Milt Fisher—they of the chilly rumble-seat ride years earlier. Following the visit, Fisher observed to his wife that Mabelle was gradually dying of grief. He added, "I thought that she just felt there was nothing more in life for her, so why struggle to live?"[13]

For many years Mabelle Lee had lived with a heart condition, brought on by a case of rheumatic fever. In January 1946, she suffered a stroke, which may have been a product of her physical constitution and the "nerves" that plagued her. After the stroke her right side was paralyzed, and she was unable to speak for a month, the only exception being the word "No." Even so, her mind remained clear. Her sister Margaret devised a method that enabled Mabelle to communicate. She cut out big letters from magazine headlines and pasted the alphabet on a large piece of cardboard. Mrs. Lee was then able to use a pointer with her unaffected left hand and indicate the message she wanted to impart. She had a large sense of relief when she learned that the Navy Department had forwarded the admiral's belongings to Rock Island. She did regain her speech, though she could not talk as rapidly as before and had trouble pronouncing some words.[14]

When she learned that a new ship would be named in honor of her late husband, she resolved to regain the strength in her right arm so she could christen the *Willis A. Lee* upon launching. She never got the opportunity. Her arm remained useless, and Mabelle Lee died of another stroke on 22 March 1949, three-plus years after her husband's passing. On 28 March, a day cherry trees blossomed, she was buried beside him at Arlington National Cemetery.[15]

■ ■ ■

Lee's legacy has continued long after his lifetime. Admiral Holloway was one of "Uncle Ching's Boys," a category that included many, many naval professionals. Lee nurtured their development, and they repaid in large measure the loyalty he extended to them. In 1944–45 Holloway commanded the *Iowa*. In the postwar years he developed the Holloway Plan that greatly extended the reach of Naval ROTC. As chief of Naval Personnel in the 1950s he facilitated the promotion to flag rank of Hyman G. Rickover, the head of the Navy's nuclear power program. In 1958, as a four-star admiral, he commanded the U.S. operation in Lebanon. Lee observed in a fitness report that Holloway had a knack for getting things done. That applied to many of his subordinates as well.

Charles Wellborn Jr. became Holloway's successor as the *Iowa*'s CO; Wellborn had served with Lee in cruisers in the 1930s, one of the "Seven Dwarfs" on Admiral Stark's staff. He commanded the ship during the Japanese surrender in Tokyo Bay in September 1945. Later he was chief of staff to CinCPac. As a vice admiral he commanded the Second Fleet and served as chairman of the U.S. delegation to the United Nations Military Staff Committee. Subsequent skippers of the *Iowa* included: Frederick Entwistle, who consulted with Lee on ordnance matters; William F. Jennings, who served with Lee in cruisers and was his handpicked chief of staff during combat operations in the Pacific; and William R. "Smeddy" Smedberg III. Smedberg, another of the "Seven Dwarfs," recommissioned the *Iowa* for Korean War duty and subsequently, as a vice admiral, was chief of Naval Personnel.

Roscoe Hillenkoetter served with Lee in the *Bushnell* shortly after World War I. He took command of the *Missouri* in late 1945. The following year he was the skipper when the ship made a groundbreaking voyage to Turkey. That trip was a forerunner of the U.S. naval presence in the Mediterranean, embodied to this day by the Sixth Fleet. In 1947 he became the first director of the Central Intelligence Agency.

Glenn B. Davis, skipper of the *Washington* at Guadalcanal, served postwar in a prime ordnance billet—as superintendent of the Naval Gun Factory in Washington, DC—and was commandant of the Potomac River Naval Command.

He retired as a "tombstone vice admiral." (That is, he was promoted on retirement to the next higher rank on the basis of awards for noteworthy performance in combat.)

Milton "Mary" Miles, whom Lee sent to China for much of the war, commanded the heavy cruiser *Columbus*. As a flag officer after the war, he was involved in Pan-American affairs; he commanded a flood relief program in Mexico following a 1955 hurricane. His last billet was as commandant of the Third Naval District. Like Davis, he retired as a tombstone vice admiral.

Two of Lee's World War II gunnery and fire control specialists, Edwin Hooper and Lloyd Mustin, both attained the rank of vice admiral on active duty. In the 1960s, Hooper commanded Service Force Pacific Fleet during the Vietnam War buildup. Mustin was in command of nuclear weapons tests in both the Atlantic and Pacific in the 1950s and 1960s. His final active-duty billet was as director of the Defense Atomic Support Agency.

William Fechteler, a longtime friend of Lee, commanded the *Indiana* when she was briefly Lee's flagship in 1943. As a four-star admiral, he served as U.S. commander in chief, Atlantic/Atlantic Fleet; Chief of Naval Operations (from 1951 to 1953); and NATO commander in chief, Allied Forces Southern Europe.

Beyond the personnel who benefited from his leadership are Lee's operational contributions. He was in on the ground floor of the use of radar in the fleet and had a rare understanding among his contemporaries of its value. He pioneered the concept of the combat information center as being the heart of warfighting for individual ships and groups of ships. He strongly emphasized the importance of antiaircraft gunnery; he constantly sought ways to make it more effective. He provided important support to James Van Allen in propagating the proximity fuze for use in 5-inch projectiles. The result was a huge leap in the success rate in shooting down Japanese aircraft.

We can well imagine that he would have had an interest in the next important step in antiair warfare, the development of the guided missile. Here again, the combat information center or combat engagement center is essential in maximizing the employment of weapons. A missile ship's commanding officer has his battle station in CIC so he can have access to an instant picture of threats and assets. Another contribution on the operational side came in the final two months of Lee's life when he directed the efforts to find a remedy for the potential danger posed by kamikazes. In July 1945 he took command of the Composite Task Force, Atlantic Fleet (renamed the Operational Development Force in 1947). It performed real-time experiments to ascertain what tactics and equipment would be effective in the hands of seagoing naval personnel. In 1952 the Tactical Development Group was formed to test and expand the evaluation of projects. The groups essentially merged in 1959 to become the Operational Test and Evaluation Force. That command, growing from the seeds planted by Willis Lee in 1945, exists to this day as a vital part of the U.S. Navy.

APPENDIX
USS *Willis A. Lee* (DL 4), 1949–1969

The christening of Admiral Lee's namesake ship took place on a chilly late-autumn day, 1 November 1949, some months after Mabelle Lee was laid to rest. The Quincy, Massachusetts, shipyard of the Bethlehem Steel Corporation laid the keel for the *Willis A. Lee*. Her original hull number designation was DD 929, part of the first generation of U.S. destroyers to be built following World War II. At 493 feet long and displacing 4,730 tons, she would be much bigger than her wartime predecessors. Comparable figures for the wartime *Gearing* class were 2,200 tons and 376 feet. In time, the new ship would be reclassified as a destroyer leader (DL 4) in recognition of her increased size.[1]

The shipyard launched the hull on 26 January 1952. In connection with the launching, the ship's sponsor did the christening honors that the admiral's widow had hoped to accomplish. In her place was Elizabeth V. Palmer, Lee's niece. She had visited the *Concord* in California in the 1930s as a graduation present. During that trip she met her future husband, Ensign Fitzhugh Lee Palmer Jr. The principal speaker at the launching ceremony was Rear Admiral Glenn Davis, who was then commandant of the Sixth Naval District. In November 1942, he had been captain of Lee's flagship, the *Washington,* during the night battle off Savo Island.[2]

The new destroyer leader, redesignated a frigate in 1955, went into commission at the Boston Naval Shipyard on 5 October 1954. She was one of only four ships of her class. Her large size made additional ships of the class too expensive to afford. The subsequent *Forrest Sherman*–class destroyers were scaled down in size. To put it kindly, the *Willis A. Lee* went through a lot of growing pains, particularly in regard to her new steam propulsion plant, which operated at a pressure of twelve hundred pounds per square inch. The boilers were more compact and weighed less per horsepower than their predecessors. Ted Litsey, one of the denizens of the engineering department, encountered a lot of setbacks in trying to deal with the new design.[3] For antisubmarine warfare the ship was equipped with the newly designed Weapon Able (later Alfa), which was a rocket launcher that enabled destroyers to fire warheads ahead of the ship rather than having to pass over submarines, as was the case with dropping depth charges.

Her operations were mostly in the Atlantic and Mediterranean, though she did take part in a celebrated inland cruise in 1959 to commemorate the opening of the St. Lawrence Seaway. In 1960 she participated in an exercise north of the Arctic Circle. In 1962 she was part of the quarantine line invoked during the Cuban Missile Crisis. During her career she served as a testbed for evaluation of new sonar capabilities. Her active career lasted only fifteen years. She was decommissioned in 1969. Her demise was part of an overall drawdown of Navy ship strength as Congress tired of the high costs of the Vietnam War.[4]

Among the thousands of men who served in the ship was Lloyd M. Mustin, who was a thoroughgoing surface warfare officer. He had served side by side with Admiral Lee during the final months of World War II. He was one who believed that Lee's preeminence was far from sufficiently recognized. He particularly saluted his mentor's mastery of radar and its uses. In 1962, by then a rear admiral, he wrote, "It was indeed a privilege to serve under him and to know him as a member of his personal staff, of which I was even more forcefully reminded when not long ago I flew my flag in USS W. A. LEE, as my flagship for operations at sea."[5]

NOTES

Chapter 1. Mischievous Mose in Kentucky, 1888–1904

1. Ruth Williamson, letter to Evan E. Smith, 12 February 1962. This letter and many others used in the book were among papers donated to the author by Mrs. Kate Smith after the death of her husband, who had started work on a biography of Lee in the early 1960s.
2. Williamson, "Big Eagle Country: Nostalgic Views of the Past Along The 99-Mile Stream That Possesses Secrets of Owen County's History," reprint of articles that appeared in the *News-Herald*, Owenton, KY, 8 and 15 February 1962.
3. Allen R. Meacham, letters to Evan Smith, 1 and 14 September 1961. "Grandison R. Lee," Find a Grave, https://www.findagrave.com/memorial/46229992/grand ison-r-lee; "Nathaniel Wiley Lee," Find a Grave, https://www.findagrave.com /memorial/16440841/nathaniel-wiley-lee.
4. Meacham, letter, 1 September 1961.
5. B. N. Griffing, et al., *An Atlas of Owen County, Kentucky.*
6. Mariam Sidebottom Houchens, *History of Owen County, Kentucky "Sweet Owen."*
7. "Susan Ireland Lee," Find a Grave, https://www.findagrave.com/memorial/67294212 /susan-ireland-lee.
8. Elizabeth V. Palmer, letter to author, 7 February 1987.
9. Allen B. Cammack, letter to author, 7 August 1976; interview with author, 21 May 1977.
10. Florence Arnold Dubs, letter to the author, 4 June 1977.
11. "Rear Admiral Lee Spent Happy Boyhood Days in Owen County," *News-Herald*, Owenton, KY, 21 September 1941.
12. Owen F. Cammack, letter to Evan Smith, 9 February 1962.
13. Allen Cammack, interview.
14. W. T. Forsee, letter to Evan Smith, 19 October 1961.
15. Elizabeth Palmer, interview with author, 2 November 1975.
16. Mary Moss Ihrig, letter to author, 17 August 1976.
17. Charles Yancey, letter to author, 24 April 1980.
18. Louise Cammack Davis, "The Lees," unpublished manuscript, January 1962.
19. Elizabeth Palmer, interview.

20. Allen Cammack, interview.
21. Davis, "The Lees."

Chapter 2. Naval Academy Years, 1904–1908

1. Oscar Smith Jr., letter to Evan Smith, 27 March 1962.
2. Jack Sweetman, *The U.S. Naval Academy*, 87–88, 142–44. Oscar Smith Jr., letter to Evan Smith, 9 May 1962.
3. Smith, letter.
4. Theodore Taylor, *The Magnificent Mitscher*, 20–22.
5. "Gov. Lloyd Crowe Stark," National Governors Association, https://www.nga.org /governor/lloyd-crow-stark.
6. Lloyd C. Stark diary, 1904.
7. John H. Earle, letter to Evan Smith, 25 March 1962.
8. Earle Buckingham, letter to Evan Smith, 25 August 1962. Earle, letter.
9. Edmund R. Norton, letter to Evan Smith, undated.
10. Earle, letter.
11. Worrall R. Carter, letter to Evan Smith, 30 March 1962.
12. John E. Meredith, letter to Evan Smith, 6 April 1962.
13. John E. Iseman Jr., letter to Evan Smith, 30 March 1962.
14. *Annual Register of the Naval Academy*, 1 October 1907, 187.
15. Lee service record.
16. *Arms and the Man*, 5 September 1907, 516–18.
17. Thomas C. Kinkaid, letter to Evan Smith, 9 April 1962.
18. William Ward Smith, letter to Evan Smith, 26 May 1962.
19. Eugene E. Wilson, letter to Evan Smith, 13 March 1962.
20. Earle, letter to Mabelle Lee, 29 August 1945.
21. William F. Kurfess, letter to Evan Smith, 28 May 1962.
22. Kinkaid, letter.
23. Wilson, letter to Evan Smith, 23 March 1962.
24. 1908 *Lucky Bag*, 324.
25. Lee service record.
26. Naval Academy, *Register of Alumni*, 1908.

Chapter 3. Junior Officer, 1908–1918

1. Lee service record.
2. Lee service record.
3. Malcolm Muir Jr., *The Capital Ship Program in the United States Navy, 1934–1945*, 14.
4. William D. Brereton, letter to Evan Smith, 5 January 1962.
5. *The Boston Sunday Globe*, 1 August 1909.
6. *Dictionary of American Naval Fighting Ships* (hereafter *DANFS*), s.v. "*Independence*."

7. *DANFS*, s.v. *"New Orleans."*

8. Eugene E. Wilson, letter to Evan Smith, 23 March 1962.

9. Lee service record.

10. W. A. Lee Jr. and A. D. Denney, "Revolver Shooting," U.S. Naval Institute *Proceedings* 36, no. 1 (1910), 249–54.

11. Lee service record.

12. *DANFS*, s.v. *"Helena."*

13. Philip Seymour, letter to Evan Smith, 9 April 1962.

14. Adolph B. Miller, letter to Evan Smith, 16 July 1962.

15. Miller, letter.

16. Harold C. Train, letter to Evan Smith, 25 May 1962.

17. Lee service record.

18. *DANFS*, s.v. *"New Hampshire."*

19. Arthur J. Sweetman, letter to author, 31 March 1977.

20. Sweetman, letter.

21. Frederick J. Egger, letter to Evan Smith, 1 July 1962.

22. Egger, letter.

23. Sweetman, letter.

24. Lee service record.

25. Jack Sweetman, *American Naval History*, 128.

26. Jack Sweetman, *American Naval History*, 128–30.

27. Jack Sweetman, *The Landing at Veracruz: 1914*, 117.

28. Lee service record.

29. This paragraph is an amalgam of two letters Earle wrote, one to Mabelle Lee on 29 August 1945 and one to Evan Smith on 25 March 1962.

30. Lee service record.

31. Lee service record.

32. Lee service record.

33. Lee service record.

34. Lee service record.

35. Lee service record.

36. Lee service record.

Chapter 4. World War I and Aftermath, 1917–1920

1. "Rear Admiral Lee, Cited in Solomons Battle, Wed Rock Island Girl in '19," *Democrat* (Davenport, IA), 18 November 1942.

2. Margaret Allen, unpublished manuscript, no date.

3. "Root and Van Dervoort," Rock Island Plow Co., http://www.rockislandplowco.com/index_files/rv.htm.

4. Lee service record.

5. Lee service record.

6. Lee service record.

7. Lee service record.

8. Lee to Mabelle Allen, 23 January 1919.

9. Lee to Mabelle Allen, 9 February 1919.

10. Lee to Mabelle Allen, 9 February 1919.

11. Lee to Mabelle Allen, 6 April 1919.

12. Lee service record.

13. Evan W. Yancey, letter to author, 15 September 1976.

14. Mabelle Elspeth Allen, baptismal certificate.

15. Margaret Allen, letter to Evan Smith, 15 June 1962.

16. "Lee-Allen Nuptials in Chicago Culmination of Pretty War Romance," *Rock Island Argus*, 19 July 1919.

17. Margaret Allen, unpublished manuscript, undated.

18. "National Rifle Matches of 1919," *Cambridge Sentinel* (MA), 14 June 1919.

19. Virtually all of the information about Lee's service in the *Bushnell* was provided by Roscoe H. Hillenkoetter in an interview with the author, 26 February 1977.

20. *DANFS*, s.v. *"Bushnell"*; Paul Silverstone, *U.S. Warships of World War I*, 202–3.

21. "Revival of Our Oldest Navy Yard," *Scientific American* (10 January 1920), 50–51.

22. *Bushnell*, deck log.

23. Hillenkoetter, interview.

24. Jim Grossman, *Olympic Shooting*, 57.

25. Lee service record.

26. Grossman, *Olympic Shooting*, 57–58.

27. Grossman, *Olympic Shooting*, 60–61.

28. Carl T. Osburn, letter to Evan Smith, 3 April 1962.

29. Margaret Allen, letter to author, 30 November 1976.

30. Albert G. Mumma, U.S. Naval Institute oral history, 11–12.

Chapter 5. Destroyer Skipper, 1920–1928

1. *DANFS*, v.s. *"Fairfax."*

2. Lee letters to Margaret (Mrs. John) Allen, 14 March 1921 and 15 March 1921.

3. Margaret Allen, letter to author, 16 April 1977.

4. Allen, unpublished manuscript, undated.

5. W. S. G. Davis, letter to Evan Smith, 20 June 1962.

6. E. H. Cope, letter to Allan Colon, 17 June 1922.

7. Jerauld Wright, letter to Willis Lee, 31 March 1924.

8. Frank A. Braisted, interview with author, 13 November 1978.

9. Braisted, interview.

10. Husband E. Kimmel, letter to Evan Smith, 6 February 1962.

11. Braisted, interview. James L. Holloway Jr., letter to author, 5 January 1976.

12. Margaret Allen, letter to author, 30 November 1976.

13. Holloway, letter.
14. Holloway, letter.
15. Wilma Miles, interview with author, 28 November 1975.
16. Miles, interview.
17. Miles, interview.
18. Horace B. Butterfield, letter to author, 12 March 1976.
19. William S. G. Davis, letter to Evan Smith, 20 June 1962.
20. Davis, letter.
21. "First Flight Around the World: The Douglas World Cruisers at Pearson Field," National Park Service, https://www.nps.gov/articles/douglasworldcruiserspearson.htm.
22. "The Race to Fly First Around the World," Historic Wings, http://fly.historicwings.com/2012/06/race-to-fly-first-around-the-world/.
23. Lowell Thomas, "Maj. McLaren's [sic] Rescue Due to America's Aid," *Chicago Daily Tribune*, 23 December 1924, 4.
24. Thomas, article.
25. Thomas, article.
26. "Round-the-World Flights," Wingnet, https://www.wingnet.org/rtw/RTW001C.HTM.
27. Richard E. Byrd, letter to Lee, 18 March 1926.
28. Morton C. Mumma Jr., letter to Evan Smith, 6 July 1962.
29. Mumma, letter.
30. Thomas H. Dyer, U.S. Naval Institute oral history, 68–73.
31. Dashiell L. Madeira, tape recording made for author, 22 September 1976.
32. Madeira, tape recording.

Chapter 6. Commander, 1928–1936

1. Henry M. Kieffer, letter to author, 2 November 1978.
2. Margaret Allen, letter to author, 3 June 1977.
3. Gerald John Kennedy, *United States Naval War College, 1919–1941*, 177–78.
4. Kennedy, 155–59.
5. Kennedy, 171–72.
6. John M. Lillard, *Playing War: Wargaming and U.S. Naval Preparations for World War II*, 48. John B. Hattendorf, B. Mitchell Simpson III, and John R. Wadleigh, *Sailors and Scholars: The Centennial History of the U.S. Naval War College*, 139.
7. Kennedy, 152–60.
8. Trent Hone, email to author, 11 September 2020.
9. Kennedy, 116, 169–71.
10. Quoted in Lillard, 1.
11. Alexander H. Hood, letter to author, 15 April 1980.
12. Walter T. Jenkins, letters to author, 18 May and 27 June 1979.

13. Jenkins, letter of 27 June 1979.

14. Harold D. Krick, letter to author, 8 April 1976.

15. George C. Dyer, interview with author, 12 December 1975.

16. *Pennsylvania* deck log.

17. Lee service record.

18. Thomas H. Dyer, U.S. Naval Institute oral history, 161.

19. Arthur W. Radford, "Aircraft Battle Force," in Paul Stillwell, *Air Raid: Pearl Harbor!*, 18–22.

20. Richard C. Steere, interview with author, unknown date.

21. Margaret Allen, letter to author, 19 March 1977.

22. Allen, letter of 19 March 1977 and undated unpublished manuscript.

23. Allen, letter to author, 19 March 1977.

24. Charles Wellborn Jr., U.S. Naval Institute oral history, 42–43.

25. John F. Davidson, U.S. Naval Institute oral history, 70–73.

26. Estelle Wright, interview with author, 21 December 1975. Margaret Allen, undated unpublished manuscript.

27. Commander Battle Force letter to Chief of Naval Operations, 4 March 1933.

28. Lee service record.

29. Military Order of the World War *National Bulletin*, November 1933, 7–8.

30. Lee service record. "Goldplaters." Destroyer History Foundation, http://destroyerhistory .org/goldplater/.

31. Malcolm F. Schoeffel, U.S. Naval Institute oral history, 164–65. Schoeffel, letter to author, 26 October 1977.

32. Schoeffel, letter.

33. Schoeffel, U.S. Naval Institute oral history, 166–68.

34. *DANFS*, s.v. "*Utah*."

35. Ernest M. Eller, U.S. Naval Institute oral history, 301–3.

36. Lee service record.

37. Mabelle Lee, postcard to her mother, 29 August 1936.

Chapter 7. Cruiser Service, 1936–1939

1. George C. Dyer, interview with author, 12 December 1975.

2. *DANFS*, s.v. "*Concord*."

3. Evan W. Yancey, letters to author, 15 September 1976 and 14 October 1976.

4. Yancey, letter to author, 14 October 1976.

5. Richard R. Bradley, interview with author, 1 October 1976.

6. Harold D. Krick, letter to author, 5 December 1976.

7. Alvin I. Malstrom, interview with author, 5 June 1976.

8. William D. Anderson, letter to author, 1 August 1976.

9. Anderson, letter.

10. Fitzhugh L. Palmer Jr., interview with author, 2 November 1975.

11. Fitzhugh L. Palmer Jr., interview.
12. Anderson, letter.
13. Marcus W. Williamson, letter to author, 6 October 1976.
14. Anderson, letter.
15. Margaret Simpson, interview with author, 27 February 1977.
16. Williamson, letter.
17. Margaret Allen, letter to author, 30 November 1976.
18. Estelle Wright, interview with author, 21 December 1975.
19. Anderson, letters to author, 1 August and 6 September 1976; Fitzhugh L. Palmer Jr., interview; Jeannette Wishard, letter to author, 12 April 1976.
20. Allen, letter to author, 31 January 1977; M. C. Fisher, letter to Evan Smith, 15 June 1962.
21. Yancey, letter, 15 September 1976; Wellborn, interview with author, 5 March 1976.
22. Anderson, letter to author, 6 September 1976.
23. *Concord* deck log.
24. Ruthven E. Libby, letter to author, 4 November 1977.
25. Fitzhugh L. Palmer Jr., interview.
26. John C. Lester, letter to author, 9 October 1976.
27. Secretary of the Navy letter to commanding officer, USS *Concord,* 5 August 1937.
28. Chief of Naval Operations letter to commanding officer, USS *Concord*, 10 August 1938.
29. Royal A. Wolverton, letter to author, 18 September 1976.
30. William R. Smedberg III, U.S. Naval Institute oral history, 42.
31. Smedberg, U.S. Naval Institute oral history, 42–44.
32. *Concord* deck log.
33. *Concord* deck log.
34. Fitzhugh L. Palmer Jr., interview.
35. Harold D. Krick, letters to author, 7 October 1976 and 5 December 1976.
36. *Concord* deck log. William F. Jennings, letter to Evan Smith, 29 November 1961.
37. Harold S. Bottomley, letter to author, 22 February 1980.
38. *Concord* deck log.
39. Fitzhugh L. Palmer Jr., interview.
40. Bradley, interview.
41. *Concord* deck log.
42. Wellborn, U.S. Naval Institute oral history, 63.
43. Wellborn, U.S. Naval Institute oral history, 63–64. Smedberg, letter to author, 18 February 1976.
44. Wellborn, letter to author, 11 March 1976.
45. Butterfield, letter.
46. Fitzhugh L. Palmer Jr., interview.
47. Nicholas G. Doukas, letter to author, 12 November 1976. Wellborn, interview.
48. *Concord* deck log.

49. *The Minute Man*, 11 June 1938.
50. *Concord* deck log.
51. Doukas, letter.
52. Krick, letter to author, 8 April 1976.
53. Doukas, letter.
54. *Concord* deck log.
55. Frank A. Zimanski, letter to author, 28 January 1980.
56. William D. Brereton, letter to Evan Smith, 5 January 1962.
57. John R. Wadleigh, letter to author, 21 February 1976.
58. Wadleigh, letter.
59. Margaret Allen, letter to author, 19 March 1976.
60. Frederick I. Entwistle, letters to author, 19 May and 13 June 1976.
61. Wellborn, U.S. Naval Institute oral history, 66–67, and letter to author.
62. Harold D. Krick, letter to author, 8 April 1976.
63. Bertha Jennings, note to Mabelle Lee, 19 December 1938.
64. Krick, letter, 8 April 1976.
65. Donald Siders, letter to author, 17 May 2008.
66. Wellborn, letter to author, 22 May 1976.
67. "FDR and Fleet Problem XX," Les Dropkin, http://usspotomac.org/education/documents/4FFleetProblemXX.pdf.
68. Butterfield, letter. Fitzhugh L. Palmer Jr., interview.
69. *Honolulu* deck log.

Chapter 8. The Washington Years: Preparing for Battle, 1939–1942

1. Malcolm F. Schoeffel, letter to author, 26 October 1977.
2. Joseph H. Wellings, interview with author, 18 November 1977.
3. Wellings, letter to author, 7 September 1977.
4. Harold R. Stark, *Organization of the Office of the Chief of Naval Operations with Duties Assigned the Divisions Thereunder*, 21–23.
5. Willis A. Lee Jr., confidential memorandum to Captain G. B. Wright, USN (Ret.), "Internal Organization of the Office of the Chief of Naval Operations." Folder (SC) A3-1, Confidential General Correspondence of the Division of Fleet Training, 1927–41, Record Group 38 (Box 299), NARA.
6. Nealy A. Chapin, letter to author, 14 July 1977.
7. Lee service record.
8. Lee service record.
9. Norman Friedman, *U.S. Battleships*, 329–43. See also Malcolm Muir Jr., *The Capital Ship Program in the United States Navy, 1934–1945*, 157–58.
10. Muir, 165–66.
11. Richard B. Frank, email to author, 1 September 2020.
12. Ernest M. Eller, U.S. Naval Institute oral history, 493–94.

13. Eller, oral history.

14. George L. Russell, letter to author, 23 February 1976.

15. Arleigh A. Burke, interview with author, 15 September 1976.

16. Dino A. Brugioni, "Naval Photo Intel in WWII," U.S. Naval Institute *Proceedings* (June 1987), 46.

17. Brugioni, article.

18. Joseph H. Wellings, *On His Majesty's Service*, edited by John B. Hattendorf, 1–2.

19. Wellings, letter.

20. Wellings, *On His Majesty's Service*, 2.

21. Wellings, *On His Majesty's Service*, 2.

22. Wellings, letter.

23. Wellings, *On His Majesty's Service*, 243.

24. Wellings, letter.

25. B. Mitchell Simpson, letter to author, 28 November 1978.

26. James L. Holloway Jr., letter to author, 29 June 1976.

27. Chester W. Nimitz, letter to Evan Smith, 8 May 1962.

28. John F. Crowe Jr., letter to author, 12 July 1977.

29. Estelle Wright, interview with author, 21 December 1975.

30. Guilliaem Aertsen III, interview with author, 14 March 1980. M. C. Fisher, letter to Evan Smith, 15 June 1962.

31. NARA, Record Group 38, Box 323 Folder (SC) QB (Boards), 9 August 1940; Box 323, Folder (SC)QB/AA, 13 August 1940.

32. NARA, Record Group 38, Box 323, Folder (SC) QB/AA, 24 February 1941.

33. Wilma Miles, interview with author, 28 November 1975.

34. James L. Holloway Jr., interview with author, 16 December 1975.

35. Holloway, letter to author, 13 July 1977.

36. NARA, Miles files, chapters 1, 2, Record Group 38 G, Box 1, Folder 1, "Personal." Quoted in Maochun Yu, *OSS in China: Prelude to Cold War*, 50–51.

37. Yu, *OSS in China*, 8–9.

38. Miles' prewar activities in relation to China are covered in much greater detail in his book *A Different Kind of War*, 1–16. Unfortunately, some of the details in the early part of the book are inaccurate because it was written after Miles' death. The manuscript was produced by Hawthorne Daniel, working from Admiral Miles' notes and the memory of Mrs. Miles.

39. Raymond A. Kotrla, interview with author, 29 May 1976.

40. Richard B. Frank, letter to author, 15 August 2008.

41. Simpson, letter.

42. FDR Presidential Library, President's Secretary's File, Department of Navy: Nov–Dec 1940 through July–Dec. 1942, Box 59.

43. Holloway, letter to author, 13 July 1977.

44. Eller, U.S. Naval Institute oral history.

45. For a detailed account of the acquisition and production of the 20-mm and 40-mm guns, see Buford Rowland and William B. Boyd, *U.S. Navy Bureau of Ordnance in World War II*, 219–31.

46. Blake D. Mills, letter to author, 9 February 1980.

47. Boynton L. Braun, interview with author, 28 August 1977.

48. Eller, U.S. Naval Institute oral history, 487–89.

49. Horacio Rivero, letter to author, 10 September 1977.

50. Trent Hone, email to author, 11 September 2020.

51. Marion E. Murphy, letter to author, 13 October 1977.

52. A much fuller description of the process is in Rowland and Boyd, 379–84. Other inputs were the author's interviews with Holloway, 10 July 1977; McDowell, 3 March 1977; and Eller's U.S. Naval Institute oral history.

53. Frederick R. Furth, letter to author, 12 March 1977.

54. NARA, Record Group 38, Box 324, Folder (SC)S67 (Radio Apparatus), 15 May 1941.

55. NARA, Record Group 38, Box 324, Folder (SC)S67 (Radio Apparatus), 25 June 1941.

56. NARA, Record Group 38, Box 324, Folder (SC)S67 (Radio Apparatus), 7 July 1941.

57. Chapin, letter.

58. McDowell, interview.

59. Miles H. Hubbard, letter to author, 15 April 1980.

60. Holloway, interview with author, 12 September 1980.

61. Holloway, interview, 12 September 1980.

62. Julius Augustus Furer, *Administration of the Navy Department in World War II*, 152–56.

63. Lee service record.

64. Holloway, interview, 12 September 1980.

65. Miles, *A Different Kind of War*, 20.

66. Maochun Yu, *OSS in China: Prelude to Cold War*, 52–56.

67. Miles, *A Different Kind of War*, 18. Considering the posthumous nature of Miles' memoirs, there must be at least some question whether the language in the book represents an exact transcript of the conversation between Miles and King. Another version of what King said to Miles is in Maochun Yu, *OSS in China*, 57.

68. George C. Dyer, interview with author, 12 December 1975.

69. John R. Waterman, letter to the author, 27 July 1977.

70. Clay Blair Jr., *Silent Victory*, 435–39.

71. McDowell, interview.

72. Lee endorsement of 18 April 1942 to Gatch letter of 8 April 1942. Eller, U.S. Naval Institute oral history, 491.

73. Holloway, letter to author, 5 January 1976.

74. McDowell, interview

75. McDowell, interview.

76. McDowell, interview.
77. NARA, Record Group 38, Box 316, Folder (SC)A13, Fleet Training Division Confidential correspondence.
78. Wilma Miles, interview. Charles H. Lyman, letter to Evan Smith, 16 June 1962.
79. Wilma Miles, interview.
80. Wilma Miles, interview.
81. Waterman, letter. McDowell, interview.
82. Chapin, letter.
83. McDowell, interview.
84. Margaret Allen, undated manuscript.

Chapter 9. Battleship Division Commander, August–October 1942

1. Thomas B. Buell, *Master of Sea Power*, 214–18.
2. Richard B. Frank, *Guadalcanal*, 30–31. Trent Hone, email to author, 11 September 2020.
3. Winston Jordan, "Man Overboard," U.S. Naval Institute *Proceedings* (December 1987), 92–95. John Cadwalader, interview with author, 9 March 1980.
4. Arthur Nicholson, email to author, 13 October 2020. Nicholson is researching and writing about the *Wasp*'s two 1942 voyages into the Mediterranean to fly off Spitfire fighters headed for Malta.
5. Richard B. Frank, "Picking Winners?" *Naval History* (June 2011), 24–30.
6. Raymond W. Thompson, interview with author, 31 January 1976.
7. Thompson, interview.
8. Paul H. Backus, "Why Them and Not Me?" in Paul Stillwell, *Air Raid: Pearl Harbor!*, 160–70.
9. *DANFS*, s.v. "*South Dakota.*"
10. Backus, U.S. Naval Institute oral history, 131.
11. William R. Smedberg III, U.S. Naval Institute oral history, 177–78. Thompson, interview.
12. Norman C. Hoffman, letter to author, 28 January 1976. James V. Claypool, letter to Evan Smith, 17 December 1962.
13. Herbert J. Preston, interview with author, 23 January 1976.
14. Thompson, interview. Backus, U.S. Naval Institute oral history. John C. Hill II, interview with author, 7 May 2002.
15. Commander Task Group 2.9 to Commander South Pacific Force dispatch, 062246 September 1942, CNO Top Secret Blue File microfilm.
16. Commander South Pacific Force dispatch to Commander Task Force 11, 080342 September 1942, Record Group 313, flag files, ComSoPac administrative files.
17. Harold T. Berc, letter to author, 3 March 1980.
18. Glenn B. Davis, remarks at USS *Washington* reunion, 16 July 1969.
19. Edward Maslanka, interview with the author, 7 June 1998.

20. Maslanka, interview.

21. John Cadwalader, interview with author, 9 March 1980.

22. Raymond Baker, letter to author, 8 April 1980.

23. Chadbourn R. Knowlton, letter to Edward Maslanka, 28 September 1996.

24. Trent Hone, *Learning War*, 328.

25. Edwin B. Hooper, U.S. Naval Institute oral history, 74. Hooper, interview with author, 13 January 1980. Thompson, interview.

26. Thompson, interview. Bentinck-Smith, letter, 3 September 1976.

27. Bentinck-Smith, letter, 3 September 1976.

28. Bentinck-Smith, letter, 3 September 1976.

29. Edwin S. Schanze, letter to Margaret Allen, 29 August 1962.

30. Ivan Musicant, *Battleship at War*, 69–70.

31. Leo R. Schwabe, letter to author, 31 January 1980.

32. Jonas M. Platt, interview with author, 19 January 1980.

33. Stanley J. Krawczyk, letter to Evan Smith, 28 August 1962.

34. Albert T. Church Jr., interview with author, 23 December 1979.

35. Church, interview.

36. Schanze, letter.

37. Church, interview.

38. Schanze, letter.

39. Thompson, interview.

40. Church, interview.

41. Davis, letter to Evan Smith, 9 July 1962.

42. James D. Hornfischer, *Neptune's Inferno: The U.S. Navy at Guadalcanal*, 151.

43. Chester Nimitz, letter to Robert Ghormley, 8 October 1942.

44. Hornfischer, *Neptune's Inferno*, 138–40.

45. Hornfischer, *Neptune's Inferno*, 157–88.

46. William F. Halsey Jr., and J. Bryan III, *Admiral Halsey's Story*, 109.

47. Church, interview.

48. Richard Frank, email to author, 2 September 2020.

49. Musicant, *Battleship at War*, 82–85.

50. Thompson, interview.

51. Lloyd M. Mustin, U.S. Naval Institute oral history, 545–46.

52. Hornfischer, *Neptune's Inferno*, 192–96.

53. Hornfischer, *Neptune's Inferno*, 206, 209; Musicant, *Battleship at War*, 91–92.

54. Samuel Eliot Morison, *The Struggle for Guadalcanal*, 182.

55. Guilliaem Aertsen III, letter to Evan Smith, 9 April 1962.

56. Aertsen, interview with author, 8 April 1979.

57. Aertsen, interview, 8 April 1979.

58. Aertsen, interview, 8 April 1979.

59. Robert Leckie, *Challenge for the Pacific: Guadalcanal—The Turning Point*, 260, 270.

60. Musicant, *Battleship at War*, 95–96. Hooper, U.S. Naval Institute oral history, 77–78.
61. Morison, *The Struggle for Guadalcanal*, 201–2.
62. Halsey and Bryan, *Admiral Halsey's Story*, 121. Richard B. Frank, *Guadalcanal*, 711.
63. Sidney Shalett, *Old Nameless*, 80.

Chapter 10. Night Action off Savo Island, November 1942

1. Edwin T. Layton, letter to author, 5 March 1976.
2. Layton, letter.
3. Layton, letter.
4. William Bentinck-Smith, letter to author, 3 September 1976.
5. Richard B. Frank, *Guadalcanal*, 428–29.
6. Frank, *Guadalcanal*, 433–34.
7. Trent Hone, email to author, 11 September 2020.
8. The description of this battle is drawn largely from Frank, *Guadalcanal*, 428–61.
9. John B. Lundstrom, *The First Team and the Guadalcanal Campaign*, 484–88.
10. Lundstrom, *The First Team*, 487–88.
11. Glenn B. Davis, interview with author, 3 September 1977.
12. Frank, *Guadalcanal*, 469–75.
13. Trent Hone, *Learning War*, 198–99.
14. Harvey T. Walsh, letter to Evan Smith, 30 July 1962.
15. Lloyd M. Mustin, U.S. Naval Institute oral history, 619.
16. James G. Ross, letter to author, 17 March 1980.
17. Davis, remarks at USS *Washington* reunion, 16 July 1969.
18. John Cadwalader, interview with author, 9 March 1980.
19. Raymond P. Hunter, interview with author, 13 January 1980.
20. Harold T. Berc, letter to author, 3 March 1980.
21. Task Force 64, action report, 18 February 1943.
22. Albert T. Church Jr., interview with author, 23 December 1979.
23. Bentinck-Smith, letter to author, 3 September 1976.
24. Hugh M. Robinson, letter to author, 14 January 1980.
25. Sidney Shalett, *Old Nameless*, 107.
26. James V. Claypool, *God on a Battlewagon*, 11–12.
27. Claypool, *God on a Battlewagon*, 11–12; Shalett, *Old Nameless*, 106.
28. Shalett, *Old Nameless*, 108.
29. Morison, *The Struggle for Guadalcanal*, 272.
30. Albert P. Kohlhas Jr., letter to author, 30 January 1980.
31. Edward J. Maslanka, interview with author, 7 June 1998.
32. Maslanka, interview.
33. William George Matton Jr., letter to author, 26 January 1980.
34. Shalett, *Old Nameless*, 111–12.
35. Erling Hustvedt, "Surface Ship Gunnery Systems in Battle."

36. Davis, letter to Evan Smith, 9 July 1962. Davis, remarks at USS *Washington* reunion, 16 July 1969.

37. Robert D. Macklin, letter to author, 4 February 1980.

38. James G. Ross, letter to author, 6 February 1980.

39. Hornfischer, *Neptune's Inferno*, 357.

40. Theodore Roscoe, *United States Destroyer Operations in World War II*, 201–4. Morison, *The Struggle for Guadalcanal*, 274–75.

41. Robert Reed, interview with author, 6 May 1995.

42. Silvic DeChristofaro, letter to author, 23 January 1980.

43. John M. Gore, letter to author, 18 January 1980.

44. William B. Fargo, letter to author, 31 January 1980.

45. Hunter, interview; Davis, interview; Morison, *The Struggle for Guadalcanal*, 275–77.

46. Davis, reunion remarks.

47. Malcolm Muir Jr., *The Capital Ship Program in the United States Navy, 1934–1945*, 293.

48. Edwin B. Hooper, interview with author, 13 January 1980.

49. Hooper, U.S. Naval Institute oral history, 80–83.

50. "*Kirishima* Battle Damage," Robert Lundgren, Navweaps.com/index_lundgren/kirishimaDamageAnalysis.php.

51. Davis, reunion remarks. Morison, *The Struggle for Guadalcanal*, 278–79.

52. Frank M. Sanger Jr., interview with author, 8 May 1980.

53. Morison, 279.

54. Task Force 64, action report, 18 February 1943.

55. Schwabe, letter to author, 31 January 1980. Matton, letter.

56. Platt, interview.

57. Schwabe, letter.

58. Bentinck-Smith, letter.

59. Matton, letter.

60. P. J. Stahnke, letter to author, 7 March 1977.

61. Robert Tate Simpson, letter to author, 8 September 1976.

62. Simpson, letter to author, 10 October 1976.

63. Fred Tucker, "Stand by for a Ram," *The Daily Press* (Newport News and Hampton, VA), 4 January 1970.

64. Walsh, letter.

65. Shalett, *Old Nameless*, 127–28.

66. R. Sargent Shriver Jr., interview in the collection of the USS *South Dakota* Battleship Memorial, circa 1969, 5.

67. Bureau of Ships, "U.S.S. SOUTH DAKOTA (BB57), Gunfire Damage, Battle of Guadalcanal, 14–15 November 1942," report dated 1 June 1947.

68. Backus, U.S. Naval Institute oral history, 147–48, 160–61.

69. John D. Wilson, letter to author, 10 September 1976.

70. Backus, U.S. Naval Institute oral history, 153–54.
71. Hoffman, letter to author, 28 January 1976.
72. Backus, letter to author, 13 February 1976.
73. Backus, U.S. Naval Institute oral history, 149, 154–55.
74. Claypool, *God on a Battlewagon.*
75. Task Force 64, action report, 18 February 1943.
76. Morison, *The Struggle for Guadalcanal,* 280.
77. Chadbourn R. Knowlton, letter to Edward Maslanka, 28 September 1996.
78. Knowlton, letter.
79. Davis, reunion remarks.
80. Hornfischer, *Neptune's Inferno,* 365.
81. Task Force 64, action report, 18 February 1943.
82. Cadwalader, interview with author, 9 March 1980.
83. Davis, interview with author.
84. Schanze, letter to Margaret Allen, 29 August 1962.
85. Hooper, U.S. Naval Institute oral history, 86.
86. Backus, U.S. Naval Institute oral history, 164–65.
87. Backus, U.S. Naval Institute oral history, 246–47.
88. Claypool, *God on a Battlewagon,* 20–25.
89. Morison, *The Struggle for Guadalcanal,* 281.
90. Raymond W. Thompson, interview with author, 31 January 1976.
91. Bentinck-Smith, letter.
92. Task Force 64, action report, 18 February 1943.
93. Schanze, letter to Evan Smith, 29 August 1962.
94. Bureau of Ships, "Gunfire Damage, 14–15 November 1942." NARA, Backus, U.S. Naval Institute oral history, 160.
95. Backus, U.S. Naval Institute oral history, 155–56. Backus, letter to author, 13 February 1976. Berc, letter to author, 3 March 1980.
96. Shalett, *Old Nameless,* 167.
97. Robert E. Harris, letter to author, 16 February 1980.
98. Halsey to Nimitz, 29 November 1942, Fleet Admiral William F. Halsey papers, Manuscript Division, Library of Congress, Box 15.
99. Lee letter to Mabelle Lee, 1 December 1942.

Chapter 11. Watchful Waiting, December 1942–October 1943

1. Robert D. Macklin, letter to author, 4 February 1980. Samuel Eliot Morison, *The Struggle for Guadalcanal.*
2. William Bentinck-Smith, letter to author, 3 September 1976.
3. Edward Maslanka, interview with author, 7 June 1998.
4. Guilliaem Aertsen III, interview with author, 14 March 1980.
5. Thomas C. Kinkaid, letter to Evan Smith, 9 April 1962.

6. Davenport, IA, *Democrat*, 18 November 1942.

7. William F. Jennings, letter to Evan Smith, 29 November 1961.

8. Jennings, letter.

9. John M. Gore, letter to Evan Smith, 14 February 1963.

10. Jennings, letter to Mabelle Lee, 15 February 1943.

11. Richard Frank, email to author, 17 November 2020; William L. Dawson, interview with author, 25 January 1980.

12. Dawson, interview.

13. James A. Van Allen, "What Is A Space Scientist? An Autobiographical Example," *Annual Review of Earth and Planetary Sciences*, no. 18 (1990), 1–26. Also at www-pi .physics.uiowa.edu/java/.

14. Van Allen, "What Is a Space Scientist?" Also Van Allen, letter to author, 26 April 1976.

15. Van Allen, letter.

16. Van Allen, letter.

17. Raymond P. Hunter, interview with author, 13 January 1980.

18. Hunter, interview. Also Van Allen, "What Is A Space Scientist?"

19. Glenn B. Davis, interview with author, 3 September 1977.

20. Samuel Eliot Morison diary, April 1943.

21. Morison, diary.

22. Morison, diary.

23. Morison, diary.

24. Davis, interview. Raymond W. Thompson, interview with author, 31 January 1976.

25. Lorenzo Russo, letter to Evan Smith, 20 June 1962.

26. Russo, letter.

27. Patrick Gormley, letter to Evan Smith, 1 July 1962.

28. Russo, letter.

29. Bentinck-Smith, letter to author, 8 September 1976.

30. Malcolm Muir Jr., *The Capital Ship Program in the United States Navy, 1934–1945*, 180.

31. Guilliaem Aertsen III, interview with author, 8 April 1979.

32. Ivan Musicant, *Battleship at War*, 168–69.

33. Jonas M. Platt, interview with author, 19 January 1980. Musicant, *Battleship at War*, 168.

34. *DANFS*, s.v. "*Washington*." Harvey T. Walsh, letter to Evan Smith, 30 July 1962.

35. Bentinck-Smith, letter to author, 3 September 1976.

36. Aertsen, interview with author, 10 October 1976.

37. Aertsen, interview, 10 October 1976.

38. Bentinck-Smith, letter of 3 September 1976.

39. Hooper, U.S. Naval Institute oral history, 94.

40. Musicant, *Battleship at War*, 173–75. Hooper, U.S. Naval Institute oral history, 92. Albert T. Church Jr., interview with author, 23 December 1979.

41. Platt, interview. Musicant, *Battleship at War*, 183–85.

42. Malcolm Muir Jr., "Misuse of the Fast Battleship in World War II." Hooper, U.S. Naval Institute oral history, 97.

43. Van Allen, "What Is A Space Scientist?"

44. Edwin S. Schanze, letter to Margaret Allen, 29 August 1962.

45. Dawson, interview.

46. Bentinck-Smith, letter to author, 3 September 1976.

47. Morison, *Aleutians, Gilberts and Marshalls*, 94–96.

48. Commander Task Force 11, "Occupation of Baker Island—Report of," 29 September 1943.

49. Frederic S. Withington, interview with author, 6 December 1975.

50. Joseph Bryan III, letter to the author, 2 December 1978.

51. Clark G. Reynolds, *The Fast Carriers*, 80–81. Morison, *Aleutians, Gilberts and Marshalls*, 92–93.

52. Lee, letter to Mabelle Lee, 11 November 1943.

53. Thomas Gatch, letter to Willis Lee, 18 November 1943.

54. Roy W. Johnson, interview with author, 4 October 1996.

Chapter 12. Central Pacific Campaign, Autumn 1943–Summer 1944

1. Blake D. Mills, letter to author, 9 February 1980.

2. "Bombardment of Nauru," Battleship *North Carolina*, http://www.battleshipnc .com/bombardment-of-nauru.

3. Jonas M. Platt, interview with author, 19 January 1980.

4. Platt, interview; Samuel Eliot Morison, *Aleutians, Gilberts and Marshalls*, 197–98.

5. Clark G. Reynolds, *The Fast Carriers*, 108.

6. Malcolm Muir Jr., *The Capital Ship Program in the United States Navy, 1934–1945*, 207–10.

7. Frederic S. Withington, interview with author, 6 December 1975.

8. Trent Hone, email to author, 11 September 2020.

9. Reynolds, *The Fast Carriers*, 119–24.

10. Guilliaem Aertsen III, interview with author, 8 April 1979.

11. Quoted in Theodore Taylor, *The Magnificent Mitscher*, 202.

12. William L. Dawson, interview with author, 25 January 1980.

13. Rafael Maza, interview with author, 7 July 1985.

14. Quoted in Reynolds, *The Fast Carriers*, 126.

15. Aertsen, interview with author, 8 April 1979.

16. Aertsen, interview, 8 April 1979.

17. Aertsen, interview, 8 April 1979.

18. Commander Battleships Pacific Fleet (ComTaskUnit 58.1.3), action report A-16-3(14), 15 March 1944.
19. *DANFS*, s.v., *"Indiana."* For an excellent detailed account of the incident, see Fred Tucker, "Stand by for a Ram," *Daily Press* (Newport News and Hampton, VA), 4 January 1970.
20. William Bentinck-Smith, letter to author, 8 September 1976.
21. Dawson, interview.
22. *DANFS*, s.v. *"Indiana."*
23. Frederic S. Withington, interview with author, 6 December 1975.
24. Glenn B. Davis, interview with author, 3 September 1977.
25. Jonas M. Platt, Marine Corps oral history, 62–63.
26. Frank M. Sanger Jr., interview with author, 8 May 1980.
27. Aertsen, interview, 8 April 1979.
28. Material on Spruance and the Truk attack is from Thomas B. Buell, *The Quiet Warrior*, 227–33.
29. Alan C. Byers, letter to author, 23 January 1980.
30. Backus, U.S. Naval Institute oral history, 199.
31. Morison, *Aleutians, Gilberts and Marshalls*, 308–9.
32. Frank L. Pinney Jr., letter to author, 4 November 1977.
33. John L. McCrea, *Captain McCrea's War*, 217–18.
34. Olaf M. Hustvedt, U.S. Naval Institute oral history, 275.
35. Pinney, letter.
36. Harry O. Reynolds, interview with author, 15 May 1983.
37. Aertsen, interview, 8 April 1979.
38. Arleigh A. Burke, interview with author, 15 September 1976.
39. Bentinck-Smith, letter.
40. Clark Reynolds, *The Fast Carriers*, 151.
41. Morison, *Aleutians, Gilberts and Marshalls*, 40–41.
42. Harold Hopkins, *Nice to Have You Aboard*, 100–104.
43. Margaret Allen, unpublished manuscript.
44. Hopkins, *Nice to Have You Aboard*, 107.
45. *New Jersey* deck log.
46. *New Jersey* deck log.
47. Trent Hone, *Learning War*, 223–24.
48. Tentative Radar Doctrine and CIC Instructions, Battleships, Pacific Fleet, Commander Battleships, U.S. Pacific Fleet, 5 June 1944. CNO files. Cited in Hone, *Learning War*, 224.
49. Hopkins, *Nice to Have You Aboard*, 137–38.
50. Morison, *Aleutians, Gilberts and Marshalls*, 179–80.
51. Quoted in Theodore Taylor, *The Magnificent Mitscher*, 217.

52. Quoted in Clark G. Reynolds, *The Fast Carriers*, 183. Arleigh Burke, interview with author, 15 September 1976.

53. Burke, interview. Clark Reynolds, *The Fast Carriers*, 183.

54. Aertsen, interview, 8 April 1979.

55. Burke, sound recording made on 20 August 1945, page 21 of transcript.

56. Morison, *Aleutians, Gilberts and Marshalls*, 244.

57. Burke, interview.

58. Allan Millett, letter to author, 23 March 1982.

59. Clark Reynolds, *The Fast Carriers*, 183.

60. Muir, *The Capital Ship Program in the U.S. Navy*, 312–13.

61. Muir, *The Capital Ship Program in the U.S. Navy*, 207–10.

62. Noble C. Harris, interview with author, 28 November 1983.

63. James G. Ross, letter to author, 6 February 1980.

64. James Van Allen, letter to author, 26 April 1976.

65. Morison, *Aleutians, Gilberts and Marshalls*, 268–70.

Chapter 13. The Battle of Leyte Gulf, Summer–Autumn 1944

1. Clark G. Reynolds, *The Fast Carriers: The Forging of an Air Navy*, 234.

2. Thomas P. Jeter biographical summary.

3. Lloyd M. Mustin, U.S. Naval Institute oral history, 823.

4. Guilliaem Aertsen III, interview with author, 8 April 1979.

5. Thomas P. Jeter, interview with Clark G. Reynolds, 1966.

6. Aertsen, interview, 8 April 1979.

7. William L. Dawson, interview with author, 25 January 1980.

8. Edward J. Mathews, letter to author, 16 September 1976.

9. William Bentinck-Smith, letter to author, 8 September 1976.

10. Mathews, letter to Evan Smith, 15 June 1962.

11. Carl Solberg, *Decision and Dissent: With Halsey at Leyte Gulf*, 17; *New Jersey* deck log.

12. William F. Halsey Jr. and J. Bryan III, *Admiral Halsey's Story*, 203.

13. *New Jersey* deck log.

14. "Stassen, Harold E.," Naval History and Heritage Command, https://www.history .navy.mil/our-collections/photography/us-people/s/stassen-harold-e.html.

15. Aertsen, interview, 14 March 1980.

16. *New Jersey* deck log.

17. Solberg, *With Halsey at Leyte Gulf*, 37.

18. Tomiji Koyanagi, "With Kurita in the Battle for Leyte Gulf," U.S. Naval Institute *Proceedings* (February 1953), 124.

19. Gerald F. Bogan, U.S. Naval Institute oral history, 108–9.

20. Bogan, U.S. Naval Institute oral history, 109.

21. Samuel Eliot Morison, *Leyte*, 195–96.

22. Aertsen, interview, 14 March 1980.

23. Evan Thomas, *Sea of Thunder*, 227–29.

24. Bentinck-Smith, letter to author, 3 September 1976.

25. Quoted in William Tuohy, *America's Fighting Admirals*, 309.

26. Arleigh Burke, interview with author, 15 September 1976.

27. Bogan, U.S. Naval Institute oral history, 110. Burke, interview.

28. James S. Russell, U.S. Naval Institute oral history, 180.

29. Reynolds, *The Fast Carriers*, 270.

30. Russell, U.S. Naval Institute oral history.

31. Jeter, interview.

32. Reynolds, *The Fast Carriers*, 270–71.

33. Russell, U.S. Naval Institute oral history.

34. Mathews, interview with author, 22 June 1977.

35. Noble C. Harris, interview with author, 28 November 1983.

36. Harris, interview.

37. Thomas J. Cutler, *The Battle of Leyte Gulf*, 237–38.

38. Chris McDougal, "Who Was in the Room Where It Happened," *Nimitz News Dispatch*, (First Quarter 2019), 4–5. Richard B. Frank, "The World Wonders," *Naval History* (October 2019), 14–19.

39. David McCampbell, U.S. Naval Institute oral history, 209–10.

40. Malcolm Muir Jr., *The Capital Ship Program in the United States Navy, 1934–1945*, 317–18.

41. Russell, U.S. Naval Institute oral history, 182.

42. Russell, U.S. Naval Institute oral history.

43. Koyanagi, "With Kurita in the Battle for Leyte Gulf," 125–29.

44. Russell, U.S. Naval Institute oral history, 184–85.

45. Reynolds, *The Fast Carriers*, 330.

46. Quoted in Hanson W. Baldwin, *Sea Fights and Ship Wrecks*, 170.

47. Aertsen, interview, 14 March 1980.

48. Quoted in Muir, *The Capital Ship Program in the United States Navy*, 319.

49. Bogan, U.S. Naval Institute oral history, 111–13.

50. Thomas Hone and Norman Friedman, "*Iowa* vs. *Yamato*: The Ultimate Gunnery Duel," U.S. Naval Institute *Proceedings* (July 1983), 122–23.

51. Mustin, "Comment and Discussion," U.S. Naval Institute *Proceedings* (November 1983), 98–99.

52. Edwin S. Schanze, letter to Margaret Allen, 29 August 1962.

53. Bentinck-Smith, letter to author, 9 January 1979.

54. Russel E. Hurd, letters to author, 13 October 1972 and 15 December 1972.

55. Mustin, U.S. Naval Institute oral history, 826–28.

56. Battleship Division Six War Diary, 21 November 1944.

Chapter 14. Closing in on Japan, November 1944–June 1945

1. Lloyd M. Mustin, U.S. Naval Institute oral history, 815–16; Raymond W. Thompson, interview with author, 31 January 1976.

2. Mustin, U.S. Naval Institute oral history, 818–19.

3. Thomas P. Jeter, interview with Clark G. Reynolds, 1966.

4. Mustin, U.S. Naval Institute oral history, 824–25.

5. Guilliaem Aertsen III, interview with author, 8 April 1979. Dino A. Brugioni, "Naval Photo Intel in WWII," U.S. Naval Institute *Proceedings* (June 1987), 46.

6. Aertsen, interview, 8 April 1979.

7. Aertsen, interview, 8 April 1979.

8. Aertsen, interview, 8 April 1979.

9. Noble C. Harris, interview with author, 28 November 1983.

10. Harris, interview.

11. Trent Hone, email to author, 10 June 2020. Hone got the information from the *Source Book on the History of Fire Control Radar*, which was probably an internal document prepared by the Bureau of Ordnance.

12. *DANFS*, s.v. "*South Dakota*."

13. Arthur P. MacArthur, letter to author, unknown date in 1980.

14. Mustin, U.S. Naval Institute oral history, 820.

15. Carl F. Stillman, letter to author, 14 December 1976.

16. *South Dakota* deck log.

17. David Gray, letter to author, 18 January 1980; Aertsen, interview, 14 March 1980.

18. Mustin, U.S. Naval Institute oral history, 896–97.

19. Aertsen, interviews, 8 April 1979 and 14 March 1980.

20. *DANFS*, s.v. "*South Dakota*."

21. *DANFS*, s.v. "*South Dakota*."

22. Thomas B. Buell, email letter to Dave Nelson, 26 July 2000.

23. Walter G. Ebert, letter to author, 19 May 1976; Mustin, U.S. Naval Institute oral history, 833.

24. Lillian Gilroy, letter to author, 27 May 1976.

25. *South Dakota* deck log.

26. *South Dakota* deck log. John C. Hill II, interview with author, 7 May 2002.

27. *DANFS*, s.v. "*South Dakota*."

28. William F. Halsey Jr., *Admiral Halsey's Story*, 233–35; Mustin, oral history, 830–33.

29. William McMillan, letter to Evan Smith, 20 June 1962.

30. *DANFS*, s.v. "*South Dakota*."

31. *DANFS*, s.v. "*South Dakota*."

32. Aertsen, interview, 8 April 1979.

33. Frederick I. Entwistle, letters to author, 19 May and 13 June 1976.

34. *DANFS*, s.v. "*South Dakota*."

35. Malcolm Muir Jr., *The Capital Ship Program in the United States Navy, 1934–1945*, 254–55.

36. Muir, *The Capital Ship Program*, 254.

37. *DANFS*, s.v. "South Dakota"; Mustin oral history, 842–46.

38. Samuel Eliot Morison, *Victory in the Pacific*, 199–209.

39. *DANFS*, s.v. "South Dakota"; *South Dakota* deck log; Samuel Eliot Morison, *Victory in the Pacific*, 242.

40. Aertsen, interview, 8 April 1979.

41. Mustin, U.S. Naval Institute oral history, 847–48, 860.

42. Trent Hone, email to author, 11 September 2020.

43. "Kamikazes at the Battle of Okinawa," History News Network, https://historynews network.org/article/174496.

44. Mustin, U.S. Naval Institute oral history, 850.

45. Mustin, U.S. Naval Institute oral history, 850–51, 859.

46. Mustin, U.S. Naval Institute oral history, 856.

47. Robert P. Foreman, interview with author, 9 October 1977.

48. Foreman, interview.

49. J. H. Murphy, *South Dakota* bomb disposal officer, letter of 1 June 1945 to the Chief of Naval Operations, via commanding officer, *South Dakota*, NARA.

50. Stillman, letter.

51. *DANFS*, s.v. "South Dakota."

52. Foreman, interview.

53. Peter Maas, *The Rescuer*, 217.

54. Aertsen, interview, 14 April 1980.

55. Aertsen, interview, 8 April 1979.

56. Aertsen, interview, 14 March 1980.

57. *DANFS*, s.v. "South Dakota."

58. McMillan, letter.

59. *DANFS*, s.v. "South Dakota."

60. Aertsen, interview, 8 April 1979.

61. Mustin, U.S. Naval Institute oral history, 868.

62. Mustin, U.S. Naval Institute oral history, 871–72.

63. Mustin, U.S. Naval Institute oral history, 872–73.

64. Aertsen, interview, 14 March 1980.

65. Edward J. Mathews, "Bombarding Japan," U.S. Naval Institute *Proceedings* (February 1979), 74–75; Mustin oral history, 874.

Chapter 15. War's End at Last, June–August 1945

1. Much of the information in this section is taken from the author's interview of Arleigh A. Burke, 15 September 1976.

2. Raymond P. Hunter, interview with author, 13 January 1980.
3. Captain Robert P. Foreman, interview with author, 9 October 1977; Mabelle Lee, letter to Margaret Allen, et al., 9 July 1945.
4. Guilliaem Aertsen III, interview with author, 10 October 1976.
5. Wilma Miles, interview with author, 28 November 1975.
6. Mabelle Lee, letter to Margaret Allen, et al., 9 July 1945.
7. Allen, unpublished manuscript; Mabelle Lee, letter to Margaret Allen, et al., 5 July 1945.
8. John B. McLean, letter to author, 7 August 1976.
9. Robert B. Pirie, letter to author, 7 January 1980.
10. Lloyd M. Mustin, U.S. Naval Institute oral history, 877–78.
11. Descriptions of the relationship with the DesLant staff and life in Mrs. Fish's rooming house are from the author's joint interview of Guiliaem and Mary Aertsen, 10 October 1976.
12. John J. O'Brien, letter to author, 24 September 1976.
13. Mustin, U.S. Naval Institute oral history, 880. Norman Zalkind, interview with author, 9 October 1976.
14. Mustin, U.S. Naval Institute oral history, 879–80.
15. Mustin, U.S. Naval Institute oral history. Foreman interview. Kinloch C. Walpole, letter to author, 17 July 1976. Bernard H. Meyer, letter to author, 10 January 1980.
16. Much of the wording in this section comes from editing Admiral Mustin provided to a rough draft of the chapter. His help was useful throughout the chapter.
17. Test results described in this and the following paragraphs are from Mustin's superbly detailed oral history.
18. Meyer, letter, 1 February 1980.
19. Mustin, U.S. Naval Institute oral history, 888–90.
20. Mustin, U.S. Naval Institute oral history, 892.
21. Mustin, U.S. Naval Institute oral history, 883–84.
22. This quotation is partly from the Mustin oral history, 885–86, and partly from material he added in reviewing a draft of the manuscript.
23. Aertsen, interview, 14 March 1980.
24. Norman Zalkind, letter to author, 6 February 1980.
25. Walpole, letter to author, 10 August 1976.
26. O'Brien, letter to author.
27. Rooming house events from Guilliaem and Mary Aertsen, joint interview with the author, 10 October 1976.
28. Aertsen, interview, 14 March 1980.
29. Mabelle Lee, letter to Margaret Allen, et al., 8 August 1945.
30. Zalkind, interview with author, 9 October 1976. Mabelle Lee letters to Margaret Allen, et al., 5 July, 9 July, 26 July, 1 August, and 4 August 1945. Aertsen, interview, 10 October

1976. In reviewing a draft of the chapter, Mustin wrote a note indicating that Lee's expertise was missing from the battleships: "As well he should have been—Shafroth loused up the long-planned BB bombardment of northern Japan."

31. Mary Aertsen, interview; Mabelle Lee letters to Margaret Allen, et al., 9 July, 16 July, 26 July, 1 August, 4 August, 8 August, and 14 August 1945.

32. Material on Lee's actions at the end of the war and in the days following is from the author's 10 October 1976 interview of the two Aertsens and a subsequent interview with Guillaem on 14 March 1980.

33. Guillaem Aertsen III, letter to author, 28 March 1980.

34. Walpole, letter.

35. James Gamage, interview with author, 4 October 1996.

36. Details of Lee's death are from John B. McLean, letter to Mabelle Lee, 31 August 1945.

Chapter 16. Epilogue, 1945–1949

1. Wilma Miles, interview with author, 28 November 1975.
2. Miles, interview.
3. Margaret Allen, letter to Evan Smith, 25 January 1962.
4. Norman Zalkind, interview with author, 9 October 1976.
5. Jonas H. Ingram, letter to William F. Halsey Jr., 27 August 1945.
6. Guilliaem Aertsen III, interviews with author, 8 April 1979 and 14 March 1980.
7. Arleigh A. Burke, interview with author, 15 September 1976.
8. James L. Holloway Jr., letter to author, 29 June 1976.
9. Glenn B. Davis, interview with author, 3 September 1977.
10. Allen, letter to author, 30 November 1976.
11. Allen, unpublished manuscript.
12. Ethel Douglas Burkhart, letter to Evan Smith, 14 December 1961; *Army & Navy Journal* (1 September 1945), 27.
13. M. C. Fisher, letter to Evan Smith, 15 June 1962.
14. Allen, unpublished manuscript; Allen letter to Evan Smith, 25 January 1962.
15. Allen, unpublished manuscript.

Appendix

1. *DANFS*, s.v. "Willis A. Lee."
2. Margaret Allen, letter to Evan Smith, 20 March 1962.
3. Warrant Officer-1 Theodore B. Litsey, letter to author, 13 April 1980.
4. *DANFS*, s.v. "Willis A. Lee."
5. Lloyd M. Mustin, letter to Evan Smith, 30 May 1962.

BIBLIOGRAPHY

Interviews with Author

Aertsen, Guilliaem, III, Mechanicsville, PA, 10 October 1976, 8 April 1979, and 14 March 1980.

Aertsen, Mary, Mechanicsville, PA, 10 October 1976.

Bradley, Captain Richard R., USN (Ret.), College Park, MD, 1 October 1976.

Braisted, Rear Admiral Frank A., USN (Ret.), Washington, DC, 13 November 1978.

Braun, Rear Admiral Boynton L., USN (Ret.), Dahlgren, VA, 28 August 1977.

Burke, Admiral Arleigh A., USN (Ret.), Bethesda, MD, 15 September 1976.

Cadwalader, Captain John, USNR (Ret.), Blue Bell, PA, 9 March 1980.

Cammack, Allen B., Burlington, NC, 21 May 1977.

Church, Captain Albert T., Jr., USN (Ret.), Alexandria, VA, 23 December 1979.

Davis, Vice Admiral Glenn B., USN (Ret.), Washington, DC, 3 September 1977.

Dawson, Captain William L., USN (Ret.), Annapolis, MD, 25 January 1980.

Dyer, Vice Admiral George C., USN (Ret.), Annapolis, MD, 12 December 1975.

Foreman, Captain Robert P., USN (Ret.), The Plains, VA, 9 October 1977.

Gamage, Chief Signalman James, USN (Ret.), Wilmington, NC, 4 October 1996.

Harris, Noble C., Jr., Annapolis, MD, 28 November 1983.

Hill, Captain John C. II, USN (Ret.), Washington, NC, 7 May 2002.

Hillenkoetter, Vice Admiral Roscoe H., USN (Ret.), Weehawken, NJ, 26 February 1977.

Holloway, Admiral James L., Jr., USN (Ret.), Virginia Beach, VA, 16 December 1975; McLean, VA, 12 September 1980.

Hooper, Vice Admiral Edwin B., USN (Ret.), Chevy Chase, MD, 13 January 1980.

Hunter, Captain Raymond P., USN (Ret.), Washington, DC, 13 January 1980.

Johnson, Roy W., Wilmington, NC, 4 October 1996.

Kotrla, Captain Raymond A., USN (Ret.), Washington, DC, 29 May 1976.

Malstrom, Rear Admiral Alvin I., USN (Ret.), Bethesda, MD, 5 June 1976.

Maslanka, Lieutenant Commander Edward J., USNR (Ret.), by telephone, 7 June 1998.

Mathews, Commander Edward J., USNR (Ret.), New York, NY, 22 June 1977.

Maza, Rafael, by telephone, 7 July 1985.

McDowell, Captain Percival E., USN (Ret.), Winchester, VA, 3 March 1977.

Miles, Wilma, Chevy Chase, MD, 28 November 1975.

Palmer, Captain Fitzhugh L., Jr., USN (Ret.), Strasburg, VA, 2 November 1975.

Palmer, Elizabeth V., Strasburg, VA, 2 November 1975.

Platt, Major General Jonas M., USMC (Ret.), Washington, DC, 19 January 1980.

Preston, Colonel Herbert J., USMC (Ret.), Annapolis, MD, 23 January 1976.

Reed, Robert, Annapolis, MD, 6 May 1995.

Reynolds, Commander Harry O., USN (Ret.), Yucaipa, CA, 15 May 1983.

Sanger, Captain Frank M., Jr., USN (Ret.), Falls Church, VA, 8 May 1980.

Simpson, Margaret, Annapolis, MD, 27 February 1977.

Steere, Captain Richard C., USN (Ret.) unknown location and date.

Thompson, Captain Raymond W., Jr., USN (Ret.), Chevy Chase, MD, 31 January 1976.

Wellborn, Vice Admiral Charles, Jr., USN (Ret.), Washington, DC, 5 March 1976.

Wellings, Rear Admiral Joseph H., USN (Ret.), Newport, RI, 18 November 1977.

Withington, Rear Admiral Frederic S., USN (Ret.), Washington, DC, 6 December 1975.

Wright, Estelle, Washington, DC, 21 December 1975.

Zalkind, Commander Norman, USNR (Ret.), Fall River, MA, 9 October 1976.

Letters to the Author

Aertsen, Guilliaem, III, 28 March 1980.

Allen, Margaret B., 30 November 1976; 31 January, 19 March, 16 April, and 3 June 1977.

Anderson, Rear Admiral William D., USN (Ret.), 1 August 1976 (tape recording) and 6 September 1976.

Audley, Lawrence M., 12 August 1996.

Backus, Commander Paul H., USN (Ret.), 20 January 1976 and 13 February 1976.

Baker, Raymond, 8 April 1980.

Bentinck-Smith, William, 3 September and 8 September 1976; 2 and 9 January 1979.

Berc, Harold T., 3 March 1980.

Bottomley, Captain Harold S., USN (Ret.), 22 February 1980.

Bryan, Joseph, III, 2 December 1978.

Butterfield, Rear Admiral Horace B., USN (Ret.), 12 March 1976.

Byers, Alan C., 23 January 1980.

Cammack, Allen B., 7 August 1976.

Chapin, Rear Admiral Nealy A., USN (Ret.), 14 July 1977.

Clark, Rear Admiral David H., USN (Ret.), 16 November 1977.

Crowe, Captain John F., Jr., USN (Ret.), 12 July 1977.

Cunningham, Father James F., 9 November 1978.

DeChristofaro, Commander Silvic, USN (Ret.), 23 January 1980.

Doukas, Captain Nicholas G., USN (Ret.), 12 November 1976.

Dubs, Florence Arnold, 4 June 1977.

Ebert, Rear Admiral Walter G., USN (Ret.), 19 May 1976.

Entwistle, Rear Admiral Frederick I., USN (Ret.), 19 May and 13 June 1976.

Fargo, Captain William B., USN (Ret.), 31 January 1980.

Flachsenhar, Captain John J., USN (Ret.), 3 December 1976.

Frank, Richard B., letter, 15 August 2008, and emails, 1 and 2 September 2020.

Furth, Rear Admiral Frederick R., USN (Ret.), 12 March 1977.

Gilroy, Lillian, 27 May 1976.

Gore, Captain John M., Supply Corps, USN (Ret.), 18 January 1980.

Gray, David, 18 January 1980.

Harris, Captain Robert E., USN (Ret.), 16 February 1980.

Hoffman, Captain Norman C., USN (Ret.), 28 January 1976.

Holloway, Admiral James L., Jr., USN (Ret.), 5 January and 29 June 1976, 13 July 1977.

Hone, Trent, emails, 10 June and 11 September 2020.

Hood, Captain Alexander H., USN (Ret.), 15 April 1980.

Hubbard, Vice Admiral Miles H., USN (Ret.), 15 April 1980.

Hurd, Commander Russell E., USN, 13 October and 15 December 1972.

Ihrig, Mary Moss, 17 August 1976.

Jenkins, Captain Walter T., USN (Ret.), 18 May and 27 June 1979.

Kieffer, Lieutenant Commander Henry M., USN (Ret.), 2 November 1978.

Kohlhas, Captain Albert P., Jr., Supply Corps, USN (Ret.), 30 January 1980.

Krick, Captain Harold D., USN (Ret.), 8 April, 7 October, and 5 December 1976.

Layton, Rear Admiral Edwin T., USN (Ret.), 5 March 1976.

Lester, Rear Admiral John C., USN (Ret.), 9 October 1976.

Libby, Vice Admiral Ruthven E., USN (Ret.), 4 November 1977.

Litsey, Warrant Officer-1 Theodore B., USN (Ret.), 13 April 1980.

MacArthur, Arthur P., unknown date in 1980.

Macklin, Captain Robert D., USN (Ret.), 4 February 1980.

Madeira, Rear Admiral Dashiell, USN (Ret.), 22 September 1976 (tape recording).

Mathews, Commander Edward J., USNR (Ret.), 16 September 1976.

Matton, Captain William George, Jr., USN (Ret.), 26 January 1980.

McCrea, Vice Admiral John L., USN (Ret.), November 1977.

McLean, Rear Admiral John B., USN (Ret.), 7 August 1976.

Meyer, Captain Bernard H., USN (Ret.), 10 January 1980.

Millett, Dr. Allan R., 23 March 1982.

Mills, Captain Blake D., USNR (Ret.), 19 February 1980.

Murphy, Vice Admiral Marion E., USN (Ret.), 13 October 1977.

Nicholson, Arthur, email, 13 October 2020.

O'Brien, John J., 24 September 1976.

Palmer, Elizabeth V., 6 October 1975 and 7 February 1987.

Pinney, Rear Admiral Frank L., USN (Ret.), 4 November 1977.

Pirie, Vice Admiral Robert B., USN (Ret.), 7 January 1980.

Rivero, Admiral Horacio, USN (Ret.), 10 September 1977.

Robinson, Captain Hugh M., USN (Ret.), 14 January 1980.

Ross, Captain James G., USN (Ret.), 6 February 1980 and 17 March 1980.

Russell, Vice Admiral George L., USN (Ret.), 23 February 1976.

Schoeffel, Rear Admiral Malcolm F. USN (Ret.), 26 October 1977.

Schwabe, Commander Leo R., USN (Ret.), 31 January 1980.

Simpson, Captain Robert Tate, USN (Ret.), 8 September 1976 and 10 October 1976.

Simpson, Lieutenant Commander B. Mitchell, III, USN (Ret.), 28 November 1978.

Smedberg, Vice Admiral William R. III, USN (Ret.), 18 February 1976.

Stahnke, P. J., 7 March 1977.

Stillman, Rear Admiral Carl F., USN (Ret.), 14 December 1976.

Sweetman, Arthur J., 31 March 1977.

Van Allen, Dr. James A., 26 April 1976.

Wadleigh, Rear Admiral John R., USN (Ret.), 21 February 1976.

Walpole, Rear Admiral Kinloch C., USN (Ret.), 17 July and 10 August 1976.

Waterman, Rear Admiral John R., USN (Ret.), 27 July 1977.

Wellborn, Vice Admiral Charles, Jr., USN (Ret.), 5 March 1976.

Wellings, Rear Admiral Joseph H., USN (Ret.), 7 September 1977.

Williamson, Captain Marcus W., USN (Ret.), 6 October 1976.

Wilson, Lieutenant John D., USN (Ret.), 10 September 1976.

Wishard, Jeannette S., 12 April 1976.

Wolverton, Captain Royal A., USN (Ret.), 18 September 1976.

Yancey, Chief Warrant Officer Charles, USN (Ret.), 24 April 1980.

Yancey, Rear Admiral Evan W., USN (Ret.), 15 September and 14 October 1976.

Zalkind, Commander Norman, USNR (Ret.), 6 February 1980.

Zimanski, Captain Frank A., USN (Ret.), 28 January 1980.

Oral Histories

Backus, Commander Paul H., USN (Ret.), U.S. Naval Institute, interview by Paul Stillwell, published in 1995.

Bogan, Vice Admiral Gerald F., USN (Ret.), U.S. Naval Institute, interview by Commander Etta-Belle Kitchen, USN (Ret.), published in 1970; later version published in 1986.

Davidson, Rear Admiral John F., USN (Ret.), U.S. Naval Institute, interview by Paul Stillwell, published in 1986.

Dyer, Captain Thomas H., USN (Ret.), U.S. Naval Institute, interview by Paul Stillwell, published in 1986.

Eller, Rear Admiral Ernest M., USN (Ret.), U.S. Naval Institute, interview by Dr. John T. Mason Jr., Volume I, published in 1986.

Hooper, Vice Admiral Edwin B., USN (Ret.), interview by Dr. John T. Mason Jr., published in 1978.

Hustvedt, Vice Admiral Olaf M., USN (Ret.), U.S. Naval Institute, interview by Dr. John T. Mason Jr., published in 1975.

McCampbell, Captain David, USN (Ret.), U.S. Naval Institute, interview by Paul Stillwell, published in 2010.

Mumma, Rear Admiral Albert G., USN (Ret.), U.S. Naval Institute, interview by Paul Stillwell, published in 2001.

Mustin, Vice Admiral Lloyd M., USN (Ret.), U.S. Naval Institute, interview by Dr. John T. Mason Jr., published in 2003.

Platt, Major General Jonas M., USMC (Ret.), Marine Corps History and Museums Division, interview by Benis Frank, published in 1984.

Russell, Admiral James S., USN (Ret.), U.S. Naval Institute, interview by Dr. John T. Mason Jr., published in 1976.

Schoeffel, Rear Admiral Malcolm F., USN (Ret.), U.S. Naval Institute, interview by Dr. John T. Mason Jr., published in 1979.

Smedberg, Vice Admiral William R. III, USN (Ret.), U. S. Naval Institute, interview by Dr. John T. Mason Jr., published in 1979.

Wellborn, Vice Admiral Charles Jr., USN (Ret.), U.S. Naval Institute, interview by Dr. John T. Mason Jr., published in 1972.

Other Interviews

Jeter, Rear Admiral Thomas P., USN (Ret.), interview by Dr. Clark G. Reynolds, 1966.

Shriver, R. Sargent Jr., interview in the collection of the USS *South Dakota* Battleship Memorial, circa 1969. http://www.usssouthdakota.com/OralHistories/pdfs/USSSDTrnscrpt_Shriver_Sargent.pdf.

Letters to Evan E. Smith

Aertsen, Guilliaem, III, 9 April 1962.

Allen, Margaret B., 15 January, 20 March, 29 March, and 15 June 1962.

Brereton, Captain William D., USN (Ret.), 5 January 1962.

Buckingham, Earle, 25 August 1962.

Burkhart, Ethel Douglas, 14 December 1961.

Cammack, Owen F., 9 February 1962.

Carter, Rear Admiral Worrall R., USN (Ret.), 30 March 1962.

Claypool, Captain James V., Chaplain Corps, USNR (Ret.), 17 December 1962.

Davis, Captain William S. G., USN (Ret.), 20 June 1962.

Davis, Vice Admiral Glenn B., USN (Ret.), 9 July 1962.

Earle, John H., 25 March 1962.

Egger, Chief Warrant Officer-4, USN (Ret.), 1 July 1962.

Fisher, Milton C., 15 June 1962.

Forsee, W. T., 19 October 1961.

Gore, Captain John M., Supply Corps, USN, 14 February 1963.

Gormley, Patrick, 1 July 1962.

Iseman, Commander John E., Jr., USN (Ret.), 30 March 1962.

Jennings, Rear Admiral William F., USN (Ret.), 29 November 1961.

Kimmel, Rear Admiral Husband E., USN (Ret.), 6 February 1962.

Kinkaid, Admiral Thomas C., USN (Ret.), 9 April 1962.

Krawczyk, Stanley J., 28 August 1962.

Kurfess, William F., 28 May 1962.

Lyman, Rear Admiral Charles H., USN (Ret.), 16 June 1962.

Mathews, Commander Edward J., USNR (Ret.), 15 June 1962.

McMillan, Commander William, USNR (Ret.), 20 June 1962.

Meacham, Allen R., 1 and 14 September 1961.

Meredith, Commander John E., USN (Ret.), 6 April 1962.

Miller, Colonel Adolph B., USMC (Ret.), 16 July 1962.

Mumma, Rear Admiral Morton C., Jr., USN (Ret.), 6 July 1962.

Mustin, Rear Admiral Lloyd M., USN, 30 May 1962.

Nimitz, Fleet Admiral Chester W., USN, 8 May 1962.

Norton, Captain Edmund R., USN (Ret.), undated.

Osburn, Captain Carl T., USN (Ret.), 3 April 1962.

Russo, Lorenzo, 20 June 1962.

Seymour, Captain Philip, USN (Ret.), 9 April 1962.

Smith, Commodore Oscar, Jr., USN (Ret.), 27 March and 9 May 1962.

Smith, Vice Admiral William Ward, USN (Ret.), 26 May 1962.

Train, Rear Admiral Harold C., USN (Ret.), 25 May 1962.

Walsh, Rear Admiral Harvey T., USN (Ret.), 30 July 1962.

Williamson, Ruth, 12 February 1962.

Wilson, Commander Eugene E., USNR (Ret.), 13 March 1962 and 23 March 1962.

Other Letters

Buell, Commander Thomas B. Buell, USN (Ret.), email to Dave Nelson, 26 July 2000.

Byrd, Commander Richard E., USN (Ret.), to Lieutenant Commander Willis A. Lee, USN, 18 March 1926.

Chief of Naval Operations to commanding officer, USS *Concord*, 10 August 1938.

Cope, Commander Elihu H., Supply Corps, USN, to Allan Colon, 17 June 1922.

Earle, John H., to Mabelle Lee, 29 August 1945.

Gatch, Rear Admiral Thomas L., USN, to Rear Admiral Willis A. Lee, USN, 18 November 1943.

Ingram, Admiral Jonas H., USN, letter to Admiral William F. Halsey Jr., USN, 27 August 1945, Fleet Admiral William F. Halsey papers, Manuscript Division, Library of Congress, Box 14.

Jennings, Bertha, to Mabelle Lee, 19 December 1938.

Jennings, Commander William F., USN, to Mabelle Lee, 15 February 1943.

Knowlton, Chadbourn R., to Edward Maslanka, 28 September 1996.

Lee, Mabelle A., to Margaret Allen, et. al., 5 July, 9 July, 16 July, 26 July, 1 August, 4 August, 8 August, and 14 August 1945.

Lee, Willis A., to Mabelle Allen/Lee, 23 January, 9 February, and 6 April 1919; 21 August, 4 September, and 1 December 1942; 11 November 1943.

McLean, Rear Admiral John B., USN (Ret.), to Mabelle Lee, 31 August 1945.

Murphy, J. H., to the Chief of Naval Operations, 1 June 1945. NARA.

Nimitz, Admiral Chester W., USN, to Robert Ghormley, USN, 8 October 1942. Fleet Admiral Nimitz papers, Naval History and Heritage Command.

Schanze, Rear Admiral Edwin S., USN (Ret.), to Margaret Allen, 29 August 1962.

Secretary of the Navy to commanding officer, USS *Concord*, 5 August 1937.

Wright, Lieutenant Jerauld, USN, to Lieutenant Commander Willis Lee, USN, 31 March 1924.

Unpublished Manuscripts

Allen, Margaret, no title, no date.

Burke, Admiral Commodore A., USN. Sound recording made on 20 August 1945.

Davis, Louise Cammack. "The Lees." January 1962.

Davis, Vice Admiral Glenn B., USN (Ret.). Remarks at USS *Washington* reunion, Wilmington, NC, 16 July 1969.

Hustvedt, Captain Erling, USN (Ret.). "Surface Ship Gunnery Systems in Battle." Paper presented 10 August 1994 at the World War II in the Pacific Conference.

Jeter, Rear Admiral Thomas P., USN (Ret.). Biographical summary, U.S. Naval Academy archives.

Morison, Lieutenant Commander Samuel Eliot, USNR. April 1943 diary.

Stark, Lloyd C. September–October 1904 diary.

Books

Annual Register of the Naval Academy, 1907–1908. 1 October 1907.

Baldwin, Hanson W. *Sea Fights and Shipwrecks: True Tales of the Seven Seas* (Garden City, NY: Hanover House, 1955).

Blair, Clay, Jr. *Silent Victory: The U.S. Submarine War Against Japan* (Philadelphia and New York: J. B. Lippincott, 1975).

Buell, Thomas B. *Master of Sea Power: A Biography of Admiral Ernest J. King* (Boston: Little, Brown, 1980).

———. *The Quiet Warrior: A Biography of Admiral Raymond A. Spruance* (Boston: Little, Brown, 1974).

Claypool, Captain James V., USNR. *God on a Battlewagon* (Philadelphia: Universal Book and Bible House, 1944).

Cutler, Thomas J. *The Battle of Leyte Gulf* (New York: HarperCollins, 1994).

Dictionary of American Naval Fighting Ships (DANFS). Available online through the Naval History and Heritage Command (NHHC).

Frank, Richard B. *Guadalcanal: The Definitive Account of the Landmark Battle* (New York: Random House, 1990).

Furer, Rear Admiral Julius Augustus, USN (Ret.). *Administration of the Navy Department in World War II* (Washington, DC: U.S. Government Printing Office, 1959).

Griffing, B. N., et al. *An Atlas of Owen County, Kentucky* (Philadelphia: D. J. Lake, 1883). Reprinted as part of special souvenir newspapers on the occasion of the Owen County sesquicentennial, 27 June–6 July 1969.

Grossman, Jim. *Olympic Shooting* (Washington, DC: National Rifle Association, 1978).

Halsey, Fleet Admiral William F., Jr., USN (Ret.), and J. Bryan III. *Admiral Halsey's Story* (New York; Whittlesey House, McGraw-Hill Book Company, 1947).

Hattendorf, John B., B. Mitchell Simpson III, and John R. Wadleigh. *Sailors and Scholars: The Centennial History of the U.S. Naval War College* (Newport: Naval War College Press, 1984).

Hone, Trent. *Learning War: The Evolution of Fighting Doctrine in the U.S. Navy, 1898–1945* (Annapolis: Naval Institute Press, 2018).

Hopkins, Captain Harold, RN. *Nice to Have You Aboard* (London: George Allen & Unwin, 1964).

Hornfischer, James D. *Neptune's Inferno: The U.S. Navy at Guadalcanal* (New York: Bantam Books, 2011).

Houchens, Mariam Sidebottom. *History of Owen County, Kentucky "Sweet Owen"* (Louisville, KY: Standard Printing, 1976).

Leckie, Robert. *Challenge for the Pacific: Guadalcanal—The Turning Point* (Garden City, New York: Doubleday, 1965).

Lillard, John M. *Playing War: Wargaming and U.S. Naval Preparations for World War II* (Lincoln: University of Nebraska Press [Potomac Books], 2016).

Lucky Bag 1908 (Naval Academy yearbook).

Lundstrom, John B. *The First Team and the Guadalcanal Campaign: Naval Fighter Combat from August to November, 1942* (Annapolis: Naval Institute Press, 1994).

Maas, Peter. *The Rescuer* (New York: Harper and Row, 1967).

McCrea, Vice Admiral John L., USN (Ret.). *Captain McCrea's War*, edited by Julia C. Tobey (New York: Skyhorse Publishing, 2016).

Miles, Vice Admiral Milton E., USN (Ret.), with Hawthorne Daniels. *A Different Kind of War* (Garden City, New York: Doubleday, 1967).

Morison, Samuel Eliot. *History of United States Naval Operations in World War II*, Volume V, *The Struggle for Guadalcanal: August 1942–February 1943* (Boston: Little, Brown, 1955).

———. *History of United States Naval Operations in World War II*, Volume VII, *Aleutians, Gilberts and Marshalls: June 1942–April 1944* (Boston: Little, Brown, 1953).

———. *History of United States Naval Operations in World War II*, Volume VIII, *New Guinea and the Marianas: March 1944–August 1944* (Boston: Little, Brown, 1953).

———. *History of United States Naval Operations in World War II*, Volume XII, *Leyte: June 1944–January 1945* (Boston: Little, Brown, 1958).

———. *History of United States Naval Operations in World War II*, Volume XIV, *Victory in the Pacific: 1945* (Boston: Little, Brown, 1960).

Musicant, Ivan. *Battleship at War: the Epic Story of the USS Washington* (New York: Harcourt Brace Jovanovich, 1986).

Naval Academy *Register of Alumni*, various editions.

Reynolds, Clark G. *The Fast Carriers: The Forging of an Air Navy* (New York: McGraw-Hill, 1968).

Roscoe, Theodore. *United States Destroyer Operations in World War II* (Annapolis: U.S. Naval Institute, 1953).

Rowland, Lieutenant Commander Buford, USNR, and Lieutenant William B. Boyd, USNR. *U.S. Navy Bureau of Ordnance in World War II* (Washington, DC: U.S. Government Printing Office, 1953).

Shalett, Sidney. *Old Nameless: The Epic of a U.S. Battlewagon* (New York: D. Appleton-Century, 1943).

Silverstone, Paul. *U.S. Warships of World War I* (Garden City, New York: Doubleday, 1970).

Solberg, Carl. *Decision and Dissent: With Halsey at Leyte Gulf* (Annapolis: Naval Institute Press, 1995).

Stillwell, Paul. *Air Raid: Pearl Harbor! Recollections of a Day of Infamy* (Annapolis: Naval Institute Press, 1981).

Sweetman, Jack. *American Naval History* (Annapolis: Naval Institute Press, 1984).

———. *The Landing at Veracruz: 1914* (Annapolis: U.S. Naval Institute, 1968).

———. *The U.S. Naval Academy: an Illustrated History* (Annapolis: Naval Institute Press, 1979).

Taylor, Theodore. *The Magnificent Mitscher* (New York: W. W. Norton, 1954).

Thomas, Evan. *Sea of Thunder: Four Commanders and the Last Great Naval Campaign 1941–1945* (New York: Simon & Schuster, 2006).

Tuohy, William. *America's Fighting Admirals* (St. Paul Minnesota: MBI Publishing [Zenith Press], 2007).

Wellings, Rear Admiral Joseph H., USN (Ret.), edited by John B. Hattendorf. *On His Majesty's Service: Observations from the British Home Fleet* (Newport: Naval War College, 1983).

Yu, Maochun. *OSS in China: Prelude to Cold War* (New Haven: Yale University Press, 1996).

Journals and Articles

Arms and the Man. A National Rifle Association-affiliated magazine (5 September 1907).

Army & Navy Journal (1 September 1945).

Boston Sunday Globe (1 August 1909).

Brugioni, Dino A. "Naval Photo Intel in WWII." U.S. Naval Institute *Proceedings* (June 1987).

Frank, Richard B. "Picking Winners?" *Naval History* (June 2011).

———. "The World Wonders." *Naval History* (October 2019).

Griffing, B. N., et al. *An Atlas of Owen County, Kentucky* (Philadelphia: D. J. Lake, 1883). Reprinted as part of special souvenir newspapers on the occasion of the Owen County sesquicentennial, 27 June–6 July 1969.

Hone, Dr. Thomas, and Dr. Norman Friedman. "*Iowa* vs. *Yamato*: The Ultimate Gunnery Duel." U.S. Naval Institute *Proceedings* (July 1983).

Jordan, Winston. "Man Overboard." U.S. Naval Institute *Proceedings* (December 1987).

Koyanagi, Tomiji. "With Kurita in the Battle for Leyte Gulf." U.S. Naval Institute *Proceedings* (February 1953).

Lee, Midshipman W. A., Jr., USN, and Midshipman A. D. Denney, USN. "Revolver Shooting." U.S. Naval Institute *Proceedings* 36, no. 1 (1910).

"Lee-Allen Nuptials in Chicago Culmination of Pretty War Romance." *Rock Island Argus* (19 July 1919).

Mathews, Commander Edward J., USNR (Ret.). "Bombarding Japan." U.S. Naval Institute *Proceedings* (February 1979).

McDougal, Chris. "Who Was in the Room Where It Happened." *Nimitz News Dispatch.* (First Quarter 2019).

Muir, Dr. Malcolm, Jr. "Misuse of the Fast Battleship in World War II." U.S. Naval Institute *Proceedings* (February 1979).

Mustin, Vice Admiral Lloyd M., USN (Ret.). "Comment and Discussion." U.S. Naval Institute *Proceedings* (November 1983).

National Bulletin. Military Order of the World War (November 1933).

"National Rifle Matches." *Arms and the Man* (5 September 1907).

"National Rifle Matches of 1919." *Cambridge Sentinel* (MA) (14 June 1919).

"Rear Admiral Lee, Cited in Solomons Battle, Wed Rock Island Girl in '19." *Democrat* (Davenport, IA) (18 November 1942).

"Rear Admiral Lee Spent Happy Boyhood Days in Owen County." *News-Herald* (Owenton, KY) (21 September 1941).

"Revival of Our Oldest Navy Yard." *Scientific American* (10 January 1920).

Siders, Donald L. "The Expert." Series on Admiral Lee. *Adventure Sports Outdoors* (September–October–November 2004).

Thomas, Lowell. "Maj. McLaren's [sic] Rescue Due to America's Aid." *Chicago Daily Tribune* (23 December 1924).

Tucker, Fred. "Stand by for a Ram." *Daily Press* (Newport News and Hampton, VA) (4 January 1970).

Van Allen, James A. "What Is A Space Scientist? An Autobiographical Example." *Annual Review of Earth and Planetary Sciences*, no. 18 (1990). Also available at http://www-pi.physics.uiowa.edu/java/.

Williamson, Ruth. "Big Eagle Country: Nostalgic Views of the Past Along the 99-Mile Stream That Possesses Secrets of Owen County's History." *News-Herald* (Owenton, KY) (8 February 1962 and 15 February 1962).

Official Documents

Annual Register of the Naval Academy. 1 October 1907.

Bureau of Ships. "U.S.S. SOUTH DAKOTA (BB57), Gunfire Damage, Battle of Guadalcanal, 14–15 November 1942." 1 June 1947.

Commander Battleship Division Six. "Report of Night Action, Task Force SIXTY-FOUR – November 14–15, 1942." 18 February 1943.

Commander Battleship Division Six War Diary. 21 November 1944.

Commander Battleships Pacific Fleet (ComTaskFor 11), "Occupation of Baker Island – Report of." CBP/A16-3. 29 September 1943.

Commander Battleships Pacific Fleet (ComTaskUnit 58.1.3). Action report A-16-3(14). 15 March 1944.

FDR Presidential Library, President's Secretary's File, Department of Navy: Nov–Dec 1940 through Jul–Dec 1942, Box 59.

Lee, Vice Admiral Willis A. Jr., USN, numerous personnel record entries.

NARA, Record Group 38, Box 299, Willis A., Lee Jr., confidential memorandum to Captain G. B. Wright, USN (Ret.), "Internal Organization of the Office of the Chief of Naval Operations." Folder (SC)A3-1, Confidential General Correspondence of the Division of Fleet Training, 1927–41.

———. Record Group 38, Box 316, Folder (SC)A13, Fleet Training Division Confidential correspondence.

———. Record Group 38, Box 323 Folder (SC) QB (Boards), 9 August 1940; Box 323, Folder (SC)QB/AA, 13 August 1940.

———. Record Group 38, Box 323, Folder (SC) QB/AA, 24 February 1941.

———. Record Group 38, Box 324, Folder (SC)S67 (Radio Apparatus), 15 May 1941.

———. Record Group 38, Box 324, Folder (SC)S67 (Radio Apparatus), 25 June 1941.

———. Record Group 38, Box 324, Folder (SC)S67 (Radio Apparatus), 7 July 1941.

Stark, Harold R. *Organization of the Office of the Chief of Naval Operations with Duties Assigned the Divisions Thereunder* (Washington, DC: Navy Department) 23 October 1940, 21–23.

Academic Studies

Kennedy, Gerald John. *United States Naval War College, 1919–1941: An Institutional Response to Naval Preparedness* (Newport, RI: Naval War College, 1975).

Muir, Dr. Malcolm, Jr. "The Capital Ship Program in the United States Navy, 1934–1945." PhD diss. The Ohio State University, 1976.

INDEX

ABOUT THE AUTHOR

Paul Stillwell graduated from Drury College, Springfield, Missouri, in 1966 with a bachelor's degree in history and in 1978 from the University of Missouri-Columbia with a master's in journalism. A Vietnam War veteran, he served on board the tank landing ship *Washoe County* from 1966 to 1969. In 1969, as a lieutenant, Stillwell was the assistant combat information center officer of the battleship *New Jersey* during operations in the Eastern Pacific. Stillwell retired as a commander in the Naval Reserve in 1992, following thirty years of service. His final active duty was in 1988, when he was sent to the Persian Gulf as a historian to document the Navy's role in Operation Earnest Will during the Iran-Iraq tanker war.

Stillwell was on the staff of the U.S. Naval Institute from 1974 to 2004 and continues to do freelance history work. During his time on the staff, he served several editorial roles with *Proceedings*; was editor of the annual *Naval Review*; was the founding editor in chief of *Naval History* magazine; and served as director of oral history and the history division. For twenty-three years he wrote a column titled "Looking Back" for *Naval History*. All told, he is author, coauthor, or editor of thirteen books.

The Naval Institute Press is the book-publishing arm of the U.S. Naval Institute, a private, nonprofit, membership society for sea service professionals and others who share an interest in naval and maritime affairs. Established in 1873 at the U.S. Naval Academy in Annapolis, Maryland, where its offices remain today, the Naval Institute has members worldwide.

Members of the Naval Institute support the education programs of the society and receive the influential monthly magazine *Proceedings* or the colorful bimonthly magazine *Naval History* and discounts on fine nautical prints and on ship and aircraft photos. They also have access to the transcripts of the Institute's Oral History Program and get discounted admission to any of the Institute-sponsored seminars offered around the country.

The Naval Institute's book-publishing program, begun in 1898 with basic guides to naval practices, has broadened its scope to include books of more general interest. Now the Naval Institute Press publishes about seventy titles each year, ranging from how-to books on boating and navigation to battle histories, biographies, ship and aircraft guides, and novels. Institute members receive significant discounts on the Press' more than eight hundred books in print.

Full-time students are eligible for special half-price membership rates. Life memberships are also available.

For a free catalog describing Naval Institute Press books currently available, and for further information about joining the U.S. Naval Institute, please write to:

Member Services
U.S. Naval Institute
291 Wood Road
Annapolis, MD 21402-5034
Telephone: (800) 233-8764
Fax: (410) 571-1703
Web address: www.usni.org